Exegesis and Spiritual Pedagogy
in Maximus the Confessor

Christianity and Judaism in Antiquity
Charles Kannengiesser, Series Editor
Volume 7

Exegesis and Spiritual Pedagogy in Maximus the Confessor

An Investigation of the *Quaestiones ad Thalassium*

by
Paul M. Blowers

University of Notre Dame Press
Notre Dame, Indiana

University of Notre Dame Press

Copyright © 1991 by

University of Notre Dame

Notre Dame, Indiana 46556

All Rights Reserved
Published in the United States of America

Paperback edition published in 2017

Library of Congress Cataloging-in-Publication Data

Blowers, Paul M., 1955-
   Exegesis and spiritual pedagogy in Maximus the Confessor : an investigation of the Quaestiones ad Thalassium / Paul M. Blowers.
    p. cm. — (Christianity and Judaism in Antiquity ; v. 7)
   Includes bibliographical references and indexes.
   ISBN 978-0-268-00927-4 (hardback)
   ISBN 978-0-268-04884-6 (paper)
   1. Maximus, Confessor, Saint, ca. 580-662. Quaestiones ad Thalassium.   I. Title.   II. Series.
BR65.M39676B46   1991
220.6—dc20
                                                            90-50973
                                                                  CIP

To the Memory of
Dean Everest Walker
(1898-1988)

... going round and surveying us, as it were, with the skill of an husbandman, and not taking notice merely of what is obvious to everyone and superficial, but digging into us more deeply, and probing what is most inward in us, he put us to the question, and proposed things to us, and listened to our replies. For whenever he detected anything in us not wholly unprofitable and useless and ineffectual, he would start clearing the soil, and turning it up and watering it. He would set everything in motion, and apply the whole of his skill and attention to us so as to cultivate us.

Gregory Thaumaturgus
Panegyric on Origen

Contents

ACKNOWLEDGMENTS xi
ABBREVIATIONS xiii

INTRODUCTION 1
   The Current State of Maximian Studies 1
   The Context and Purview of the *Quaestiones ad Thalassium* 2
      Maximus' Monastic Formation 3
      The Historical Foreground of the *Ad Thalassium* 6
      The Immediate Occasion of the *Ad Thalassium* 9
   The Critical and Interpretative Problem
   of the *Quaestiones ad Thalassium* 13
   Notes 17

CHAPTER 1. THE *QUAESTIONES AD THALASSIUM*:
GENRE AND CONTEXT IN THE BYZANTINE
MONASTIC PEDAGOGICAL TRADITION 28
   The *Aporiai* Tradition of Patristic Exegetical "Questions and
   Responses" and the Literary Genre of the *Ad Thalassium* 29
   The *Quaestio-Responsio*, Scriptural *Aporiai*, and Spiritual
   Pedagogy in the Byzantine Monastic Tradition before Maximus 36
      The *Apophthegmata patrum* 37
      The Monastic *Regulae* of Basil of Caesarea 39
      The *Collationes* of John Cassian 40
      The Spiritual-Doctrinal Writings of Pseudo-Macarius,
      Mark the Hermit, and Isaac the Syrian 42
      A Return to the Pragmatism of the Desert: The *Quaestiones
      et responsiones* of the Palestinians Barsanuphius and John 47

The *Quaestiones et responsiones* of Anastasius Sinaïta 49

The *Quaestio-Responsio* in Maximus' Earlier Monastic Writings 52

The *Quaestiones ad Thalassium* in the Tradition of Monastic
Pedagogical *Quaestiones et responsiones* 56

    Monastic *Topoi* in the *Ad Thalassium* 57

    Scriptural *Aporiai* and Spiritual Pedagogy
    in Maximus' Responses to Thalassius 61

Recapitulation: Scriptural *Aporiai*, Monastic Use of Scripture,
and the *Quaestiones ad Thalassium* 69

Notes 73

CHAPTER 2. *DIABASIS*: THE THEOLOGICAL AND
HERMENEUTICAL FRAMEWORK OF MAXIMUS'
EXEGESIS OF SCRIPTURE IN THE *QUAESTIONES
AD THALASSIUM* 95

The Terminological and Thematic Significance
of *Diabasis* in the *Quaestiones ad Thalassium* 96

The Objective and Macrocosmic Dimensions of the *Diabasis*:
Access to the Logos-Christ through Creation and Scripture 100

    Creation, Scripture, and the Symbolic Structure
    of the *Diabasis* 102

        A *Locus Classicus*: *Ambiguum* 10 102

        The *Logoi* of Scripture and Maximus' Notion
        of Accommodation in the *Ad Thalassium* 106

    A *Diabasis* from Letter to Spirit in Scripture 112

The Christological *Skopos* of Creation and Scripture:
The Mystery of the Incarnate Logos-Christ 117

    The Three Laws and the Three Incarnations 117

    The Mystery of the Incarnation and the Eschatological
    Scope of Scriptural Symbols 122

The Subjective and Microcosmic Dimensions of the *Diabasis*:
The Integration of the Spiritual Life 131

    Πρᾶξις—Θεωρία—Θεολογία in the *Ad Thalassium* 133

Natural (φυσική) and Scriptural (γραφική) Contemplation 137

Recapitulation: Communion with the Incarnate Logos-Christ
as the Goal of the Spiritual *Diabasis* 145

Notes 149

CHAPTER 3. ANAGOGICAL EXEGESIS AS A THEOLOGICAL
AND PEDAGOGICAL USE OF SCRIPTURE IN THE
QUAESTIONES AD THALASSIUM 184

Anagoge and Multiple Meanings of Scripture
in Maximus' Exegesis 185

Anagogical Exegesis as a Use of Scripture
in the *Quaestiones ad Thalassium* 192

Forms of Anagogy in the *Quaestiones ad Thalassium* 196

    Typology, Allegory, and Tropology 197

    Etymology 203

    Arithmology 211

    Extrapolations from Biblical Terms or Language 219

Notes 228

CONCLUSION 249

    Notes 256

BIBLIOGRAPHY 259
GENERAL INDEX 273
INDEX OF THE WORKS OF MAXIMUS THE CONFESSOR 279
INDEX OF BIBLICAL REFERENCES 283

Acknowledgments

This study is the fruit of many years of interest and research in the thought and writings of Maximus the Confessor. In substance it is the revision of a doctoral dissertation submitted to the Department of Theology of the University of Notre Dame in the summer of 1988. A special word of thanks must go to Charles Kannengiesser, Huisking Professor of Theology, for his kind supervision and encouragement, and to another esteemed teacher, Robert L. Wilken, now of the University of Virginia, who helped me define my interests in patristic studies. I also want to express my deep appreciation to Harry Attridge for his advice on a few *aporiai* in Maximus the Confessor's Greek text, to Jean Laporte for his assistance with a number of bibliographical resources, and finally to George Berthold of St. Anselm College, a specialist in Maximian studies, who kindly agreed to serve as a visiting reader of the original dissertation. I am also greatly indebted to Jeannette Morgenroth Sheerin of the University of Notre Dame Press for her critical expertise and thoughtful interest in editing my manuscript.

Certainly my gratitude goes out to my wife Polly, and to my children Leslie and Colin, for exercising much patience during the long term of my research, writing, and rewriting. And to my parents back in Indianapolis, my thanks for many a daily prayer for their son.

Emmanuel School of Religion
Johnson City, Tennessee

Paul M. Blowers
June, 1991

Abbreviations

AB	*Analecta bollandiana*
ACW	Ancient Christian Writers
BGL	Bibliothek der griechischen Literatur
BZ	*Byzantinishe Zeitschrift*
col(s).	column(s)
CCSG	Corpus christianorum, series graeca
CS	Cistercian Studies
CSEL	Corpus scriptorum ecclesiasticorum latinorum
CWS	Classics of Western Spirituality
DS	*Dictionnaire de spiritualité*
EB	*Études byzantines*
Ep.	*Epistula(e)*
ET	English translation
frag.	fragment
GCS	Die griechischen christlichen Schriftsteller der ersten drei Jahrhunderte
GCSO	GCS–Origenes Werke
GNO	Gregorii nysseni opera
Heb.	Hebrew
Ir	*Irénikon*
JTS (N.S.)	*Journal of Theological Studies* (New Series)
LPGL	*A Patristic Greek Lexikon* (ed. G. W. H. Lampe)
OCA	Orientalia christiana analecta
OCP	*Orientalia christiana periodica*
PG	Patrologia graeca
PL	Patrologia latina
PO	Patrologia orientalis
PTS	Patristische Texte und Studien
RAC	*Reallexikon für Antike und Christentum*
RAM	*Revue d'ascétique et de mystique*
RB	*Revue biblique*
RSPhTh	*Revue des sciences philosophiques et théologiques*

SA	Studia anselmiana
SC	Sources chrétiennes
schol.	scholium
StPatr	*Studia patristica*
Théol	Théologie
ThH	Théologie historique
trans.	translation
TU	Texte und Untersuchungen
VigChr	*Vigiliae christianae*

Works of Maximus the Confessor

Amb.	*Ambiguorum liber (Ambigua)*
Cap. car.	*Capita de caritate (Chapters on Charity)*
Cap. theol.	*Capita theologica et oeconomica (Chapters on Knowledge)*
Ep.	*Epistulae 1-45*
Myst.	*Mystagogia*
Opusc. theol. et polem.	*Opuscula theologica et polemica*
Qu. et dub.	*Quaestiones et dubia*
Q. Thal.	*Quaestiones ad Thalassium*

Note on Citation of Primary Sources

All references to primary sources either in the PG or PL collections include volume number in the series, followed by column(s) and section(s). All references to material in the GCS, GCSO, CSEL, CCSG, GNO, PO, and SC collections include volume number in the series, followed by page(s) and, where appropriate, lines. For ease of reference with our major primary source, the *Quaestiones ad Thalassium*, I have simplified the citations. All citations from the critical edition of *Quaestiones* 1-55 in CCSG, no. 7 (ed. Laga-Steel) include simply CCSG followed by page(s) and lines. All citations from *Quaestiones* 56-65 in the earlier edition of Combefis in PG, vol. 90, simply include PG followed by column(s) and section(s). I regret that the second volume of the Laga-Steel critical text was not yet available for use in this study.

All translations of primary sources (and of non-English secondary sources, where quoted) are my own unless otherwise noted. My translations of passages from Maximus are not, I would add, intended to oversimplify his occasionally prolix Greek. I have opted for a conservative rendering that is fair to his heavy use of technical philosophical, theological, and ascetic terms.

Introduction

The Current State of Maximian Studies

Maximus the Confessor has been called by patristic scholars past and present a theological genius of the early Eastern Church, a grand synthesizer of Greek patristic thought, and yet one of the most difficult theologians to read in his original texts, not to mention one of the most difficult to translate. Critical research on the career and writings of Maximus will doubtless profit richly from the coming publication of all his major writings in critical editions.[1] The results, it is hoped, will be a readier access to his literary corpus and a deepening of our understanding of the fine points of his scholarly output. To date, there has been a serious deficit in the analysis of Maximus' works individually. Polycarp Sherwood, who single-handedly introduced Maximus to English-speaking readers, signaled this problem over thirty years ago, when, in the foreward to his classic study of the *Ambigua ad Joannem*, he lamented the lack of knowledge of the Confessor's individual writings in their own context and scope. Scholars "have written of his doctrine, and written well, but taking here a text, there a text on which to build their structure."[2]

Sherwood certainly moved positively toward filling this gap through his close critical work on the earlier *Ambigua*, as did Hans Urs von Balthasar in his annotations to Maximus' *Mystagogia, Chapters on Charity*, and *Chapters on Knowledge*.[3] But there has been little concentration since then on illuminating the particularities of Maximus' works as individual productions. A look at secondary studies published in the last two decades confirms this pattern. Brief articles on the sources, doctrine, and spirituality of Maximus abound.[4] Even the outstanding series of dissertations, directed by M.-J. le Guillou, which build on the foundational work of pioneering specialists on Maximus the Confessor like Sherwood, von Balthasar,

Dalmais,[5] and Thunberg,[6] all focus on doctrinal themes that comprehend the full gamut of Maximus' corpus.[7] Vittorio Croce's very useful study of Maximus' theological method likewise treats the Confessor's works comprehensively.[8]

Yet there have been occasional indications of a greater interest in the contextual, literary, stylistic, and methodological characteristics of Maximus' writings. The 1980 international Symposium on Maximus in Fribourg, Switzerland, included a series of presentations not only on the manuscript traditions but also on philological, literary, and methodological concerns.[9]

Sherwood attested some time ago the need for a close study particularly of the *Quaestiones ad Thalassium,* along the lines of his own work on the earlier *Ambigua*.[10] This need has been echoed more recently by Jaroslav Pelikan.[11] The absence of a major critical study of this work is particularly unfortunate since it is second in size only to Maximus' *Ambigua* and by far the most extensive of his so-called spiritual writings. No doubt its length, its weighty style, the density of its exegetical expositions, and the diversity of its theological and ascetic themes have combined to discourage concentrated study of the *Ad Thalassium*. Characterizing the work as a premier piece of monastic spiritual pedagogy, I hope here to make a beginning toward understanding more fully its literary style and intentionality, as well as its appropriation of earlier sources and exegetical traditions, and its theological and pedagogical scope. But before setting out the main directions of this inquiry, let us first attempt to locate the *Quaestiones ad Thalassium* within Maximus' career as a monastic scholar and within the broader parameters of Byzantine monastic culture in the seventh century.

The Context and Purview of the *Quaestiones ad Thalassium*

The life of Maximus the Confessor can roughly be divided into four significant periods: his early years and service in the imperial court of the emperor Heraclius (580-c. 614); the formative monastic period leading to his relocation in Carthage (c. 614-c. 628); an intermediate monastic period of intense literary activity in Carthage (c. 628-c. 638); and his later theological career, dominated by his involvement in the monothelite controversy and his eventual arrest, torture, exile, and death (c. 638-662).[12] Our principal concern here is the two middle monastic periods, which form the background of the *Quaestiones ad Thalassium*.

Maximus' Monastic Formation

Maximus' biographer leaves us no clear motive for the Confessor's retirement from imperial service to the monastery of Philippicus near Chrysopolis (on the Asiatic shore of the Bosphorus, opposite Constantinople) save the lure of the life of quietude (ὁ καθ' ἡσυχίαν βίος).[13] Yet the impending siege of Constantinople from the east by the Persians and from the north by Avars and Slavs[14] would force Maximus in 626 from a second monastic residence at St. George's in nearby Cyzicus. After a period of intermittent travel east to Crete and perhaps Cyprus,[15] he settled at Carthage, probably between 628 and 630.[16]

North Africa at the time was, in fact, a haven of refugee monks from the east, who were looking for safe haven in the numerous monasteries that proliferated there during the sixth and seventh centuries.[17] As the eminent Byzantinist Charles Diehl has noted, Africa was one of the few flourishing and tranquil parts of the empire during the Persian campaigns.[18] Maximus took up residence in the monastery of Eukratas, under the tutelege of his spiritual father Sophronius. In one of his opuscula, Maximus specifically mentions "Sophronius, who, with me and all the foreign monks (*mecum et cum omnibus perigrinis monachis*), spent time in the land of the Africans."[19] In a related allusion, he remembers "many other pious monks who are in exile there (ἐνταῦθα ἐπιξενουμένων) and, in particular, the blessed servants of God, our fathers who are called Eukratades (οἱ ἐπίκλην Εὐκρατάδης)."[20] Christoph von Schönborn asserts that this group whom Maximus calls "our fathers," called Eukratades, was the original circle of monks that was gathered together by the renowned Palestinian John Moschus (surnamed Eukratas) and that in exile was led by John's favored disciple, Sophronius. The group based itself at Carthage and was ostensibly deeply involved in the struggle for christological orthodoxy.[21]

Maximus himself leaves us all too little information on the particulars of his early monastic formation, and what we know must be inferred from his writings, his relationship with Sophronius, and from scanty external evidence. Like other literate Byzantine monks, his training surely included an immersion in scripture and in the writings of the Greek Fathers. A critical factor in Maximus' monastic paideia, at one time heavily debated in Maximian scholarship, was his access to the works of Origen and his contact with the Origenist tradition. His monothelite biographer asserted that Maximus had actually been trained at the monastery of Palaia Lavra (St. Chariton) in Palestine, under a certain "wicked Origenist" by the name of Panteleon.[22] This tendentious account is of course highly suspect.[23] Yet we know from Maximus' own writings that he was deeply influenced both by Origenist doctrine and by Origenian biblical hermeneutics. This Alexandrian legacy of allegorical interpretation was, through such key figures as Didymus and Evagrius, the shared inheritance of Byzantine monasticism.[24] Von Balthasar, however, has sufficiently proved that Maximus, at least in his *Chapters on Knowledge*, had read Origen's works firsthand.[25] The hypothesis of an "Origenist crisis" in Maximus' early career, occasioned perhaps by a trip with Sophronius to Alexandria and by fascination with Origen's writings, has generally been overturned.[26] Yet the impact of Origen's thought, even negatively in Maximus' refutation of the more recent strains of radical Origenism in the earlier *Ambigua ad Joannem*, was decisive in his developing understanding of the monastic life. As Sherwood remarks rightly, Maximus appears, not as having undergone an Origenist crisis, "but as deliberately endeavoring to give the assimilable elements in the Alexandrian master's thought a secure place in monastic tradition."[27]

The impact of the Cappadocians on Maximus' monastic formation was no less fundamental.[28] Earlier evidence indicates that the Cappadocians were widely read by literate monks throughout the Christian East during the fifth and sixth centuries. Barsanuphius and John, the strongly anti-Origenist Palestinian monks of the early sixth century, report how one monk, having been reading the Greek Fathers, consulted them over seemingly problematic passages in the works of Gregory of Nyssa.[29] The monk Maximus had the same sorts of questions. In one of his *Quaestiones et dubia*, he asks about the sensitive issue of Gregory of Nyssa's doctrine of the apokatastasis.[30] Moreover, he recalls having worked out his answers to difficult passages in

Gregory of Nazianzus' *Orations* precisely while in monastic solitude at Cyzicus[31] (the fruit of which was his *Ambigua ad Joannem*, completed mainly in Carthage). Throughout this period, especially in the wake of the Origenist controversy, the works of the Cappadocians and other Greek Fathers were consulted and assimilated by the Byzantine spiritual writers. Gregory of Nyssa's works were decisive in helping to shape the ascetic doctrine of Evagrius, Pseudo-Dionysius, and beyond them the likes of Diadochus of Photice (fifth century) and the representatives of the Palestinian-Sinaitic school. Maximus thus inherited a much wider tradition through which to interpret the original works of the great Cappadocians and Origen.[32]

A final, and certainly decisive, factor in Maximus' monastic development was his personal association with Sophronius, which, by the latter's relation to John Moschus, linked Maximus indirectly to the desert spirituality of the Palestinian-Sinaitic ascetic tradition. Sophronius had been schooled by John in the "philosophy" of monastic exile, the *xeniteia*[33] in which the monk became a foreign pilgrim on earth, during their travels together between Palestine, Egypt, and Rome.[34] As monastic types, John and Sophronius (whose epithet was "the Sophist") sharply differed in social standing and education.[35] John was not a gifted theologian but a zealot whose anecdotal ascetic treatise, the *Pratum spirituale* or "Spiritual Meadow," was intended mainly to inspire admiration for the holy men;[36] Sophronius was a trained philosopher and rhetorician whose passion for book learning was never ultimately extinguished by monastic exile.[37] This did not hinder a deep and abiding relationship between the two men, John Moschus calling Sophronius his "holy and faithful son," "lord," "brother," "companion,"[38] and Sophronius praising John as his "spiritual father and teacher."[39]

Having opted for monastic exile (albeit circumstantially) under the direction of an older master of monastic paideia, Maximus assumed a similar relationship of spiritual patronage under Sophronius.[40] Moreover, just as John had led Sophronius to combine his monastic vocation with struggles over Christology, Sophronius inspired Maximus' participation in the fight for Chalcedonian orthodoxy in North Africa, a campaign that would dominate much of the Confessor's later career.

In contrast with John Moschus and Sophronius, Sophronius and Maximus were equally refined scholar-monks, well grounded in Greek philosophy and Christian theology,[41] both accommodating this learning to their monastic professions. Both enjoyed personal influence even in imperial echelons, as exemplified by their common friendship with George, eparch of Africa.[42] Both were destined to become highly visible figures, earning wide repute for their championing of Chalcedonian orthodoxy during the monothelite controversy: Sophronius as patriarch of Jerusalem, Maximus as a leader in the Lateran Synod in Rome in 649.

The actual extent of Sophronius' influence on Maximus' ascetic formation can only be inferred. It would be interesting indeed if we could positively identify the "grand old man" ($μέγας$ $γέρων$), to whom Maximus defers in his *Mystagogia* (and in other of his writings), as Sophronius.[43] This was the very title used by desert monks in Palestine and Egypt for their spiritually gifted sages.[44] Juan Miguel Garrigues has argued plausibly that it was precisely Sophronius who, through his close association with Palestinian-Sinaitic monachism, introduced Maximus to that hesychast tradition which, inspired by Pseudo-Macarius and typified in the work of Maximus' contemporary John Climacus, was to give Byzantine mystical theology its proper distinction.[45] "This Macarian and Sinaitic inspiration is very visible," adds Garrigues, "in the *Quaestiones ad Thalassium*," which "constitutes an attempt at correcting the intellectualism of Evagrius with the help of Macarian themes centered on affection, the synergy of our will, the heart, the development of baptismal grace, charity...."[46]

The Historical Foreground of the Ad Thalassium

Maximus' tenure in Carthage, part of which he spent under Sophronius' tutelege, was a time of great literary productivity. In less than a decade, he composed or completed his *Orationis dominicae expositio* (*Commentary on the Lord's Prayer*) (c. 628-630), *Ambigua ad Joannem* (c. 628-630), *Mystagogia* (c. 628-630), *Quaestiones ad Thalassium* (c. 630-633), and *Capita theologica et oeconomica* (*Chapters on Knowledge*) (c. 630-634).[47]

Yet this was also a period of social and political turbulence, as reported by Maximus himself in the end of a letter to Sophronius. Protesting Heraclius' decision, in the wake of new Jewish insurgency, to impose baptism on all Jews and Samaritans in Africa (and throughout the empire) on Pentecost of 632, he denounces the idea of compromising the holy sacrament on unbelievers.[48] For Maximus, these drastic imperial measures were in fact capable of inaugurating the "great apostasy" (2 Thess. 2:3).[49] In another letter a short time later, Maximus decries the barbarous desert hordes (of Arabs) who were invading Africa from the east and threatening civilized society. In the same letter he complains of the Jews, who were ostensibly rejoicing over the spilling of Christian blood in these Arab incursions.[50] These instructive allusions may help to illuminate a strong anti-Jewish current running through the *Quaestiones ad Thalassium* itself. In certain passages, Maximus merely deploys traditional sorts of anti-Jewish polemic, claiming that the Jews are an antitype of spiritual truth, an acute example of the general human preoccupation with the carnal and the material;[51] but at other points in the *Ad Thalassium*, his polemic against Judaism is so virulent that it would seem to hint of some concrete historical crisis in which the Jews were again perceived to be menacing the Church. Maximus calls upon a host of typological[52] and biblical-historical[53] arguments to demonstrate that the Jews are now what they always have been, an intransigent and proud people who have rejected the light of the incarnate Logos. Carl Laga surmises that this invective may have arisen from actual disputations between Christian theologians and Jewish intellectuals in which the Bible was being cited on both sides.[54]

A more immediate problem in the purview of Maximus' writings from this period was a purely Christian affair: the perceived threat of a recalcitrant Origenism in the Byzantine monasteries. Origenism by no means died out completely after the conciliar condemnation of Origen, Didymus, and Evagrius at Constantinople in 553. Having been given tremendous philosophical and theological impetus in the work of Evagrius, the Origenist system had provided the first comprehensive philosophical rationale for the monastic life. Indeed, Evagrius was single-handedly responsible for putting the ideology of desert monasticism into writing and, through such works as his *Praktikos*, had become the premier theoretician of Origenist spirituality.[55] After the expulsion of the Palestinian Origenist monks from the New Lavra in 555,[56] it is quite probable that some of them fled west, perhaps even into North Aftrica itself. The anti-Origenist treatise *De sectis* would seem to presuppose the active presence of Origenist teaching even into the early seventh century.[57] Maximus, therefore, may very well have known or encountered Origenist sympathizers within monastic circles during the earlier part of his career. The postulation of an "Origenist crisis" in his life, though reasonably overturned upon closer scrutiny,[58] is not *a priori* unimaginable.

As Irénée-Henri Dalmais points out, the Origenism (or more accurately "Evagrianism") in the purview of Maximus' early writings—namely, the earlier *Ambigua*, the *Chapters on Knowledge*, and, to a lesser extent, the *Quaestiones ad Thalassium*—is never concretely described or identified. "But the place that the refutation of this alleged monastic Origenism maintained in the thought and work of Maximus shows us that in the second quarter of the seventh century, these errors retained all their virulence."[59]

The Origenist danger was not the inheritance of the monks alone, but it remains true nonetheless (and significant for the present study) that Maximus worked out his corrections of Origenism in the context of resolving monks' questions and in clarifying patristic authorities to a monastic audience.[60] Moreover, Maximus developed this correction precisely by rejecting the problematic premises of Origenism and applying its positive elements to his synthetic understanding of the spiritual life. The main source for this correction of Origenism, of course, is the earlier *Ambigua* addressed to John of Cyzicus,[61] but we find clear evidence of it in the *Quaestiones ad Thalassium* as well.

Two of Maximus' responses, in particular, explicitly target Origenism. In a long exposé in *Quaestio* 59 on how the prophets searched out and investigated the salvation of souls (1 Pet. 1:10-11), he deals with the problematic Origenist equation of the beginning ($ἀρχή$) and end ($τέλος$) of human existence. Characteristically, he denies such an equation on a purely ontological level (i.e., rejecting the Origenist idea of a primitive henad of pure spirits that is to be realized again at the end) but accepts it on a moral and cognitive level, insofar as humanity truly discovers the original purpose of its creation only teleologically.[62] In another response as well, Maximus contests those Origenists who would speculate that a natural creature could have enjoyed primordial foreknowledge, as in a preexistent state:

Indeed, we reject the argument of some who say that Christ was foreknown before the foundation of the world, to those to whom he was later manifested at the end of time, as though those beings were themselves present with the foreknown Christ before the foundation of the world, and as though the Word, being estranged from the truth, were teaching that the essence of rational beings (λογικοί) is coeternal with God.[63]

Besides these explicit references to Origenism, Maximus reveals in many of his moral and spiritual exegeses in the *Ad Thalassium* a more subtle, implicit criticism of the radical intellectualism posed by the later Origenist tradition in the representative figure of Evagrius Ponticus, though Maximus still attempts to rehabilitate its more positive aspects. Of this more will be said further on in the analysis of specific texts in the *Ad Thalassium*.

Most important for our purposes here is the fact that Origenism, in its most sophisticated Evagrian rendition, was still being perceived as a viable option for reflective monks when Maximus composed the *Quaestiones ad Thalassium* in the second quarter of the seventh century. Any new treatise addressed to a monastic audience would have to deal, in Maximus' mind at least, with the residual effects of a system that seemed at once to picture human corporeal and "historical" existence as quasi-accidental, and to minimize the centrality of the historically incarnate Christ in the spiritual life of humanity. In this Maximus would join his voice with a chorus of Greek Christian ascetic theologians who, from the time of the Cappadocian Fathers on, struggled to redirect and rehabilitate certain of the fundamental intuitions of Origen's worldview.

The Immediate Occasion of the Ad Thalassium

Maximus' relationship with Thalassius is another matter that we are forced to infer from the Confessor's writings. Certainly his own introduction to the *Ad Thalassium* presupposes a warm and mature friendship, as do his letters to Thalassius.[64] The evidence does not clearly indicate, however, whether Maximus had been a disciple of Thalassius, or vice versa. In his correspondence with "the presbyter and hegumen Thalassius,"[65] Maximus addresses him as "venerable father" (τίμιε πάτερ),[66] and refers to himself as "your servant (δοῦλος) and disciple (μαθητής) Maximus,"[67] or "Maximus, a humble monk (ταπεινὸς μονάζων)."[68] There is no reason to take these salutations absolutely literally. Sherwood suggests that the correspondence "supposes a relation of friendship between the two as between an older (Thalassius) and younger man...; it is sufficient that Thalassius was abbot and priest. Maximus simple monk."[69] Even if Maximus, in the *Quaestiones ad Thalassium*, was the younger man, put in the position of teaching an elder monk, this ostensibly set no utterly new precedent. Two centuries before, Basil of Caesarea had addressed just this sort of situation in one of his monastic rules.[70]

The origin of Maximus' acquaintance with Thalassius is also elusive. M.-Th. Disdier has reasonably conjectured that the two monks probably met either in the Libyan Pentapolis or the province of Africa, at some point during Maximus' long monastic exile, when he had occasion to travel through these regions in the fight against an emergent monotheletism.[71]

Attempts have been made to establish their relationship on the basis of a comparison of their writings, and on the possible dependence of Thalassius' *Centuries on Charity and Self-Control* on Maximus' own *Chapters on Charity*. The comparison is precarious from the outset since both rely on a very influential common source: Evagrius.[72] Yet clear thematic parallels do exist and are rich enough to suggest that Thalassius had probably already perused Maximus' *Chapters*,[73] and even the *Quaestiones ad Thalassium* itself,[74] before finally redacting his own *Centuries*. Though not merely a passive imitator of the Confessor, Thalassius did develop, in his own way, spiritual themes that were basic to Maximus.[75]

The two were apparently in frequent correspondence about their shared interests, the elder deferring to the theological acumen of his younger contemporary. Maximus addresses one of his letters "to Thalassius the presbyter, who asked how it was that some of the pagan kings would sacrifice their children and kinsmen to appease the wrath of God on the mass of their subjects, and that the wrath would stop, just as it is recorded in many of the ancients."[76] As it so happens, the *Quaestiones ad Thalassium* itself arose from a letter from Thalassius enjoining Maximus to resolve a list of scriptural difficulties.[77] Maximus already alluded to this injunction in his *Epistulae* 40 and 41.

Maximus tells us of this original request in his introduction to the *Ad Thalassium*, indicating also his tremendous esteem for Thalassius' spiritual maturity:

> Hence after the complete removal of any inclination toward sense and the flesh, strenuously navigating the infinite sea of the oracles of the Spirit with an intellectual science, you searched the deep things of the Spirit with the help of the Spirit. Receiving from him a manifestation of hidden mysteries, on account of your great, so it seems, humility of mind, you were filled with many difficult topics from Holy Scripture, and you sent me a note, seeking from me, one bereft of all virtue and knowledge, a written response to each topic in terms of an anagogical interpretation.[78]

With characteristic self-abasement, Maximus further expresses his reticence to undertake such an enterprise, submitting only on account of his abiding friendship with Thalassius:

> Having received and read what you sent, I was overwhelmed in mind, hearing, and thought. Earnestly entreating you about it, I begged your pardon. I said that the questions were scarcely approachable even for those who have made the greatest strides in contemplation, and for others who have attained to a knowledge of the highest and unattainable goal, let alone for myself, one cast down to the earth, who, like the other serpent, as in the ancient curse (cf. Gen. 3:14), has no food besides the dirt of the passions and crawls like a worm in the decay of the pleasures. I did this repeatedly for a long time, when I discovered that you would not accept my excuse about it. I feared that something would happen to our love, whereby we are welded together and have one soul, even if we bear two bodies. I feared that you would consider my excuse a pretext for disobedience. Not wishing for things beyond

> my ability, I dared rather to be marked and scorned for rashness, better led by my own desires, than for our love to be disrupted and diminished for any reason. There is nothing apart from God more honorable for those who have a mind, nor more pleasant to God, than this love, since it unites those divided into oneness and can create a single factionless identity of will among many or among all.
>
> Being alone preeminent, venerable father, pardon me for this undertaking and ask the others to forgive me for rashness. Insure by your prayers that God will be gracious to me and a partner in the things I say; that he will become a patron of the complete and correct response for every topic in question. For "every good endowment and perfect gift" (James 1:17) is from God, Source and Father of all enlightened knowledge and abilities being supplied proportionately to those who are worthy. Being confident in you, I accepted your injunction, and as payment for consenting I am receiving your good will.[79]

There is more in Maximus' self-abasement here than a rhetorical convention. Throughout the *Ad Thalassium* it is obvious that he does not consider himself principally an exegete. Many times he urges his readers to investigate alternative, loftier interpretations of the topic in question and not to consider his own interpretations exhaustive.[80] Yet Maximus has a strong sense of obligation to his readers. Clearly he has in view a larger audience than Thalassius, desiring to address his answers to "you (pl.) who are truly gnostic and precise seers of divine realities."[81] He insists also on his refusal to cast aside a task set before him by "you (pl.) who enjoined and imposed on me this labor of speaking about things beyond my ability."[82]

We can assume that Thalassius has sent Maximus these sixty-five "diverse difficulties" from scripture as a result of his own meditation, or perhaps more likely (since Maximus envisions a plural audience) through collective discussion of the scriptures in conferences with his subordinates. At any rate, Maximus at the outset finds himself in the position of a spiritual father who is addressing the needs of a specific community of monks.

The Critical and Interpretative Problem
of the *Quaestiones ad Thalassium*

Even a cursory glance at the list of sixty-five questions on scripture sent by Thalassius to Maximus shows that there is no apparent arrangement or progression in the topics at hand. As in Maximus' *Quaestiones et dubia*, the scriptural texts cited and the queries posed are highly variegated, as in a random collection. From a purely superficial perspective, then, Dalmais has concluded of the *Quaestiones ad Thalassium* that

> the very most that can be said is that the responses to the later questions are clearly longer, more serious, and that they furnish one or several explanations of each of the details of the text and of the whole altogether. None of its characteristics is original, and when it is noted that the interpretation remains closely within the tradition of Origen, it appears that everything has been said. In fact, the essential factor has not yet been touched: the constancy of perspectives which form *a complete treatise of spiritual anthropology* from a collection which is at very first sight incoherent.[83]

Dalmais finds the closest formal parallel to the *Quaestiones ad Thalassium* in the famous *Moralia on Job* of Gregory the Great, insofar as both exhibit a remarkable and mature instance of that interpretation of scripture for monastic usage that the Benedictine tradition came to call the *lectio divina*.[84]

Without doubt, scriptural commentary plays a subordinate role to spiritual-doctrinal exposition in the *Ad Thalassium*. More than half of Maximus' introduction to the text is devoted to Thalassius' initial list of queries about the origin and nature of the passions.[85] Moreover, moral and ascetic motifs dominate the individual exegeses in the responses to the questions on scripture. Gustave Bardy suggested early on that the work was actually more interesting for the history of spirituality than for the history of exegesis.[86] Later studies have also simply acknowledged this preponderance of spiritual doctrine and ascetic themes in the *Ad Thalassium*. In a brief early article on Maximus' exegesis of scripture, Sherwood bluntly contended that the Confessor's use of scripture in this work could be called "exegesis" only in the most qualified sense, its aim being primarily to render all scriptural texts tributary, through anagogical interpretation, to the central mystery of Christ.[87] Walther Völker has furthermore claimed that scriptural anagogy in the *Ad Thalassium* belongs primarily within the context of Maximus' developing understanding of the formation of the Christian "gnostic."[88]

Given this consensus, it is little wonder that Maximus' exegeses in the *Quaestiones ad Thalassium* have been cited in secondary studies mainly just as another source for his doctrine.[89] My purpose will first be to investigate these extensive exegetical scholia on their own terrain in the *Ad Thalassium*, that is, as *a peculiar medium of monastic spiritual pedagogy* with particular heuristic intentions. Such an approach—seeking to understand this immense work from the standpoint of its own purview and trying to capture something of its special occasion and purpose—has never been undertaken. Nor has a close consideration of its *monastic* provenance and context as yet been attempted. Christoph von Schönborn has indirectly hinted at the same problem in a 1980 study of the *Ad Thalassium*, in noting the fact that the preoccupation of modern scholars with Maximus' sources (and, I would add, with the development of his overarching theological themes) has run the risk of overshadowing the simple appreciation of Maximus in his role as "a spiritual guide" who is prescribing "a course of Christian *praxis*" or "an initiation in a spiritual way of life."[90] Georges Florovsky has suggested of Maximus that "it is the rhythm of the spiritual life rather than a logical connection of ideas which defines the architechtonics of his vision of the world."[91] It would indeed seem that one cannot fully comprehend the *Quaestiones ad Thalassium* as a "treatise of spiritual anthropology," to use Dalmais' phrase, without taking account of its original form as commentary on scripture intended to lead inquisitive monks over certain difficult or obscure passages to those larger truths of spiritual or mystical doctrine which were believed to lie behind the text. The *Ad Thalassium* is, at the most basic level, a spiritual father's response to the need to show that all of scripture—including, indeed especially its difficult passages, its $ἀπορίαι$—is indispensible to the soul in its struggle to attain to deification.

Drawing from the already interconnected traditions of monastic devotion to the Bible, Origenian hermeneutics, the sophisticated symbolic theology of Pseudo-Dionysius, the rich spiritual anthropology of Greek Christian asceticism inspired by the Cappadocian Fathers, Maximus would develop a form of exegesis that was consummately pedagogical, and "theological" in the broader sense of preparing monks for the way of true θεολογία. Our descriptive task in this study is to understand the fusion of spiritual pedagogy and biblical exegesis in the *Ad Thalassium* by considering integratively its form or genre, its theoretical and hermeneutical principles, and its practical exegetical methods.

Chapter 1 extends the analysis of the context of the *Quaestiones ad Thalassium* by specifically considering its genre and its links to earlier forms of monastic catechesis, namely, to the tradition of monastic pedagogical *quaestiones* in earlier Byzantine monastic literature. Against this background, the *Ad Thalassium* comes to light more within a concrete, albeit dynamic, *Sitz im Leben*, which further enhances our understanding of Maximus' exegesis as grounded in its own monastic culture and in the emergent patterns of the use of scripture—and scriptural ἀπορίαι—in Byzantine monasticism.

Chapter 2 attempts to outline what might best be termed Maximus' hermeneutical theology. Here I shall concentrate on the theme of spiritual διάβασις as an organizing principle of Maximus' theology of exegesis. This will spawn a consideration of how Maximus integrates cosmological, scriptural, anthropological, and ascetic perspectives on the fundamental "transit" from sensible to intelligible reality. Creation (the natural law) and scripture (the written law) are for Maximus, as for his major predecessors, analogous mediums or economies of revelation, each by its inherent structure capable of conducting the mind to the level of intelligible truth (the spiritual law), or more precisely, to the μυστήριον of the incarnate Christ. But if the incarnate Christ is the substance and σκοπός of all of creation and scripture, this raises the further hermeneutical problem, as we shall observe, of the nature of the correspondence between the "three laws," the correlation or "difference of degrees" (to use Lars Thunberg's terms) between the Logos' "incarnations" in creation, in scripture, and in the historical Jesus. How is it that Jesus Christ holds the key to the intelligible truth behind the world and scripture? Maximus answers this question in a way which indicates both his fidelity to, and innovation upon, the hermeneutical principles of his significant precursors, Origen and Evagrius.

But that is only the objective order, the "macrocosmic" dimension. There is also the subjective and "microcosmic" dimension, the *diabasis*, or transition, that human beings are summoned to undergo both cognitively, through the interchangeable contemplation of creation (φυσικὴ θεωρία) and scripture (γραφικὴ θεωρία), and morally, through the practice (πρᾶξις) of virtue. These two mutually co-inherent aspects find their culmination in the higher "theological" (θεολογικῇ) aspect of the spiritual *diabasis*, the deifying encounter with the mystery of Christ.

At the outset of chapter 3, I shall demonstrate the implications of this vision of spiritual *diabasis* for Maximus' "anagogy" itself. His anagogical interpretation (ἀναγωγικὴ θεωρία) of scripture seeks not to exhaust scripture of this mystery, but to introduce multiple possibilities from the text that, in principle at least, would lead up from the literal to the most mystical and ineffable meaning of scripture—the one, it would seem, to be disclosed by the Logos himself in the culmination of his self-revelation. In actual practice, as we shall see, Maximus normally negotiates among a variety of spiritual or theological interpretations, not necessarily in a precise order nor even with obvious thematic consistency, but all, in his view, anchored in the mystery of Christ.

The remainder of chapter 3 analyzes some of the more consistent anagogical methods employed by Maximus in the *Quaestiones ad Thalassium*, most of which find a precedent in earlier patristic exegesis: typology, etymology, arithmology, and extrapolations from biblical terminology and discourse. Here Maximus' dependence on Origenian hermeneutics will be most conspicuous; yet I would seek to move a step beyond considering these methods only as exegetical techniques aimed at extracting spiritual meanings from scripture and view them as pedagogical tools enabling Maximus to use scripture in framing and developing his own ascetic doctrine for the monks. Anyone who reads the more substantive of his *responsiones* sees that these are more than concise exegetical scholia; they are, in many instances (especially in the later and longer responses to Thalassius) thoroughgoing spiritual catechisms. By means of these anagogical methods, then, all of scripture, even its discrepancies and obscurities, is rendered transparent to the cosmic drama of the history of salvation—both its fulfillment in the deifying activity of the Logos-Christ and its gradual unfolding in the lives of the spiritually diligent.

Notes

1. Already a first volume of the *Quaestiones ad Thalassium* has appeared: *Maximi Confessoris Quaestiones ad Thalassium, I: Quaestiones I-LV una cum latine interpretatione Ioannis Scotti Eriugenae*, ed. Carl Laga and Carlos Steel, Corpus christianorum, series graeca 7 (Turnhout: Brepols—Leuven University Press, 1980). Part II (*Quaestiones LVI-LXV*), ed. idem, has just appeared (though too late for use in my study), and all of Maximus' other major works are also in preparation and slated for publication in CCSG.

2. Polycarp Sherwood, *The Earlier Ambigua of Maximus the Confessor and His Refutation of Origenism*, SA 36 (Rome: Herder, 1955), vii.

3. See the German translations with extensive annotations in Hans Urs von Balthasar, *Kosmische Liturgie: Das Weltbild Maximus' des Bekenners*, 2nd ed. (Einsiedeln: Johannes-Verlag, 1961), 361-643 ("Texte und Studien").

4. See my bibliography below.

5. See the articles of I.-H. Dalmais listed in my bibliography below.

6. See especially the still-pivotal study of Lars Thunberg, *Microcosm and Mediator: The Theological Anthropology of Maximus the Confessor* (Lund: C. W. K. Gleerup, 1965); cf. also his recent work, *Man and the Cosmos: The Vision of St. Maximus the Confessor* (Crestwood, N.Y.: St. Vladimir's Seminary Press, 1985).

7. Cf. Alain Riou, *Le monde et l'église selon Maxime le Confesseur*, ThH 22 (Paris: Beauchesne, 1973); Juan Miguel Garrigues, *Maxime le Confesseur: La charité, avenir divin de l'homme*, ThH 38 (Paris: Beauchesne, 1976); François-Marie Léthel, *Théologie de l'agonie du Christ: La liberté humaine du Fils de Dieu et son importance sotériologique mises en lumière par saint Maxime le Confesseur*, ThH 52 (Paris: Beauchesne, 1979); and Pierre Piret, *Le Christ et la Trinité selon Maxime le Confesseur*, ThH 69 (Paris: Beauchesne, 1983).

8. See his *Tradizione e ricerca: Il metodo teologico di san Massimo il Confessore*, Studia patristica mediolanensia 2 (Milan: Vita e Pensiero, 1974).

9. In particular, see the following studies from the volume *Maximus*

Confessor: Actes du Symposium sur Maxime le Confesseur, Fribourg, 2-5 septembre 1980, ed. Felix Heinzer and Christoph von Schönborn, Paradosis 27 (Fribourg: Éditions Universitaires, 1982): A. Ceresa-Gestaldo, "Tradition et innovation linguistique chez Maxime le Confesseur," 123-137; Carl Laga, "Maximus as a Stylist in *Quaestiones ad Thalassium*," 139-146; and N. Madden, "The *Commentary on the Pater Noster*: An Example of the Structural Methodology of Maximus the Confessor," 147-155. Cf. also the recent study of Carl Laga, "Maximi Confessoris ad Thalassium Quaestio 64," in *After Chalcedon: Studies in Theology and Church History Offered to Professor Albert van Roey for His Seventieth Birthday*, ed. Carl Laga, J. A. Munitz, and L. van Rompay, Orientalia lovaniensia analecta 18 (Leuven: Departement Oriëntalistiek, 1985), 203-215.

    10. See Polycarp Sherwood, *An Annotated Date-List of the Works of Maximus the Confessor*, SA 30 (Rome: Herder, 1952), 35: "A thorough doctrinal analysis of this work is needed." See also *Earlier Ambigua*, vii-viii.

    11. See his essay, "Council or Father or Scripture: The Concept of Authority in the Theology of Maximus the Confessor," in *The Heritage of the Early Church: Essays in Honor of Georges Florovsky*, ed. David Neiman and Margaret Schatkin, OCA 195 (Rome: Pontifical Institute of Oriental Studies, 1973), 281.

    12. Our basic source for Maximus' career is the Greek *Vita* in a number of recensions: see the *Acta* in PG 90.109-172; and Robert Devreesse, "La vie de s. Maxime le Confesseur et ses recensions," *AB* 46 (1928): 5-49. Cf. the rather derisive, monothelite Syriac *Vita* of Maximus published by Sebastian Brock, "An Early Syriac Life of Maximus the Confessor," *AB* 91 (1973): 299-346. See also the fundamental reconstruction of Sherwood, *Annotated Date-List*, 1-22; and his introduction to *Maximus the Confessor: The Ascetic Life and Four Centuries on Charity*, ACW 21 (Westminster, Md.: Newman Press, 1957). A good summary of research on Maximus' biography may be found in Thunberg, *Microcosm and Mediator*, 1-20.

    13. *Vita ac certamen* (PG 90.72D). See also Thunberg, *Man and the Cosmos*, 21.

    14. See George Ostrogorsky, *History of the Byzantine State*, rev. ed., trans. Joan Hussey (New Brunswick, N.J.: Rutgers University Press, 1969), 87-103. Ostrogorsky notes that the Persians advanced toward Constantinople precisely via the Bosphorus (i.e., through the region of Chrysopolis and Cyzicus).

    15. See Sherwood, *Annotated Date-List*, 5.

    16. From the end of Maximus' *Ep.* 8, with its reference to the forced baptism of Jews and Samaritans in Carthage in 632, it is clear that he was in

Carthage at least by that date; cf. the text published with discussion by Robert Devreesse, "La fin inédite d'un lettre de saint Maxime: Un baptême forcé de juifs et de samaritains à Carthage en 632," *Revue des sciences religieuses* 17 (1937): 25-35. Sherwood (*Annotated Date-List*, 6), however, rightly supposes a period of adjustment, thus setting the relocation in Carthage back to c. 628-630.

17. Cf. Charles Diehl, *L'Afrique byzantine: Histoire de la domination byzantine en Afrique (539-709)*, vol. 2 (Paris: E. Leroux, 1896), 427-430. He observes that the sixth and seventh centuries in Africa witnessed a tremendous flowering of churches and monasteries, with recruitment of monks from both Africa and abroad.

18. Ibid., 522, 526, 527. Even the emperor Heraclius temporarily considered moving his capital to Carthage in the wake of the Persian threat.

19. *Opusc. theol. et polem.* 12 (a Latin extract from a letter written from Maximus to Peter the Illustrious) (PG 91.142A).

20. *Ep.* 12 (PG 91.461A).

21. See Schönborn's study, *Sophrone de Jérusalem: Vie monastique et confession dogmatique*, ThH 20 (Paris: Beauchesne, 1972), 75. Schönborn further notes (56-57, n. 13) that Sophronius shared the surname "Eukratas" with John Moschus, and the two were called (in one MS of the hagiographical *Life of John the Almsgiver*) οἱ Εὐκρατάδης.

22. Syriac *Vita* 4-7, ed. and trans. by Brock, "Early Syriac Life," 304-305, 315.

23. See Dalmais, *DS* 10, s.v. "Maxime le Confesseur," cols. 836-837. Brock ("Early Syriac Life," 340-342) is nonetheless more willing to concede some element of truth in this account of a Palestinian provenance of Maximus, given the Syriac biographer's confirmed credentials. Brock suggests that the Greek *Vita*, with its eulogistic descriptions of Maximus' aristocratic origins in Constantinople, must equally be held suspect from an historical-critical perspective.

24. Cf. Denys Gorce, *La lectio divina des origines du cénobitisme à saint Benoît et Cassiodore*, vol. 1 (Wépion-sur-Meuse, Belgium: Monastère du Mont-Vièrge; Paris: Libraire A. Picard, 1925), 63ff; Georges Florovsky, *The Byzantine Ascetic and Spiritual Fathers*, The Collected Works of Georges Florovsky 10, trans. Raymond Miller et al. (Vaduz: Büchervertriebsanstalt, 1987), 135; Thunberg, *Man and the Cosmos*, 21-22.

25. See the annotations to his German translation of the *Chapters on Knowledge* in *Kosmische Liturgie*, 482-643. It is less likely that Maximus was reading the works of Origen firsthand earlier, when formulating his refutation of Origenism in the *Ambigua ad Joannem*, where his knowledge of Origen's thought is dependent mainly on the pejorative caricatures of the myth

of a primordial spiritual henad, as they were recorded in the conciliar anathemas of 553. Cf. here Sherwood, *Earlier Ambigua*, 72-102.

26. Von Balthasar first postulated such a crisis, contingent on an alleged trip of Maximus to Alexandria in 633, in his *Die Gnostischen Centurien* (Freiburg, 1941), and in the first edition of his *Kosmische Liturgie* (Freiburg, 1941), 42. Diehl (*L'Afrique byzantine*, 547) also affirmed that Maximus had been in Alexandria. Yet Sherwood (*Annotated Date-List*, 28-29, 39-40) has pointed out that the only evidence of Maximus' being in Alexandria, *Opusc. theol. et polem.* 12 (PG 91.143C-D), with its description of Sophronius refuting monothelites in Alexandria, need not assume an eyewitness account. Moreover, *Ep.* 12 (PG 91.532D-533A) presupposes Sophronius' presence in Alexandria in 633 without Maximus. Von Balthasar himself, in the second edition of *Kosmische Liturgie* (12-13), took notice of Sherwood's criticism of his hypothesis of an "Origenist crisis" in Maximus, which he claims to have presented "only as a hunch."

27. *Annotated Date-List*, 4-5. Sherwood showed (ibid., 4) that the initial ten sentences of the *Gnostic Centuries* constituted a summary of Maximus' anti-Origenist stance (paralleling the *Ambigua*), to be contrasted with his more positive evaluation of Origenian motifs further on in the *Centuries*.

28. Juan Miguel Garrigues has suggested the possibility that Maximus had spent some time in a (Palestinian?) monastery of the Basilian cenobitic type. He bases this hypothesis on Maximus' letters to a certain John of Cyzicus, who may be the same John of Cyzicus mentioned by John Moschus (*Pratum spiritualis* 187) as having resided at a monastery on the Mount of Olives. See Garrigues, "La Personne composée du Christ d'après Maxime le Confesseur," *Revue thomiste* 74 (1974): 183. Cf. also Dalmais, "Maxime le Confesseur," col. 837.

29. See Barsanuphius and John, *Quaestiones et responsiones* 600-607, cited by Derwas Chitty in *The Desert a City: An Introduction to the Study of Egyptian and Palestinian Monasticism under the Christian Empire* (Oxford: Basil Blackwell, 1966), 136-137. As Jacques Rousse notes (*DS* 9, s.v. "Lectio divina et lecture spirituelle" [I. La lectio divina], cols. 477-478), this correspondence clearly indicates that the monks were encouraged to read the Fathers as well as scripture for the edification of the soul.

30. *Quaestiones et dubia* 19 (I,3) (CCSG 10.17-18; ed. José Declerck [Turnhout: Brepols–Leuven University Press, 1982]).

31. Cf. his preface to *Amb.* II (*ad Joannem*) (PG 91.1064A). See also Sherwood, *Annotated Date-List*, 31-32; Garrigues, *Maxime le Confesseur*, 36-37. On Maximus' assimilation of Cappadocian thought directly into his

own work, see George Berthold, "The Cappadocian Roots of Maximus the Confessor," in *Maximus Confessor: Actes du Symposium sur Maxime le Confesseur, Fribourg, 2-5 septembre 1980*, ed. Felix Heinzer and Christoph von Schönborn, Paradosis 27 (Fribourg: Éditions Universitaires, 1982), 51-59.

32. Garrigues (*Maxime le Confesseur*, 45, n. 10) has rightly called attention to the Macarian tradition as a context in which Maximus knew and read the works of Gregory of Nyssa (see below). Maximus' dependence on Evagrius, especially in the *Chapters on Charity*, was originally demonstrated by Marcel Viller, "Aux sources de la spiritualité de s. Maxime: Les œuvres d'Évagre le Pontique," *RAM* 11 (1930): 156-184, 239-268, 331-336. Unfortunately, as von Balthasar has pointed out (*Kosmische Liturgie*, 12), Viller tended to view Maximus more as a compiler than as a creative synthesizer in his own right.

33. On this principle of the monastic *xeniteia* as eschatological vocation, see Garrigues, *Maxime le Confesseur*, 41; and Schönborn, *Sophrone*, 61-62; and the more extensive study of Hans von Campenhausen, "The Ascetic Idea of Exile in Ancient and Medieval Monasticism," in *Tradition and Life in the Church*, trans. A. V. Littledale (Philadelphia: Fortress Press, 1968), 231-251.

34. On the details of Sophronius' relationship with John Moschus, see Henry Chadwick, "John Moschus and His Friend Sophronius the Sophist," *JTS* N.S. 25 (1974): 49-74. Cf. also Norman Baynes, "The *Pratum Spirituale*," *OCP* 13 (1947), repr. in *Byzantine Studies and Other Essays* (London: University of London–Athlone Press, 1955), 261-270.

35. See Chadwick, "John Moschus," 59.

36. See ibid., 64-68. Chadwick adduces as evidence of John's intent a number of relevant chapters from the *Pratum spirituale*.

37. See Schönborn, *Sophrone*, 54-60.

38. Cited from the *Pratum spirituale* by Chadwick, "John Moschus," 59.

39. *Miracula Cyri et Joannis* (PG 87.3668B).

40. Maximus refers to Sophronius as "my blessed master ($\delta\epsilon\sigma\pi\delta\tau\eta\varsigma$), my father ($\pi\alpha\tau\dot{\eta}\rho$) and teacher ($\delta\iota\delta\dot{\alpha}\sigma\kappa\alpha\lambda o\varsigma$) and senior abbot Sophronius" (*Ep.* 12, PG 91.533A).

41. Most scholars concur that if we accept the account of Maximus' Greek biographer, his training in Constantinople must have included the study of Plato, Aristotle, and their Neoplatonic commentators. Cf. Sherwood, *Annotated Date-List*, 1-2; and Devreesse, "La vie," 14, n. 2 ("Maximus is a philosopher. His works...reveal a dialectician's temperament").

42. Cf. Sophronius' remarks about George in PG 87.3080D-3084A; also Schönborn, *Sophrone*, 77. On Maximus' relation to George, see *Ep.* 1 (PG 91.364A-392B), a word of encouragement for George on the occasion of his dismissal.

43. Cf. *Mystagogia*, prooemium (PG 91.657C) and passim. If he is a real figure, he may be the same γέρων mentioned in *Amb.* 5 (PG 91.1044B), and in the dialogue in the *Liber asceticus*. That this "grand old man," if not a literary artifice, might well be Sophronius, is suggested by Sherwood, *Earlier Ambigua*, 9; and again by George Berthold in his translation of the *Mystagogia* in *Maximus Confessor: Selected Writings*, CWS (Mahwah, N.J.: Paulist Press), 215, n. 4.

44. On the term γέρων, see J.-C. Guy, "Les *Apophthegmata patrum*," in *Théologie de la vie monastique: Études sur la tradition patristique*, Théol 49 (Paris: Aubier, 1961), 75-76, n. 9; also Benedicta Ward in the glossary of her translation of *The Sayings of the Desert Fathers*, CS 59 (Kalamazoo: Cistercian Publications, 1975), xvii. For a parallel usage of the title μέγας γέρων, see *Barsanuphius and John: Questions and Responses*, Greek text edited with ET by Derwas Chitty, PO 31.3 (Paris: Firmin-Didot, 1966). Here Barsanuphius is himself called by the title of μέγας γέρων.

45. *Maxime le Confesseur*, 44-45.

46. Ibid., 45, n. 10.

47. Here I am following Sherwood's datings in *Annotated Date-List*, 31-35.

48. *Ep.* 8, the end of which is published by Devreesse, "La fin inédite," 34-35. See also the further study of this letter, with ET of the Greek text given by Devreesse, in Joshua Starr, "St. Maximos and the Forced Baptism at Carthage in 632," *Byzantinisch-neugriechisches Jahrbuch* 16 (1940): 192-196. Starr notes (193) that the text of this letter in PG 91 is defectively edited as no. 8 and incorrectly addressed to John the Chamberlain instead of Sophronius.

49. *Ep.* 8, in Devreesse, "La fin inédite," 35.

50. *Ep.* 14 (PG 91.540A): ...καὶ λαὸν Ἰουδαϊκὸν, καὶ ἀνέθακεν ἀνθρώπων αἵμασι χαίροντα, καὶ μόνην θείαν εὐαρέστησιν τὸν φόνον τοῦ πλάσματος. As Garrigues suggests (*Maxime le Confesseur*, 42-43), these ominous signs of the times virtually had an eschatological aura for the monk Maximus.

51. See, e.g., *Q. Thal.* 53 (CCSG 433,45-54), where Maximus compares compares the Jews with Saul sitting in the cave (1 Kings 24:4ff), i.e., in the present age, or in the dark letter of the law, "a truly earthly people that cherishes corporeality and limits the promises of incorruptible gifts to the

corruption of transitory things..." (The scriptural citations that I supply in parentheses are given according to the traditional names and ordering of the books of the Bible in the Septuagint recension. Thus here, for example, 1 Kings 24:4 in LXX = 1 Sam. 24:4 in other recensions). Cf. similarly, ibid. 65 (PG 737B-C); ibid. 63 (PG 668Dff). The Jews are the archetype of pride (τύφος), "an accursed passion which is a composite of the two evils of arrogance (ὑπερηφανία) and vainglory (κενοδοξία)" (ibid. 64 [PG 716A-B]). Finally, see also ibid. 20 (CCSG 123,50-125,64), where the Jews are compared to the fruitless tree (cf. Matt. 21:18ff), whose outward conceit is accursed by the Logos.

52. See ibid. 64 (PG 712A-720B). In this long section, Maximus articulates his typology of Jonah as representing the "derangement" (παραφροσύνη) of the Jews. In 712A he writes: "Even if the malicious Jewish people, that thoughtless, ungrateful, and misanthropic people that is the enemy of the love of humankind, dares to fight against the very goodness of God, and is cut to pieces, it renounces life (cf. Jon. 4:8) and considers the salvation of the gentiles in Christ an occasion for sorrow; because of its folly, it considers the gourd to be much better than the salvation of the gentiles, and grieves when it sees the gourd withered by the worm (cf. Jon. 4:6-9)." To the Jews Maximus opposes the "spiritual Nineveh," the Church of the gentiles which transcends the earthly Jerusalem (712Df, 717C-720B).

53. See ibid. 23 (CCSG 151,54-153,71), where Maximus in no uncertain terms declares: "It was this Israel that rose up in the manner of Cain, and through envy murdered the intelligible Abel (cf. Gen. 4:8). In the manner of Ishmael, it mocked the divine character of the intelligible Isaac (cf. Gen. 21:9ff). Like Esau, it went mad with rage against the intelligible Jacob (cf. Gen. 27:41). In the manner of Er and Onan, this unbelieving Israel poured the seed of faith, and of the righteousness of faith, on the ground of error and passion (cf. Gen. 38:7-10). Like those two men, who denied Tamar, this Israel denied God's Church. Like Manasseh, it characterized itself by forgetting the virtues (cf. 4 Kings 21:1-18). Like Eliab, it was consumed with contempt for the intelligible David for having acquired the kingdom, and for this reason was set at naught (cf. 1 Kings 17:28). In the manner of Ammon, it produced an alien sort of iniquity (cf. 2 Kings 13:11-21). God did not make his promise to these 'foreign sons who were lame in their tracks' (Ps. 17:46), those who breathe madness and murder (cf. Acts 9:1), the really carnal sons of the flesh alone, strangers to grace 'whose god is their belly and whose glory is their shame' (Phil. 3:19), and the very 'memory' of whose unbelief 'is destroyed with a roar' (Ps. 9:7)."

54. "Maximi Confessoris," 215.

55. See Antoine Guillaumont, *Les 'Kephalaia gnostica' d'Évagre le Pontique et l'histoire de l'origénisme chez les grecs et chez les syriens*, Patristica sorbonensia 5 (Paris: Éditions du Seuil, 1962), 163. On Evagrian anthropology as a groundwork for Origenist spirituality in the fourth century, see ibid., 102-119; and the comprehensive study of Michael O'Laughlin, "Origenism in the Desert: Anthropology and Integration in Evagrius Ponticus" (Th.D. dissertation, Harvard Divinity School, 1987), chs. 2-4, 72-244.

56. On the events and circumstances surrounding this ouster, see Chitty, *Desert a City*, 129-130.

57. See Sherwood, *Earlier Ambigua*, 87-88. Real Origenist adversaries are certainly indicated in some of the *Ambigua* of Maximus as well: cf. *Amb.* 7 (PG 91.1089C); ibid. 15 (PG 91.1216C, 1217B-1220B); ibid. 42 (PG 91.1336C; 1337B).

58. See above, n. 25-27 and related text.

59. Irénée-Henri Dalmais, "Saint Maxime le Confesseur et la crise de l'origénisme monastique," in *Théologie de la vie monastique: Études sur la tradition patristique*, Théol 49 (Paris: Aubier, 1961), 411-412.

60. See ibid., 412.

61. See Sherwood, *Earlier Ambigua*, chs. 2-6 (103-221), for an extensive study of Maximus' criticism of the Origenist notions of preexistence, satiety (κόρος), ecstasy, Logos-logoi, and apokatastasis. Cf. also Sherwood's paper "Maximus and Origenism: Ἀρχή καὶ Τέλος," *Berichte zum XI. internationalen Byzantinisten-Kongreß* (Munich, 1958), 1-27. On the specifically philosophical dimensions of this anti-Origenism, see Endre von Ivánka, "Der philosophische Ertrag der Auseinandersetzung Maximos des Bekenners mit dem Origenismus," *Jahrbuch der Österreichischen Byzantinischen Gesellschaft* 7 (1958): 23-49; and José J. Prado, *Voluntad y naturaleza: La antropología filosófica de Maximo el Confesor* (Rio Cuarta, Argentina: Ediciónes de la Universidad Nacional de Rio Cuarta, 1974), 83-97.

62. *Q. Thal.* 59 (PG 613B-D). See also the discussion of this text below, ch. 3.

63. Ibid. 60 (PG 625A-B).

64. Cf. ibid. introduction (CCSG, especially 17,1-18); and *Ep.* 9 (PG 91.445C-449A); *Ep.* 26 (PG 91.616A-617B); *Ep.* 40 (frag.) (PG 91.633C-636A); *Ep.* 41 (PG 91.636B-C); *Ep.* 42 (frag.) (PG 91.636C-637B).

65. Cf. the salutations in his *Epistulae* to Thalassius, and in *Q. Thal.* intro. (CCSG 17).

66. Cf. *Ep.* 9 (PG 91.449A); *Ep.* 40 (PG 91.636C); *Q. Thal.* intro. (CCSG 19,53); and ibid. 65 (PG 737A).

67. *Ep.* 9 (PG 91.449A); cf. *Opusc. theol. et polem.* 1 (*ad Marinum*) (PG 91.29D), where Maximus, referring to the *Q. Thal.* itself, speaks of Thalassius as his "senior" (κύριος) and "teacher" (διδάσκαλος).

68. *Q. Thal.* intro. (CCSG 17, greeting).

69. *Annotated Date-List,* 33. Cf., however, Viller, "Aux sources," 262, n. 199: "I am not inclined to see in this designation any sign of deference regarding persons older than himself and with whom he is united in a close friendship." Basically the same position is more recently adopted by Michel van Parys, "Un maître spirituel oublié: Thalassios de Libye," *Ir* 52 (1979): 218.

70. See the *Regulae brevius tractatae* (*Shorter Rules*) 169 (PG 31.1193), which treats the question of how a younger brother should behave in the event that he is ordered to teach something to one who is his senior in years.

71. "Le témoignage spirituel de Thalassius le Lybien," *EB* 2 (1944): 81.

72. See Viller ("Aux sources," 263, n. 199), who postulates that Thalassius had not merely read Evagrius through Maximus but had known the Evagrian texts directly. Disdier ("Le témoignage," 80) further asserted that Thalassius' use of Evagrius was, on the whole, "more personal" than that of Maximus, "who renders him religiously almost *ad verbum.*" Van Parys ("Un maître spirituel," 216) rightly observes, however, that Disdier never proves this highly subjective assertion on the basis of the texts themselves, which would merit a study in itself.

73. See again Viller ("Aux sources," 262, n. 199), who concludes that the dependence of Thalassius' *Centuries* on those of Maximus could be born out stylistically, Thalassius showing more perfect form and terseness than Maximus' highly diffuse style. "The parallel, even if not always conclusive, allows us to affirm that Maximus came first and that he was utilized by Thalassius." H.-G. Beck is more reticent to argue for the priority of either Maximus or Thalassius, both because their similarities in expressions do not demonstrate dependence on the other and because the similarities may be traceable to their common reading of Evagrius (see his *Kirche und theologische Literatur im byzantinischen Reich,* Handbuch der Altertumswissenschaft, section 12, Byzantinisches Handbuch 2.1 [Munich: C. H. Beck, 1959], 355).

74. The Romanian translator of the *Philokalia,* P. D. Staniloae, demonstrated that the acrostic in Thalassius' third *Century* was a resumé of *Q. Thal.* 58 of Maximus (cited by van Parys, "Un maître spirituel," 22). This would of course prove its redaction after Thalassius' reception of the *Q. Thal.*

75. This would include such themes as the reciprocity of the soul and

body in human salvation and deification, "self-love" as the basis for the disorder in human nature, etc. On Thalassius' personal development of such themes, see Disdier, "Le témoignage," 83-118; cf. also van Parys, "Un maître spirituel," 220-240.

76. *Ep.* 26 (PG 91.616A). Sherwood (*Annotated Date-List*, 34), queries whether this piece could be from some collection (presumably lost) of "questions and responses."

77. The traditional title, *Quaestiones ad Thalassium*, is thus misleading, and is better rendered *To Thalassius, Most Holy Presbyter and Hegumen, Concerning Diverse Difficulties from Holy Scripture* (Πρὸς Θαλάσσιον, ὁσιώτατον πρεσβύτερον καὶ ἡγούμενον περὶ διαφορῶν ἀπόρων τῆς ἁγίας γραφῆς).

78. *Q. Thal.* intro. (CCSG 17,19-19,29). Cf. also ibid. 65 (PG 737A), where Maximus honors Thalassius for "suffering" (πάσχων) divine truths, and for coming to possess the knowledge of them "by experience" (τῇ πείρᾳ), whereas his own knowledge has been tainted by passions.

79. Ibid. intro. (CCSG 19,30-21,63).

80. Cf. ibid. (CCSG 21,89-23,98); ibid. 10 (CCSG 87,96-98); ibid. 50 (CCSG 391,203-205); ibid. 54 (CCSG 453,191-455,202).

81. Ibid. intro. (CCSG 21,70-71); cf. ibid. 40 (CCSG 269,40).

82. Ibid. 65 (PG 737B); cf. ibid. 50 (391,209-211), where Maximus again admits to not comprehending the entire power of the scriptures, which is "infinitely beyond my own ability."

83. Irénée-Henri Dalmais, introduction to Astérios Argyriou, trans., *Saint Maxime le Confesseur: Le mystère du salut* (Namur: Les Éditions du Soleil Levant, 1964), 24. Emphasis added.

84. Ibid.

85. See *Q. Thal.* intro. (CCSG 23,108-43,432). The actual list of Thalassius' questions on the passions is preserved in Maximus' discussion, ibid. (23,108-27,183).

86. "La littérature patristique des 'Quaestiones et Responsiones' sur l'Écriture sainte," *RB* 42 (1933): 336.

87. "Exposition and Use of Scripture in St. Maximus as Manifest in the *Quaestiones ad Thalassium*," *OCP* 24 (1958): 204, 207. Cf. the remarks of a skeptical Photius, who declared in his ninth-century *Bibliotheca* that he could find nothing of a graceful style or method of exegesis in the *Ad Thalassium* and that the Confessor's solutions were "far from the text and known history, and even farther from the difficulty itself" (PG 103.645B-C).

88. See his *Maximus Confessor als Meister des geistlichen Lebens* (Wiesbaden: Franz Steiner, 1965), 272-286, on "Der Gnostiker als Deuter des

geheimen Schriftsinnes."

89. As an example of this kind of treatment of Maximus' exegesis, see the section on "The Trichotomy (of the Soul) and Maximus' Allegorical Interpretations," in Thunberg, *Microcosm and Mediator*, 206ff.

90. "Plaisir et douleur dans l'analyse de saint Maximus d'après les *Quaestiones ad Thalassium*," in *Maximus Confessor: Actes du Symposium sur Maxime le Confesseur, Fribourg, 2-5 septembre 1980*, ed. Felix Heinzer and Christoph von Schönborn, Paradosis 27 (Fribourg: Éditions Universitaires, 1982), 273.

91. *The Byzantine Fathers of the Sixth to Eighth Century*, The Collected Works of Georges Florovsky 9, trans. Raymond Miller et al. (Vaduz: Büchervertriebsanstalt, 1987), 213.

Chapter One

The *Quaestiones ad Thalassium*: Genre and Context in the Byzantine Monastic Pedagogical Tradition

The rich history of the *quaestio-responsio* as a literary genre in antiquity has been studied by classicists and historians of Christianity alike for the light that it sheds on philosophical and theological heuristics in the ancient world. As Hermann Dörries notes, however, patristic authors did not merely assume a prefabricated literary model from pagan antiquity and fill it with a Christian content; the *quaestio-responsio* genre had its own rich formal history in the Christian tradition as well.[1] Bardy's classic study of the flowering of the genre in patristic literature certainly confirms this observation.[2] Indeed, the inherent plasticity of the *quaestio-responsio* insured its continued vitality—and diversity—in early Christian literature, for authors could easily adapt the genre to their own prerogatives.

In this chapter I shall explore the generic background and character of the *Quaestiones ad Thalassium*, in hopes of demonstrating that, in a unique way, the work bridges and fuses two antecedent *quaestio* traditions: (1) the patristic exegetical ἀπορίαι tradition, a relatively uniform literary genre of collections of scholia on difficult passages of scripture; and (2) the spiritual-pedagogical tradition of monastic questions and responses, where the *quaestio-responsio* was never destined to be a pure literary genre *per se* but primarily a teaching device adaptable to a wide variety of literary formats.

As a collection of exegetical scholia formally addressing scriptural difficulties posed to Maximus by Thalassius, the affinities of the *Quaestiones ad Thalassium* with the ἀπορίαι tradition are fairly self-evident. This is the genre in which Bardy has located it, and most Maximian scholars have simply deferred to his judgment.[3] Our aim in this chapter will be, not to dispute such a generic identification with the ἀπορίαι tradition, but to suggest that it is too general to enhance our understanding of the ethos and content of a work like the *Ad Thalassium*, in which scriptural ἀπορίαι are not merely "resolved" but reworked into elaborate expositions of ascetic or spiritual doctrine. This will lead to an investigation, further on in the chapter, of the formal connection of the *Quaestiones ad Thalassium* with the Greek monastic *quaestio* tradition, which, despite its embracing a wide-ranging literature, has the advantage, from a critical perspective, of attaching to a reasonably distinctive and clearly more identifiable *Sitz im Leben* of monastic pedagogy and use of scripture.

The *Aporiai* Tradition of Patristic Exegetical "Questions and Responses" and the Literary Genre of the *Ad Thalassium*

As was noted above, the *Quaestiones ad Thalassium* has an obvious kinship with the genre of patristic exegetical *quaestiones et responsiones*, a fertile tradition in Latin as well as Greek Christian literature. Constituting a variety of scholia, or notations, on scripture, this literature survived the decline of the commentary proper in the patristic period and rivaled the emerging and increasingly popular *catenae* commentaries.[4] Bardy has identified two general strands of this genre, one of "artificial" questions, wherein an exegete invented his own queries about the text as a way of regulating his commentary, and another of "authentic" ἀπορίαι wherein the exegete attempted to resolve self-evident scriptural difficulties posed by others or by himself.[5] Nonetheless, those collections of authentic ἀπορίαι to which the *Ad Thalassium* may be more directly compared are relatively few.

Eusebius' *Quaestiones evangelicae ad Stephanum*, which answered a variety of queries posed on discrepancies in the gospel narratives of Jesus' childhood, and the adjoining *Quaestiones evangelicae ad Marinum*, on the resurrection narratives, survive only in fragments[6] but represent, as Bardy has indicated, the first patristic work actually bearing the technical title of ζητήματα καὶ λύσεις.[7] A later epitome gives us an idea of the kind of difficulties raised in the *Ad Stephanum*: e.g., Why do the evangelists give the genealogy of Joseph and not that of Mary? Why does the one evangelist (Matt.) begin with Abraham and follow Jesus' genealogy descending from him, whereas the other (Luke), instead of stopping with Abraham, proceeds to show it going even back to Adam and to God? The *Ad Marinum* deals with similar kinds of questions: e.g., Why is it that according to Matthew, the Savior was resurrected on Saturday evening, whereas Mark has it early in the morning on the day after the Sabbath?[8] Eusebius' responses endeavor to resolve the discrepancy precisely through clarification of the literal meaning of the biblical text, and—unlike Maximus—without recourse to an allegorical interpretation.[9]

In the same mold with Eusebius' work on the harmony of the gospels is Hesychius of Jerusalem's fifth-century collection of some sixty-one *Quaestiones ex evangelica consonantia*,[10] which cover the whole gamut of the gospel narratives. They are the work of an erudite monk well versed in the classic problems of gospel exegesis.[11] His responses aim not to be innovative, so much as to set forth in brief terms an outline of the major difficulties in the gospels.[12]

Theodoret's two works of *Quaestiones in Octateuchum* and *in libros Regnorum et Paralipomenon*, composed in the mid-fifth century, exploit the use of scriptural ἀπορίαι for deliberately apologetic purposes. In the preface to his questions on the Octateuch, Theodoret expressly states his desire to refute those who inquire into scripture in order to uncover its contradictions; he determines instead to defend the harmony (συμφωνία) of the Bible.[13] Similarly in the preface to his work on Kings and Chronicles, he sets out to clarify that which might be obscure to the readers.[14] Whether the scriptural difficulties he thereupon raises are artificial or authentic is open to critical judgment; it is sufficient that Theodoret himself sees them as alleviating potential misinterpretations. "Why," he asks in the first of his *Quaestiones in Genesim*, "did the author not mention God prior to recounting the creation of the world?" His response reflects his typical preference for a solution based on the literal sense: Moses had already delivered his teaching on God to the Hebrews while they were still in Egypt, and later on, during the sojourn in the desert, he recorded the creation account.[15] Many of Theodoret's questions and responses—such as his treatment of the hardening of Pharaoh's heart—proved to be of great value to later exegetes and compilers of exegetical florilegia.[16]

Theodoret's less familiar collection of *Quaestiones et responsiones ad orthodoxos*[17] takes an even stronger apologetic stance. It treats of a very wide variety of doctrinal, ethical, exegetical, and other problems. Moreover, many of its questions, as Bardy has shown, deal not only with familiar problems in the Christian ἀπορίαι tradition but also with the kinds of scripture-related discrepancies that figured in earlier pagan polemic against Christianity (e.g., Celsus, Porphyry, Julian).[18]

Turning to the *Quaestiones ad Thalassium* itself, we again confront the problem, from a critical perspective, of discerning between "artificial" and "authentic" difficulties from scripture. There is a restricted number of questions, in the list of sixty-five, that broach what would likely be judged as genuine or self-evident scriptural and scripture-related discrepancies. Listed below is a selection of nineteen such questions (keeping in mind that any such list is bound to be arbitrary to some extent):

Q. 2: If the Creator made (ἐποίησε) all the species which fill out the world in six days (cf. Gen. 1:31-2:2), what is the Father effecting (ἐργάζεται) now beyond these things? For the Savior says, "My Father is working (ἐργάζεται) even now, just as I am working" (John 5:17). Is he therefore speaking of a preservation (συντήρησις) of the forms of things that have been produced once for all?[19]

Q. 4: How is it that the Lord commanded the disciples not to have two tunics, when, according to St. John the Evangelist, he himself had five of them, as it appears from when they were divided (Matt. 10:10; Mark 6:9; Luke 9:3; cf. John 19:23)? And what did these garments consist of?[20]

Q. 6: If, as St. John says, "he who is born of God does not sin, because his seed dwells in God, and he cannot sin" (1 John 3:9), while he who is born of water and Spirit is himself born of God (cf. John 3:5), then how are we who are born of God through baptism still able to sin?[21]

Q. 8: Since St. John says that "God is light" (1 John 1:5), and then a few lines later "if we walk in the light, as he is in the light" (ibid. 1:7), how is he said to "be" light, and yet also "in" the light as one thing in another?[22]

Q. 9: Why does St. John say, "Brethren, we are children of God now; what we shall be did not yet appear" (1 John 3:2)? If what we shall be did not appear yet, how is it that St. Paul says that "God revealed to us through the Spirit. For the Spirit searches everything, even the depths of God" (1 Cor. 2:10)? How too does Paul treat (φιλοσοφεῖ) such things concerning "what we shall be"?[23]

Q. 10: If "he who fears is not perfected in love" (1 John 4:18), how is it that "there is no deficiency in those who fear him" (Ps. 33:10)? If there is no deficiency, it appears that one would be perfect. How, then, is he who fears not perfect?[24]

Q. 15: What does the scripture mean, "For your incorruptible spirit is in all things. Therefore you reproach trespassers little by little" (Wisd. 12:1)? If it is speaking of the Holy Spirit, how can he be in a foolish heart when it also says that "Wisdom will not enter nor dwell in a body consumed in sin" (ibid. 1:4)? I noted this because it clearly says "in all things."[25]

Q. 17: If God sent Moses to Egypt, for what reason did the angel of God seek to kill him when he had been sent by God? He would have killed him, had the anxious woman not circumcised her young son and thereby curbed the angel's wrath (Exod. 4:24ff). And if the circumcision of the little boy was necessary, why did God not kindly enjoin Moses to circumcise the boy before he ever sent Moses out? Why indeed, seeing that there was a blunder, did the good angel not kindly warn Moses when he was sent by God for such a service?[26]

Q. 18: If, as the Apostle says, "The doers of the law will be justified" (Rom. 2:13), how can he further say, "You who are justified by the law have fallen away from grace" (Gal. 5:4).[27]

Q. 19: What does the scripture mean, "All who have sinned without the law will also perish without the law, and all who have sinned under the law will be judged by the law"

(Rom. 2:12)? And how is it that he still speaks of "that time when, according to my gospel, God will judge the secrets of men through Jesus Christ" (ibid. 2:16)? If they are to be judged by the law, how can they still be judged through Jesus Christ?[28]

Q. 20: What is the meaning of the withered fig tree (cf. Matt. 21:18ff; Mark 11:12-14), which, in appearance at least, is abnormal in the gospel? And what is to be made of the incontinence of (Jesus') hunger in seeking fruit out of season? And what is meant by the curse of something that is senseless?[29]

Q. 22: If "in the coming ages" God "will show his riches" (Eph. 2:7), how is it that "the end of the ages has come upon us" (1 Cor. 10:11)?[30]

Q. 27: Since the Lord, after his resurrection, clearly enjoined (us) "to make disciples of all the nations" (Matt. 28:19), how is it that Peter needed the revelation concerning the gentiles in the presence of Cornelius (cf. Acts 10:11-48)? Or, how is it that the apostles who heard about it back in Jerusalem criticized Peter for his dealings with Cornelius (cf. Acts 11:2)?[31]

Q. 28: To whom did God say, "Come, let us go down and confound their language" (Gen. 11:7)?[32]

Q. 29: What is the meaning of the statement found in Acts, "Through the Spirit they told Paul not to go up to Jerusalem" (Acts 21:4)? Why did he disregard the Spirit and go up to the city?[33]

Q. 37: It says of St. Paul in Acts, "...so that handkerchiefs and aprons were taken from his body and applied to the sick, and their distresses were removed from them" (Acts 19:12). Did this happen for the sake of his ministry and unbelievers, or did Paul accomplish these things with his body simply because his body was sanctified? And if, for this same reason, Paul suffered nothing from the viper (ibid. 28:5), why did the saint's body not succumb to the beast's poison but did succumb to the sword? I seek to know the same thing about the body of Elisha. Moreover, what is the significance of the "aprons"?[34]

Q. 42: How is it that we are said to commit sin and know it (cf. 1 John 1:8), when it is said that the Lord became sin, but did not know it? How is it not more serious to become sin and not know it, than to commit sin and know it? For the scripture says, "God made him sin who knew no sin" (2 Cor. 5:21).[35]

Q. 43: If the "tree of life" is said to be "wisdom" in scripture (Prov. 3:18), while a work of wisdom is to discern and to know ($\gamma\nu\hat{\omega}\nu\alpha\iota$), how does the "tree of life" differ from the "tree of the knowledge ($\tau\grave{o}\ \gamma\nu\omega\sigma\tau\acute{o}\nu$) of good and evil" (Gen. 2:9)?[36]

Q. 44: To whom did God say, "Behold, Adam has become like one of us" (Gen. 3:22a)? If to his Son, how did he compare Adam with God when he was not of the divine being? But if to the angels, how again did he compare the angel with himself, as if to say "like one of us" to his equal in essence?[37]

A few of Thalassius' questions here hint of topics well grounded in patristic exegetical tradition. Question 2 on God's creative activity (John 5:17) after resting from his original work (Gen. 2:2), for example, recalls a *topos* that recurs consistently in earlier apologetic exegesis.[38] Question 4 on the apparent contradiction about Jesus' tunics adds itself to a long tradition of patristic interpretation of Jesus' divided vestments in John 19:23-24.[39] Questions 28 and 44 are both indicative of the kinds of problems raised in earlier anti-Marcionite or anti-Gnostic exegesis, where an allegorical interpretation was called for in order to dismiss possible anthropomorphisms or plural significations of God in scripture. Certain other of the queries are reminiscent of topics of discussion in the earlier tradition of monastic *quaestiones,* and of these more will be said below.

Still other questions, not listed here, broach rather typical cross-cultural or linguistic obscurities in the biblical text: e.g., Question 25 on the reasoning of Paul's ruling on women praying with their heads covered, and women "having authority on account of the angels" (1 Cor. 11:3-5, 10). In a number of these cases, Thalassius already appeals implicitly or explicitly for an anagogical interpretation of an odd scriptural term or passage.[40] How else, for instance, could one understand the curse placed on Adam, enjoining him to eat the ground and to eat bread "in the sweat of his face" (Gen. 3:17, 19)?[41] In Question 64, Thalassius complains openly of not finding anything edifying from the literal meaning of Jonah 4:11, on men who "do not know their right hand or their left." In other cases he petitions for extended anagogical expositions of whole narrative blocks from 2 Chronicles[42] and from 1 Esdras.[43] Still other questions seem clearly to be inviting a theological exposition,[44] while numerous others appear to be fully open-ended, with Thalassius revealing no explicit reason or motive for his inquiry.[45]

Despite the fact that it embraces a wide variety of biblical questions and does not focus on any particular books of the Bible, nor any particular classification of scriptural difficulties, the *Quaestiones ad Thalassium* appears, with its closest antededents in the Greek ἀπορίαι tradition, as part of a fairly pure genre of exegetical scholia designed principally to establish scholastic solutions to scriptural discrepancies.[46] Standing in this tradition, Maximus occasionally appeals to earlier, usually unnamed sources for the purpose of resolving certain difficulties or offering an authoritative alternative exegesis.[47]

Precise comparisons between works in this ἀπορίαι tradition are hard to make because, again, of the inherent plasticity of the *quaestio-responsio* literature itself and because of the tremendous variation in the content of these compilations of exegetical scholia. For this reason, one wonders whether, after all, this generic ascription has any decisive value for illuminating our understanding of the *Ad Thalassium*. The other, and, in our view, far more revealing trajectory in which to study this work is that of the distinctly monastic *quaestio* tradition.

A certain evolution is observable in the emergence of the *quaestio-responsio* as a didactic device in Byzantine monastic pedagogy. Yet our special focus in the analysis below will be on how *scriptural* ἀπορίαι, in particular, became an increasingly formalized teaching technique, as the way was open for scripture itself to be used more and more "speculatively" in the pedagogical tradition to which Maximus and Thalassius were so heavily indebted. The tradition-historical links between the *Ad Thalassium* and the monastic *quaestio* tradition can then be substantiated by considering three relevant factors: the use of the *quaestio-responsio* in certain of Maximus' earlier monastic writings, the presence of established monastic *topoi* in Thalassius' list of questions, and, most significantly, the adaptation of scriptural $ἀπορίαι$ for monastic pedagogy in Maximus' responses to Thalassius.

The *Quaestio-Responsio*, Scriptural *Aporiai*, and Spiritual Pedagogy in the Byzantine Monastic Tradition before Maximus

The evolution of the *quaestio-responsio* in Greek monasticism was part of the larger, gradual transition from the oral culture of the charismatic desert sages to an ever richer and variegated tradition of monastic sapiential and hagiographic literature: e.g., compilations of *sententiae*, often as "centuries"; recensions of the *apophthegmata patrum*; written *regulae*; biographies; monastic histories, and the like.[48] In its use as a monastic pedagogical form, the *quaestiones-responsiones* first comes into view within the *Sitz im Leben* of the eremitic conferences conveyed to us in the traditions of the sayings of the desert fathers. These collections of apophthegms, emerging from the fourth century and having extensive influence in the formative period of Byzantine monasticism, initiated a long process of generic development in the monastic *quaestio* tradition—from the actual questions of monastic ethics raised in the early conferences of spiritual fathers and their disciples, to the increasingly artificial use of the question-and-response as a didactic tool in a variety of Greek monastic literatures. One can see this evolution in such representative texts as Basil of Caesarea's longer and shorter *Regulae*; in monastic dialogues like John Cassian's *Conferences* or Maximus the Confessor's own *Liber asceticus*; in spiritual homilies like those of Pseudo-Macarius or Isaac the Syrian; in discourses on ascetic theology like Mark the Hermit's *De baptismo*, among others.

The Apophthegmata patrum

The *Apophthegmata patrum* relate primitive monastic conferences, episodic dialogues with one or more interrogators under the direction of a spiritual master (an abba or γέρων).[49] They offer a glimpse of the procedure of earliest monastic teaching, wherein less experienced monks would defer to their charismatic leaders for practical instruction in monastic life. In the classic format of the *Apophthegmata*, the monk solicits the sage for an inspired "word" of salvation: Εἰπέ μοι ῥῆμα πῶς σωθῶ,[50] or similarly, as is asked of Abba Poemen, "What ought I to do?"[51] or "How do you advise me to behave?"[52] Numerous queries treat of persistent problems in monastic ethics,[53] while still others deal with the novel circumstances arising from eremitic life.[54] The sages' responses in turn represented, as Benedicta Ward says, "words given by a spiritual father to his sons as life-giving words that would bring them to salvation."[55] In this way, the question and response provided a consistent framework of spiritual direction, presupposing a strong mutual bond between the authoritative γέρων and his disciple.

An outstanding feature of the questions-and-responses in the *Apophthegmata* is their virtually total orientation toward the pragmatic, rather than speculative, concerns of monastic life. The practical exigencies of penitence take almost complete precedence over intellectual matters. Interestingly enough in the apophthegms, the reading of scripture for more than an immediate practical application ranks among such speculative extravagances. Jean-Claude Guy comments:

> This distrust of all intellectual speculation manifested itself in the use the monks made of Holy Scripture. Scripture, according to their teaching, must not be considered an *object* of discussion, like a word whose mystery man could claim to pierce. It is the Word of God, to which man must conform himself by refusing categorically to exercise any curiosity about it.[56]

This stern attitude is related in a brief conference attributed to Abba Zeno in which some monks have been reflecting on dark sayings in the text of Job:

Some brothers came to see him and asked him, "What does this saying in the book of Job mean: 'Heaven is not pure in his presence'?" (Job 15:15) The old man replied, "The brothers have passed over their sins and inquired about heavenly things. This is the interpretation of the saying: 'God alone is pure,' therefore he said, 'heaven is not pure.'"[57]

The sage's response throws the "literal" sense of the text in the face of any further speculative interest in it and serves simply to remind the monks that they are still impure before God. Abba Zeno presumes indeed that there is a mysterious profundity in the "heavenly things," but it simply is not the monks' business.

The same principle holds true in an anecdote from Abba Copres, who refuses to countenance a query about Melchizedek in scripture, insofar as it is a topic about which God does not mean for him to know.[58] Abba Poemen and others are said to have refused to entertain questions about the "spiritual and heavenly things"[59] of scripture or of the fathers because of the immediate urgency of combatting the passions[60] or because these lofty things might prove too precarious for discussion.[61] Even where an allegorical or typological interpretation of scripture is presented by a sage, it invariably holds a direct practical consequence for the monks.[62] The "desert hermeneutic," as Douglas Burton-Christie has called it, carried the conviction precisely that the Bible was something lived; its words were to be fulfilled, appropriated. The sages' "straight talk regarding the priority of practice served to remind all those who came to the desert that their primary responsibility was to realize the words of scripture by weaving them into the fabric of their transformed lives."[63]

The urge, in these primitive conferences, to orient the whole process of interrogation and response to the practical exigencies of monastic life, even if it meant stifling the monks' more speculative theological inquiries, clearly highlighted the importance of the question-and-response method as a means of regulating monastic life. Besides its didactic utility, the method served to secure the actual authority of the sages over the monks' affairs. Thus the sage is portrayed in the *Apophthegmata* as exercising absolute control over the whole process of interrogation and response.[64] Even when a question is judged too speculative and refused an answer, as in the case of the questions from scripture cited above, the abba's silence is instructive. Indeed, the refusal to entertain such questions further indicates the ultimate authority of the sage and his logia, sometimes even above that of written scripture,[65] in the regulation of monastic affairs; for the sage's dictum, as well as scripture itself, was legitimately a "word of God."[66]

The Monastic Regulae *of Basil of Caesarea*

Basil of Caesarea's fourth-century *Regulae fusius* and *Regulae brevius*, which issued originally from conferences between abbots and their subordinates, are the work of a master sensitive to the whole range of practical and intellectual questions of the monks, yet preoccupied mainly with crucial issues of monastic praxis. Basil himself alludes to the process by which monks would gather and ask questions of their superiors, the more difficult of which were in turn referred by the abbots to higher authorities in conferences of representatives from the different coenobia.[67] As Basil remarks, this process prevented monks from disputing with each other and from all asking questions at once, and guaranteed the use of the questions and responses for the edification of the whole community.[68] The *Regulae* thus testify directly to the transition from *quaestio-responsio* as an actual heuristic procedure in early monastic teaching, to its deployment as an artificial literary technique, in this case formatted as precise pieces of legislation for regulating the coenobia.[69]

Predominant in the *Regulae brevius* are those questions and responses, scriptural and not, which address concrete issues of monastic practice. "Generally speaking, is it good to practice silence?"[70] "If a man is cross or angry when awakened from sleep, what does he deserve?"[71] "What does, 'Sing psalms intelligently' (Ps. 46:8), mean?"[72] Many times the questions address very specific sorts of circumstances. "Is it necessary that all should be gathered together at the hour of lunch? and how shall we treat him that stays behind and comes after the meal has begun?"[73]

Questions from scripture are abundant in the *Regulae brevius*. Many deal with passages from the gospels and the Pauline epistles and seek an explanation of biblical terms,[74] an elucidation of peculiar scriptural phrases,[75] or, especially frequently, as in the *Apophthegmata* traditions, an exposition of the practical application of a certain passage.[76] Less frequent though still included in the *Regulae brevius* are questions of real discrepancies, or ἀπορίαι, within scriptural texts, like Rule 243:

> What does the apostle mean by saying, "Be ye angry and sin not; let not the sun go down on your wrath" (Eph. 4:26), while elsewhere he says, "Let all bitterness, and wrath, and anger be put away from you" (Eph. 4:31)?[77]

Rarer still, but represented nonetheless, are scriptural queries that evoke a potential dogmatic problem, such as Rule 267: "If one man shall be beaten with many, another with few stripes (Luke 12:47), how do some say that there is no end of punishment?"[78] Indicating that this difficulty can be resolved by other, more lucid passages of scripture on this issue (namely, sayings of Jesus on eternal punishment for sinners), Basil's response to this question seeks to obviate the possibility, implied in the question, of an end to eschatological punishments. God's justice in meting out different eternal lots according to the merits of sinners or saved precludes any such inference. Basil seems clearly to have been aiming his question and response here against the Origenist doctrine of a final apokatastasis.[79] Though such a use of scripture, or of scriptural *quaestiones*, as a means of setting forth peculiar points of monastic doctrine is still fairly rare in the *Regulae*, it anticipated a trend that would gain greater momentum in other later works in the monastic *quaestio* tradition.

The Collationes *of John Cassian*

Given Cassian's close relation and indebtedness to the desert monks of the Christian East, he can justly be included in an analysis of the literary tradition of Greek monasticism. His *Collationes*, or *Conferences*, dating from the early fifth century, represented a decisive new shift toward exploiting the *quaestio-responsio* as an artificial pedagogical device. The result was the stylized monastic dialogue,[80] in Cassian's case directed precisely toward an ascetic and mystical instruction[81] that would accommodate, within reason, the speculative problems that were capturing the interest of monks influenced by Origenist-Evagrian spirituality. Thus questions of monastic practice or ethics, though important in their own right in the *Collationes,* appear at times to provide merely a platform for larger discussions of spiritual anthropology.[82]

Scriptural questions in the *Collationes* also exemplify this urge to accommodate authentic intellectual problems, or, as Cassian himself calls it, the "theoretical knowledge" that embraces both historical interpretation and spiritual sense.[83] In *Conference* 8 with Serenus, for instance, Cassian poses a whole series of questions concerning the fall of the Principalities and of humanity in Genesis, which lead into extended discourses of theological interpretation. How could fallen angels have had intercourse with "the daughters of men" (Gen. 6:1-4)? If not literally, then how? Answer: the seed of the righteous Seth, called "angels" or "sons of God" so long as they were true to their lineage, were gradually seduced and caused to fall by the lineage of the wicked Cain, called in scripture "children" or "daughters of men." Such further explains the human fall from God-given "natural philosophy" to demonic enchantments and magic.[84] Elsewhere, in *Conference* 11, Cassian has Germanus quizzing the sage Chaeremon on how, in view of certain scriptural texts (Ps. 33:10; Ps. 118:112; Heb. 11:24-26), he could maintain that perfect love of God exceeds the fear of God and hope of reward. The response is an exposition from scripture of the different levels of perfection, rising from perfect fear to perfect love.[85]

Cassian's questions and responses on scripture in the *Collationes* reflected his desire to deal with the new problems occasioned by the monks' study of the Bible.[86] From the beginning, the monks had been admonished to memorize the scriptures as inspiration for the practical life,[87] a discipline that Cassian too advocated.[88] But with meditation had come more profound questions of the sense of the text. As one anchorite in the *Apophthegmata patrum* had complained to another, "When I read the Scriptures, my mind is wholly concentrated on the words so that I may have something to say if I am asked."[89] Cassian determined to uphold the older *ruminatio* on scripture as a means for overcoming vice or warding off demons,[90] but also to make provision for reasonable inquiry into its deeper spiritual meaning ($\theta\epsilon\omega\rho\iota\alpha$; *scientia spiritualis*).[91] In so doing, he confirmed a new precedent in monastic spiritual pedagogy, sanctioning scripture as an object of deeper intellectual reflection as well as a guide to practice.[92]

The Spiritual-Doctrinal Writings of Pseudo-Macarius, Mark the Hermit, and Isaac the Syrian

From the fifth century on, one sees a remarkable proliferation in the use of the *quaestio-responsio* as a pedagogical artifice adopted in a variety of monastic literatures. The Pseudo-Macarian homilies are an important case in point. Their authorship has been an object of continued debate. More recent scholarship has revealed the author's connections with the Messalian heresy, although it is now widely believed that Pseudo-Macarius was himself less a Messalian extremist than a critic attempting to salvage its more constructive elements.[93] Werner Jaeger's thesis that the author of the homilies was an influential Eastern monastic leader and devotee of Gregory of Nyssa, whose sermons aimed at applying themes from Gregory's spiritual writings to monastic practice,[94] has given way to new reconstructions which clearly demonstrate an opposite dependence: Gregory was to some extent a disciple of Pseudo-Macarius.[95] At any rate, Jaeger correctly observes that in the Pseudo-Macarian corpus we are dealing with a seasoned monastic pedagogue directly involved with a community of monks.

> Some of these homilies are real sermons, but others are in reality mere starting points (ἀφορμαί) for a discussion in the question and answer style, while still others consist exclusively of questions and answers. It is obvious that this is not merely a literary form that the author has chosen at will, but that this mixture of homilies with questions and answers reflects the actual teaching of the spiritual leader of a monastic community.[96]

Both in the diverse sermons edited by Heinz Berthold,[97] and in the better known collection of Pseudo-Macarian *Spiritual Homilies* edited by Dörries et al.,[98] the question-and-response is a methodical tool for setting theological themes in relief and obviating potential doctrinal error. The author uses his questions to elucidate a host of consistent themes: among them, the opposition between satanic and divine powers in the life of the soul,[99] the interplay between human effort and divine grace in the achievement of moral perfection,[100] and the related classical problem of how the monk could be, as it were, *simul justus et peccator*.[101]

The fortieth *Spiritual Homily* is exemplary of the way that Pseudo-Macarius uses the question-and-response method to eliminate theological problems that emerge in the course of his discussion. The author postulates here a doctrine of sanctification in terms of progressive degrees ($\beta\alpha\theta\mu o\iota$) and modulates it for a monastic audience.[102] In the process, he treats three prospective difficulties. "Since there are some who sell their possessions, liberate their slaves, and perform the commandments, yet do not seek to receive the Spirit in this world, do they not, by living so, enter into the kingdom of heaven?"[103] Pseudo-Macarius' response introduces the notion of the many degrees ($\beta\alpha\theta\mu o\iota$), differences ($\delta\iota\alpha\phi o\rho\alpha\iota$), and measures ($\mu\epsilon\tau\rho\alpha$) both in the kingdom and in hell, God being a just judge who rewards each $\kappa\alpha\tau\grave{\alpha}$ $\tau\grave{o}$ $\mu\epsilon\tau\rho o\nu$ $\tau\hat{\eta}s$ $\pi\iota\sigma\tau\epsilon\omega s$.[104] Such an idea dismisses the viewpoint of those who think purely in either-or terms about heaven and hell.[105] This leads to a second possible objection: "If prayer is repose, how do some say, 'We cannot pray,' and will not continue in prayer?"[106] In other words, if there are in fact levels of perfection, how is it that some who have reached the exalted state of prayer have not remained in its repose but found themselves unable to continue in that state? The author's answer carries a surprising ethical implication: they cannot stay in that lofty repose because in prayer they rediscover the need to return to the world, as it were, and perform deeds of charity.[107] The discussion then turns to a final query arising from the idea of graded perfection: "How can the two things ($\pi\rho\acute{o}\sigma\omega\pi\alpha$), grace and sin, coexist in the heart?"[108] Again the author answers on the existential level, from which perspective grace and sin do not really coexist in the heart but are two dimensions of a dynamic moral struggle in the soul. Only by tasting bitterness and death does the soul come to discern the sweetness of life.[109]

Scriptural imagery and citations permeate Pseudo-Macarius' responses, but occasionally he interjects questions on scripture to make his point. Thus, for example, he asks a number of questions of the Pauline epistles in order to elucidate his concept of grace as a power only gradually appropriated. "What is the meaning," he asks, "of 'the things which the eye has not seen nor the ear heard, nor have they entered into the heart of man' (1 Cor. 2:9)?" Christians, he replies, despite their unique joy, are still subject to fear and trembling (cf. 2 Cor. 7:15). "To what fear and trembling are they subject?" The fear and trembling, he explains, of not faltering in anything, but of acting in harmony with grace.[110]

Scriptural imagery, theological elucidation, and moral exhortation go hand in hand in the questions and responses of the Pseudo-Macarian homilies. Thus any sharp distinction between "theoretical" and "practical" questions disappears, since the author, as spiritual teacher and father, aims both to ground monastic ethics in sound doctrine and to resolve intellectual difficulties through pragmatic application.

A further development of the method of *quaestio-responsio* as a pedagogical form in the early monastic literature may be found in the ascetic opuscula of Mark the Hermit, a spiritual master ostensibly from the fifth century whose historical identity, like that of Pseudo-Macarius, remains very much shrouded.[111] Mark's *De baptismo*, which bears some close thematic parallels with the homilies of Pseudo-Macarius, is a full-fledged discourse, composed in the question-and-response form, and taking up a series of theological and ethical issues raised by the Messalian theory of baptism. The questions reproduce the point of view of his opponents, who have not only calumniated baptism by considering it ultimately ineffectual in rooting out the evil demon residing in us, but who have also used scripture to defend their point of view. Thus his first query, the second half of which recalls a key Messalian testimonium:

> Question: Some say that holy baptism is complete, and rely on scripture, which says, "Rise and be baptized, and wash away your sins" (Acts 22:16); and also, "Wash yourselves and become clean" (Isa. 1:16); and again, "But you were washed, you were sanctified" (1 Cor. 6:11). They also cite many other such passages as testimony. Others, on the other hand, say that old sin is cleared away through ascetic struggles (ἐξ ἀγώνων), and they too use the testimony of scripture, when it says, "Let us cleanse ourselves of

all defilement of the flesh and spirit" (2 Cor. 7:1), at once finding in themselves the very same efficacy ($\dot{\epsilon}\nu\dot{\epsilon}\rho\gamma\epsilon\iota a$) of sin after baptism. What shall we say to these arguments? Are we to believe them?[112]

Another question similarly brings forward the opponents' use of a Pauline text: Did not Paul sin after baptism, because he was exerted to sin not of his own will? For he says, "I see another law warring against the law of my mind" (Rom. 7:23).[113] Other texts, like Hebrews 12:22, come into play as crucial points of contention capable of being used by both sides: "How is it that scripture speaks of the 'heavenly Jerusalem,' yet you have said that it is in the heart?"[114] In other words, how can the pure grace of the "heavenly Jerusalem" be both immediate and eschatological?[115]

Like Pseudo-Macarius, Mark stages a dialectical argument and seeks through his questions and responses to come to terms with the either-or mentality of Messalian ethics. "If we have been freed in baptism, why do we not know the air of freedom as (spiritual) combatants ($oi\ \dot{a}\gamma\omega\nu\iota\zeta\dot{o}\mu\epsilon\nu o\iota$) see?"[116] Or again, "Why is it that I, *who am baptized*, beseech the name of the Lord, and call upon his grace, and wish to be cleansed in my whole will and to be rid of evil thoughts, but am unable?"[117] These and other questions enable Mark to counter the Messalian teaching point by point, and to articulate his own ideas on the ever-unfolding mystery of baptismal grace.

In the introduction to his German translation of Mark's *Opuscula*, Otmar Hesse follows Dörries' designations[118] in suggesting that Mark's work represents a distinct progression from the old monastic "eisagogic Erotapokriseis" (e.g., Basil) arising from the immediate *Sitz im Leben* of monastic teaching, his *De baptismo* being a thoroughgoing "polemical discourse" (*Streitgespräch*).[119] Yet, even though it constitutes a more formalized treatise whose *quaestiones* are artificially introduced, such a distinction does not obscure the distinctly monastic and spiritual-pedagogical purview of the *De baptismo* as it addresses problems raised among monks who have been influenced positively or negatively by the Messalian heresy.

Mark further employs the *quaestio-responsio* method in his *Disputatio cum quodam causidico*. The first part of the work presents a dialogue between a $\gamma\dot{\epsilon}\rho\omega\nu$ and a lawyer disgruntled that his vocation is being rendered obsolete by the monks' preaching against lawsuits. The lawyer's questions, which set forth a number of traditional secular arguments against the perceived antinomianism of monastic philosophy, afford Mark the opportunity to set forth his own apologia for the ascetic life.[120] The monk's central "work" is the fulfillment of the spiritual law (Rom. 7:14) and unceasing prayer, an assertion that he supports with abundant New Testament testimonia.[121] This in turn sets up the second part of the *Disputatio*, a fictional conference between the same γέρων and his students concerning the prior dialogue with the lawyer. Here Mark takes on a variety of potentially problematic issues emerging from the lawyer's accusations. On the whole a masterpiece in the literature of monastic pedagogical *quaestiones*, the *Disputatio* draws on the patterns of the earlier tradition and exploits them for the author's own purposes.[122]

One further example to be mentioned here is the work of Isaac the Syrian, the seventh-century master of Syriac Christian spirituality who, in the manner of Pseudo-Macarius, adapts the *quaestio-responsio* as a method of spiritual-doctrinal discourse in certain of his *Ascetical Homilies*.[123] Here again, practical questions of monastic ethics are interwoven with weightier issues of spiritual anthropology.[124] One set of questions, for example, deals in depth with the passions and anticipates the very kinds of questions on the passions posed to Maximus by Thalassius in the beginning of his entreaty.[125] Scriptural ἀπορίαι are also used, in some cases, as starting points for expositions of spiritual teaching, as in a passage from Isaac's third homily:

> Question: How does "Pray that ye enter into temptation" (Matt. 26:41) agree with "Strive to enter in at the narrow gate" (Luke 13:24)? And again, with "Fear not them that kill the body" (Matt. 10:28), and "He that loseth his life for My sake shall find it" (Matt. 10:39)? Why is it that the Lord everywhere urges us to temptations, yet here He enjoins us to pray not to enter into them? Indeed, what virtue is without affliction and trial? Or what kind of trial is greater than for a man to lose his very self, a trial into which He has bidden us all to enter on His account?...Concerning

what sort of temptations dost Thou command us to pray that we enter not into them?[126]

The question allows Isaac to explain how one must only pray not to enter into temptations of faith itself, induced as they are by the demon of blasphemy and pride. As for bodily temptations, a common-sense approach obtains: the Lord has enjoined us to pray to avoid these as well, lest we be overwhelmed by them, yet they are not to be shirked in the cause of virtue.[127] Overall, this mixing of *quaestiones* into a homiletic format closely parallels the style of Pseudo-Macarius, whose works may have been known to Isaac.

A Return to the Pragmatism of the Desert: The Quaestiones et responsiones *of the Palestinians Barsanuphius and John*

If, amid an earlier generation of monks, Cassian's *Collationes* had betrayed a cautious optimism about the gnostic trend of Origenist spirituality and biblical exegesis, a trend he sought to keep in balance by maintaining the equal value of $\pi\rho\hat{\alpha}\xi\iota\varsigma$ and $\theta\epsilon\omega\rho\acute{\iota}\alpha$,[128] a later monastic text, from the sixth century, fiercely reacted to the perceived intellectualism of the Origenist-Evagrianist tradition, and called for a return to the rigorously practical asceticism of the early desert fathers. The *Quaestiones et responsiones* of Barsanuphius and John reveal the direction of monastic pedagogy in the Palestinian-Sinaitic school in the wake of the Origenist controversy.[129] This huge collection of letters, reedited by an anonymous monk in the form of *quaestio-responsio*,[130] amasses over eight hundred responses of two venerable $\mu\epsilon\gamma\acute{\alpha}\lambda o\iota\ \gamma\acute{\epsilon}\rho o\nu\tau\epsilon\varsigma$ to the inquiries of other monks, devout laymen,[131] and even bishops.[132] Overall, they aim at dispensing practical wisdom, at moral exhortation, and at admonition in the practical life.

Here again we find, as in earlier monastic *quaestiones,* numerous problems arising from the monks' daily experience and their moral or spiritual dilemmas. A correspondence between Barsanuphius and an elderly and infirm monk Andrew is typical:

Question of the same (brother Andrew) to the same Great Old Man:
—Since I have severe rheumatism in my feet and hands, and am

cautious lest it be of the demons, tell me, father, if it is so. And what shall I do, that I am altogether in distress at not being able to fast, and that I am compelled to take food very many times? And what is it that I see in dream[ing of] wild beasts? I entreat thee, master, for the Lord's sake, to send me a little blessing from thy holy food and water, that by them I may receive comfort.[133]

Barsanuphius' response urges Andrew to identify himself with Job, and to know that his bad health is but a redemptive chastening; that his fasting is no failure since God does not test a man beyond his power; and that the bad dreams are caused by demons who will be dispelled through the prayers of the saints.[134]

In a manner reminiscent of the *Apopthegmata patrum*, the monks sometimes beseech Barsanuphius or John for a "rule" (κανών) by which they might properly fulfill their religious duties and be saved.[135] The two γέροντες strive to be strictly pragmatic in the teaching they mete out.[136] In one instance, some monks asking about who it was that gave the devil his rule and power are censured for their speculation: "You should not be meddling with unnecessary questions."[137]

Questions and responses on scripture in Barsanuphius and John also tend toward this strictly practical orientation. The monk John of Beersheba petitions Barsanuphius, "If the Lord has given 'power to tread on serpents and scorpions' (Luke 10:19), how is it that I am moved?" The answer is merely an exhortation to awareness of one's inadequacy, to meekness, long-suffering love (1 Cor. 13:4), and identification with Christ.[138] Another exchange has Barsanuphius advising the same John about a dispute he has had with an abbot over a text in 1 Thessalonians. Rather than interceding with an authoritative interpretation, the Grand Old Man merely gives him a list of further scriptural readings that will clarify the passage and urges him to examine them closely "for the profit of the soul" (ὠφελείας ψυχῆς χάριν).[139]

Especially telling, however, is a set of thirteen questions and responses between Barsanuphius and a γέρων Euthymius who is caught up in allegorical interpretation of scripture.[140] Barsanuphius, as Chitty comments, treats Euthymius with his own allegorical medicine[141] and ultimately suspends the correspondence, telling the old monk to enter into quiet (ἡσυχία) and not to trouble him with further queries.[142] The Grand Old Man's admonition here clearly recalls the same disparagement of any speculative interest in the scriptures that is found in numerous instances in the earlier *Apophthegmata patrum*.[143]

The Quaestiones et responsiones *of Anastasius Sinaïta*

There remains one last important example in the Greek monastic tradition of questions and responses. The large collection of *Quaestiones et responsiones* attributed to the seventh-century Egyptian abbot Anastasius Sinaïta confronts us with a complicated textual history. In its final form, it constitutes, as Marcel Richard has ably demonstrated, a Byzantine monastic spiritual florilegium from the ninth or tenth century.[144] Of its 154 questions and responses, only the initial 22 are considered by Richard as authentically authored by Anastasius,[145] while some of the others are identifiable as having been taken by the redactors from other earlier patristic sources.[146]

Whether Anastasius' questions come from troubled monks within his community, or are his own platform for addressing pressing issues, their character is much the same as those we have seen before: practical or ethical problems which occasion a moral admonition, a teaching from scripture, or an exposition of spiritual anthropology.

> Question: Through how many means do fornication and nocturnal illusions enter a man?

> Response: As the fathers say, they enter by four means: through a natural inflammation ignited by excessive eating and drinking, excessive sleep and idleness; or through haughtiness; or through judging others to be sinners; or through the demons' envy when they see us making progress in the godly life. But it is also possible to suffer a nocturnal illusion on the basis of vanity and feeble power. Moreover, such an illusion derives from a wicked habit (συνήθεια) of the flesh, once it has been compelled into

defilement and fornication. For there are two existent streams running from the body: one of them frequently defiles—that is, sperm; and one sanctifies—that is, tears. And just as every sin a man ever commits is outside the body—the fornicator offering his own sperm as a sacrifice as though from his body to the Evil One—so too, as many good things as a man does are outside the body. But tears are offered to God from our very being, just like the blood of martyrs...[147]

Another classic quandary long on the minds of the monks, and addressed again by Anastasius, is this:

Question: If a man has a wife, and children, and is concerned with worldly affairs (βιωτικὰ πράγματα), how can he be pleasing to God and keep the commandments?

Response: Unless such men as these, of every kind—that is, I mean, men who live in the world, with wealth, marriage, and enjoyment—are pleasing to God, then perhaps those who make excuses for such men in their sins would have some defense. Now we see in the divine scriptures, however, that nearly all those beloved to God, who pleased God, lived in the world with wealth and children. I am speaking of Abraham, Job, David, and the like. For it is said that wealth is good for whom it is not sin. Let us, then, take heed of the Apostle, when he writes to Timothy about such matters, saying, "Exhort those who are wealthy in the present age not to be arrogant, nor to set their hopes upon the uncertainty of riches but upon the living God, who richly furnishes us with everything to enjoy. Exhort them to do what is good, to be rich in good works, to be generous and liberal, laying for themselves a good foundation for the future, that they may attain eternal life" (1 Tim. 6:17-19). And elsewhere he furthermore says, "I am saying, brethren, that the present time has grown short. Henceforth, let those who have wives live as though they had none, and those who mourn as though they were not mourning, and those rejoicing as though they were not rejoicing, and those who deal with the world as though they had no dealings with it. For the form of this world is passing away" (1 Cor. 7:29-31).[148]

Another of Anastasius' queries reveals how the monks continued to be concerned with larger speculative problems related to their own ethical life:

Question: What is fate (τύχη)? Is a Christian allowed to confess (the reality of) fate?

Response: Fate is said among the Greeks to be the administration of the world without divine providence. But the Christian confesses the God who administers and provides for all things. If he also confesses (the reality of) fate, he deviates from Christian doctrine and belief, like the feeble-minded Greeks. For they senselessly ascribe everything that happens to humanity to fate and to the stars, and the Pharisees too foolishly think that necessity (είμαρμένη) is the beginning of things. Holy Scripture, speaking about those who worship this so-called fate, reproaches their folly and impiety, and mentions "those who prepare a table for the demon and prepare a mixture for fate" (Isa. 65:11). About the astrologers, it says, "Let the astrologers of the heavens stand and save you," and so on. "Behold, all of them shall be burned up like firewood on a fire, and have no chance of removing their life from the flame" (Isa. 47:13-14). Likewise the Lord, triumphing over their foolishness, says, "Where are your astrologers? Let them declare the things that are happening to you" (Isa. 19:12).[149]

The larger mass of non-Anastasian questions and responses in this spiritual florilegium covers many different topics which, having been culled from earlier patristic and monastic writings along with the Fathers' authoritative interpretations, reveal the urge in later Byzantine monasticism to fix orthodox teaching on problematic ethical, theological, and scriptural issues.[150] Many are familiar topics drawn from scripture. "Is paradise a sensible and corruptible place, or an intelligible and incorruptible one?"[151] "What does 'in the image and likeness' (Gen. 1:26) mean?"[152] "How is the phrase 'I will harden Pharaoh's heart' (Exod. 4:21, etc.) to be interpreted?"[153] The tendency in this and in other monastic florilegia (e.g., the Pseudo-Athanasian *Quaestiones ad Antiochum*[154]) to harmonize and standardize doctrine represented the last, and certainly degenerative, phase in the Byzantine monastic tradition of spiritual-pedagogical *quaestiones-responsiones*. It signaled their divorce, as a didactic tool, from the dynamic engagements between teacher and students, abbot and subordinates, preacher and audience.

As was noted at the outset of this chapter, we have to do, in these collections of monastic pedagogical *quaestiones-responsiones*, not with a pure literary genre *per se*, but with a didactic tool that found its way into different literary formats (sayings traditions, rules, dialogues, homilies and discourses). Their "generic" continuity, their consistency as a tradition, lay in their "eisagogic" value (as Dörries calls it[155]), their capacity to address the practical and theoretical difficulties of monastic existence, whether the specific problems be pragmatic, doctrinal, or scriptural. For our purposes they are a decisive indicator of how scripture, in particular, came to be, more than a practical guide for the monastic life, an object and source of speculative reflection on the salvation of the soul. Having often been discouraged in the earliest monastic conferences, questions of obscure or discrepant scriptures came to play a fundamental role either as a means of fleshing out scriptural teaching on issues of monastic ethical discipline and doctrine, or as an artificial platform for working out important themes of spiritual anthropology.

The *Quaestio-Responsio* in Maximus' Earlier Monastic Works

Unlike its demonstrable generic conformity with the exegetical $ἀπορίαι$ literature, the continuity of the *Quaestiones ad Thalassium* with the literature of monastic didactic *quaestiones* does not, of course, rest on any purely literary-generic criteria, but, again, on the peculiar pedagogical function served by the *quaestio-responsio* method itself, namely, monastic ascesis and spiritual doctrine. Before moving on to the *Ad Thalassium* itself, however, it is necessary, in establishing this continuity, to consider Maximus' extensive use of the *quaestio-responsio* as a mode of spiritual pedagogy in certain of his earlier writings whose primary audiences were apparently Christian monks.156

His *Liber asceticus* is, in the same mold as Cassian's *Collationes* or Mark the Hermit's *Disputatio,* a stylized monastic dialogue, in question-and-response form, between a γέρων and a novice.157 The unmistakably monastic purview of the *Liber asceticus* is born out in the themes of its questions and responses, covering the whole range of ethical and contemplative concerns of the monastic life: the fall, the passions, renunciation of the world, prayer, scripture reading, the ongoing battle with the demons, ἀγάπη and the virtues, deification as the culmination of the monk's spiritual quest, and so on.

The *Liber asceticus* is a careful and deliberate imitation of the didactic format of the early desert "conferences," with the inexperienced young monk petitioning the elder sage for an inspired word of salvation.158 The very first two questions posed in the *Liber asceticus* evoke Maximus' peculiar intention in this dialogue to integrate the doctrine of the incarnation into his understanding of the the ascetic life. "I beseech you, father, tell me: What was the purpose of the Lord's incarnation?"159 and, "What are the commandments I ought to perform, father, that through them I might be saved?"160 Throughout the treatise, the responses place profuse scriptural citations in the mouth of the γέρων that are aimed at casting the monk's struggle in scriptural imagery and identifying it with the exemplary suffering of Christ and of the divine Apostle. The upshot, as Dalmais has shown, is a systematic effort to portray monastic ascesis within the larger framework of the economy of salvation, the incarnation itself being the focal mystery and the paradigm of the life of charity.161

Two other texts from among Maximus' earlier monastic works are of particular importance for illuminating the adaptation of the *quaestio-responsio* in the *Quaestiones ad Thalassium* itself. The little-known *Quaestiones ad Theopemptum,* which gives us no details of its occasion, elucidates three New Testament texts posed to Maximus by a certain Theopemptus the Scholastic: Luke 18:6 on the "unjust judge"; Luke 6:29 on the striking of the cheek; and John 20:17 on Jesus' saying "I have not yet returned to my Father."162

The more revealing *Quaestiones et dubia* is a collection of Maximus' own ἀπορίαι, mostly on scripture but occasionally on the teachings of earlier patristic authorities, especially the Cappadocian Fathers. Except for the obvious difference that these are his own queries, the text has very clear affinities to the *Quaestiones ad Thalassium*, the questions often being quite open-ended, providing Maximus a point of departure for extrapolating spiritual-anthropological ideas. As in the *Ad Thalassium*, the individual exegeses are moral and anagogical expositions of texts that appear sometimes to be only *prima facie* problematic. Question 77 is a good preliminary example of how Maximus renders a biblical text as a virtual inventory of monastic spiritual teachings:

> Question: What is the anagogical interpretation (ἡ θεωρία κατ' ἀναγωγήν) of the figures of Cain and Abel (Gen. 4:1-16)?
>
> Response: Cain stands for "the setting of the mind on the flesh" (Rom. 8:6), while Abel stands for sorrow (πένθος), or rather repentance (μετανοία). Whenever therefore the mind, having not yet perfectly amended its practical habit, mocks itself by "the setting of the mind on the flesh" (Rom. 8:6), and goes by itself out "into the field" (Gen. 4:8)—that is, out onto the plain of natural contemplation (φυσική θεωρία)—it dies; for it is not strong enough to pass beyond the mere appearances of created beings and instead dwells on them. Hence, whoever kills Cain (representing as he does "the setting of the mind on the flesh," which is but a compliance [συγκατάθεσις] with the flesh since whoever murders sorrow consents to evil) "unleashes sevenfold vengeance" (Gen. 4:15), or in other words, abolishes the seven spirits of wickedness, or also the seven evil passions that they activate. But the curse of bemoaning Cain (Gen. 4:12) signifies the upheaval of the conscience which ever beats and shakes the thought of him.[163]

Even the seemingly most obscure or insignificant passage of scripture is for Maximus, in the *Quaestiones et dubia*, a potential treasury of spiritual instruction for the ascetic life. In the following question, for example, he selects some texts from Genesis as a point of departure for an exposition of natural contemplation (φυσικὴ θεωρία) and the dangers of demonic deception:

Question: What are the rods off of which Jacob peeled bark and placed in the watering troughs (Gen. 30:37-38)? And what does it mean that Rachel stole the idols (Gen. 31:19), and what is the terebinth in which Jacob hid them (Gen. 35:4)?

Response: Every "Jacob" (meaning "vanquisher") peels rods—that is to say, he strips the principles (λόγοι) of created beings clean of the material appearances which build up on them—and sets them in watering troughs (that is, in the habit of knowledge [ἡ ἕξις τῆς γνώσεως]) so that those who, like cattle, learn by demonstration, might conceive in this habit (cf. Gen. 30:39) and form themselves on the imitation of it. Thus every soul that is so instructed steals the idols from his own father who formerly ill-begat him in evil. They are idols which do not inhere naturally in visible things but are schemes of deceit fashioned into idols by "the devil" who is "father" (John 8:44) of evil. Likewise, in a good sense, one who steals these things "takes (them all) captive in order to obey Christ," as the Apostle says (2 Cor. 10:5). But these idols were hidden in the saddles of camels (cf. Gen. 31:34). Interpret the camel here as the body. For because of its crooked frame, and because, in general, its feet make footprints in the ground, the camel signifies our human body after having become crooked and infused with passion because of transgression. The saddles are different modes of ascetic training (τρόποι τῆς ἀσκήσεως). The soul that sits on them escapes the father of evil who is tracking down and seeking the idols he intends to use for deception (cf. Gen. 31:33ff). Through elevated anagogy and contemplation of these very "idols," the soul truly tears them from him and hides them in the saddles of self-control (ἐγκράτεια) which hold fast our body. But when the soul enters the land of promise (that is, perfect knowledge), it is then commanded to be stripped of these idols too (that is, the things stolen in a good sense according to our anagogical interpretation), whether they be, like a garment, more ethical modes of conduct, or, like earrings, those modes which, through the more ethical ones, give ear to natural principles (cf. Gen. 35:1-4). For when the discerning mind ($νοῦς$) laid hold of these things, he hid them in the terebinth tree (Gen. 35:4)—that is, in the mystery of the cross, for all practice ($πρᾶξις$) and knowledge ($γνῶσις$) is concealed within that mystery. The cross bears a resemblance to the terebinth tree because, while in the winter it is altogether unpleasant, in the spring it is entirely fragrant and pleasant; so too the Lord's cross, while in the present life appearing to have the form of nothingness, displays, in the better life to come, a more fragrant and glorious beauty.[164]

Such moral and tropological exegeses, densely packed with the technical terminology of Maximus' ascetic doctrine, indicate a deliberate and artificial use of scriptural $ἀπορίαι$, but one that suits the peculiar intentions of a monastic spiritual father whose responsibility is to maximize the salvific value of every passage of scripture for the monastic life.[165] The exegesis (*responsio*), as it were, logically precedes the scriptural $ἀπορία$ (*quaestio*), which is a mere starting point for some targeted moral or spiritual lesson. The *Quaestiones et dubia* is an exaggeration of the kind of use of *quaestiones* found in some cases in the homilies of Pseudo-Macarius or Isaac the Syrian, where questions were employed as a means to open up new propositions in the author's parenesis or doctrinal instruction.[166] In the *Quaestiones et dubia*, they enable Maximus to illuminate even the most remote corners of scripture, unfolding from them new insights into the dynamics of the ascetic life.

The *Quaestiones ad Thalassium* in the Tradition of Monastic Pedagogical *Quaestiones et responsiones*

Given the grounds of Thalassius' association with Maximus, compelling the Libyan hegumen to petition his more erudite friend for an anagogical interpretation of difficult passages of scripture,[167] the distinctly monastic *Sitz im Leben* of the text—and its "formal" location within the tradition of monastic pedagogical *quaestiones*—are indicated from the outset. Moreover, even though, as Thunberg has emphasized,[168] Maximus probably envisions his spiritual teaching as paradigmatic for a wider audience than the monks, he leaves little doubt that they are the immediate object of his exegeses of scriptural ἀπορίαι. Responding, for example, to a question from 1 Esdras, Maximus describes how the demons deceptively share the zeal of spiritual combatants in order to wrest control of their good intentions:

> The malefactors (demons) say, "We, like you, obey your Lord" (1 Esdras 5:69). For they neither despise temperance, nor detest fasting. Nor do they hate *the distribution of goods, hospitality, singing of psalms, the discipline of scripture reading, the higher disciplines of the mind, sleeping on the ground, vigils, and all the rest of the things which characterize the godly life*, so long as the object and source of one's actions inclines toward them. The monk (ἀσκητής) who detects the foreign demons ahead of time easily avoids injury from them.[169]

Clearly the "godly life" here is the monastic life, and its *dramatis persona* is the individual monk in his ongoing inner struggle with demons.

Yet there are some other key indicators which must enter into a consideration of the *Ad Thalassium* within the Byzantine monastic *quaestiones* tradition. First, taking content itself as a consideration in literary genre in this instance, one cannot ignore the presence of demonstrably monastic *topoi* in certain of the scriptural problems posed to Maximus by Thalassius. Second, it remains for us to examine how Maximus himself adapts scriptural ἀπορίαι as a proper form of monastic spiritual pedagogy—in much the same fashion as in the *Quaestiones et dubia*.[170]

Monastic Topoi *in the* Ad Thalassium

It has been noted earlier that the scriptural ἀπορίαι that Thalassius sent to Maximus were in fact the second part of a larger solicitation, the first part of which posed a variety of questions on the classic monastic theme of the origin and nature of the passions.[171] Moreover, the first entry in the main body of scriptural problems further addresses the question, "Are the passions evil in themselves or only with use?"—a question on which Maximus has occasion to apply to monastic ascesis the teaching of Gregory of Nyssa on the positive transformation of the soul's passible faculties.[172]

Many of Thalassius' scriptural ἀπορίαι, moreover, also broach diverse topics already having special moral, spiritual, or theological import for the monks. I would note here some of the more salient examples. Of particular interest are a set of ἀπορίαι on problems that, in the evolving struggle against Messalian spiritual doctrine, continued to be reopened in Byzantine monastic "philosophy" through repeated consideration and discussion in the influential works of prominent monastic teachers—the likes of Pseudo-Macarius, Mark the Hermit, John Cassian, Dorotheus of Gaza, and Diadochus of Photice. Thalassius asks how the baptized can still sin in the light of John's affirmations that one who is born of God, that is, of water and Spirit (John 3:5), does not sin (1 John 3:9).[173] Such a query is reminiscent of Pseudo-Macarius' extensive questions, in his homilies, on how it is possible for the soul to fall *post gratiam*,[174] or of Mark the Hermit's own dilemma as to how he can be baptized and enjoy baptismal grace but still remain unable to put away evil thoughts.[175] Similarly, Thalassius inquires as to how, in Paul's terms, the doers of the law, who are already justified (Rom. 2:13) could still fall away from grace (Gal. 5:4),[176] a problem that Maximus resolves by a classic patristic exegetical maneuver. Paul, he says, has the *spiritual* law in mind in speaking of those who are justified by the law in Romans 2:13, while in Galatians 5:4 it is those who hold to the *literal* law who fall from grace.[177]

One of Thalassius' questions from scripture similarly reflects the abiding threat of an all-or-nothing tendency in monastic ethics, and the speculation, fueled by radical Messalianism, that perfection is a state either fully possessed and experienced, as a sort of final and eternal security, or not possessed at all:

> If "he who fears is not perfected in love" (1 John 4:18), how is it that "there is no deficiency in those who fear him" (Ps. 33:10)? If there is no deficiency, it appears that one would be perfect. How then, is he who fears not perfect?[178]

Cassian had already raised this exegetical problem in his eleventh *Conference*, noted above,[179] in the course of an exposition of the varying levels or progressive grades of perfection among the saints. Having quoted the very same texts, Psalm 33:10 and 1 John 4:18, Cassian emphasizes the qualitative distance between that fear which is the treasure of wisdom and knowledge (Ps. 33:10), and the quite inferior fear of punishment (1 John 4:18).[180] We discover the same scriptural *topos* in a discussion of "perfect love" in Diadochus of Photice's *Centuries on Spiritual Knowledge*,[181] and in a brief discourse περὶ θείου φόβου of the sixth-century Palestinian Dorotheus of Gaza, who opens his discussion with a query remarkably similar to Thalassius' own:

> Saint John says in the catholic epistles, "Perfect love casts out fear" (1 John 4:18). What does the saint signify to us by this? What kind of love and what kind of fear is he speaking of? The Prophet in the Psalms says, "Fear the Lord all of you who are his saints" (Ps. 33:10), and we find scores of similar statements in Holy Scripture. If, therefore, the saints who love him in this way fear him, how can he say, "Love casts out fear?"[182]

Dorotheus, like Cassian and Diadochus, resolves the apparent discrepancy between the two fears by taking up again the idea of different levels of perfection, and *ipso facto* of fear. Beginners form a desire for God through a kind of preliminary fear (εἰσαγωγικὸς φόβος) of punishment, while those who are perfected in holiness, attaining the true love of God, have the healthier fear of losing the sweetness of being with God.[183]

Maximus too, in his response to Thalassius' question on these scriptures, has recourse to this traditional line of thinking. Distinguishing between an impure and pure fear,[184] he differentiates the "fearers" (οἱ φοβούμενοι), the beginners in virtue who have not yet been released from the mere fear of divine retribution to a pure intellectual love of God, and the "lovers" (οἱ ἀγαπῶντες), whose perfect love of God includes an equally pure fear, an innate natural reverence, for the transcendence of God.[185] John and the Psalmist thus do not contradict one another. The "perfect" can indeed still "fear," granted this qualitative difference between the two sorts of fear.[186]

Numerous other of Thalassius' scriptural ἀπορίαι introduce individual themes of enduring importance in monastic ascesis. Questions 33 and 34 probe Jesus' teaching on answered prayer (Mark 11:23-24), and are taken by Maximus as a basis for explaining the inner psychological and ascetical dimensions of faith and prayer.[187] Question 58 raises the problem of involuntary sufferings,[188] a prevalent theme in earlier Greek monastic literature,[189] and one that receives from Maximus a thoroughgoing exposition of the psychological substructure of pain and pleasure consequent upon the fall of humanity. Question 43 inquires into the distinction between the "tree of life" and the "tree of the knowledge of good and evil," a central motif particularly in the speculations of Gregory of Nyssa and Pseudo-Macarius on the nature of paradise and the fall.[190] Question 44, and possibly also Question 28, explore passages from Genesis which had traditionally called for an allegorical interpretation to avoid potential anthropomorphisms or to explicate plural significations of God in scripture. It is not unreasonable to suppose that such scriptural accounts as these had remained exegetically sensitive among the monks in the wake of the earlier historic disputes between alarmed Origenists and the alleged "Anthropomorphites," Egyptian monks who were unwilling to rule out some sort of "literal" significance to these narratives where God is cast in corporeal imagery.[191] The perennial issue of this controversy was whether monks could legitimately integrate such "sensible" imagery, derived from the literal text of scripture, into their deeper meditative and prayer life. The question was still a live one in Maximus' time, as monks continued to debate the spiritual validity of sensible images or knowledge in the quest for a state of pure prayer.

Question 37 inquires about the healing power of the body of St. Paul demonstrated in the handkerchiefs and aprons taken from his body and applied to the sick (Acts. 19:12). Did God bring this about purely to enhance Paul's ministry and to impress unbelievers or did the divine Apostle's body have some immanent miraculous power? If it had such a power, why was his body not harmed by the viper (Acts 28:5), but did thereafter succumb to the sword?[192] The question is obviously asked out of a monk's interest in the miraculous powers of the holy men, of whom Paul was himself a venerated prototype. Biographies of wonderworking saints contemporary with Maximus and Thalassius reflect just this kind of fascination with the saints' hallowed bodies,[193] thought to possess miraculous power in life as well as in death.[194] Maximus, no doubt aware of the monks' proneness to excessive preoccupation with such wonders, answers Thalassius' query here by pointing to the agency of grace, which transcends the human nature even of the wonder-working saint whose body is sanctified.[195] As a supplement to this theological interpretation, he further offers Thalassius the "spiritual" sense of the text that brings "greater joy to the soul of the pious," and thus sets forth an elaborate allegory on the Apostle's "body" as "piety," his "handkerchiefs" as "principles of gnostic contemplation," his "aprons" as "modes of virtuous practical philosophy," and so on.[196]

Scriptural Aporiai *and Spiritual Pedagogy* in Maximus' *Responses to Thalassius*

Whether posed to authoritative γέροντες by novice monks, or deployed artificially by monastic teachers to obviate prospective misinterpretations or to expound moral or spiritual doctrine, questions and responses on scripture played, as we have seen, an important role in earlier monastic literature. The determinative element identifying the *Quaestiones ad Thalassium* within this tradition of monastic didactic *quaestiones* is of course Maximus' own actual adaptation of scriptural ἀπορίαι as a medium of spiritual pedagogy. We have observed the way in which he used scriptural ἀπορίαι as a didactic form in his earlier writings, namely the *Quaestiones et dubia*. Again in the *Ad Thalassium*, as Laga and Steel observe, "a difficult passage, an *aporia*, is on the whole a point of departure for a speculative thought which introduces us to the very mystery of revelation: the deification of man in Christ."[197] Such comports with Maximus' underlying notion of a purposeful obscurity in scripture, and with the more radical hermeneutical principle (the legacy of the Alexandrian tradition) that the Logos or Spirit may indeed even deliberately pose obstacles in the text of scripture in order to quicken the mind toward spiritual truth.[198] But more important here, it is in keeping with Thalassius' own expectations, since he petitions Maximus not merely for a scholastic resolution of the problems posed, even though that may at times be necessitated,[199] but for ἡ ἀναγωγικὴ θεωρία,[200] and for a spiritual father's keen insights into the nature of the human condition and the way of salvation.

This spiritual-pedagogical valuation of scriptural ἀπορίαι becomes especially clear in those instances where Maximus is presented with a valid discrepancy from scripture[201] and must turn such an obstacle to spiritual profit. In Question 4, for example, Thalassius asks how Jesus could have enjoined his disciples not to have two tunics (Matt. 10:10 and par.) when he himself ostensibly had five of them (John 19:23).[202] Maximus only briefly mentions the literal interpretation: Jesus had not five tunics, but only a small inner tunic (χιτώνιον) and an exterior wrap, or garment (ἱμάτιον).[203] This distinction in turn becomes the basis for a fuller exposition of the spiritual sense:

> However, through the Spirit the great John the Evangelist has mystically given the ineffable truth of the spiritual meaning through the literal wording of the text, in order to guide our mind through the literal narrative to the things understood spiritually. Therefore, the Savior's tunic, which was woven completely from above, and which those who crucified him did not tear apart though they were allowed to strip it off him, is the indissoluably interwoven conjunction of the virtues one with another, the appropriate and proper interface between us and the Logos. Or, it may be seen as the grace of the new man, woven, after the manner of the Logos' tunic, from on high by the Spirit. The outer garment is the sensible world, which is divided into the four elements. Those (demons) who crucify the Lord noetically within us divide up this sensible world like four garments.
>
> Accordingly, the demons are dividing the phenomenal creation into four elements and are preparing us, who have ignored the divine principles (λόγοι) in it, for the passion of seeing it sensibly. But even if the demons strip the tunic of virtues from us through our failure to perform good acts, they cannot persuade virtue to be evil.
>
> Let us not, therefore, make the Savior's "five" garments a basis for greed, but rather know the true intention of scripture, and

how the Lord is crucified in those of us who neglect what is good, and is stripped naked by our laziness in performing good deeds, while the demons divide up his creation, like his garments, with a view to serving the passions through us. Let us become steadfast guardians of the good gifts given us by God; let us look upon creation with a view to his glory alone; and let us, by zeal in good works, preserve the tunic of the principle of knowledge, which cannot be stolen—namely, the virtues.[204]

Such an allegorical interpretation of Jesus' garments not only removes a seeming discrepancy in scripture, more importantly it uses the ἀπορία to illuminate the monk's spiritual combat with the demons who are operative through the carnal passions.

In another instance, Thalassius, citing an alleged divine injustice in Exodus, asks why Moses, en route to Egypt under God's own commission, and without prior warning, incurred the angel's wrath at the inn because his son by Sephora (Zipporah) was uncircumcised (Exod. 4:24ff).[205] In his response, Maximus turns immediately to an allegorical resolution of the problem in question, appealing to "the power of the literal meaning in the Spirit" (ἡ τῆς ἱστορίας ἐν πνεύματι δύναμις), since this power is constantly being realized and abounding into its fullness."[206] At this level, the plight of Moses on his way to Egypt becomes transparent to the plight of the mind (νοῦς) in its ascetic struggle to detach itself from passion and to secure itself in virtue:

The desert (Exod. 3:1) from which Moses was sent to Egypt to lead out the sons of Israel represents either human nature, or this world, or the habit (ἕξις) that is stripped of the passions. The mind which, in this habit, is instructed, in this world, in knowledge through the contemplation of created beings, receives from God a secret mystical commission invisibly to lead out of the Egypt of the heart—that is, from the flesh and sense—divine thoughts of beings, in the manner of the Israelites.... Yet the mind that is faithful in this divine ministry—with gnostic wisdom attached to it like a companion, and with the noble manner and thought that arises from that wisdom—invariably travels in a holy way of life the road of the virtues, which in no way admits of any stalling on the part of those who walk in it. Rather, this mind runs the ever-moving, swift race of the soul "toward the goal of the upward call" (Phil. 3:14). For the immobility of virtue is the beginning of evil. When the mind is vexed about material obstacles from each side in its way, it pollutes and makes uncircumcised the pure and wholly circumcised conduct and thought of the pious way of life.

Interpreted spiritually, the convicting Word, posing directly as an angel, threatens death in the conscience, and testifies that the cause of that threat is the immobility in virtue that likewise produces the uncircumcision of thought. The wisdom that dwells with the mind wins over thought, and like Sephora, uses the small stone of the word of faith to circumcise the little boy, the material fantasy that arises in thought, and dries up every contrivance of sensible life. For Sephora said, "the blood of the boy's circumcision is fixed" (Exod. 4:25), meaning that the life beset with passion ceased its fantasy and movement, since it was cleansed of defiled thought by the wisdom of faith. Thereafter the Word ceases the cleansing, and, like an angel, smites the errant mind through the conscience and frustrates every thought save that which befits it. For the way of the virtues is in truth filled with many holy "angels" who are effective in every virtue in kind—(I mean the principles [λόγοι] and modes [τρόποι] of virtue)—and with angels who cooperate with us invisibly to realize good things, and who promote such principles of virtue in us.

Therefore the word of Holy Scripture is good and noble, always offering spiritual truth in place of the literal facts in those who grasp sound truths in the eyes of their soul. It calumniates neither God nor his angels. For Moses, who was sent out by God, did not have, according to the spiritual meaning of the scripture, an uncircumcised son, or thought (λογισμός), otherwise God would have originally sent him with orders to circumcise. Moreover, the divine angel was not harsh when he warned Moses of the death that would befall him through an errant immobility in the way of the virtues. In the moral race course, weakness in performing the virtues may result in just this death.

Those of you who rely more precisely on the literal narrative (ἡ ἱστορία) will clearly discover how the angel who came to meet Moses and threatened him with death for the passion that secretly arose in his mind, did so not at the beginning nor middle nor end of the road, but in the inn. Had Moses not desisted from his course and ceased his journey he would not have been discredited and been blamed by the angel for the boy's being uncircumcised.[207]

Maximus has carefully interfused the resolution of the scriptural ἀπορία (viz., the alleviation of the apparent injustice of God toward Moses) with a thoroughgoing exposition of the unceasing progress of the soul toward virtue. The ascetic's conscience, not God or his angels, stands convicted by the scripture in question. Prefiguring the impassible νοῦς, Moses had no "uncircumcised thought" to impede his journey in virtue, but his conscience remained constantly threatened by the "angel," the Word ever poised to smite an errant mind. Even the literal interpretation (which Maximus sets forth only *after* his allegorical one) supports such an allegory: if Moses incurred the angel's wrath it was because of some secret vice or because, by taking lodging in the inn, he interrupted the progress of the journey for which God commissioned him.

In a similar pedagogical adaptation of a scriptural ἀπορία, Maximus answers the question of why Peter needed a revelation about the gentiles (Acts 10:11-48) after the Lord had already clearly given his commission to make disciples of all the nations (Matt. 28:19). For the same reason, why would the apostles have criticized Peter for his dealings with Cornelius (Acts 11:2)?[208] Maximus' response, reminiscent of Origen's interpretation of Peter's vision,[209] describes how Peter needed to be shown by example (παράδειγμα) the new spiritual mystery of Christ which superseded the old corporeal worship. The apostles back in Jerusalem who criticized Peter's relations with Cornelius had been ignorant of this mystery "until they too learned, in secret ways, that the richness of God's goodness is for all men."[210]

More significantly, however, Peter, in his vision, is a model of the ascetic, indeed of all humanity, in the struggle to transcend attachment to sensible objects, discovering that the visible creation must be perceived not through mere appearances but through its divine principles (λόγοι), the invisible world inhering in the visible one.[211]

> For this reason God said, "Rise, Peter, kill and eat" (Acts 10:13). Whence was he commanded to rise? He was commanded to rise from something else: from his sensible habit and attachment, from his rather meager preconception of created beings, or from his alleged righteousness of the law, in order that, being able to observe the principles (λόγοι) of sensible forms (σχήματα) with the mind alone, a mind freed from every sensual fantasy, he might know the figures (τύποι) of intelligible realities and learn that none of God's creatures is unclean. For having contemplated, from the perspective of the intelligible world, the visible creation manifested in its principles, or the figures of intelligible realities from the perspective of the phenomenal order—in the manner of the sheet lowered from heaven—he would believe that no visible thing is unclean and see that no contrariness is reflected in the principles of created beings. For corruption and hostility between creatures is based on sense, but there is no opposition at all among principles.[212]

Every discrepancy or seeming offense in scripture is for Maximus the medium of some higher spiritual teaching. Why did Paul go up to Jerusalem when others had warned him "through the Spirit" not to go (Acts 21:4)?[213] The explanation lies in the diversity of charisms in the Church (cf. 1 Cor. 12:8ff), the Holy Spirit existing proportionately, either more or less, in every individual gift.[214] Those prophets who warned Paul through the Spirit possessed a gift of neighborly love, but Paul favored "the divine and super-intellectual love incomparably over the others' spiritual love for him."[215] But in having this superior love, says Maximus, Paul did not actually disregard these prophets by going to Jerusalem, rather, he attracted them, through the activity of the Spirit that was proportionately given to them as their charism, to that higher spiritual desire (πόθος) which transcends everything.[216] "The great Apostle therefore did not disregard the Spirit but taught those who prophesied about him through their gift of love to be transferred from the lesser to the higher spirit, or charism."[217] The Confessor concludes:

> The great Apostle's apparent disobedience is therefore observant of the beneficial order that administers and preserves all divine things, and... also clearly instructive of the different grades (βαθμοί) in the Church, which are well-distinguished by the Spirit and in no way to be confused with one another.[218]

These examples demonstrate how Maximus uses scriptural ἀπορίαι as an effective form of spiritual pedagogy that moves beyond merely resolving discrepancies or alleged offenses in the text of scripture, exploiting these difficulties precisely to elucidate the higher coherence of scripture as regards ascetic practice, or the soul and its salvation.

It is in this adaptation of scholia on scriptural ἀπορίαι for purposes of spiritual and theological instruction that the *Quaestiones ad Thalassium* finds perhaps its closest monastic literary antecedent in certain of Evagrius' *Scholia on Proverbs* framed in the style of *quaestio-responsio*. Here too we find scriptural discrepancies set forth precisely for their prospective spiritual profit. In *Scholium* 13, for example, Evagrius illuminates Proverbs 1:26 ("Therefore I will laugh at your destruction, and will rejoice when ruin befalls you") by raising and answering a question cross-scripturally:

> How is it, then, that Solomon can say further on that "he who rejoices over another's destruction will not be held guiltless" (Prov. 17:5)? Or perhaps this is rather the way Wisdom rejoiced when it rejoiced over the destruction of Matthew the tax collector (cf. Matt. 9:9), and over the destruction of the thief who believed in Christ; for Wisdom destroyed the robber in the one, and the tax collector in the other.[219]

Elsewhere, commenting on Proverbs 2:17 ("My son, do not be overtaken by an evil decision, which forsakes the teaching of your youth, and forgets the divine covenant"), Evagrius writes:

> If a "decision" (βουλή) is a kind of activity of the mind, how can it forsake the teaching of one's youth and forget the divine covenant? For the scripture is speaking to us of evil counsel as though it pertained to a rational being. Or perhaps now it calls the devil an "evil decision." For he made an evil decision when he said, "I shall set my throne above the stars. I will be like the Most High" (Isa. 14:13-14). He also forsook divine knowledge when he abandoned the teaching of his youth, that "youth" obviously indicating the original condition he enjoyed when he was envied by the trees of paradise (cf. Ezek. 31:9).[220]

One further example can be seen in Evagrius' *Scholium* on Proverbs 9:13 ("A foolish and rash woman becomes needy of a morsel of bread; she does not know her shame"):

> The scripture says that "she does not know her shame" as though it could be taught. David also says that the fear of God can be taught: "Listen to me, children," he says, "and I will teach you the fear of the Lord" (Ps. 33:12). If fear and shame are natural passions of the soul, how can they be taught? Or perhaps the scripture is rather calling "the fear of the Lord" the teaching about the fear of the Lord, which teaches us how to turn away from evil, since "every man turns away from evil by the fear of the Lord" (Prov. 15:27). Perhaps also the scripture, in speaking of "shame," is referring to the principles (λόγοι) of repentance and shame that lead us to a consciousness of our own sins. In the same manner David says, "I shall see the heavens, the works of your fingers, the moon and stars which you have founded" (Ps. 8:4), that is to say, I shall see the principles that concern the heavens, moon, and stars.[221]

Scriptural difficulties, for Evagrius as well as Maximus, therefore constitute a peculiarly effective technique for accentuating the moral or spiritual interpretation of a particular text. Evagrius remains much more careful throughout the *Scholia on Proverbs* to restrict his scholia to very concise notations on the scriptural passage under consideration.[222] Maximus' exegetical responses in the *Quaestiones ad Thalassium*, by contrast, frequently present a whole variety of possible alternative explanations of a particular scriptural ἀπορία.[223] Yet Maximus too strives to keep his expositions under control and to set forth, in these exegetical scholia, a pointed and trenchant spiritual lesson, even if in the end it entails multiple and diverse levels of meaning, and often lengthy excurses. The heuristic purpose is always capital in his mind. Florovsky has observed accurately of Maximus' writings in general:

> Most of all he loved to write chapters in the form of exhortations. Most of his writings are just that—theological fragments, "chapters," notes. He loved to write in fragments. He discourses only when he has to, and in debates—most frequently, he explains. He prefers to go into depth, to lay bare the heart of each theme, as opposed to covering things in breadth. In this way he was able to develop the dialectical substance of his conclusions.[224]

Recapitulation: Scriptural *Aporiai*, Monastic Use of Scripture, and the *Quaestiones ad Thalassium*

As a didactic device, already proved in pagan and Christian paideia, the *quaestio-responsio* thrived within the monastic milieu as a form of spiritual pedagogy adapted in a variety of monastic literatures. One is tempted to distinguish, as in the wider scholia tradition of exegetical *quaestiones et responsiones*, between "authentic" questions (raised from within the actual *Sitz im Leben* of ascetic instruction)[225] and the "artificial" questions used in monastic dialogues,[226] discourses, and homilies, and found in abundance in the *Quaestiones et dubia* of Maximus. Such a distinction is at times obscured, however, where monastic authors raise questions pedagogically that evoke or anticipate real practical or theological problems from within their communities.[227] In the case of the *Quaestiones ad Thalassium*, Maximus has taken over numerous authentic scriptural ἀπορίαι, referred to him by another erudite monk, and produced solutions that serve principally to highlight his major spiritual-pedagogical concerns. At this point, the designations of authentic and artificial become more or less ineffectual: it is enough that Maximus considers his own spiritual teaching as the appropriate response to the inquiries conveyed to him by Thalassius. As a particular form of the *quaestio-responsio,* the scriptural ἀπορία thus becomes in Maximus a stylized mode of moral and spiritual instruction, used in much the same manner as in the *Scholia on Proverbs* of his celebrated predecessor Evagrius.

As I have consistently reiterated in this chapter, there is no uniform literary genre of monastic *quaestiones et responsiones.* It is rather the distinctly *monastic* σκοπός and spiritual-pedagogical function served by the *quaestio-responsio* that establishes the continuity of the *Ad Thalassium* with the earlier monastic tradition, and that provides us with a deeper insight into its original horizon. Already among Thalassius' scriptural ἀπορίαι, I have cited a number of ἀπορίαι that resume demonstrably monastic topics, some of which come up in the earlier collections of monastic *quaestiones.* In its turn, the *Quaestiones ad Thalassium* itself would contribute to later scriptural and doctrinal discussions in the monastic tradition, being one of the most often quoted and influential of Maximus' works in the later Byzantine monastic florilegia. I have found two selections from it, for example, in the Pseudo-Anastasian *Quaestiones et responsiones.* One of these, not noticed by Marcel Richard in his important study,[228] is but an abridgement of *Ad Thalassium Quaestio* 26, borrowing both Thalassius' question and a portion of Maximus' response concerning another favorite *topos* long raised in monastic exegesis, the allegorical interpretation of the king of Babylon (Nebuchadnezzar) as the devil.[229] Elsewhere, Maximus' response to *Ad Thalassium Quaestio* 57 is quoted, with other authorities, in the florilegium appended to the authentically Anastasian *Quaestio* 6 on the confession of sin.[230]

In evaluating the earlier literature of monastic pedagogical questions and responses, I have of course focused special attention on scriptural ἀπορίαι in the monastic tradition. In an important respect, these ἀπορίαι are simply a guage of emerging patterns in the pedagogical use of scripture in the concrete religious life of Byzantine monasticism—ranging from the practical and meditative, to the speculative and increasingly expository use of scripture by the monks. Such an access to these original patterns of monastic Bible study is, in the end, far more crucial for our purposes than the prospect of isolating a uniform literary genre.

It has been shown that many of the early γέροντες quoted in the recensions of the *Apophthegmata patrum*, followed once more by rigorous pragmatists like Barsanuphius and John, discouraged the very thought of questioning the obscurities and discrepancies of scripture, judging the Bible principally as a practical guide for the ascetic life. Basil's *Regulae* also show, amid the majority of scriptural questions used purely to adduce the biblical basis of monastic life and practice, a fairly restricted number of scriptural queries that evince deeper theological issues occasioned by the monks' contemplation of scripture.

Inspired by Origen and Evagrius, Cassian's *Collationes*, in a new and decisive way, placed scripture at the very center of intellectual speculation. While by no means forsaking the older discipline of *ruminatio* on the Bible, or the practical concerns of monastic ascesis, Cassian sanctioned the use of scripture as a springboard for speculative inquiry into the problems of the fall, sin, the soul, and the economy of salvation. With the likes of Pseudo-Macarius, Mark the Hermit, and Isaac the Syrian, carefully crafted scriptural *quaestiones* were exploited as a means of elucidating points of moral or spiritual doctrine, and for clarifying potentially contentious biblical texts. One finds in the questions and responses of Mark the Hermit's *De baptismo* a premier example of a thoroughgoing dogmatico-polemical use of scripture to expound monastic spiritual doctrine and ethics.

Maximus' works comprehend both patterns. In his *Liber asceticus*, where he adapts formulas of question and response imitative of the *Apophthegmata patrum*, Maximus' use of scripture likewise emulates the norm of the desert fathers, appealing to scripture almost exclusively as a mirror on the monk's spiritual ἀγών and as a practical weapon to be invoked against the demons.

> The brother said: "So it is, father. For out of my carelessness the demons always take occasion against me. I entreat you, then,

father: tell me how I ought to lay hold of soberness." The old man answered: "Complete lack of concern for earthly things and continuous meditation (συνεχὴς μελέτη; =*ruminatio*) on the divine Scriptures bring the soul to fear of God; and fear of God brings soberness. Then the soul begins to see the demons warring against it through its own thoughts and begins to fight back."[231]

By contrast, in the *Quaestiones ad Thalassium* (and in the *Quaestiones et dubia* before it), Maximus follows on Cassian and Evagrius, who opened the devotional use of scripture among the monks to the new horizons of an Origenian hermeneutics, in fully exploiting a *lectio divina* as a means to elaborate the grand theological themes on which the spiritual life was to be grounded: the fall and origin of the passions, the grace of the incarnation, and the struggle against the passions toward the attainment of deification. Obscurities and ἀπορίαι are of the very nature of the economy of scripture, and serve only to prosper the monk in his ongoing search for spiritual illumination.

Yet it would be inappropriate to exaggerate the distinction between "practical" and "contemplative" uses of scripture in Maximus. As will become clearer further on in this study, Maximus himself would doubtless have insisted that the application of scripture to monastic πρᾶξις and the contemplative (θεωρητική) or gnostic speculation into its deeper senses are "anagogically" inseparable. For "every syllable of divine scripture," he says, "is capable of being understood in multifarious ways (πολυτρόπως) for the benefit (ὠφέλεια) of those who long *for virtue (ἀρετή) and knowledge (γνῶσις)*."[232] His anagogical interpretation of scripture (ἡ ἀναγωγικὴ θεωρία) responds to the monk's perennial need to have the whole of scripture, obscurities and all, applied to the full compass of his struggle for salvation and deification.[233]

An inquisitive urge and a pious deference to the mystery of scripture are curiously inseparable in this approach to scripture. In this respect, Jean Kirchmeyer's remark on the use of scripture in the *Liber asceticus* could as well be referred to the *Quaestiones ad Thalassium*, for each work in its own way reveals "a remarkable specimen of a common exercise in the monastic tradition: the soul searches the scriptures, not in order to reconstruct the sense envisioned by the sacred writers, but in order to await the Spirit's response to its questions."[234]

Notes

1. *RAC* 6, s.v. "Erotapokriseis (B. christlich)," col. 366. See also the review of this genre's development in the classical pagan literature, ibid. (A. nichtchristlich), by Heinrich Dörrie, cols. 342-347.

2. See Bardy, "La littérature patristique," *RB* 41: 210-236, 341-369, 516-537; and 42: 14-30, 211-229, 328-352; cf. also Hermann Jordan, *Die Geschichte der altchristlichen Literatur* (Leipzig: Quelle und Meyer, 1911), § 69 ("Die Aporienliteratur"), 409-411.

3. See Bardy, "La littérature patristique," *RB* 42: 332ff; cf. Carl Laga and Carlos Steel in the introduction to their CCSG edition of the *Q. Thal.*, ix and n. 2; Croce, *Tradizione e ricerca*, 30 and n. 1.

4. Most notable are the *catenae* commentaries of Procopius of Gaza (460-526). See also Beck (*Kirche und theologische Literatur* 413-414), who notes the proliferation of these exegetical florilegia right along with the dogmatic ones; cf. also the study of Gilles Dorival, "Des commentaires de l'Écriture aux chaînes," in *Le monde grec ancien et la Bible*, dir. Claude Mondésert, Bible de tous les temps 1 (Paris: Beauchesne, 1984), 361-383.

5. Bardy, "La littérature patristique," *RB* 42: 351 and passim. As Bardy himself notes, these are only loose categorizations. It is not always clear whether the questions posed are artificial or authentic in those cases where an exegete is asking them from his own peculiar point of view.

6. See PG 22.879-1006.

7. Bardy, "La littérature patristique," *RB* 41: 228.

8. See also the abridgement in PG 22.880-958, which is followed by the Greek fragments; also Bardy, "La littérature patristique," *RB* 41: 229-230.

9. Bardy, "La littérature patristique," *RB* 41: 231.

10. PG 93.1391-1448.

11. E.g., *Qu. ev.* 1 (PG 93.1392B): "Why does Mark, after having said 'the beginning of the gospel of Jesus Christ,' add, 'as it is written in Isaiah...'? The citation, with some variants, is not in Isaiah, but in Malachi." Or again, ibid. 2 (PG 93.1393B): "Why does John the Baptist, questioned by the Pharisees 'Are you Elijah,' say 'No,' whereas Christ says 'He is Elijah who is to come'?"

12. See Bardy, "La littérature patristique," *RB* 42: 228.
13. PG 80.76.
14. PG 80.528B-529A.
15. PG 80.77A-B; cited by Bardy, "La littérature patristique," *RB* 42: 221. For further examples of Theodoret's questions and responses, see ibid., 221-225.
16. See the extracts from the *Quaestiones* of Theodoret in the Ps.-Anastasian *Qu. et resp.* 26-29 (including 29 on the hardening of Pharaoh), 35-37, 39, 41, 44-45; noted by Marcel Richard, *DS* 5, s.v. "Florilèges spirituels grecs," repr. in *Opera Minora* 1, ed. E. Dekkers et al. (Turnhout: Brepols–Leuven University Press, 1976), col. 500.
17. A text originally found among the spurious works of Justin (PG 6.1249-1400), which Johannes Quasten (et al.) has attributed to Theodoret. For the reasons for this attribution, see Quasten's *Patrology*, vol. 3 (Westminster, Md.: Newman Press; repr. ed., Westminster, Md.: Christian Classics, 1960), 548-549.
18. See the detailed examples adduced by Bardy, "La littérature patristique," *RB* 42: 214-217.
19. *Q. Thal.* 2 (CCSG 51,1-6).
20. Ibid. 4 (CCSG 61,1-5).
21. Ibid. 6 (CCSG 69,1-7).
22. Ibid. 8 (CCSG 77,1-5).
23. Ibid. 9 (CCSG 79,1-7).
24. Ibid. 10 (CCSG 83,1-5).
25. Ibid. 15 (CCSG 101,1-6).
26. Ibid. 17 (CCSG 111,1-11).
27. Ibid. 18 (CCSG 117,1-4).
28. Ibid. 19 (CCSG 119,1-6).
29. Ibid. 20 (CCSG 121,1-5).
30. Ibid. 22 (CCSG 137,1-3).
31. Ibid. 27 (CCSG 191,1-6).
32. Ibid. 28 (CCSG 203,1-3).
33. Ibid. 29 (CCSG 211,1-4).
34. Ibid. 37 (CCSG 247,1-11).
35. Ibid. 42 (CCSG 285,1-6).
36. Ibid. 43 (CCSG 293,1-5).
37. Ibid. 44 (CCSG 299,1-6).
38. This *topos* figured significantly in anti-Manichaean argumentation, where the ostensible tension between Gen. 2:2 and John 5:17 was resolved by showing that God's "rest" was merely allegorical and that his continued creative "working" was only an ongoing perfection of what he originally

made: cf. Ps.-Archelaeus, *Acta disputationis cum Manete* 31 (PG 10.1476B-1477A); Augustine, *De Genesi contra Manichaeos* 1.22.33 (PL 34.189). In a christological context, the *topos* was used to assert Christ's essential activity in the continuing preservation (συντήρησις) and economy (οἰκονομία) of God's original creation: see Gregory of Nazianzus, *Or. theol.* 4.11 (PG 36.117A-B). In a nonpolemical setting too, exegetes argued that there was no contradiction here, and that John 5:17 merely conveyed God's ongoing sustaining of his hexaemeral works: cf. Origen, *Hom. in Num.* 23.4 (GCSO 7.215-216); Augustine, *De Genesi ad litteram* 4.11.21-4.12.22 (CSEL 28.107-109); Procopius of Gaza, *Comm. in Gen.* 2.2 (PG 87.140B-141C). Thalassius apparently knows of this traditional interpretation, given the mention of the term συντήρησις in his question.

39. See Michel Aubineau, "Dossier patristique sur Jean XIX, 23-24: La tunique sans couture du Christ," in *La Bible et les pères (Colloque de Strasbourg, 1er-3 octobre 1969)* (Paris: Presses Universitaires de France, 1971), 9-50 (and especially 34-35 on *Q. Thal.* 4).

40. Cf., e.g., *Q. Thal.* 23 (CCSG 149,1-7): "If David ruled only the carnal Israel, and the carnal Israel rejected the kingdom of Christ–(for which reason it went over to the gentiles)–, how will it be established that, as the archangel said, 'God will give him the throne of his father David, and he will rule over the house of Jacob forever' (Luke 1:32-33)?" Or, ibid. 26 (CCSG 173,1-13): "If the king of Babylon is interpreted allegorically as the Devil, what is the meaning of God's word, uttered through the prophet Jeremiah, which threatened the gentile kings and king of Judah with yoke-bars, chains, famine, death, sword, and captivity unless they served the king of Babylon, but said that those who voluntarily served him would be left on their own land (cf. Jer. 34:2, 8, 11)?" Cf. similarly, ibid. 31, 35, 36, 38, 40. Questions 62 (PG 645C-D) and 63 (PG 666A-B) appeal implicitly for a typological or anagogical interpretation of Zechariah's visions of the "flying sickle" (Zech. 5:1-4) and the "golden lampstand" (ibid. 4:2-3). Such an appeal is of course in keeping with Thalassius' original request for an *anagogical* interpretation of the scriptures (ibid. intro, CCSG 17,19-19,29).

41. Ibid. 5 (CCSG 65,1-8).

42. Ibid. 48 on 2 Chron. 26:4-10 (CCSG 331,1-16); 49 on 32:2-4 (CCSG 351,1-9); 50 on 32:20ff (CCSG 379,1-8); 51 on 32:23 (CCSG 395,1-6); 52 on 32:25-26 (CCSG 415,1-8); and 53 on 32:33 (CCSG 431,1-5).

43. Ibid. 54 on 1 Esd. 4:48-60 (CCSG 443,1-9); 55 on 5:41-43 (CCSG 481,1-14); 56 on 5:66-71 (PG 576D-577A).

44. E.g., ibid. 35 (CCSG 239,1-6): "'The Logos became flesh' (John

1:14), and not only flesh, but also blood and bones. We are commanded to eat the flesh and to drink the blood, but not to crush the bones (cf. Exod. 12:46; John 19:31-36). I seek to learn what is the tripartite power of the Word made man." Or, ibid. 60 (PG 620B-C) on who it was that foreknew Christ according to 1 Pet. 1:20; ibid. 61 (PG 626D-628A) on the coming judgment; perhaps too, ibid. 59 (PG 604A-B) on how, in 1 Pet. 1:10-11, the prophets would have "researched" and "investigated" the salvation of souls, when they were taught directly by the Holy Spirit.

45. Cf. ibid. 30, 32, 33, 39, 41, 45, 46, 47, 57.

46. This genre of course came to thrive in in the Middle Ages, both as a method of teaching and a formal means of resolving contradictions in scripture: see, e.g., Abelard's *Problemata Heloissae* or Robert of Melun's *Quaestiones de divina pagina*. See also the excellent study of G. R. Evans, *The Language and Logic of the Bible: The Earlier Middle Ages* (Cambridge: Cambridge University Press, 1984), 125-163, on the proliferation of the medieval *quaestiones* and *disputationes* literature.

47. Cf. *Q. Thal.* 59 (PG 613Bff), where he appeals to an exegetical explanation from "a certain sage" ($\tau\iota\varsigma\ \sigma\acute{o}\phi o\varsigma$); also ibid. 60 (PG 624A: $\phi\acute{a}\sigma\iota\nu\ o\acute{\iota}\ \sigma\acute{o}\phi o\iota$); and similarly ibid. 7 (CCSG 73,9ff); ibid. 38 (CCSG 255,5ff); ibid. 40 (CCSG 269,61ff); ibid. 54 (CCSG 465,383ff). See also ibid. 43 (CCSG 293,6ff), where Maximus follows $o\acute{\iota}\ \tau\tilde{\eta}\varsigma\ \dot{\epsilon}\kappa\kappa\lambda\eta\sigma\acute{\iota}\alpha\varsigma\ \delta\iota\delta\acute{a}\sigma\kappa\alpha\lambda o\iota$ in remaining silent about the deepest and most mystical interpretation of the text in question. Only in *Q. Thal.* 1 (CCSG 47,7ff) does he explicitly name an authority on whom he depends–Gregory of Nyssa.

48. Behind the emergence of a monastic "literary" culture is the problem of the slow willingness of the monks to embrace secular forms of education. On this see the study of Gerhard Podskalsky in the section on "Mönchtum und weltliche Bildung" in his *Theologie und Philosophie in Byzanz: Der Streit um die theologische Methodik in der spätbyzantinischen Geistesgeschichte (14./15. Jh.), seine systematischen Grundlagen und seine historische Entwicklung*, Byzantinisches Archiv 15 (Munich: C. H. Beck, 1977), 34-48. I have already noted the studies of Bardy and Dörries on the appropriation of the *quaestio* as a pedagogical tool in early Christian literature. On the pagan antecedents and monastic appropriation of *sententiae* or *capita*, see Endre von Ivánka, "$K\epsilon\phi\acute{a}\lambda\alpha\iota\alpha$: Eine byzantinische Literaturform und ihre antiken Wurzeln," *BZ* 47 (1954): 285-291; cf. also Irénée Hausherr, *DS* 2.1, s.v. "Centuries," cols. 416ff. On the wide spectrum of early monastic literary genres, see Jean Leclercq, *The Love of Learning and the Desire for God: A Study of Monastic Culture*, 3rd ed., trans. Catharine Misrahi (New York: Fordham University Press, 1982), 153-190.

49. On the early history of these "conferences" and monastic instruction, see Michel Olphe-Galliard, *DS* 2.2, s.v. "Conférences spirituelles," cols. 1390-1394.

50. Int. al., from the *Apophthegmata,* Ares 1 (PG 65.132C); Hierax 1 (PG 65.232C-D); Anthony 19 (PG 65.81B). Cf. also the variants adduced by Wilhelm Bousset, *Apophthegmata: Studien zur Geschichte des ältesten Mönchtums* (Tübingen: J. C. B. Mohr, 1923; reprint ed., Aalen: Scientia-Verlag, 1969), 79. See too the discussion of Dörries, "Erotapokriseis" (B. christlich), col. 353.

51. Poemen 153 (PG 65.360B); cf. ibid. 162 (PG 65.361A).

52. Ibid. 163 (PG 65.361B).

53. Cf., e.g., Sisoes 3 (PG 65.392C-D), on avoiding women; Amoun of Nitria 2 (PG 65.128C), on avoiding conversation about "worldly subjects"; Poemen 137 (PG 65.356C), on the propriety of laughter.

54. E.g., Sisoes 2 (PG 65.392C), on how much wine is appropriate for a monk to drink on days when he takes the Eucharist at church and attends an ἀγάπη meal afterward.

55. Preface to *The Sayings of the Desert Fathers,* xiii. On the saving "word" of the sages, see also the excellent recent study of Douglas Burton-Christie, "Scripture and the Quest for Holiness in the *Apophthegmata Patrum*" (Ph.D. dissertation, Graduate Theological Union, 1988), 65-66.

56. "Les *Apophthegmata patrum,*" in *Théologie de la vie monastique: Études sur la tradition patristique,* Theol 49 (Paris: Aubier, 1961), 81. On this determination to use scripture only for practical, rather than intellectual, purposes by the monks, see Guy's analysis in *DS* 4.1, s.v. "Écriture sainte et vie spirituelle" (II. A. 4. Le monachisme), cols. 161-163.

57. Zeno 4 (PG 65.176D; trans. Ward, 56).

58. Copres 3 (PG 65.252D).

59. Poemen 8 (PG 65.321D).

60. Cf. ibid. (PG 65.324A), where a visiting anchorite seeks to question Poemen on scripture but is sidetracked by one of Poemen's disciples. "Then the brother came out and said to the visitor, 'The old man (Poemen) does not readily speak of the Scriptures, but if anyone consults him about the passions of the soul, he replies.' Filled with compunction, the visitor returned to the old man and said to him, 'What should I do, Abba, for the passions of the soul master me?' The old man turned towards him and replied joyfully, 'This time, you come as you should'" (trans. Ward, 140-141).

61. Amoun of Nitria 2 (PG 65.128C). This pious silence toward scripture is seen also in Anthony 17 (PG 65.80D) and Pambo 9 (PG 65.369D-372A); cf. Palladius, *Historia Lausiaca* 10 (Pambo) (PG 65.1033B).

62. E.g., Chronius 2 (PG 65.248A-B), where the capture of the ark by foreigners, who brought it into their god's temple, at which point the god was destroyed (1 Kings 5), is taken as a figure of the human spirit being captured by the demons and led to an invisible passion, where, if it is penitent, the passion is vanquished. On the sages' use of scripture in this fashion, reducing interpretation (*Umdeutung*) to application (*Anwendung*), see Hermann Dörries, "Die Bibel im ältesten Mönchtum," *Theologische Literaturzeitung* 72 (1947): col. 218.

63. Burton-Christie, *Scripture and the Quest for Holiness*, 231-232. On πράξις as the focal principle of the desert hermeneutic, see ibid., 238-243, 365-414.

64. This is clearly exemplified by Poemen in the anecdote quoted above, note 60.

65. Dörries argues ("Die Bibel," cols. 218-222) that the real locus of the sage's pneumatic authority was not the interpretation or application of scripture itself but the very power he claimed freely to use scripture to clothe, support, or sharpen his own logia, and to apply this or that word of scripture to this or that monk. The sage needed the authority of scripture in his own rulings, and the mastery of scripture–even if he concealed it in dialogues with his subordinates–figured into his own charismatic aura (cf. cols. 220-221). But those instances where the sage refused to answer queries about scripture sufficiently show that the logia themselves stood their own ground as authoritative; and scripture, like dogma, though not questioned or impugned in these early apophthegms, played a definitely subordinate role, a role thoroughly modified by the dicta of the desert fathers (col. 222). Cf. Burton-Christie (*Scripture and the Quest for Holiness*, 173-174, 177-182, 228-229), who likewise indicates that the desert sages, while upholding the sacredness of the written Bible, by and large rejected a purely bookish authority of scripture, desiring to let the Word perpetuate its power in their own words and lives; to the extent that they succeeded, their own logia could even be considered new sacred texts that sometimes stood above the written Word.

66. Ares 1 (PG 65.133A); cf. Dörries, "Die Bibel," col. 220; also Guy, "Les *Apophthegmata patrum*," 75-76. Cf. Bousset, *Apophthegmata*, 80: "The Abba's word was considered an oracular word."

67. A process encouraged by Basil himself in *Reg. brev.* prooemium (PG 31.1080A-B); and of the gatherings of representatives, *Reg. fus.* 54 (PG 31.1044A-B). Cf. the discussion of the *Sitz im Leben* of Basil's *Regulae* in Hermann Dörries, *Symeon von Mesopotamien: Die Überlieferung der messalianischen Makarios-Schriften*, TU 95.1 (Leipzig: J. C. Hinrich, 1941), Appendix, 454-455; and his "Erotapokriseis" (B. christlich), col. 354.

68. *Reg. fus.* 49 (PG 31.1040A): "For if in every matter there is need of knowledge and experience, much more so in such matters as these. And if no one would entrust the use of tools to inexperienced persons, much more it is necessary to put the management of speech in the hands of competent men, who will be able to distinguish accurately the place, time, and manner of the questions, answering without contention and wisely and listening prudently to preserve the solutions of the problems for the edification of the community" (trans. W. K. L. Clarke, *The Ascetic Works of Saint Basil* [London: S. P. C. K., 1925], 222).

69. Dörries, *Symeon von Mesopotamien*, 454, 455.

70. *Reg. brev.* 208 (PG 31.1221A; trans. Clarke, 306).

71. Ibid. 44 (PG 31.1109C; trans. Clarke, 245).

72. Ibid. 279 (PG 31.1280A; trans. Clarke, 336).

73. Ibid. 136 (PG 31.1172C; trans. Clarke, 279).

74. E.g., *Reg. brev.* 51 (PG 31.1117A): "What is 'raka' (Matt. 5:22)?" and ibid. 49 (PG 31.1116C): "What does it mean 'to vaunt oneself' ($\pi\epsilon\rho\pi\epsilon\rho\epsilon\acute{u}\sigma\theta\alpha\iota$) (1 Cor. 13:4)?"

75. E.g., ibid. 197 (PG 31.1213A-B): "How does the right hand act so that the left hand knows not (Matt. 6:3)?" and ibid. 250 (PG 31.1249B): "How does one give what is holy to the dogs, or cast pearls before swine (Matt. 7:6)?"

76. E.g., ibid. 54 (PG 31.1117A-B): "What is self-love ($\phi\iota\lambda\alpha\nu\tau\acute{\iota}\alpha$), and how can the lover of self recognize himself (2 Tim. 3:2)?" and ibid. 62 (PG 31.1124C): "What must a man do to be condemned for hiding his talents (Matt. 25:18)?"

77. Ibid. 243 (PG 31.1245A; trans. Clarke, 319). Cf. also ibid. 248 (PG 31.1248C). See also Dörries, *Symeon von Mesopotamien*, 458.

78. Ibid. 267 (PG 31.1264B-C; trans. Clarke, 329).

79. Dörries, *Symeon von Mesopotamien*, 457.

80. The *Collationes* comprise a series of conferences between Cassian's companion, Germanus, the interrogator, and some fifteen different Egyptian anchorites. The material has of course been thoroughly reworked by Cassian on the basis of his own experiences in Egypt with the sages.

81. See Olphe-Galliard, "Conférences spirituelles," col. 1391.

82. E.g., *Coll.* 7.2ff (CSEL 13.180ff, ed. M. Petschenig [Vienna: C. Giroldi, 1886]), where the question of whether perfect chastity is obtained wholly of one's own efforts leads to an extended deliberation (with intermittent objections) on the relation between human free will and divine grace in salvation.

83. Ibid. 14.8 (CSEL 13.404). In this passage Cassian actually refers to

the Greek term θεωρητική, learned in his discussions with the Eastern monks.

84. Ibid. 8.20-21 (CSEL 13.236-241).

85. Ibid. 11.11-12 (CSEL 13.325-328).

86. Owen Chadwick remarks: "The study was more devotional than critical. It was intended more to touch the heart than to inform the head. But it intended also to inform the mind. It could throw up constant problems of interpretation that could be handled only with such elementary tools of exegesis as were then available. Part of the purpose of Cassian's Conferences was to help minds over certain hard passages that they found in their biblical reading and that caused them difficulty" (intro. to *John Cassian: Conferences,* trans. Colm Luibheid, CWS [Mahwah, N. J.: Paulist Press, 1985], 22).

87. Cf., e.g., the *Excerpta regulae Pachomii* 6, 28, 37, 59, 139, in *Pachomian Koinonia,* vol. 2: *Pachomian Chronicles and Rules,* trans. Armand Veilleux, CS 46 (Kalamazoo: Cistercian Publications, 1981), 146, 150, 151, 156, 166; and Basil, *Reg. brev.* 235 (PG 31.1240B-C), on the expediency of memorizing scripture; also Palladius, *Hist. Laus.* 4 (PG 34.1017A); ibid. 12 (PG 34.1034B), on the reverence for sages who had committed most or all of scripture to heart.

88. *Coll.* 14.10 (CSEL 13.411).

89. Sisoes 17 (PG 65.397B; trans. Ward, 181).

90. Cf. *Coll.* 14.13 (CSEL 13.414-416); ibid. 2.11 (CSEL 13.51); 7.23 (CSEL 13.201-202); *De institutis coenobiorum* 5.14 (CSEL 17.91); ibid. 6.1-2 (CSEL 17.115-116). See as well Guy's analysis of Cassian's principles for the use of scripture, "Écriture sainte et vie spirituelle" (II. A., Époque patristique, 4. Le monachisme), by Jean-Claude Guy and Jean Kirchmeyer, cols. 163-164; also García Colombás, "La biblia en la espiritualidad del monacato primitivo," *Yermo* 2 (1964): 113-129. On the early monastic tradition of *ruminatio* on scripture, see Burton-Christie, *Scripture and the Quest for Holiness,* 189-193.

91. *Coll.* 14.10 (CSEL 13.411,11-23).

92. See Philip Rousseau (*Ascetics, Authority, and the Church in the Age of Jerome and Cassian* [Oxford: Oxford University Press, 1978], 191), who notes also the greater teaching authority of scripture that this implied: "It could no longer be taken for granted that masters would reproduce in their own behaviour the discipline and insight that the Bible contained–translating it, so to speak, from word to action, in a form at once impelling and readily available to disciples. The master would now interpret Scripture as a text to be discussed–a third and quite separable element between teacher and pupil. He became 'one who sings with great learning the songs of God', exercising 'the patronage of the interpreter'; and Scripture itself became a work of reference, against which to check the opinions of men." Contrast this with the authority

invested in the early logia of the early desert sages, as mentioned above, n. 65.

93. In his *Symeon von Mesopotamien,* Hermann Dörries (working on the basis of earlier research by L. Villecourt) argued that the author of the Macarian corpus was the Messalian theologian Symeon, since Symeon's name appears in certain of the homilies in some Greek MSS, and since there are themes in the homilies strongly hinting of Messalian spiritual doctrine. Indeed, Dörries showed (ibid., 425-441) compelling textual parallels between the homilies of Ps.-Macarius and Messalian literature. See also Dörries' more recent study, *Die Theologie des Makarios/Symeon,* Abhandlungen der Akademie der Wissenshaften in Göttingen (philosophisch-historische Klasse), series 3, no. 103 (Göttingen: Vandenhoeck und Ruprecht, 1978). Pseudo-Macarius' Messalian background was thrown into doubt, however, by Werner Jaeger in his *Two Rediscovered Works of Ancient Christian Literature: Gregory of Nyssa and Macarius* (Leiden: E. J. Brill, 1954), especially part II, chs. 1-4. Jaeger sought to prove the dependence of Macarius' *Great Letter* and *Spiritual Homiles* on the ascetic works of Gregory of Nyssa (notably *De instituto christiano*), thereby establishing his orthodox identity. As for parallels with Messalianism, Jaeger asserts that "it seems much more likely that Macarius interpreted those of his beliefs that scholars have compared with what little we know of the Messalian sect in a more spiritual sense, and did not take them from this heretic group but from some common monastic tradition" (p. 255). Further support for Jaeger's dissociation of Ps.-Macarius from Messalian radicalism comes from Florovsky, *The Byzantine Ascetic and Spiritual Fathers,* 151ff; and John Meyendorff, *Christ in Eastern Christian Thought* (Crestwood, N.Y.: St. Vladimir's Seminary Press, 1975), 123-126; idem, "Messalianism or Anti-Messalianism: A Fresh Look at the 'Macarian' Problem," in *Kyriakon: Festschrift Johannes Quasten,* ed. Patrick Granfield and Josef Jungmann (Münster: Aschendorff, 1970), 585-590. On the more recent state of the question of Ps.-Macarius' identity, see Vincent Desprez and Mariette Canévet, *DS* 10, s.v. "Macaire" (8. Pseudo-Macaire, Macaire-Symeon), cols. 20-43, and especially cols. 23-27.

94. *Two Rediscovered Works,* 227-230.

95. Cf. Reinhart Staats, *Gregor von Nyssa und die Messalianer,* PTS 8 (Berlin: Walter de Gruyter, 1968).

96. Jaeger, *Two Rediscovered Works,* 211.

97. *Makarios/Symeon: Reden und Briefe: Die Sammlung I des Vaticanus Graecus 694 (B),* 2 vols., ed. Heinz Berthold, GCS (Berlin: Akademie-Verlag, 1973).

98. *Die 50 geistlichen Homilien des Makarios,* ed. Hermann Dörries, et al., PTS 4 (Berlin: Walter de Gruyter, 1964).

99. See, e. g., *Logos* 2.2 (ed. Berthold [vol. 1], 3): "What is Satan and when did he sin so that he became Satan?" In his response (pp. 3-5), Ps.-Macarius defines Satan as a rational and inner-worldly spirit who utters evil, an evil which exists not as essence but as will or choice (προαίρεσις). He demonstrates, by a "more mystical and deeper" (μυστικώτερον καί βαθύτερον) interpretation of the scriptures, how Satan appeared before the creation of Adam and after falling from angelic glory became jealous of humanity's being created in God's image and sought to lure humanity into evil. The allusion to the deceit of the tree of knowledge (Gen. 2:16-17) in turn leads to a further question (ibid. 3, p. 5): "So then was the 'tree of knowledge' Satan?" The answer constitutes a long spiritual interpretation of the fall from paradise. As Dörries observes (*Symeon von Mesopotamien*, 13-14), this second question, like an excursus on a motif only briefly covered in the preceding response, continues the author's train of thought. The *quaestio-responsio* lends structure to his pedagogy, as new theological problems emerge from within his discussion. Many further questions about Satan's domain are presented in the *Spiritual Homilies*: cf., e.g., 7.2 (ed. Dörries et al., 71): "Is Satan together in one place with God or in the air or in men?" and ibid. 26.3 (p. 206): "Is Satan unleashed on us by measure or does he fight us as he wills?" and ibid. 26.9 (p. 209): "Does Satan know the whole of a man's thoughts and intentions?" and ibid. 26.14 (p. 211): "Is Satan ever quiet, and a man freed from his hostility, or does a man suffer his hostility his whole life?"

100. Cf. *Logos* 2.4 (ed. Berthold, 14): "Why is it that some who strive at ascesis are quickly found worthy of grace, while others who persist at it for a long time still do not attain such an efficacious visitation?" and *Spir. hom.* 15.41 (ed. Dörries, 151): "Is it gradually (κατά μέρος) that evil is diminished and uprooted, and one progresses unto grace, or is the uprooting of evil and the visitation of grace immediate?" and ibid. 26.5 (p. 207): "Does one who has received divine power, and who is partially changed, remain in the state of nature?" and ibid. 27.5 (p. 221): "Do they (i.e., graced Christians) therefore know that they have received something additional and have acquired what they did not have, what was alien to their nature?"

101. Cf. *Spir. hom.* 7.4 (ed. Dörries, et al., 73): "And how is it that those who receive the action of grace ever fall?" and ibid. 15.16 (p. 136): "Can a man who has the gift of grace fall?" and ibid. 15.17 (p. 137): "Does grace remain after one falls?" and ibid. 27.9 (p. 223): "How is it that some men fall after the visitation of grace? Is Satan not shown to be much weaker? For, where it is day, how can there be night?"

102. Cf. Jaeger, *Two Rediscovered Works*, 212-213.

103. *Spir. hom.* 40.3 (ed. Dörries, 276).
104. Ibid. (276-277).
105. Jaeger, *Two Rediscovered Works*, 212.
106. *Spir. hom.* 40.6 (ed. Dörries, 278).
107. Ibid. Though Jaeger's thesis about the dependence of Ps.-Macarius on Gregory of Nyssa may in the end be based on a faulty understanding of the relation of the *Spiritual Homilies* to the *De instituto christiano*, he is surely correct in his basic analysis of the question-answer format of the homilies as serving constantly to adapt monastic spiritual doctrine to the practical questions that were bound to arise in the life of the monastery. This sort of format "makes the theory more real and shows that the tradition of monasticism is indeed both simultaneously: the general doctrine and the ever new problems created by application to the reality of the daily practice" (*Two Rediscovered Works*, 216).
108. *Spir. hom.* 40.7 (ed. Dörries, 278).
109. Ibid. (ed. Dörries, 278-279).
110. Ibid. 27.17-18 (ed. Dörries, 227-228).
111. The splintered MS tradition of Mark's works, coupled with the piecemeal historical testimonies to him, have made it extremely difficult to identify him directly. Complicating the problem is the fact that his dogmatic (christological) writings do not show clear points of contact with his ascetic works. For this reason Henry Chadwick ("The Identity and Date of Mark the Monk," *Eastern Churches Review* 4 [1972]: 125-130), has opted to idenify him as the Mark pressed by Severus of Antioch to deny both dyophysite Christology and Messalianism, which would in turn date Mark to the early sixth century. Otmar Hesse (trans., *Markus Eremita: Asketische und dogmatische Schriften*, BGL 19 [Stuttgart: Anton Hiersemann, 1985], 106-111), has argued instead that Mark is an abbot of the Egyptian desert in the early fifth century. For a review of this historical problem, see Jean Gribomont, *DS* 10, s.v. "Marc le moine," cols. 274-283.
112. *De baptismo* 1 (PG 65.985A).
113. Ibid. 4 (PG 65.992D). Such statements of Paul in Romans seem to have played an instrumental role in the classic Messalian doctrine of the postbaptismal metaphysical opposition between sin and grace.
114. Ibid. 8 (PG 65.1009A).
115. For Mark, the grace conferred by the Spirit in baptism is already perfect or complete, its fullness being continually and gradually revealed to the believer in his ascetic life. Did not Heb. 12:22 say that "you *have arrived* (perfect tense) at Mt. Zion," the heavenly Jerusalem? (*De bapt.* 8, PG 65.1009B; cf. ibid. 4, 993C). For the Messalians, however, such a grace

could be found only when ascetic struggles had ceased and a state of utter impassibility was experienced. Worried that this might produce complacency, Mark appealed also to the futuristic aspect of the "heavenly Jerusalem," attainment to which could not be exhausted in any spiritual experience in this earthly life (ibid. 5, PG 65.1008A-B). See also the study of Timothy Ware, "The Sacrament of Baptism and the Ascetic Life in the Teaching of Mark the Monk," *StPatr* 10, TU 107 (Berlin: Akademie-Verlag, 1970), especially 442-445. Ware notes some of the important links between Mark and Ps.-Macarius on the outworking of grace in the ascetic life.

116. *De baptismo* 3 (PG 65.989A-B).
117. Ibid. 14 (PG 65.1020C). Emphasis added.
118. Cf. "Erotapokriseis" (B. christlich), cols. 348ff, 352ff.
119. *Markus Eremita*, 70 and n. 248.
120. E.g., Question 1: Why do monks not seek to bring wrong-doers to justice, which failure is illegal? Why do the monks refrain from visible works, an inactivity which is unnatural? (*Disputatio* 1, PG 65.1072A). Response: The monks have taken up a life modeled on the servanthood of Christ in Phil. 2:5-8 and "work" as such not for earthly food but for the food lasting to eternity (John 6:27) (ibid., 1072B-1073A). Thus the lawyer's second query: What is the nature of this work? (ibid. 2, 1073A). Response: The monks seek the kingdom of God and his righteousness (Matt. 6:23), which is indeed a thoroughly "natural" activity. Moreover, they need not bring evil-doers to justice, since God will execute his own judgment (so Rom. 12:19; 14:4; 1 Cor. 4:5; Luke 6:7). How can this be against the law? (ibid., 1073A-B).
121. Notably 1 Thess. 5:17 (*Disputatio* 4 [PG 65.1076D]; ibid. 6 [1080C]; ibid. 7 [1081B]); Luke 18:1-7 (ibid. 7 [1081B]); and Eph. 6:18 (ibid. 4 [1077A]), as cited by Hesse, *Markus Eremita*, 83.
122. Hesse suggests (*Markus Eremita*, 81, n. 272) that the *Disputatio* brings together two forms of *Erotapokriseis*: "Thus the work begins as a polemical discourse (*Streitgespräch*), which can be formally compared with op. IV (*De baptismo*)...and ends, in the basic form of the monastic Erotapokriseis, as the discussion of a monastic father with his students."
123. See the recent translation, dependent on Greek and Syriac MSS, *The Ascetical Homilies of Saint Isaac the Syrian*, trans. Holy Transfiguration Monastery (Boston: Holy Transfiguration Monastery, 1984). Interestingly, Isaac employs not only the *quaestio-responsio* in certain of his homilies, but also the "conference" (e.g., *Hom.* 21, 105-112), and even *sententiae* (*Hom.* 1, 3-9). On the historical background of Isaac's work, see the important introduction to *The Ascetical Homilies*, lxii-cxii, and epilogue, 487-515; also

Florovsky, *The Byzantine Ascetic and Spiritual Fathers*, 230-240. On his spirituality itself, see the recent study of Constantine Tsirpanlis, "Praxis and Theoria: The Heart, Love and Light Mysticism in Saint Isaac the Syrian," *Patristic and Byzantine Review* 6 (1987): 93-120.

124. See, int. al., *Hom.* 3 on the soul's attainment of self-knowledge. Here Isaac moves from one question and excursus to the next: "What is the nature of the soul? Is it, then, something passionless and filled with light, or something passionate and dark?" Or again, "What is the natural state of the soul, what is the state contrary to nature, and what is the state above nature?" Or still further, "Is the soul's desire natural when it is kindled by divine things, or by the things of earth and the flesh? And is anger natural when it is said that by anger the soul's nature is excited to zeal on account of bodily desire, envy, vainglory, and the rest, or when it is on account of things opposed to these?" (*The Ascetical Homilies*, 17-18). Others of Isaac's sermons using the method of question and response include *Hom.* 23 on prayer (ibid., 115-122); *Hom.* 28 on the vision of the nature of incorporeal beings (137-141); *Hom.* 37 on diverse subjects (163-186); *Hom.* 62 on a man's knowledge of his own stature (297-301); and *Hom.* 71 on virtue (344-350).

125. Ibid. "Do the bodily passions belong to the soul by nature, or by accident? And are the passions of the soul which she possesses by reason of her connexion with the body said to be hers naturally, or by a figure of speech?" And again, "Why does the (filling of the) bodily passions strengthen and make the body grow, while those of the soul harm the soul, if they are proper to her? And for what reason does virtue torment the body but enrich the soul?" (*The Ascetical Homilies*, 19). Cf. Thalassius' queries to Maximus (*Q. Thal.* intro., CCSG 23,109ff): "How many passions are there, and of what sort are they? Where do they originate? What is their end through their proper mean? What kind of faculty of the soul or part of the body gives rise to each passion? (etc.)"

126. *Hom.* 3 (*The Ascetical Homilies*, 25).

127. Ibid., 25-27.

128. See *Coll.* 14.9 (CSEL 13.407).

129. On the background of this text, see Chitty's remarks in *Desert a City*, 132-133.

130. See ibid., 132.

131. See Chitty's examples of their correspondence with laymen, ibid., 137-138.

132. Ibid., 137.

133. *Quaestiones et responsiones*, letter 79 (PO 31.3, ed. Chitty, 558;

trans. Chitty, 559). Translation correction added.

134. Ibid. (PO 31.1, 558-560).

135. Ibid., letter 88 (PO 31.3, p. 566); ibid., letter 93 (p. 572).

136. On Barsanuphius' pragmatism as a reaction to Evagrianist intellectualism, see Lucien Regnault, "Théologie de la vie monastique selon Barsanuphe et Dorothée (VIe siècle)," in *Théologie de la vie monastique: Études sur la tradition patristique*, Théol 49 (Paris: Aubier, 1961), 315-316.

137. *Quaestiones et responsiones*, qu. 63 (not included in Chitty's edition in PO), cited by Chitty in *Desert a City*, 134.

138. Ibid., letter 20 (PO 31.3, 476).

139. Ibid., letter 24 (PO 31.3, 482).

140. Ibid., letters 60-72 (PO 31.3, 518-548); cf. also Chitty, *Desert a City*,133.

141. Cf. especially ibid., letter 63 (PO 31.3, 530-534), where Euthymius queries about two separate figures in scripture, the "worm," which he christologizes in reference to Ps. 21:7 ("I am a worm and no man"), and the "mustard" to which Jesus likens the kingdom of heaven in Matt. 13:31 (and par.). Euthymius already has cited the *topos* of Christ as the worm who makes himself bait for the "dragon" (Job 40:20) in order to redeem humanity, and save it from the "corruptible worm" that infests the flesh. Barsanuphius embellishes the allegory and unites the two figures of "worm" and "mustard." He graphically describes how the heavenly worm (Christ), nailed to the hook of the Cross, was let down into the mouth of the great fish, or dragon, which had consumed the corrupted flesh of humanity, and how he pulled out the flesh and with it the dragon's entrails, and healed the flesh with the seasoning of "mustard." The worm/bait/dragon *topos* was a favorite one in early monastic spirituality, developed by Maximus too in *Q. Thal.* 64 (PG 713A) in his christological typology of Jonah and the whale.

142. *Quaestiones et responsiones*, letter 62 (PO 31.3, p. 548).

143. See above, The *Apophthegmata patrum*.

144. See Richard's "Florilèges spirituels grecs," cols. 500-501; cf. also his "Les véritables 'Questions et réponses' d'Anastase le Sinaïte," *Bulletin de l'Institut de Recherche et d'Histoire des Textes* 15 (1967-1978), repr. in *Opera Minora* 3, ed. E. Dekkers et al. (Turnhout: Brepols–Leuven University Press, 1977), 40-41.

145. Richard, "Florilèges spirituels grecs," col. 500. Richard further notes that the florilegia to these responses are not Anastasius' own, but are added by the same person who compiled the florilegia for the later questions and responses in the collection.

146. Ibid. Some of these Richard has positively identified, others he has not.

147. Anastasius Sinaïta, *Qu. et resp.* 8 (PG 89.389D-392B). Cf. Basil's similar question in *Reg. brev.* 22 (PG 31.1097C): "Where do indecent nocturnal fantasies originate?"

148. Ibid. 15 (PG 89.468B-D); cf. ibid. 5 (361B): "If a man is old, or disabled, and feeble-minded, and unable to live in solitude, how can he repent and be saved?"

149. Ibid. 19 (PG 89.513B-C).

150. Beck (*Kirche und theologische Literatur*, 91) describes these *Erotapokriseis* as "general catechisms" (*Allerweltskatechismen*) designed for all levels of believers.

151. Ibid. 23 (PG 89.540Bff).

152. Ibid. 24 (PG 89.541Cff); cf. similarly Maximus, *Qu. et dub.* III,1 (CCSG 10.170).

153. Ibid. 29 (PG 89.561Bff); excerpted from Theodoret, *Quaestiones in Exodum* 12 (PG 80.233Bff).

154. A florilegium that borrowed some of its questions from the *Qu. et resp.* of the Ps.-Anastasian florilegium: cf. Richard, "Les véritables 'Questions et réponses,'" 55, n. 1; and Bardy, "Les littérature patristique," *RB* 42: 328-332, 341-342.

155. "Erotapokriseis" (B. christlich), col. 352 and passim. This category he opposes to the "$ζητήματα$-Literatur," which aimed at resolving real difficulites in ancient texts (what I have termed the $ἀπορίαι$ tradition in this chapter).

156. Maximus used other monastic didactic techniques as well, including *sententiae* (the *Chapters on Charity* and *Chapters on Knowledge*), and the *expositio*, or commentary, on the Lord's Prayer. Even his *Ambigua* on problematic passages in Gregory of Nazianzus' *Orations* is, as Sherwood notes (*Earlier Ambigua*, 5-6), a variant of the *quaestio-responsio* genre. Sherwood suggests that its format combines the old scholastic method of solving $ἀπορίαι$ in ancient authors with the question-response technique that was quite probably an actual type of hortatory instruction in the Byzantine monasteries. (It is to be noted too that *Ambigua* 1-5 [PG 91.1032-1060] is directed precisely to a monastic abbot, Thomas. The questioning of difficult passages in patristic authorities was apparently a major preoccupation of the monks whom Maximus addressed, as was discussed in my introduction).

157. As Sherwood remarks in the introduction to his translation of the *Liber asceticus* in ACW 21 (99), the actual dialogue continues only in sections 1-26, while the second part (sections 27-45) consists in successive monologues (27-39, an extended digression on compunction; 40-45, an exhortation to hope and trust).

158. Cf. also Maximus' *Mystagogia*, a contemplation (θεωρία) of the holy mystery of the synaxis, which, though not integrating the method of question and response, also pretends to have arisen, according to Maximus, from a conference with an esteemed and knowledgeable γέρων (Sophronius? a literary fiction?). See *Myst*. prooemium (PG 91.657C- 661D), and passim.

159. *Liber asceticus* 1 (PG 90.912A): Παρακαλῶ σε, πάτερ, εἰπεῖν μοι, τίς ὁ σκοπὸς ἦν τῆς τοῦ Κυρίου ἐνανθρωπήσεως.

160. Ibid. 2 (PG 90.913A): Ποίας οὖν ἐντολὰς ὀφείλω ποιῆσαι, πάτερ, ἵνα δι' αὐτῶν σωθῶ... Note, as in the first one, the formula of the question, reminiscent of such formulas in the *Apophthegmata patrum* (see above, n. 50-52 and related text); cf. also ibid. 6 (PG 90.916B): "But the Lord's commands are many, father, and who can keep them all in mind, so as to strive for all of them. And especially myself, who have such a poor memory? I would like to hear a brief explanation, that I may retain it and be saved by it" (trans. Sherwood, ACW 21, 106).

161. See his "La doctrine ascétique de saint Maxime le Confesseur d'après le *Liber Asceticus*," *Ir* 26 (1953): 18-26. Dalmais contrasts Maximus' style of justifying his moral exhortation with doctrinal exposition with Basil's more practically-oriented instruction in the *Regulae fusius* and in another *Ascetic Discourse* whose Basilian authorship is doubted.

162. PG 90.1393-1400. Sherwood (*Annotated Date-List*, 37) speculates its dating roughly in the same time period with the *Q. Thal.* and notes its generic likeness to the same text.

163. *Qu. et dub.* 77 (I,53) (CCSG 10.58,1-17).

164. Ibid. 30 (CCSG 10.25,1-26,39).

165. This is not, however, to deny that numerous of the *Qu. et dub.*, notably those on patristic authorities, deal in genuine theological ἀπορίαι.

166. See above, n. 102-109 and related text.

167. See my introduction above, n. 64-82 and related text.

168. *Man and the Cosmos*, 22-23; cf. also Dalmais, "Maxime le Confesseur et la crise de l'origénisme monastique," 415.

169. *Q. Thal.* 56 (PG 581C-D). Emphasis added.

170. See Dörries ("Erotapokriseis" [B. christlich], col. 359), who places the *Q. Thal.* in line with the "eisagogic" *Erotapokriseis* rather than in conjunction with the classic ζητήματα-literature. Nonetheless, his treatment of the *Q.Thal.* is too cursory to show definitively its links with the earlier monastic "eisagogic" *quaestiones-responsiones*.

171. See my introduction, n. 85 and related text. Maximus indicates (*Q. Thal.* intro., CCSG 23,108-27,183) the topics of the questions on the passions, then launches into his own brief discourse on the nature of evil as

metaphysically "nonexistent," and of the fall and its consequences for the emergence of the passions (ibid. 29,209-43,432), though suggesting that this deserves a treatise of its own, and should not deter him from the main task of dealing with the scriptural difficulties in question (cf. ibid. 27,186-190).

172. *Q. Thal.* 1 (CCSG 47,2-4). Specifically citing Gregory of Nyssa as his authority, Maximus responds: "The passions...become good in those who are earnest, once they have wisely severed them from corporeal objects, and used them to gain possession of heavenly things. It is possible, on the one hand, for them to make desire (ἐπιθυμία) the appetitive movement of the intellectual longing for divine objects, while, on the other hand, making pleasure (ἡδονή) the sheer gladness of the mind's operation when it is lured toward divine objects. Moreover, they make fear (φόβος) the cautious concern for imminent punishment for errors commited, while they make grief (λύπη) the corrective repentance for a present evil.... They use the passions to destroy a present or seeming wickedness, and to apprehend virtue and knowledge." Cf. Gregory of Nyssa, *De virginitate* 18 (GNO 8, pt. 1, 315-322).

173. *Q. Thal.* 6 (CCSG 69,2-7). See also Garrigues (*Maxime le Confesseur*, 45, n. 10), who notes the strong Macarian theme in this text.

174. See above, n. 101 and related text.

175. See above, n. 117 and related text.

176. *Q. Thal.* 18 (CCSG 117,2-4).

177. Ibid. (CCSG 117,5-14).

178. Ibid. 10 (CCSG 83,2-5).

179. See above, n. 85 and related text.

180. *Coll.* 11.13 (CSEL 13.329-330).

181. Cf. *Cent. gnost.* 16 (ed. Édouard des Places, *Diadoque de Photiké: Œuvres spirituelles*, SC 5, rev. ed. [Paris: Éditions du Cerf, 1966], 92,15-93,16). Citing the "perfect love" mentioned in 1 John 4:18, Diadochus quotes Ps. 33:10 ("O fear the Lord, all you who are his saints") and Ps. 30:24 ("O love the Lord, all you who are his saints), in order to demonstrate an intermediate stage of spiritual growth known by moderate love and godly fear; this, however, is to be distinguished from that state of perfection in which purified believers know only pure love without any trace of fear.

182. *Didaskaliai* 4.47 (trans. from the Greek text of *Dorothée de Gaza: Œuvres spirituelles*, SC 92, ed. L. Regnault and J. de Préville [Paris: Les Éditions du Cerf, 1963], 220,1-8).

183. Ibid. 4.47-49 (SC 92.220-224). Dorotheus further cites Basil of Caesarea's distinction (*Reg. fus.*, prooemium [PG 31.896]) between those who, like slaves, please God out of a fear of punishment; those who, like servants, please him to earn the wages of self-advancement; and those who,

like sons, please God because they are assured of his love.

184. *Q. Thal.* 10 (CCSG 85,44-87,68). Cf. the same distinction of "fears" in *Cap. car.* 1.81-82 (PG 90.977C-980A); also *Or. dom.* prol. (PG 90.873A-C). See also Dalmais, "Un traité de théologie contemplative: Le commentaire du Pater Noster de saint Maxime le Confesseur," *RAM* 29 (1953): 126-127.

185. *Q. Thal.* 10 (CCSG 83,25-85,43).

186. Ibid. (CCSG 87,69-79): "Therefore, the prophet and the evangelist agree with one another. The former says there is no deficiency in one who fears the Lord with a pure fear (Ps. 33:10), while the latter says that one who fears God as Judge out of a foul conscience is not perfect in love (1 John 4:18). Perhaps this interpretation applies to the passage that says that God is fearful to all those who are round about him (Ps. 88:8), since he creates the love that is mixed with fear for those who love him and will come to exist round about him. For love in itself, without fear, leads to contempt, such that it changes radically. The boldness that naturally stems from love would not be restrained by fear."

187. See ibid. 33 (CCSG 229,26-231,40), where Maximus allegorizes the "mountain" to be moved as the arrogance and law of the flesh, which the true and impassible ($ἀπαθής$) faith, a faith bringing deification or union with God, is able to uproot. Cf. ibid. 34 (CCSG 235,19ff), where "whatever you ask for in prayer" (Mark 11:24) is interpreted in terms of the inward, ascetic benefits of deliverance from the passions, patience amid temptation, virtue and the means for performing virtue, detachment of the soul from the flesh, withdrawal of the mind from everything created (etc.). Cf. also ibid. 57 (PG 589D) on how the righteous man's prayer "is effective" ($ἐνεργουμένη$, James 5:16), Maximus replying that "the reality ($ὑπόστασις$) of a prayer of petition is obviously its fulfillment through the virtues, whereby the righteous man has the prayer that is strong and thoroughly empowered, since it is effective in the commandments."

188. Ibid. 58 (PG 592C-D): "'In this rejoice, though now for a little while you must be grieved by various trials' (1 Pet. 1:6). How can one who is grieved by trials still rejoice in this?"

189. Cf., int. al., Ps.-Macarius, *Spir. hom.* 9, (ed. Dörries, 83-91); ibid. 16 (157-166).

190. Cf. especially Gregory of Nyssa, *De hominis opificio* 19-20 (PG 44.196C-201A); *Comm. in Cant.* Or. 12 (GNO 6, 348-349). Maximus, in *Q. Thal.* intro. (CCSG 35, 323ff), and in his response *Ad Thalassium* 43, appears to have directly in view Gregory's distinction of the trees in terms of life and death and his interpretation of the "tree of the knowledge of good and

evil" as producing a "mixed knowledge." See other similar kinds of speculation in Ps.-Macarius, *Logos* 2.3 (ed. Berthold, 5); and Ps.-Anastasius, *Qu. et resp.* 23 (PG 89.540Bff). See also Maximus' treatment in *Qu. et dub.* 44 (II,22) (CCSG 10.37,1-38,27): "What is the anagogical significance of the garden which grew in the East (Gen. 2:8)?" Maximus' response includes a discussion of τὰ δύο ξύλα as signifying the intelligible and the sensible worlds.

191. Gen. 1:26-27 was a locus classicus in this dispute, because of the seeming offensiveness of God likening human beings to himself. See John Cassian, *Coll.* 10.2-5 (CSEL 13.286-291). On this controversy and its historical implications, see Georges Florovsky, "The Anthropomorphites in the Egyptian Desert," in *Creation and Redemption,* The Collected Works of Georges Florovsky 4 (Belmont, Mass.: Nordland, 1975), 89-96.

192. *Q. Thal.* 37 (CCSG 247,2-11).

193. The biographer of Theodore of Sykeon (late sixth and early seventh century) tells how he healed a man by lending him his tunic to wear, and how his disciples tore off pieces of his robe for a blessing. See the *Life of St. Theodore of Sykeon* 31, 73, trans. Elizabeth Dawes and Norman Baynes, in *Three Byzantine Saints* (Oxford: Basil Blackwell, 1948; repr. ed., Crestwood, N.Y.: St. Vladimir's Seminary Press, 1977), 110, 137. The earlier biography of St. Daniel the Stylite (fifth century) similarly narrates miracles accomplished through contact with the holy man's body: see the *Life and Works of Our Holy Father, St. Daniel the Stylite* 81, on a snake who coiled around the saint's foot and then burst into pieces (*Three Byzantine Saints,* 56); ibid. 82, on a barren woman who, having received from Daniel a cord that had touched his inflamed foot, became pregnant and bore a son (*Three Byzantine Saints,* 57).

194. As Norman Baynes recapitulates: "The saint's healing could be carried to the sick by many different means: just as 'from Paul's body were brought unto the sick handkerchiefs or aprons, and the diseases departed from them,' so the Byzantine saint would send the towel with which he had washed his hands, telling the sufferer to tear up the towel and make little crosses of it; when these had been nailed up on the door and window in the name of the Trinity the demon would find entry barred. Or the saint would send a 'benediction' of consecrated bread and water, or the water in which he had washed his hands or a fragment of his leathern girdle...it mattered not provided that the 'power' of the saint was conveyed to the sufferer, the 'power' which was God's gift" (introduction to *Three Byzantine Saints,* xii-xiii). On the phenomenon of the ancient holy men and their miracles, see the important studies of Peter Brown in his *Society and the Holy in Late Antiquity* (Berkeley: University

of California Press, 1982), especially 142-143, 228-229.

195. *Q. Thal.* 37 (CCSG 247,12-18; 249,35-42): "Paul's body did not accomplish these healings by the handkerchiefs and aprons merely because of his sanctity, nor only for the sake of the faith of those who received healing, but because divine grace, imparting itself both to him and to them, made the Apostle's sanctity effective in them through faith.... Were the principle of grace and nature one and the same, then that which is created would be miraculous or amazing by nature. But if there is rather one principle of nature and another principle of grace, it is clear and obvious that saints work miracles on the basis of grace, while men suffer on account of nature, since grace has not abolished the passible element from nature."

196. Ibid. (CCSG 249,49-251,78).

197. Editors' introduction to *Q. Thal* (CCSG), xii. Cf. Basile Tatakis (*La philosophie byzantine*, Histoire de la philosophie, fasc. suppl. 2, ed. Émile Bréhier [Paris: Presses Universitaires de France, 1949], 83), who wants to see in Maximus' commentaries on scripture a rather sophisticated philosophical and mystical eisegesis: "Maximus looks in the text only for an objective expression of what he himself has grasped by intuition; the text, so to speak, has nothing for him to apprehend."

198. On this idea of scriptural σκάνδαλα, see below, chapter 3.

199. See above, n. 46-47 and related text.

200. *Q. Thal.* intro. (CCSG 19,28).

201. As opposed, that is, to those instances where Thalassius poses merely an open-ended question on the meaning of a particular scriptural text.

202. *Q. Thal.* 4 (CCSG 61,2-5).

203. Ibid. (CCSG 61,6-9).

204. Ibid. (CCSG 61,9-63,38). As Michel Aubineau observes ("Dossier patristique sur Jean XIX, 23-24," 34-35), such an interpretation accrues to a long tradition of patristic exegetical speculation about the symbolic value of Jesus' garments in John 19:23-24. John Chrysostom, Isidore of Pelusium, and other early monastic exegetes moralized the text by noting the paltry value of Jesus' garment as a kind of prototype of the monk's habit; Thalassius' observation of the ostensible contradiction with Matt. 10:10 doubtless grew out of this monastic tradition.

205. Ibid. 17 (CCSG 111,2-11).

206. Ibid. (CCSG 111,19-21).

207. Ibid. (CCSG 111,22-115,80).

208. Ibid. 27 (CCSG 191,2ff).

209. See *Contra Celsum* 2.1 (GCSO 2.127), where Origen explains how Peter's vision of the descending sheet was necessary because he had not yet learned from Jesus to ascend from the letter of the law to its spiritual

interpretation. Even the Apostles themselves had, as it were, to learn their spiritual lessons.

210. *Q. Thal.* 27 (CCSG 191,7-26).
211. Ibid. (CCSG 193,36-48).
212. Ibid. (CCSG 193,48-64).
213. Ibid. 29 (CCSG 211,2-4).
214. Ibid. (CCSG 211,5-34).
215. Ibid. (CCSG 213,35-45).
216. Ibid. (CCSG 213,45-49).
217. Ibid. (CCSG 213,49-53).
218. Ibid. (CCSG 215,67-72).
219. Trans. from the Greek text of *Évagre le Pontique: Scholies aux Proverbes*, ed. Paul Géhin, SC 340 (Paris: Les Éditions du Cerf, 1987), 106.
220. Ibid. 23 (SC 340.116).
221. Ibid. 113 (SC 340.208-210). Two other such examples are *Schol.* 71 (p. 166) and 275 (p. 370). Géhin notes that the question-and-response is one of the variable formats of the *Schol. in Prov.*: "when the text on which he comments seems to be in contradiction with another passage of scripture or truly presenting some difficulty, the scholium takes the characteristic form of a question introduced by πῶς followed by a response beginning with ἤ, ἤ τάχα or ἤ μήποτε. Then it obviously falls under the well-known genre of 'questions and responses on scripture,' which itself derives from the ἀπορίαι καὶ λύσεις of pagan antiquity" (intro., 17-18). One sees a similar technique occasionally in Gregory of Nyssa, raising a question in the course of his exegetical discourse as a means to clarify the sense of a passage: see, e.g., *De vita Moysis* 2.210, GNO 7, pt. 1, 106,11-19: "While, then, there is a contradiction (because how is it possible to take in a good sense Moses' meeting with Aaron who became the Israelites' servant in making an idol?), nevertheless Scripture, in a limited sense, gives an indication of the double-meaning of brotherhood...." (trans. E. Ferguson and A. Malherbe, CWS [Ramsay, N.J.: Paulist Press, 1978], 109).
222. In fact most of Evagrius' scholia are no longer than *sententiae*. Evagrius himself insists that "the genre of scholia (τὸ εἶδος τῶν σχολίων) does not allow for prolixity" (*Schol. in Prov.* 317 [SC 340.408]; see also Géhin, intro., 13).
223. See below, chapter 3.
224. *The Byzantine Fathers of the Sixth to Eighth Century*, 213.
225. Some of the more striking examples are the *Apophthegmata patrum*, Basil's *Regulae*, Barsanuphius and John's *Quaestiones et responsiones*, and the authentic *Quaestiones et responsiones* of Anastasius Sinaïta.

226. Cf. Cassian's *Collationes*, and Maximus' own *Liber asceticus*.

227. This pattern is especially in evidence in *quaestiones* observed in the works of Ps.-Macarius, Mark the Hermit, and Isaac the Syrian.

228. See his "Florilèges spirituels grecs," col. 500, where Richard admits that he was unable to identify all the sources for the OT questions and responses compiled in Ps.-Anastasius, *Qu. et resp.* 23-53.

229. Ps.-Anastasius, *Qu. et resp.* 32 (PG 89.569B-571B) = *Q. Thal.* 26 (CCSG 173,2-175,54; 181,153-166). Ps.-Anastasius has condensed Thalassius' question: "If the king of Babylon is interpreted allegorically as the Devil, how is it that God calls him his servant, saying 'I have given all the land to Nebuchadnezzar, king of Babylon, my servant, and I have given him the beasts of the field to serve him' [Jer. 27:6]?" He then gives only a brief selection from Maximus' response. The allegorization of Nebuchadnezzar (and other gentile kings in the OT) as the Devil had been common since Origen (*Hom. in Jer.* 19.14 [GCSO 3.171,1-3]: βασιλεὺς δὲ Βαβυλῶνος κατὰ μὲν τὴν ἱστορίαν Νεβουχοδονόσαρ, κατὰ δὲ τὴν ἀναγωγὴν ὁ πονηρός; also *Sel. in Ps.* 8.3, PG 12.1184C) and Cassian (*Inst.* 5.14 [CSEL 17.92]; ibid. 6.17 [CSEL 17.125]).

230. Anastasius, *Qu. et resp.* 6 (PG 89.380A-B, Μαξίμου ἐκ τῶν Ἀπόρων) = *Q. Thal.* 57 (PG 589C-592B).

231. *Liber asceticus* 18 (PG 90.925A-B, trans. Sherwood, ACW 21, 113). Cf. also John Cassian, *Coll.* 14.10, et al., discussed above, n. 86-88 and related text; and for the same principle of meditation in Evagrius, and before him Antony, see the discussion of Jean Kirchmeyer, *DS* 4.1, s.v. "Écriture sainte et vie spirituelle" (II. F. Dans l'église orientale–1. Maxime le Confesseur), col. 165.

232. *Q. Thal.* 47 (CCSG 315,63-317,65). Emphasis added.

233. Vittorio Croce (*Tradizione e ricerca*, 184) deduces that Maximus' whole interpretation of scripture can be summed up precisely as "a response to the exigency of showing that all Scripture is divinely inspired, and that therefore every word of it can and must be useful for our salvation."

234. Jean Kirchmeyer, "Écriture sainte et vie spirituelle," col. 242.

Chapter Two

Diabasis: The Theological and Hermeneutical Framework of Maximus' Exegesis of Scripture in the *Quaestiones ad Thalassium*

Maximus hints at a fundamental integrating principle of the whole of the *Quaestiones ad Thalassium* when, in his opening greeting, he extols his friend Thalassius for having already attained to a level of gnostic stature, a depth of insight into spiritual truth, exemplary for the astute interpreter of scripture:

> Having separated rationally your soul (ψυχή) from the flesh (σάρξ) in view of its carnal proclivity (κατὰ τὴν σχέσιν), and having completely extracted your mind (νοῦς) from sense (αἴσθησις) through the Spirit, man of God, you made your soul the prolific mother of virtues, and made your mind an inexhaustible source of divine knowledge.[1] Toward the implementation merely of an arrangement of better proportions, you realized the partnership (συζυγία) of the soul and the flesh and seized sense as a tool for comprehending the magnificence of visible things. In practical deeds (πρακτικῶς), your flesh is taking on the glory of your virtuous soul, a glory molded into form through habit, and manifesting it externally, such that we would have an image of virtue—your own life—as an example to be imitated. Your sense, on the other hand, is symbolically engraving the principles (λόγοι) of intelligible things (τὰ νοητά) in the external forms (σχήματα) of visible things, and through them is elevating your mind to the simplicity of intelligible visions (νοητὰ θεάματα). Your mind is completely freed of all the variety and complexity of visible things,

such that we would have an inerrant way of truth: your own knowledge (γνῶσις) of the passage (διάβασις) to intelligible realities.[2]

The Terminological and Thematic Significance of *Diabasis* in the *Quaestiones ad Thalassium*

The term διάβασις and its cognate verb διαβαίνειν recur frequently in the *Quaestiones ad Thalassium*. They are an important part of the collective vocabulary of spiritual progress and ascent that Maximus by and large inherits from the likes of Philo, Origen, Gregory of Nyssa, and Pseudo-Dionysius. To be sure, διαβαίνειν-διάβασις are often for Maximus, as well as for his predecessors,[3] employed quite fluidly or even interchangeably with ἀναβαίνειν-ἀνάβασις, μεταβαίνειν-μετάβασις, and other related terms, to describe, in general, the ascent or spiritual *transitus* of the soul toward perfection.[4] For example, in one of his other monastic works, the *Chapters on Knowledge*, he plays with a number of compounds of βαίνειν to describe the different interrelated aspects of the spiritual ascent:

> So long as the soul makes the passage (ποιεῖται μετάβασιν) from strength to strength and "from glory to glory" (2 Cor. 3:18), progress (προκοπή) from virtue to greater virtue, and makes the ascent (ἀνάβασις) from knowledge to higher knowledge it does not cease being a sojourner, as it is stated, "My soul has long been a sojourner" (Ps. 119:6). For great is the distance and the multitude of steps of knowledge to be passed (διαβαθῆναι) until it "comes to the place of your wondrous tabernacle, up to the house of God, in a voice of exultation and thanksgiving, and of those keeping festival" (Ps. 41:5), ever adding a voice to voices, a spiritual one to spiritual ones, as it progresses in divine contemplations with rejoicing over the spiritual contemplations, that is, with joy and proper thanksgiving. These festivals are celebrated by all those who have received the Spirit of grace who cry out in their hearts, "Abba, Father" (Gal. 4:6).[5]

The one who prays ought never to halt his movement of sublime ascent (ἀνάβασις) toward God. For just as we should understand the ascents (ἀναβάσεις) "from strength to strength" as the progress (προκοπή) in the practice of the virtues, "from glory to glory" (2 Cor. 3:18), as the advance (ἐπανάβασις) in the spiritual knowledge of contemplation, and the transfer (μετάβασις) from the letter of Holy Writ to its spirit, so in the same way the one who is settled in the place of prayer should lift his mind from human matters and the attention of the soul to more divine realities. This will enable him to follow the one who has "passed through the heavens, Jesus the Son of God" (Heb. 4:14), who is everywhere and who in his incarnation passes through all things on our account. If we follow him, we also pass through all things with him and come beside him if we know him not in the limited condition of his descent (συγκατάβασις) in the incarnation but in the majestic splendor of his natural infinitude.[6]

This play in compounds (ἀνα-, δια-, μετα-, ἐπανα–βαίνειν, -βασις) is a fairly common stylistic feature in Maximus' writings, including the *Quaestiones ad Thalassium*,[7] and clearly serves here to highlight the dynamism and the multiple dimensions of movement that he envisions in the soul's spiritual progress.

Yet closer inspection of his use of such terms in the *Ad Thalassium* reveals a certain urge toward a more concentrated terminology. Διαβαίνειν-διάβασις are consistently used in the *Quaestiones ad Thalassium* to describe the interrelated aspects of the spiritual *transitus* from sensible to intelligible truth. Maximus of course reveals no direct reason for this terminological preference, but I would conjecture that he concentrates on διαβαίνειν-διάβασις because they can convey for him both a sense of *transcendence*—in keeping with the need to "pass over," or to "ascend beyond," sensible objects and the passions which they can spark[8]—and yet also a crucial sense of *continuity*, namely, the necessity of first "passing through" or "penetrating" sensible objects en route to the intelligible or spiritual truth that inheres, by grace, in those sensible things.

Having already in his introduction extolled Thalassius for achieving this spiritual *diabasis*,[9] Maximus sets up as an example the one "who has penetrated to the spiritual principles (λόγοι) and modes (τρόποι) inhering in (corporeal or sensible) things" (τοὺς ἐν αὐτοῖς πνευματικοὺς διαβὰς λόγους τε καὶ τρόπους).[10] The spiritually mature in the Church are those who, by virtue and knowledge, have penetrated the λόγοι of time and nature and "crossed over (διαβάντες) to the magnificence of eternal and intelligible realities."[11] In Question 55 Maximus speaks in terms of the νοῦς passing over (διαβὰς) nature and time and being restored to impassibility (ἀπάθεια),[12] which means also that the mind cannot be impeded by sense or by the passions in realizing this *diabasis*. True Christian "gnostics" are those "who pass beyond the perturbation of the passions" (τῶν παθῶν διαβάντες);[13] moreover, says Maximus, the power of sensibility, left unchecked, can actually bring to a stop the passage (διάβασις) of the operation of our rational functioning in relation to intelligible objects.[14] Thus the true spiritual Sabbath is the complete sedation of the passions, the cessation of the mind's movement toward created things, and the perfect passage (διάβασις) to God.[15]

Integrating the natural and scriptural aspects, Maximus indicates that the transcendence of the passions is crucial as well for the *diabasis* to the spirit of scripture, or, as he says, for "penetrating intellectually to the divine beauty that inheres, through the Spirit, in the letter of the law" (διαβαίνων κατὰ νοῦν πρὸς τὴν ἔνδον ἐν πνεύματι τοῦ νομικοῦ γράμματος θείαν εὐπρέπειαν).[16] Indeed, whoever is totally preoccupied with the letter of scripture is dominated by sensibility (αἴσθησις), for the letter is expressed only sensibly, which can prevent the true power of the scriptures from passing over (διαβῆναι) to the mind (νοῦς).[17]

This prevalence of διαβαίνειν-διάβασις as terms designating the transition from sensible to intelligible reality in created nature and in scripture invites a further speculation into the terms' special significance for Maximus. Again, though he never gives in the *Ad Thalassium* any direct explanation of this concentration of terms, his larger cosmology and epistemology would seem to hold the key. In the background lies Maximus' rather characteristic emphasis, in his polemic against extreme Origenism or Evagrianism, on the original purposefulness of the sensible cosmos in the divine will and the reciprocity between the sensible and intelligible realms according to a common universal principle (λόγος) of all *created* nature.[18] The tension between the sensible and intelligible dimensions of creation is, in the context of Maximus' system, one of the "economically" based and intrinsic polarities in the natural world that the human subject, *qua* microcosm, is summoned to mediate in the *vita practica* and *vita contemplativa*.[19]

There is already a natural coinherence or copenetration (περιχώρησις) between the sensible and intelligible dimensions of creation, and the tension thus established is a creative tension, resolved only by the Logos himself according to a "mystical principle" (μυστικὸς λόγος).[20] Before the mind can achieve its full ascent (ἀνάβασις) from created reality to God, it must first cognitively penetrate, or cross through, the medium of sensible things—a literal *diabasis*.[21] Sensible appearances and the letter of scripture, in all their diversity, are the requisite first step toward intelligible truth.[22] As Maximus himself writes, "It is impossible for the mind (νοῦς) to cross over (διαβῆναι) to intelligible realities (τὰ νοητά), to which it is naturally akin, without contemplating intermediary sensible things," even though, of course, "it is also absolutely impossible for contemplation (θεωρία) to take place, without sense (αἴσθησις), which is naturally akin to sensible things, being joined with the intellect."[23]

As a human vocation, an active mediation of the sensible and the intelligible creations, and an ongoing process of assimilation to God, such a spiritual *diabasis* not only involves the intellect but integrates the whole of human nature. The body must by its virtue ascend to and mirror the soul,[24] while sense too, by its synthetic power to apprehend the sensible symbols of the λόγοι of things,[25] must rise to the service of reason and the mind.[26] Yet while, as Sherwood observes of the *diabasis* within human nature, "the real motion is from the lower (faculties) to the higher,"[27] Maximus can also speak, as he does on two occasions in the *Quaestiones ad Thalassium*, of a converse or reciprocal *diabasis*—the crossing over or descent of reason (λόγος) to the level of the lower soul or the flesh in order to fulfill practical virtue.[28] Consistently Maximus strives to reflect the hierarchy and harmony, but also the dynamism and continuity, inherent in the created order and in holy scripture. This profound sense of symmetry informs his analysis of the spiritual life as a whole and of the exegesis of scripture in particular.

The remainder of this chapter will demonstrate how this spiritual *diabasis* is an integrating leitmotif of Maximus' entire hermeneutics. Scripture and the interpretation of scripture are part of a larger picture, embracing, on the one hand, Maximus' "macrocosmic" and thoroughly christocentric understanding of the symbolic structure of the world and of scripture and, on the other hand, his "microcosmic," and no less christocentric, vision of the spiritual life in its ascetic, contemplative, and mystagogical aspects. In his exegesis Maximus presupposes that in interpreting scripture one is actually participating in a much larger mystery of revelation and that the *diabasis* from sensible to intelligible reality incorporates not only scripture but also creation, human nature, and indeed the moral life of the soul as well, since all of these properly tend toward one and the same Logos-Christ.[29]

In the next chapter, then, I shall have the opportunity to show more precisely how the *diabasis* principle influences Maximus' understanding both of "anagogical" interpretation and of the task of scriptural exegesis itself. I shall investigate the extent to which it is possible to draw from Maximus' theme of spiritual *diabasis* a working theory of anagogical exegesis in the *Quaestiones ad Thalassium*.

The Objective and Macrocosmic Dimensions of the *Diabasis*: Access to the Logos-Christ through Creation and Scripture

The multifaceted nature of the spiritual *diabasis* and the correspondence between the different facets are concisely set forth by Maximus in his response to Question 32. Commenting on what it means for one to "grope after and discover God" (Acts 17:27), he writes:

> He who "gropes after God" properly has discretion ($\delta\iota\acute{a}\kappa\rho\iota\sigma\iota\varsigma$). Therefore he who comes upon the law's symbols intellectually ($\gamma\nu\omega\sigma\tau\iota\kappa\hat{\omega}\varsigma$), and who contemplates the phenomenal nature of created beings scientifically ($\dot{\epsilon}\pi\iota\sigma\tau\eta\mu o\nu\iota\kappa\hat{\omega}\varsigma$), discriminates within scripture, creation, and himself. He distinguishes, that is, between the letter ($\gamma\rho\acute{a}\mu\mu a$) and the spirit ($\pi\nu\epsilon\hat{u}\mu a$) in scripture, between the inner principle ($\lambda\acute{o}\gamma o\varsigma$) and the outward appearance

($ἐπιφάνεια$) in creation, and between the intellect ($νοῦς$) and sense ($αἴσθησις$) in himself, and in turn unites his own intellect indissoluably with the spirit of scripture and the inner principle of creation. Having done this, he "discovers God." For he recognizes, as is necessary and possible, that God is in the mind, and in the inner principle, and in the spirit; yet he is fully removed from everything misleading, everything that drags the mind down into countless opinions, in other words, the letter, the appearance, and his own sense.... If someone mingles and confuses the letter of the law, the outward appearance of visible things, and his own sense with one another, he "is blind and short-sighted" (2 Pet. 1:9) and suffers from ignorance of the true Cause of created beings.[30]

The parallelism thus established between creation, scripture, and human nature, and the correlation between the intelligible and sensible content in each, is a familiar one in Maximus' theology,[31] but of particular interest here is the "necessary" integration implied with respect to the three aspects of the *diabasis* from the sensible to the intelligible reality: from letter to spirit in scripture, from surface appearance to inner logos in creation, from sense to intellect in human nature. The first two aspects evince the inner symbolic structure of creation and scripture, the interrelated economies of revelation, while the third, human nature, incorporates *ipso facto* the human subject's inner spiritual life. In each case, it is the spiritual or intelligible element—the $λόγος$ of creation, the $πνεῦμα$ of scripture, the $νοῦς$ in human beings— which must prevail toward the fulfillment of salvation and deification. As Maximus expresses it in the *Mystagogia*,

> Thus if any of these three men—the world, holy Scripture, and the one who is ourselves—wishes to have a life and condition that is pleasing and acceptable to God let him do what is best and noblest of all. And let him as best he can take care of the soul which is immortal, divine, and in process of deification through the virtues, and let him disdain the flesh which is subject to corruption and death and able to soil the soul's dignity by its carelessness.[32]

Applied to Maximus' interpretation of scripture, this will mean, as George Berthold has noted, that "because of the close connection of the logoi of nature, Scripture, and moral life, whoever falls away from fullness of biblical understanding and adheres to the letter alone will suffer in the other two areas as well."[33]

Creation, Scripture, and the Symbolic Structure of the Diabasis

The integration of the first two dimensions of the *diabasis*, creation and scripture, and their mutual access to the Logos-Christ merit their own investigation. Inspired by the philosophical-theological constructs of Origen and Pseudo-Dionysius, Maximus envisions creation and scripture as objective economies of divine revelation that stand in a perfect analogous relation to the Logos-Revealer.[34] Von Balthasar has observed, nevertheless, how Maximus goes beyond certain of his predecessors in setting the "natural law" (creation) and the "written law" (scripture) on an utterly equal par vis-à-vis the Logos. The written law is thus no longer an intermediate degree between natural revelation and the revelation of Christ; rather, nature and history are equal poles that complement one another eschatologically. Christ, embodying the third, spiritual law, fulfills both of the first two laws, uniting them while ultimately transcending them.[35]

A Locus Classicus: Ambiguum 10. Perhaps nowhere in all of Maximus' writings is this interrelation between creation and scripture and their mutual, even interchangeable, relation to the Logos more clearly illustrated than in a passage from *Ambiguum* 10, a sort of opusculum on spiritual *diabasis*. Clearly inspired by Origen's interpretation of the transfiguration scene in Matthew 17,[36] Maximus develops his own θεωρία, a text so fundamentally important to his understanding of the symbolic structure of spiritual *diabasis* in the *Quaestiones ad Thalassium* that I translate the bulk of it here. There on the mountain, says Maximus, having witnessed the transfigured Christ with Moses and Elijah flanking him on each side, Peter, James, and John crossed over (μετέβησαν) from the flesh to the spirit, having already put off their carnal life. The Spirit brought about a transformation of their sensible energies and stripped away the veils of passions from their intellectual faculty. Having been cleansed by the Spirit in their psychic and bodily senses, they were taught the spiritual principles (πνευματικοὶ λόγοι) of the mysteries that had been exhibited to them. They were mystically taught that the wholly blessed splendor that beamed radiantly from the Lord's face, as though excelling all their eyes' energy, is a symbol of his divinity, which transcends intellect (νοῦς), sense (αἴσθησις), essence (οὐσία), and knowledge (γνῶσις). They were guided from the fact that he had neither form nor beauty (cf. Isa. 53:2), and from the knowledge of the Logos begotten in the flesh, to the fact that he is more beautiful than the sons of men (cf. Ps. 44:3), and to the notion that he was in the beginning, and was with God, and is God (John 1:1). They were led up intellectually (γνωστικῶς), through the theological negation (διὰ τῆς θεολογικῆς ἀποφάσεως) that praises him who is utterly incomprehensible to everyone, to that glory which, since it belongs to the Only-Begotten of the Father, is full of grace and truth (cf. John 1:14). His whitened garments bear a symbol of the words (τὰ ῥήματα) of holy scripture,[37] since at that moment they became luminous, clear, and distinct to the disciples, and were comprehended apart from every dark riddle (αἴνιγμα) and symbolic shadow (σκιά), disclosing the Logos who exists and is hidden in them, at which point the disciples attained to the plain and correct knowledge of God, and were freed from any inclination (προσπάθεια) toward the world and the flesh. Or, the garments were a symbol of creation itself, rid of the foul repute of that which is deceitful and bound only to sense, a repute which meanwhile seems to be reflected in that creation. Through the wise variety of different species that fill it out, creation proportionately reveals, in the manner of a garment, the dignity of what conveys the power of the Logos, its Creator. For what I am saying will suit both scripture and creation to the Logos, since he has rightly been concealed in obscurity in both for our sake, so that we will not dare to approach incomprehensible things unworthily: neither the word of holy scripture, insofar as he is its Logos, nor creation, insofar as he is its Creator, Author, and Artificer. For this reason, I assert that whoever wishes to advance straightforward blamelessly to God necessarily requires both scripture and creation: he needs both the knowledge of scripture in the Spirit, and the natural contemplation, through the Spirit, of created beings. So too whoever desires to become the consummate lover of perfect wisdom is able to demonstrate, so it seems, that the two laws, the natural law and the written law, are of equal honor and reciprocally teach the same things, and that neither one has more or less value than the other.

A Contemplation of the Natural and the Written Law,
and of the Interchangeable Concurrence between Them:

I am thinking here, on the one hand, of the natural law, which is ordained as uniformly as possible according to reason, and which, in the manner of a bible contains through its interrelated wonders, the harmonious web of the universe (τὸ ἐναρμόνιον τοῦ παντὸς ὕφασμα).[38] This "bible" has, as its "letters" and "syllables," the things that are primary, immediate, and particular to us, and the bodies that become thick through the conjunction of numerous qualities; its "words" are the more universal of these things, which are distant and thinner. The Logos, who reads this book, having wisely written on these things and ineffably inscribed himself in them, completes the book, providing us the idea only that God is, not what he is; he leads us through pious accumulation of diverse appearances unto a single representation of the truth, proportionately offering himself for us to behold through visible things as Creator. On the other hand, I also have in mind the written law, which is ordained for our instruction. Through the things it wisely dictates, the written law is constituted, like another "cosmos," of heaven and earth, and the things in between—that is, of ethical, natural, and theological philosophy. It displays the unspeakable power to make known its Dictator, and demonstrates that the two laws are interchangeably the same in relation to each other: the written law is potentially (κατὰ τὴν δύναμιν) identical with the natural law, while the natural law is habitually (κατὰ τὴν ἕξιν) identical with the written law. It shows that the two laws disclose and conceal the same Logos: disclosing him through the utterance (τῇ λέξει) and appearance (τῷ φαινομένῳ), and hiding him through the thought (τῇ νοήσει) and through what is concealed (τῷ κρυπτομένῳ). For just as, when we call the words of holy scripture the garments of the Logos, and interpret its ideas as his flesh, we conceal him with the former and reveal him with the latter, so too when we call the visible species and external forms of created things garments, and interpret the principles (λόγοι) according to which they were created as flesh, we likewise conceal him with the former and reveal him with the latter. For the Logos, who is Creator of the universe and Lawgiver and by nature invisible, in appearing conceals himself, and in hiding manifests himself; and is not confiding in the wise that he is thin by nature. It is up to us to reveal, through negation (δι' ἀποφάσεως), what is hidden, to go beyond all the power of outward forms and enigmas to provide a likeness of what is true, and better yet to be elevated (ἀναβιβάζεσθαι) ineffably from the letter and from phenomena to the Logos himself, by the power of the Spirit. Or, on the other hand, it is up to us to conceal, through affirmation (διὰ θέσεως), what is apparent. Otherwise we, like the Greeks, will become murderers of reason and worship the creation rather than the Creator (cf. Rom. 1:25) and not have faith that he is higher than visible things and more magnificent than sensible objects; or, otherwise, like the Jews, seeing only as far as the letter, we will magnify the body alone, and, deifying the belly and finding glory in shame (cf. Phil. 3:19), claim the same inheritance as those who slew God, because we did not discern the Logos, who—having come to us in his incarnate body and become like us, for our sake—also became thick in syllables and letters, for the sake of human sensibility (αἴσθησις), which inclined our intellectual faculty (τὸ νοερόν) wholly toward itself. For the divine Apostle says, "The letter kills, but the spirit gives life" (2 Cor. 3:6).[39]

I would call attention to two decisive principles from this text that will figure heavily in my discussion. First, again, is the fundamental reciprocity, and indeed interchangeability, established between creation (natural law) and scripture (written law) in virtue of their underlying symbolic structure and their common access to the intelligible mystery of the incarnate Logos. This mutuality is reinforced here by Maximus' application of the garments-symbolism equally to creation and scripture, and his reciprocal transference of metaphors: creation as "bible," and scripture as "cosmos".

Second is the symbolic epistemology that, in classic Origenian terms, Maximus roots in the incarnational mystery itself, offset here by his paradoxes of the Logos' concealing himself by appearing, and disclosing himself by hiding—paired also with our subjective disclosure of him "apophatically" and our concealment of him "affirmatively." The Logos becomes "thick," incarnating or inscribing himself in the sensible words (ῥήματα) or letters (γράμματα) of scripture, and the appearances (φαντασίαι) of creation, without violating the "thinness," or subtlety, of his ineffable divinity. Yet the spirit (πνεῦμα) of scripture and the principles (λόγοι) of creation still yield a genuine, if meanwhile relative, knowledge of the Logos-Christ in his economic self-manifestation as Lawgiver and Creator. These scriptural and natural symbols therefore convey, in terms quite reminiscent of Pseudo-Dionysius,[40] the double movement of the procession and return of the Logos, and, respectively, the affirmative (kataphatic) and negative (apophatic) predications of the human mind—οἰκονομία and θεολογία.

The Logoi *of Scripture and Maximus' Notion of Accommodation in the* Ad Thalassium. The symbolic structure of the mutual access of creation and scripture to the Logos is undergirded by Maximus' theory of the unification of differentiated λόγοι in the divine Logos, a theory that by itself has been examined thoroughly in earlier studies and need not be elaborated in detail here.[41] Maximus' λόγοι doctrine ties together his cosmic and salvation-historical perspectives on the spiritual *diabasis* and provides the foundation of his whole structure of natural and scriptural symbolism.

He speaks of the λόγοι in several respects. Strongly influenced in this regard by Origen, Evagrius, and Pseudo-Dionysius, as a number of specialists have pointed out, Maximus develops in depth his doctrine of the natural λόγοι of creatures, the intelligible principles of creaturely particularity that preexist in the mind of the Logos and stabilize the created world.[42] Though stable and irreducible from the human perspective, these natural λόγοι are fully dynamic from the divine perspective and constitute the underlying "intentions" (θελήματα) of God for his creation.[43] They prefigure God's providential σκοπός for the world and assure that the free divine counsel, which precedes any ontological or symbolic hierarchy, will be eschatologically consummated by the "incarnate" Logos himself.[44] In turn Maximus also speaks, in a more salvation-historical light, of the governing λόγοι of divine providence and judgment, another notion taken over from Evagrius but recast by the Confessor in distinctly anti-Origenist terms.[45]

At the heart of Maximus' λόγοι doctrine one can see the double orientation, the differentiation and unification, expansion (διαστολή) and contraction (συστολή), of the λόγοι in creation,[46] which directly reflect the condescension and ascension—or, in the classic Pseudo-Dionysian terms, "procession" (πρόοδος) and "return" (ἐπιστροφή)—of the Creator-Logos himself. Clearly by contemplating these differentiated λόγοι, the sensible world becomes transparent to the intelligible economy of salvation, and the mind is led ever deeper to a knowledge of God's attributes and, to some limited degree, his divinity.[47]

Profoundly important for our purposes here, however, is Maximus' subtle coapplication of this doctrine of natural λόγοι ("principles"), and its conceptual framework, to the λόγοι ("words" and "meanings") of scripture,[48] for this provides, in effect, the theoretical basis for Maximus' understanding of the very nature of scripture and of the task of exegesis: its diversity and unity; its total underlying orientation to the Logos-Christ; and its accommodation to human knowledge through the infusion of the true spiritual λόγοι of scripture in the sensible ῥήματα and συλλαβαί of written and utterable words.

In principle, Maximus envisions, as he does for the λόγοι of creation, a total concentration and convergence of all the diverse words and meanings of scripture in the Logos. Scripture is itself a veritable world of different people, places, times, terms—the πράγματα of scripture—all of which find their way, through spiritual contemplation and interpretation of the λόγοι contained therein, to the ineffable mystery of the Logos. In an extraordinary text from *Ambiguum* 37, Maximus describes in ideal terms how, through scriptural contemplation (γραφικὴ θεωρία), all these differentiated λόγοι of scripture might be viewed from the perspective of their "contraction" into one comprehensive logos,[49] the universal purpose or meaning hidden away in the Logos himself:

> Those who are true experts on such mysteries and are devoted to the contemplation of the spiritual meanings (πνευματικοὶ λόγοι) contained therein say that the logos of scriptural contemplation (γραφικὴ θεωρία), which is one in general, is, when it expands itself, contemplated in a tenfold (δεκαχῶς) manner: by place (τόπος), time (χρόνος), genus (γένος), person (πρόσωπον), dignity (ἀξία) or occupation (ἐπιτήδευμα); practical (πρακτική), natural (φυσική), and theological (θεολογική) philosophy; present (ἐνεστώς) and future (μέλλον), or type (τύπος) and truth (ἀλήθεια). When the logos contracts itself, it encompasses the initial five into three tropes (τρόποι); the three into the two; and draws the two into the one and utterly irreducible logos. In other words, the logos contracts the first five tropes of time, place, genus, person, and dignity into the second three: practical, natural, and theological philosophy. These three it contracts into the next two, which signify present and future. And these last two are drawn into the perfecting and simple and, as they say, ineffable logos that comprehends them all. For it is from it (ἐξ οὗ), according to its procession (κατὰ πρόοδον), that the general decad of tropes subject to the contemplation of scripture emerges; and it is to it (εἰς ὅν), as comprehensive source (ὡς ἀρχὴ κατὰ περιγραφήν), that this same decad contracts, in ascending order (ἀνατατικῶς), back into a monad again.[50]

Again it is clear how scripture is for Maximus a "cosmos" in itself, authored by the Logos who indwells its λόγοι and, through a comprehending logos, draws them back to himself. These λόγοι, the words of scripture pregnant with spiritual meanings that can be penetrated only through scriptural contemplation along the lines described above, are nonetheless rendered accessible only through the mass variety of sensible symbols, the actual words (ῥήματα) on the page of scripture. Just as the λόγοι of created nature are "types" (τύποι) and "foreshadowings" (προχαράγματα) of God's future benefits,[51] so too the true meanings of scriptural words are veiled by "figurative signs" (τυπικὰ συνθήματα).[52] Only the true gnostics, says Maximus, "see the meanings (λόγοι) of scripture stripped of the figurative signs which veil them" and never make use of those sensible symbols

> save where they wisely choose to express the words in a corporeal way (σωματικῶς) for those who, out of intellectual immaturity, are unable to rise above sense, in order that they might be trained first in a sensible way through figures (τύποι), and then yearn to approach the archetypal meanings (ἀρχέτυποι λόγοι) without sense.[53]

Maximus certainly betrays here his indebtedness to the Alexandrian hermeneutical tradition in distinguishing between a more public and a more hidden and esoteric (or "gnostic") access to the Logos through scripture.[54] In his actual exegetical practice, however, Maximus is less disposed purely to delineate the "gnostic" meaning of texts than to set forth a variety of spiritual insights useful to readers at various levels of initiation in scriptural mysteries. And even the saints must start with sensible symbols in creation and scripture before penetrating their more sublime truths.[55]

This principle is directly connected with Maximus' view that, not only has the ineffable Logos created access to himself through the spiritual λόγοι in scripture, but the Holy Spirit, through the unlimited bounty of the Word,[56] has also providentially accommodated the whole of the sensible, *literal* text of scripture to the variegated spiritual needs of human subjects.[57] As the Confessor says in the opening of his response to Question 31,

God, who wisely cares for the mutual harmony (ἀναλογία) of the things under his providence, leading them firstly through figures (τύποι), using the things that are administered through sense in a way conforming to human nature, has mingled himself (ἐγκατέμιξεν) with all these figures that were given to the ancient people, therein bringing about the ascent (ἀνάβασις) of those whom he is training (οἱ παιδαγωγούμενοι).[58]

Similarly in Question 51, Maximus confirms that

this was the peculiar plan of God's consummate goodness: not only did the divine and incorporeal essences of intelligible things constitute representations (ἀπεικονίσματα) of God's ineffable glory, acquiring legitimately and proportionately within themselves the whole incomprehensible loveliness of inapproachable beauty, but, in addition, traces (ἀπηχήματα) of God's own majesty intermingled with sensible things, things that fall far short of intelligible essences. These traces of God's majesty are able to transport (διαπορθμεύειν) the human mind, which uses them as a vehicle, infallibly to God.[59]

Elsewhere, in a text clearly influenced by a number of earlier patristic sources, Maximus describes more precisely how, through a sort of providential preexistence of scripture, its words have been accommodated to *individual* human needs:

We find that holy scripture portrays God in relation to the underlying condition (ἡ ὑποκειμένη διάθεσις) of those under his providence. For this reason, though God is none of these things, scripture calls him "lion," "bear," "leopard," "panther," "man," "cow," "sheep," "sun," "stars," "fire," "wind,"[60] and scores of other things, and he is contemplated according to the designation (ἐπίνοια) of each word.[61] Indeed, when God appeared to Abraham, who was perfect in knowledge, he taught Abraham, whose mind had already fully transcended matter and material types, that the immaterial principle of the Trinity inheres in the principle of the Monad. It was for this reason that God appeared to him as three but conversed with him as one (cf. Gen. 18:1ff). Lot, however, had not yet purged his mind of the composite nature of corporeal things, but was still caught up in the origin of corporeal things from form and matter, and believed that God was the Creator only of the visible creation. Therefore God appeared to Lot as two but not three (cf. Gen. 19:1), and by exhibiting himself through the two gave an indication that Lot's ascending mind had not yet transcended (ἐκβεβηκέναι) matter and form.[62] So too for every passage of scripture that fashions God in multifarious ways (πολυτρόπως), you will find, when you examine the words scientifically, that the reason for the rich diversity of figures of the divine is the condition of those under his providence.[63]

Maximus gives other examples as well of this divine accommodation of scriptural language. In explaining the nature of the plural signification of God in Genesis 11:7 ("Come, *let us* go down and confound their language"), he suggests that this was not only a reference to the Trinity, directed toward the truly pious,[64] but was also suited to the condition (διάθεσις) of those masses of polytheists lapsed into multiple opinions about the deity, providentially obviating their error.[65] In the same respect God said, "Adam has become *like one of us*, knowing good and evil" (Gen. 3:22), scripture using irony (εἰρωνεία) against the polytheism taught to Adam by the devil.[66] The very syntax of the text obviously bears this out: "Unless scripture included God's saying 'like one of us' for the purpose of opposing Adam's error, it would have added the subsequent phrase 'knowing good and evil' in a way that seemed as if God had a composite knowledge composed of contrary things."[67]

Maximus thus follows very closely on the Pseudo-Dionysian principle of the absolute efficacy even of the most unseemly parlance in the literal text of scripture,[68] since, as he insists, "it is customary in scripture for the unspeakable and hidden intentions (βουλαί; =λόγοι) of God to be represented in corporeal terms, so that we can perceive divine realities through the words

($ῥήματα$) and sounds ($φωναί$) that are conformable with our nature."[69] Moreover, like both Origen[70] and Pseudo-Dionysius,[71] Maximus affirms that the Spirit may even deliberately insert obstacles in the literal narrative ($ἡ ἱστορία$) of scripture in order to goad the mind and quicken it in its pursuit of spiritual truth,[72] an idea that is certainly fundamental to his understanding of scriptural $ἀπορίαι$ in general. Thus even the literal text of scripture can be seen always to provide a "beneficial order" ($εὐταξία$),[73] by virtue of the underlying spiritual $λόγοι$. But it is only through spiritual interpretation that we discover "how the Spirit determines the meaning of the scriptures which is proper and fitting for every human being, such that every person who desires to be a pupil of the divine Word...can become another Hezekiah or another Isaiah in spirit."[74]

A Diabasis from Letter to Spirit in Scripture

Maximus affirms that the "letter" of scripture and "appearance" of natural creation are not harmful of themselves but become a source of delusion only with respect to the third, subjective and moral, element, when $νοῦς$ and $αἴσθησις$ are thrown out of balance and the mind becomes caught up in externals.[75] Of this more will be said further on.

It is therefore fully possible for Maximus simultaneously to decry the letter that kills (cf. 2 Cor. 3:6),[76] the seeming "corruption" ($φθορά$) of past events,[77] the literalists ignorant of the mystery of the incarnation,[78] and yet to affirm the positive value of the literal meaning of scripture for those who are penetrating its spirit. Both in their "natural contemplation" and "scriptural mystagogy," the saints "use sense ($αἴσθησις$), appearances ($ἐπιφανείαι$), external forms ($σχήματα$), letters ($γράμματα$), and syllables ($συλλαβαί$)," albeit "only for the purpose of acquiring the blessed knowledge of God."[79] The basic healthiness of the letter of scripture is a crucial corollary of the natural wholeness, the copenetration and mutuality of intelligible and sensible reality, that is constitutive for creation, human nature, and scripture alike.[80]

In actual practice Maximus pays little attention to the literal record in scripture. There is no need to defend his neglect of the recorded history ($ἡ ἱστορία$)[81] any more than Maximus himself found it necessary to defend his appeal to allegory and anagogy. Like Origen and Evagrius, and like other earlier monastic exegetes, he merely finds little use for it in his own demonstration. He concentrates rather on what he calls "the power of the literal meaning in the spirit ($\dot{\eta}$ τῆς ἱστορίας ἐν πνεύματι δύναμις), which is constantly being realized and abounding into its fullness."[82] The letter finds its true value when it is giving way to higher spiritual meanings in a dynamic process of spiritual *diabasis*, or penetration.

At times the literal meaning of a text provides merely a negative starting point for an anagogical interpretation. Obviously this is the case where the Spirit has inserted σκάνδαλα in the text to rouse the mind toward deeper senses of scripture. Moreover, the solution of ἀπορίαι, as we saw in the preceding chapter, warrants an allegorical exposition in order to establish the absolute propriety of scripture. Question 52 is an excellent case in point.[83] In other instances the literal sense itself invites its own spiritual interpretation, such as Zerubbabel's futuristic vision of the "plummet of tin" in Zechariah 4.[84] In still other places, the literal sense provides a support for the spiritual sense. Noting again the text from Question 52, Maximus suggests that if "Judah" and "Jerusalem," which together appear to have suffered unjustly God's wrath upon Hezekiah's pride (2 Chron. 32), are allegorized respectively as the πρᾶξις and θεωρία of the contemplative νοῦς, then

> the spiritual interpretation agrees with the literal reading (τὸ ῥητόν) of the scripture, neither slandering God's decree of judgments, nor overturning any other divine commandment. For, according to the given interpretation of the text, only Hezekiah (that is, the mind) is proud and haughty over his accomplishments, while those from Judah and Jerusalem (or, respectively, practice and contemplation) are not proud along with him, because they were not naturally disposed to suffer from this pride, nor to be interpreted hypostatically by themselves. Moreover, wrath did not come upon Hezekiah (that is, upon the mind) alone, but also upon Judah and Jerusalem. For practice and contemplation are completely defiled along with the mind that is in any way polluted, yet they do not share the blame for incurring wrath.[85]

Another salient example comes in Question 17,[86] concerning the seeming injustice whereby Moses, on a mission from God, incurred the angel's wrath because his son by Sephora (Zipporah) was uncircumcised (Exod. 4:24-26). Moses' journey is interpreted allegorically in terms of the soul's ongoing struggle with impassioned thoughts, and the angel's seemingly unjustified wrath is rendered as the Word of God that is always prepared to smite passion or an ill conscience. In his brief literal exposition to shore up his allegory, Maximus adds that Moses incurred the angel's wrath, among other things, "for the passion that secretly arose in his mind"[87]—a fact obviously not in the text itself, suggesting that Maximus has in effect read his moral-spiritual interpretation back into the literal one.

These cases indicate a relatively artificial appeal to the literal sense as a mere support for the higher spiritual meaning, yet they convey Maximus' ideal of multiple anagogical meanings that would lead up from (and not exclude) the letter of scripture. In fact, in his treatment of numerous New Testament texts, it is precisely the *literal* meaning of scripture that is the locus of dogmatic or theological interpretation.[88] In Question 7, where Maximus is asked to identify the "dead" to whom the gospel was preached (1 Pet. 4:6), he first enters upon a detailed speculation about the νεκροί as those who had died before the incarnation,[89] before he moves on to the spiritual interpretation, where the "dead" are those who engage in ascetic mortification.[90] The miraculous nature of Paul's body in Acts 19:12 is explained through a digression on the distinction of nature and grace, before the exegesis proceeds to the spiritual sense.[91] The literal sense is the grounds too for showing how John the Evangelist and Paul concur over the nature of the end times.[92]

Nonetheless, past history, whether of the Old Testament or the New, can only be recovered on the moral and spiritual level, and here the letter must give way absolutely to the spirit. "For the historical past (τὸ διὰ τῆς ἱστορίας πάρελθον)," Maximus claims, "always stands as present fact (ὡς παρόν) mystically, through spiritual interpretation (διὰ τῆς θεωρίας)."[93] Maximus assumes here a fundamental principle of Origenian allegory and tropology: the moral or spiritual internalization or actualization of the biblical history through a "transposition" (μετάληψις)[94] of the literal sense of scripture.⁹⁵ To become a "son of Abraham," writes Origen, "every person must, by interpreting the whole Abrahamic history allegorically, perform all of Abraham's deeds spiritually."⁹⁶ Long before Maximus, this spiritual transposition of biblical events had become a mainstay of monastic exegesis.⁹⁷ In a classic passage from his *Epistles,* the spiritual writer Nilus of Ancyra (early fifth century) indicates how such a transposition would conceivably recover the contemporary spiritual significance of the ancient τύποι without rejecting the literal history itself. His summary demonstrates how the Origenian principle of transposition came to thrive in Byzantine monastic exegesis, and captures the essence of the Confessor's own use of typological transposition:

> If something has been recorded in the Old or New Testament to have happened historically, and this or that deed was manifestly accomplished, and we interpret it for our own purposes, using ideas and thoughts for our own spiritual edification, do not suppose that we have disregarded the letter, or rejected the history. By no means! We neither condemn nor reject the perceptible event (τὸ αἰσθητῶς πεπραγμένον) that has been committed to history. Since, however, we *are* the world, we benefit today by interpreting everything that happened yesterday for our own purposes (Ἀλλ' ἐπειδὴ ἡμεῖς ἐσμεν ὁ κόσμος, πάντα τὰ πρώην γενόμενα, σήμερον εἰς ἑαυτοὺς νοοῦντες ὠφελούμεθα). For, since today there is no Joseph, no Egypt, no King Hezekiah, no Judas the betrayer, no Lazarus dead and raised, no Simon Magus, etc., for this reason, if (today) we see someone prudent, we call him "Joseph"; an adulterous woman, we call her "Egypt"; if a ruler is faithful to God and pious, he is named "Hezekiah." Everyone who betrays the word of truth and casts others to death is acknowledged a "Judas." If the noblest man, having become negligent, sins, and afterward repents and is made alive, clearly his mind died through error and was raised through repentance. But him who approaches the Church of God hypocritically and is baptized merely with water but not with the Holy Spirit we are wont to call a "Simon Magus." Therefore, holding to the standard of what we have said

here and everything we say in an intellectual manner, you shall in no way be scandalized against us. So interpret for your own purposes all the things that happened figuratively to the ancients and were performed by them. For the Apostle says, "We are the temple of the living God" (2 Cor. 6:16), not the one built by Solomon of stone (cf. 3 Kings 6:1). "For everything is yours, whether the world, or the present, or the future" (1 Cor. 3:22).[98]

Maximus deploys this spiritual transposition of biblical events to the fullest in Questions 49-53 on the exploits of Hezekiah in 2 Chronicles 32. In Question 49 (on 2 Chron. 32:2-4), for example, the struggle over Jerusalem between King Hezekiah and the forces of Sennacherib gives way to an extended anthropological typology of the mind's inner combat with intelligible enemies for rule of the soul.[99] Therein Hezekiah (the νοῦς) has as his "elders and captains" the rational faculty (ἡ λογικὴ δύναμις), the concupiscible faculty (ἡ ἐπιθυμητικὴ δύναμις), and the irascible faculty (ἡ θυμικὴ δύναμις), which contend for control of the "waters from outside the city" (i.e., concepts [νοήματα] which stream from sense into the mind in the process of natural contemplation) with Sennacherib (the devil) and his demonic forces.[100] Thus as Maximus says later in Question 51, "every person can become a 'Hezekiah' by imitating Hezekiah spiritually (κατὰ πνεῦμα). Every person can, through prayer, cry out to God and be heard and receive an angel (cf. 2 Chron. 32:20-21)—that is, a greater word of wisdom and knowledge—at the moment when the wicked demons attack."[101]

> For even if these things "happened to them figuratively (τυπικῶς)" according to the the historical account but nevertheless "were written down for (spiritual) admonition" (1 Cor. 10:11), the events recorded are continually happening to them, while, on an intelligible level (νοητῶς), the hostile power stands ever poised against us. These events continue to happen so that, if possible, having transferred (μεταβιβάσαντες)[102] all of scripture over to the mind, we would enlighten the mind with divine thoughts and cleanse the body with the tropes (τρόποι) of the more divine

meanings (θειότεροι λόγοι) of scripture interpreted spiritually, so making the body a rational factory of virtue by abolishing its innate passions.[103]

The Christological *Skopos* of Creation and Scripture: The Mystery of the Incarnate Logos-Christ

The Three Laws and the Three Incarnations

In assessing earlier the fundamental symbolic structure of spiritual *diabasis* in Maximus' hermeneutics, I have already called attention to the emphasis laid on the mutual access of creation and scripture to the Logos, articulated on the one hand in terms of the λόγοι doctrine, but described also in the conceptual framework of the three "laws"—the natural law and written law that are mutually fulfilled and transcended in the spiritual law of Christ.

> Jesus Christ the Logos of God, insofar as he is Creator of all things, is also Author of the law of nature; and insofar as he is Provident and Lawgiver, he is clearly also the Giver of the law in letter and in spirit (that is, in grace). "Christ is the end of the law" (Rom. 10:4) obviously refers to the literal law interpreted spiritually. If, then, the natural law, the written law, and the law of grace converge in Christ (εἰς Χριστὸν συνάγεται), insofar as he is Creator, Provident, Lawgiver, and Redeemer, the divine Apostle is being truthful when he says that God is about to judge the secrets of men according to his gospel (cf. Rom. 2:12-16)— that is, just as he preaches it, through Jesus Christ, God's only-begotten Logos by essence; that God, who is present throughout all things, reproves them on the one hand, but receives them back on the other; and that, according to the natural law, the written law, and the law of grace, God distributes to them according to merit through his ineffable, only-begotten Logos, who is present with him in essence. For the Logos of God is the Author of every nature, of every law, regulation, and order, and the Judge of those

who live under nature, law, regulation, and order. Apart from the Logos who promulgates it, there is no law. So if someone is judged by the law (Rom. 2:12), he will be judged as being in Christ; if he is judged without the law, he will still be judged entirely as in Christ. For the Logos, as Creator, is beginning (ἀρχή), middle (μεσότης), and end (τέλος) of everything existent, spoken, and thought.[104]

Maximus assumes for his own purposes an ancient and venerable *topos* of Pauline, Origenian, and Augustinian usage: the dual laws (natural and written) in their subservience to the saving law of Christ. The natural law and the written law, creation and scripture, are grounded in the preexistent and transcendent Logos. In Maximus' thought, however, the transcendent Logos is never conceptually separate from the *historically* incarnate Christ. As the Confessor says at the opening of the response to Question 19, it is *Jesus Christ* who is Creator, Provident, Lawgiver, Redeemer, and Author of the three laws.

In observing more precisely the interrelation between the "three laws" in Maximus' thought, I should perhaps first point out what this interrelation is not. First, it is not merely another notion of dispensational or progressive revelation, though Maximus can also speak on occasion (in a way reminiscent of Origen, Augustine, and other earlier authorities) of dispensational "laws" leading up to Christ.[105] His aim is rather to explicate (and in plainly anti-Origenist terms) how the incarnate Logos, who is in himself the law of grace, being *ontologically anterior*, yet *historically posterior*, to the natural and written laws, is the common σκοπός of them both; and that the historical incarnation is not merely another provisional economy but carries in itself, from the beginning of time, the eschatological key both to the destiny of creation and the fulfillment of scripture. It is, in a neo-Irenaean sense, a principle of "recapitulation" (ἀνακεφαλαίωσις).[106]

Second, the interrelation between the three laws is not a pure philosophical synthesis. Therefore in calling it a "synthesis of the three laws,"[107] von Balthasar hastens to emphasize that it is not merely a collapsing of the two laws into the one in a virtually mechanistic process of revelation. It is at bottom a christological and soteriological synthesis, at which level each law is properly irreducible and plays its own necessary role cooperatively toward the goal of human deification. This fact becomes especially clear in Question 64[108] and Question 15,[109] where Maximus relates the three laws more specifically to salvation and the spiritual life.

The interrelation or "synthesis" of the three laws, as a fundamental theological and hermeneutical construct of Maximus, is perhaps best summarized, drawing again on von Balthasar's analysis, in terms of three constitutive aspects or simultaneous moments: first, the circumincession between the natural and written laws[110] (seen in the establishment of creation and scripture as interchangeable symbolic structures, which was observed above in conjunction with the key text from *Ambiguum* 10);[111] second, an elevation or transference in the two laws to a higher, spiritual level by their relation to the law of grace[112] (represented, in our discussion, in the *diabasis* from $\dot{\epsilon}\pi\iota\phi\dot{\alpha}\nu\epsilon\iota\alpha$ to $\lambda\acute{o}\gamma os$ in creation, and from $\gamma\rho\acute{\alpha}\mu\mu\alpha$ to $\pi\nu\epsilon\hat{v}\mu\alpha$ in scripture); and third, the transcendence of the two laws by the law of grace[113] (which is the full unfolding of the $\mu\nu\sigma\tau\acute{\eta}\rho\iota o\nu$ of the incarnation). In each of the three aspects it is the Logos himself who has the initiative: first, by accommodating himself through natural and scriptural symbols; second, by gradually disclosing himself in the $\lambda\acute{o}\gamma o\iota$ of creation and scripture; and third, by consummating his self-revelation in his historical incarnation.

Maximus describes this self-disclosure of the Logos-Christ even more graphically in his celebrated idea of the "three incarnations" of the Logos:[114] in the principles of creation, in the words of scripture, and in the person of Jesus Christ.[115] A *locus classicus* is *Ambiguum* 33, where, commenting on Gregory of Nazianzus' curious phrase "The Logos becomes thick,"[116] Maximus elucidates the three incarnations in the order of historical, cosmic, scriptural:

> The Logos, being simple and incorporeal, spiritually nurturing all the divine powers in heaven in succession, deemed it worthy also to thicken himself through his incarnate presence—as born from us, for our sake, and like us yet without sin—and fittingly to teach us, through sounds and paradigms, the power of ineffable things, which transcends all human speech. (For it is said that everything

has been taught through parables, and that nothing is explained without a parable. For so it pleases teachers to use parables whenever their pupils have not understood what they originally said and to lead them from what is said to comprehension). Or it could be said that the Logos "becomes thick" in the sense that, having ineffably hidden himself in the principles (λόγοι) of created beings for our sake, he indicates himself (ὑποσημαίνεται) proportionately through each visible thing, as through certain letters, present in his utter fullness in the universe and wholly present in individual things. He is wholly present and undiminished. Remaining, as always, without difference, he is present in different things; simple and not composite, he is present in composite things; having no beginning, he is in things that have a beginning; invisible, he is in visible things; intangible, he is in tangible things. Or, it could be said that the Logos "thickens himself" in the sense that, for the sake of us who are dense of mind, he consented to embody himself for our sake and to be represented (τυπωθῆναι) through letters and syllables and sounds, so that, following him little by little through these things, we would be led to him, being united to his Spirit, entering into subtle and non-relative thought about him. Thus the more he drew us together (συστείλας) into union with him for himself, the more for our sake he would expand (διέστειλαν) himself by reason of his condescension.[117]

Yet just as the concept of the three laws raises the question of precisely how the three are interrelated and how the law of grace transcends the other two, so also the idea of the three incarnations raises the issue of how the historical incarnation surpasses the other two "incarnations" in creation and scripture. As Thunberg puts it, there is a persistent question of "difference of degree and, as it were, historical culmination" in the three incarnations.[118]

From the *economic* perspective, the framework of salvation history, the incarnation in scripture is indeed an imperfect anticipation of the historical incarnation. This is illustrated, for example, in Question 62 (an allegory on the prophet Zechariah's elusive vision of the "flying sickle," Zech. 5:1-4), as the Confessor reflects on the Logos' incarnation in the τύποι of the prophets:

> (The Logos) who formed himself (ἑαυτὸν διαπλάσας) mystically in the various figures (τύποι) for the prophet's visions taught that he was in truth about to submit voluntarily, and by nature, to our human formation (διάπλασις) in order to reveal factually (τοῖς πράγμασι) the present truth (παροῦσα ἀλήθεια) predicted through the figures.[119]

Here the qualitative superiority of the historical incarnation is clearly implied in the tension of τύπος-ἀλήθεια.

From the perspective of the *ontological* priority of the Logos-Christ, nevertheless, the "three incarnations" appear to be simultaneous self-manifestations, or, as it were, common aspects of the one μυστήριον of incarnation. This comes out, also in Question 62, where Maximus depicts the Logos-Christ's "incarnation" in the commandments of scripture. Interpreting the "flying sickle" allegorically as the Logos-Christ, he writes:

> The scripture states that the sickle was "twenty cubits long and ten cubits wide" (Zech. 5:2). As God and Logos, therefore, Christ is naturally disposed to broaden himself by the processional manner of his providence (τῷ τῆς προνοίας τρόπῳ κατὰ πρόοδον), into "ten cubits"—that is, into the ten efficacious and divine commandments. For God's Logos spreads himself out into a decad of commandments, through which God, having legislated the performance of what is proper and idleness in what is improper, encompassed all voluntary movement of the beings under his providence. On the other hand, insofar as he assumed flesh and fully became a man, he elongated himself (μηκύνεται) into "twenty cubits," in view of the composition of the four elements into senses at the origination of his (incarnate) body. For there are five senses and four elements, the combination of which produces human nature. Five multiplied by four obviously makes twenty. By "length" (μῆκος), scripture designates the manner (τρόπος) of

the economy of the incarnation, because the sublimity (τὸ ὕψος) and the mystery (τὸ μυστήριον) of the divine incarnation are utterly supernatural.[120]

In this text, with the incarnation in the commandments and the historical incarnation standing side by side, it is less clear precisely how the incarnation in the historical person of Jesus surpasses the other incarnation in scripture— or, one could add, the incarnation in creation. Thus the question of a difference of degrees persists: How does the historical incarnation, or the "law of grace," transcend and so also consummate the other two incarnations, or laws? The secret, as a number of Maximian scholars have already hinted,[121] appears to lie in Maximus' christological and soteriological notion of μυστήριον.

The Mystery of the Incarnation and the Eschatological Scope of Scriptural Symbols

As Thunberg has pointed out, when Maximus speaks of the central μυστήριον of the incarnation of the Logos-Christ, as he does repeatedly throughout the *Quaestiones ad Thalassium,* he has in view a proleptic truth hidden in natural and scriptural symbols, one that must be unfolded *by the Logos himself* through the economy of salvation.[122]

Again, on the order of this economy, the historical incarnation surpasses the incarnation in the Law and Prophets as a fulfillment of the ancient τύποι. This is the familiar pattern of early Christian typology, which Maximus merely takes for granted, as when Thalassius raises the classic query of why Jesus would have caused the fig tree to wither for lack of fruit when in fact it was out of season (Matt. 21:18ff; Mark 11:12-14). Maximus replies:

> The divine Logos, who governs everything with wisdom for the sake of human salvation, originally trained (παιδαγωγήσας) human nature with a more corporeal worship —(for human nature was not able to receive the truth stripped of figurative veils [τυπικὰ προσκαλύμματα] because of the ignorance and estrangement arising in it toward the Archetype [ἀρχετυπία] of divine actions). Afterwards, since humanity was visibly created by him,

the Logos came in the incarnation, having an intellectual and rational soul, and, as Logos, converted human nature to the immaterial and gnostic worship in the Spirit. Since the truth (ἀλήθεια) shines through in this life, he did not wish for the shadow (σκιά) to have control. The fig tree was the figure (τύπος) of that shadow. For this reason the scripture speaks of Jesus' "returning from Bethany to Jerusalem" (Matt. 21:18; Mark 11:11ff), referring to his sojourning anew through flesh in human nature after his figurative and shadowy presence (ἡ τυπικὴ καὶ σκιώδη παρουσία) in the Law, which is invisible (for the "return" must be interpreted in this way). It says that "he saw a fig tree on the way, having nothing but leaves" (Matt. 21:19; Mark 11:13), the tree being the obviously corporeal observance of the Law, which exists in shadows (σκιαί) and figures (τύποι), based on the unstable and transient tradition that, as it were, lies "in the way"; it is one of the merely passing patterns (τύποι) and orders (θεσμά). Having examined it delicately and copiously, like a fig tree, adorned outwardly, as with leaves, with the garments of the corporeal conditions of the Law, the Logos, finding no fruit (clearly no fruit of righteousness, since it would not cultivate reason), cursed it, or better yet commanded the truth (ἀλήθεια) that is held in the figures of the Law no longer be hidden. That which has already gone by was demonstrated through works; the ripeness of the Law, which exists merely in external forms (σχήματα), was completely dried up and the cloud of the Jews that hung over it was extinguished. For it was neither reasonable nor seasonable, since the truth of the fruits of righteousness was manifestly displayed. The appetite of those who traversed the present life, like a road (cf. Matt. 21:19), and who bore the good and edible fruitfullness of the Word, was deceived into being persuaded with mere "leaves." Therefore it says that "it was not the season for figs" (Mark 11:13). The time when the Law prevailed over human nature was not that of the fruits of righteousness, but was rather representative of the fruits within righteousness and indicative of the future ineffable grace of God that is capable of saving all. Because the ancient people did not arrive at this grace, it was lost through unbelief. For the divine Apostle says that "Israel, which pursued the righteousness based on the Law (referring, of course, to the Law in shadows and figures) did not arrive at the righteousness in the Law" (referring, of course, to the Law fulfilled in the Spirit by Christ) (Rom. 9:31).[123]

In this flourish of typological parallels, Maximus contrasts the Logos' presence in σκιαί, τύποι, and σχήματα with the ἀλήθεια of his historical appearance, a fulfillment of the ancient types and shadows. Yet clearly the "incarnation" in the ancient figures of scripture does not lose its force *after* the historical person of Jesus, the timeless Logos being, as it were, simultaneously incarnate in creation/scripture/Jesus. Rather, after Jesus, the ancient types gain a new and spiritual value for the soul or for the Church in the present, opened up by the Savior himself. This, in a word, is the μυστήριον of the incarnation, which, says Maximus, "bears the power of all the hidden meanings (αἰνίγματα) and figures (τύποι) of Scripture as well as the knowledge of visible and invisible creatures," and which can only be grasped by those who participate eschatologically in the mystery of the cross and resurrection.[124] In this μυστήριον lies the clue to the "difference of degree" in the incarnations: it is precisely the historically incarnate and risen Christ who unfolds eschatologically the intelligible content of scripture, the "symbols of his mysteries."[125]

Maximus has a very precise understanding of how this principle obtains in scripture and scriptural symbols. The New Testament fulfills and transcends the Old, and the πνεῦμα outstrips the γράμμα, yet this does not destroy the continuity or the symbolic development that exists between them: the New Testament remains mystically embedded in the Old, just as the spirit still inheres by grace in the letter.[126] Here again we are reminded of Maximus' comparisons of scripture to human nature, the copenetration of the intelligible and the sensible, soul (NT) and body (OT).[127] But such a "natural" analogy can only extend so far. In a striking passage from Question 63, Maximus adds an important caveat:

The two Testaments completely agree with one another (ἀλλήλαις συμφωνοῦσιν), but they do so more *by grace* (κατὰ τὴν χάριν), *toward the fulfillment of a single mystery* (εἰς ἑνὸς μυστηρίου συμπλήρωσιν), than by synthesis (κατὰ τὴν σύνθεσιν), as is the case with the soul and the body, which synthetically combine toward the formation of a single human being.[128]

This principle of the μυστήριον, implying as it does the eschatological reality whereby the incarnate and glorified Christ (and, of course, the Holy Spirit, his agent in the Church) will disclose κατὰ χάριν the ultimate spiritual senses of scripture, in turn becomes determinative for Maximus' theology of scriptural symbolism.

René Bornert, in his study of parallels between scriptural and liturgical symbolism in Maximus, has distinguished three phases in the Confessor's subordination of scriptural symbols: first, the Old Testament "figures" (τύποι) (one could add "shadows," σκιαί, and "riddles," αἰνίγματα[129]) which have as their counterpart the fulfilling truth (ἀλήθεια);[130] second, the New Testament, which is an "image" (εἰκών) of the future or eschatological "archetype" (ἀρχέτυπος) (parallel to the relation between liturgical σύμβολα and future μυστήριον);[131] and third, the eschatological archetype itself.[132] What Bornert's analysis does not make clear, however, is the precise scheme of fulfillment between the phases. Is the fulfilling truth (ἀλήθεια) of the ancient figures and shadows the New Testament εἰκών, or the future ἀρχέτυπος?[133] Here, in effect, lies the difficulty of holding Maximus too formalistically to a hierarchical symbolism like that of Pseudo-Dionysius, when, as Dalmais has reiterated, Maximus more often prefers "the dialectic of preparation-realization to the antithesis of figure-reality."[134] Thunberg has made an important observation in this regard: rather than just a subordination of the Old Testament figure to the New Testament image, and of New Testament image to its archetype, Maximus concentrates more decisively on a development from Law to Prophets to Gospel,[135]—a development, I might add, not far off Origen's scheme of "law"/"gospel"/"spiritual gospel."[136]

What is striking here is that it is "the Gospels" and "the Gospel" that are singled out, not the New Testament as such. Is it not an indication that the bodily Incarnation of the Logos in the man Jesus is seen as decisive also for the letters and symbols, which are used as vehicles of a higher spiritual insight? And in addition to that, it seems self-evident that the very fact that there is available for believers within the Church an interpretation of higher quality (such as Maximus himself represents through tradition) is due to the presence in the Christian community of Christ Himself through his Spirit. It is thus within the community of the Church, and its tradition of insight, that the deeper meaning of Scripture can be communicated.[137]

Throughout the *Quaestiones ad Thalassium*, Maximus insists on the μυστήριον of the incarnation as the rallying point of all the diverse senses of scripture. He uses an entire response in Question 60—a much celebrated text in Maximus and in Neo-Chalcedonian Christology in general—to recount the depth and comprehensiveness of the so-called Christic mystery (τὸ κατὰ Χριστὸν μυστήριον):

It was fitting for the Creator of the universe, the one who by the economy of his incarnation became what by nature he was not, to be preserved in an immutable state both with respect to what he himself was by nature, and what he became by his incarnation. For it is not natural to consider any mutability in God, nor to conceive of any movement in him. Being changed belongs to those who are moved. This is the great and hidden mystery (μυστήριον). This is the blessed end (τέλος) for which all things are ordained. This is the divine objective (σκοπός) conceived before the beginning of created beings. In defining it, we would say that it is the preconceived goal for which everything exists but which itself exists on account of nothing. With a clear view to this goal, God created the essences of created beings. It is, properly speaking, the terminus (πέρας) of providence and of the things under its care. Inasmuch as it leads to God, it is the recapitulation (ἀνακεφαλαίωσις) of the things he has created. It is the mystery that circumscribes all the ages and that reveals the grand plan of God (cf. Eph. 1:10-11), a superinfinite plan infinitely preexisting the ages of time....

...This mystery was known to the Father, the Son, and the Holy Spirit before all the ages of time. It was known to the Father by his approval ($εὐδοκία$), to the Son by his own personal working ($αὐτουργία$), and to the Holy Spirit by his cooperation ($συνέργεια$). There is one knowledge shared by the Father, the Son, and the Holy Spirit, since they have one essence and power. The Father and the Holy Spirit were not ignorant of the incarnation of the Son, because the whole Father is by essence in the whole Son, who by his incarnation brought about the mystery of our salvation. The Father himself did not become incarnate but approved the incarnation of the Son. Moreover, the whole Holy Spirit is by essence in the whole Son, not by becoming incarnate himself, but by cooperating with the Son in his ineffable incarnation for our sake. Whether, then, one speaks of Christ, or of the mystery of Christ, only the Holy Trinity—Father, Son, and Holy Spirit—foreknew it. And no one will be in doubt that Christ, who is one of the Holy Trinity, was foreknown by the Trinity. Christ knew that he was foreknown not as God but as man. In other words, it was his incarnation in the economy of salvation for humanity's sake that was foreknown (cf. 1 Pet. 1:20).... For it was necessary in truth for him who is by nature Creator of the essence of created beings to become in himself, by grace, the author of the deification of those whom he created, in order for the Giver of being ($τὸ εἶναι$) to appear also as gracious Giver of eternal well-being ($τὸ ἀεὶ εὖ εἶναι$).[138]

It is exactly this comprehensive $μυστήριον$—variously described by Maximus as "the mystery of the incarnation" ($τὸ μυστήριον τῆς ἐνανθρωπήσεως$),[139] "the mystery of (the Logos') embodiment" ($τὸ τῆς ἐνσωματώσεως μυστήριον$),[140] "the new mystery" ($τὸ καινὸν μυστήριον$),[141] "the mystery of his ineffable plan" ($τὸ τῆς ἀπορρήτου βουλῆς μυστήριον$),[142] "the mystery based on faith" ($τὸ κατὰ τὴν πίστιν$

μυστήριον)[143]—that dominates Maximus' scriptural symbolism in the *Quaestiones ad Thalassium*.[144] He shows this quite clearly in Question 64, for example, where he sees an important development in scripture between (1) the "three days" Jonah spent in the whale's belly (Jon. 2:1); (2) the "three days still (ἔτι)" before Nineveh was to be destroyed (Jon. 3:4);[145] and (3) the "three days" spent by the Savior in the heart of the earth between his burial and resurrection (Matt. 12:40). By Maximus' account, 1 is a simple τύπος of 3, 3 being the ἀλήθεια realized in actual events (πραγματειωδῶς); but 2 is the μυστήριον that is going to indicate 3 "in a completely novel way" (παντῶς καινοπρεπῶς), evincing the "three days still of a more mystical (μυστικωτέρα) burial and better resurrection" that will be inaugurated by the three days of Christ's historical burial and resurrection.[146]

This μυστήριον of Christ thus embraces the ancient figures, the New Testament truth, and the future culmination all within the eschatological moment of the self-revelation of the Logos-Christ. Following Origen and Evagrius, Maximus reinforces the principle that the Logos-Christ is himself both the content and the revealer of this saving μυστήριον. But in contrast with Evagrius, whose strong Origenist theology, in Maximus' eyes, sets in relief the transcendent cosmic work of the Logos-Mediator, the Confessor clearly determines to present the historical Christ as the initiator of the mystery of his own incarnation and embodiment in the soul and in the Church.[147] The deeper intelligible or spiritual senses of scripture, interpreted anagogically (as we will have more occasion to see in the next chapter) will thus be rendered transparent to the work of Christ in salvation history, an unfolding drama of preparation and fulfillment that Maximus eloquently portrays, in Question 22, in terms of the two "ages" (αἰῶνες) of "incarnation" (σάρκωσις) and "deification" (θέωσις), or "activity" (τὸ ποιεῖν) and "passivity" (τὸ πάσχειν).[148]

> He who, by the sheer inclination of his will, laid the foundation of all creation, visible and invisible, had an ineffably good plan (βουλή) for created beings long before the ages and before those beings. The plan was for him to mingle, without change on his part, with human nature by true hypostatic union, to unite human

nature to himself while remaining immutable, so that he might become a man, as he alone knew how, and might make humanity divine in union with himself. Also, according to the plan, it is plain that God wisely divided and distinguished the ages between those intended for the purpose of God becoming a man, and those intended for the purpose of man being made divine.

The end of those ages that were predetermined for the purpose of them was fulfilled in the incarnation. The divine Apostle, having fully examined this very matter, observed the end of the ages intended for God to become man in the very incarnation of God the Logos; he thus said that the end of the ages had come upon us (1 Cor. 10:11). Obviously he did not mean the ages from our own perspective, but the ages that were manifestly intended for the purpose of the mystery of the Logos' embodiment, which have received their proper conclusion ($\pi\acute{\epsilon}\rho\alpha\varsigma$) in the purpose of God.

Seeing, then, that the ages that were predetermined in God's purpose for the realization of God's becoming a man have reached their end for us, and since God worked for and actually fulfilled his own perfect incarnation, it was necessary for the other ages, the ones that are to come upon us for the purpose of the mystical and ineffable deification of humanity, henceforth to follow. In these new ages God "will show the immeasurable riches of his goodness toward us" (Eph. 2:7), having completely realized the deification of those who are worthy. For if he has fulfilled the goal of his mystical effort for becoming a man, having become like us in every respect save without sin, and even descended into the lower regions of the earth where the tyranny of sin was pressing humanity, then God will also completely fulfill the goal of his mystical effort to deify humanity, in every respect, of course, short of an identity of essence with God, and assimilate humanity to himself and elevate it to a position above all the heavens. It is to this exalted position that the greatness of God's grace, and of his infinite goodness, summons lowly humanity. The great Apostle teaches this very thing when he says that "in the ages to come the immeasurable riches of his goodness will be shown to us" (Eph. 2:7).

We too should therefore divide the ages conceptually, and distinguish between those intended for the mystery of the divine incarnation and those intended for the grace of human deification, and we shall discover that the former have already reached their proper end, while the latter have not yet arrived. In short, the former have to do with God's descent (κατάβασις) to human beings, while the latter have to do with humanity's ascent (ἀνάβασις) to God. By interpreting these texts in this way, we do not embroil ourselves in the obscurity of the divine words (ἡ ἀσάφεια τῶν θείων λόγων), nor assume that the divine Apostle has made this very mistake.

Or rather, since our Lord Jesus Christ is the beginning (ἀρχή), middle (μεσότης), and end (τέλος) of all the ages, past and future, it would be fair to say that the "end of the ages"—specifically that end which will in actuality come about by grace for the deification of those who are worthy—"has come upon us" in the potency of our faith (δυνάμει τῆς πίστεως).

Or again, since there is one principle of activity (τὸ ποιεῖν) and another principle of passivity (τὸ πάσχειν), we could say that the divine Apostle has mystically and wisely distinguished the active principle from the passive principle respectively in the past and future ages. For example, the ages of the flesh, in which we now live (for scripture also knows the ages of time, as when it says that man "toiled in this age and shall live until its end" [Ps. 48:10]) are characterized by activity, while the future ages in the Spirit, which are to follow the present life, are characterized by the transformation of humanity in its passivity. Existing here and now, we arrive at the ends of the ages precisely as active agents and reach the end of the exertion of our power and activity. But in the coming ages, we shall undergo transformation into the grace of deification and no longer be active but passive; and for this reason we shall not cease from being deified. At that point our passivity (τὸ πάθος) will be supernatural, and there will be no limit to the divine activity in infinitely deifying those who are passive.[149]

The Subjective and Microcosmic Dimensions of the *Diabasis*: The Integration of the Spiritual Life

Heretofore I have presented the objective and "macrocosmic" dimensions of the spiritual *diabasis*, the symbolic structure of creation and scripture in their mutual access to the Logos-Christ and their accommodation to human apprehension. For Maximus the mystery of the historical incarnation constitutes the unifying σκοπός of this symbolic structure, Jesus Christ fulfilling his other two "incarnations" in scripture and creation.

In this section, I turn to the other side of the mystery, its subjective and its "microcosmic" dimensions. Maximus consistently seeks to integrate the macrocosmic and microcosmic, objective and subjective perspectives in a common vision of the spiritual *transitus*. The natural tension within the macrocosm between the sensible and the intelligible reality—that is, between ἐπιφάνεια and λόγος in creation, between γράμμα and πνεῦμα in scripture, and thus too between sense (αἴσθησις) and intellect (νοῦς) in human nature[150]—must be mediated in the human microcosm through the individual's own spiritual vocation of ascetic practice (πρᾶξις) and contemplation (θεωρία).

In Question 65, Maximus makes it clear that, in spite of the fundamental natural dignity of the sensible element in creation and in scripture, it can become a snare and a source of passion for the spiritually infirm, who do not contemplate the phenomenal and the literal, as it were, from above. This is the legacy of Saul and his offspring (cf. 2 Kings 21:8-9), interpreted allegorically as ὁ ἐν γράμματι νόμος ("Saul"), which can engender a worldly proclivity of the will and passion ("Ermonthi"), preoccupation of the mind with worldly things ("Memphibosthe"), and the aberrant or unnatural use of the senses (Saul's "five grandsons" by Merob).[151] Contrasted with Saul is the figure of Peter in his vision of the descending sheet (Acts 10:11-48), who learns from God to penetrate the principles (λόγοι) hidden beneath sensible forms (σχήματα) and types (τύποι) by contemplating them "from the perspective of the intelligible world" (ἐκ τοῦ νοητοῦ κόσμου).[152]

Even, then, with his abiding philosophical sense of the unity and proportion of the sensible and intelligible elements in creation and scripture,

Maximus is first a monk and an ascetic whose vision for the world is always tempered by his vision of the world.[153] The literal and the phenomenal must be transcended because of the reality of human passion and weakness, the perversion of the sensible that stigmatizes humanity in consequence of the fall. Maximus describes this tragedy in detail in Question 61[154] and in his introduction to the *Ad Thalassium*.[155] The *diabasis* toward the intelligible truth of creation and scripture in turn presupposes for Maximus the integration and reorientation of humanity's whole moral and spiritual development. He indicates this in his interpretation of Peter's vision and of the injunction to "rise, kill, and eat" (Acts 10:13):

> The sheet held by four corners (cf. Acts 10:11) signifies the sensible world, itself held together by four elements. So too the reptiles, wild animals, and birds of the air (cf. ibid. 10:12) represent the different principles (λόγοι) of creatures, principles that are unclean as regards sense, but clean, nutritious, and life-sustaining as regards the mind. The voice heard three times (cf. ibid. 10:16) respectively teaches *practical, natural, and theological philosophy* (πρακτικὴ καὶ φυσικὴ καὶ θεολογικὴ φιλοσοφία). For he who "arises" not once, but twice and a third time, must "kill" the phenomenal creation and eat it intellectually (γνωστικῶς), obeying God wholly and sincerely. First, he who "rises" from a disposition impassioned over phenomenal things "kills" the movement of phenomena and by performing virtue "eats" virtue (ἀρετή). Second, he who "rises" from false opinions about created beings "kills" the external forms of phenomena and, "eating" the invisible principles, practices natural contemplation in the Spirit (ἡ ἐν πνεύματι φυσικὴ θεωρία). Third, he who "rises" from the error of polytheism sacrifices the very essence of created beings and by faith "eats" the Cause of those beings and is filled with a theological power (θεολογικὴ δύναμις). Therefore every contemplative mind (θεωρητικὸς νοῦς), having in hand "the sword of the Spirit, which is the word of God" (Eph. 6:17), and having within itself cut off the movement of the phenomenal creation, establishes

virtue and, having destroyed its fantasy of sensible forms, discovers truth in the principles of created beings—the very truth that is constitutive for natural contemplation. Moreover, by transcending the essence of created beings, the mind is enlightened by the divine and impregnable Monad—the very enlightenment that is constitutive for the mystery of true theology (τῆς ἀληθοῦς θεολογίας τὸ μυστήριον).[156]

Πρᾶξις—Θεωρία—Θεολογία in the Ad Thalassium

While contemplation (θεωρία) is clearly the primary medium of the penetration of the intelligible principles of creation or the spiritual senses of scripture, and the special object of our interest here, it cannot be separated from the whole program of the spiritual life in the Confessor's thought. As J. Lemaître remarks of Maximus, "One will become a contemplator of nature just as one becomes a spiritual exegete of scripture: by *praxis*, by purity, by the virtues, by grace."[157] By now it is quite clear that Maximus' hermeneutics cannot be studied, properly speaking, in isolation from his larger spiritual anthropology and his asceticism.

Numerous Maximian scholars have already observed the Confessor's indebtedness to Evagrius for his triad of spiritual development,[158] which embraces the three phases of πρᾶξις (variously referred to as πρακτικὴ φιλοσοφία, or simply ἀρετή); θεωρία (or θεωρητικὴ φιλοσοφία, with its higher form being a πνευματικὴ θεωρία, or simply γνῶσις); and θεολογία (μυστικὴ θεολογία, θεολογικὴ μυσταγωγία, etc.).[159] The interrelations between these three phases of the spiritual life have been an object of dispute in studies of Maximus' spirituality, some claiming to find a "chronological" sequence or progression such as we find in Evagrius,[160] others noting the inseparability between πρᾶξις and θεωρία (or ἀρετή and γνῶσις). Thunberg has authoritatively argued from a general analysis of Maximus' works that, wanting to avoid making the *vita practica* only a preparatory stage for the *vita contemplativa*, the Confessor places the two in a mutual relation, distinguished but indissoluably united.[161]

In the *Quaestiones ad Thalassium* this συζυγία of πρᾶξις and θεωρία is asserted fairly consistently throughout. To be sure, Maximus will, on occasion, make allusion to a movement from ethical practice to contemplation that could, if isolated, be taken to indicate a sequential development.[162] Moreover, honoring Evagrius' view, he will sometimes admit a relative superiority in contemplation or knowledge based on its proximity to loftier mystagogy,[163] as is evinced by his pairing of πρακτικὴ φιλοσοφία and θεωρητικὴ μυσταγωγία.[164] Yet this is balanced out by those instances where Maximus seems to suggest a certain superiority of πρᾶξις to θεωρία, clearly in an effort to curb the perceived intellectualism of the Evagrianist scheme. In Question 49, he casts Hezekiah as ὁ διαγνωστικὸς νοῦς, who, at the moment of the assault of the passions, orders his faculties to "cease from natural contemplation (φυσικὴ θεωρία) and engage in prayer (προσευχή) alone and in the mortification (κακοπάθεια) of the body through practical philosophy (πρακτικὴ φιλοσοφία)."[165] Contemplation and γνῶσις carry the danger of vainglory that must be balanced out by the humilty of πρᾶξις, though the "practical mind" too can, if not perfected with knowledge, lead to conceit (οἴησις).[166] "Whoever seeks the Lord by contemplation without practice does not discover the Lord, since he has not sought him in the fear of the Lord."[167]

Overall Maximus vigorously seeks to demonstrate the ideal balance and coinherence between πρᾶξις and θεωρία:[168]

> In my view, practice (πρᾶξις) and contemplation (θεωρία) mutually cohere with each other, and the one is never separated from the other; on the contrary, practice shows forth through conduct the knowledge (γνῶσις) derived from contemplation, while contemplation, no less than reason, fortifies itself with the virtue (ἀρετή) derived from practice.[169]

Maximus illustrates this pairing or συζυγία, and again the relative superiority of contemplation by its relation to mystical knowledge, but also the absolutely mutual functioning of both, in an extensive allegory of Peter and John en route to join the Logos in the upper room (Luke 22:7-13):

Peter is a symbol of ascetic practice (πρᾶξις) while John is a symbol of contemplation (θεωρία). Fittingly, then, the first man to meet them, who was carrying the jar of water, signifies in himself all those who, by practical philosophy (πρακτική φιλοσοφία), carry on the shoulders of virtue, as in a jar, the grace of the Spirit, which both keeps watch by mortifying the body's members on earth and cleanses them of defiling things. Next to him, then, the second man, the householder who showed the disciples the furnished upper room, likewise demonstrates in himself all those who, according to contemplation, furnish, like an upper room, the purest and noblest reflection, for the purpose of entertaining the great Logos with gnostic thoughts and dogmas, in a way that befits God. The household, moreover, is the habit of true piety, toward which the practical mind travels when it performs virtue. But the contemplative mind, radiant with the divine light of mystical knowledge, masters virtue as though having made it henceforth naturally its own, and for this reason is deemed worthy, together with the practical mind, of the presence and gladness of the transcendent and saving Logos.[170]

But in an even more striking illustration drawn from the vision of the lampstand in Zechariah 4, Maximus bases the reciprocity between πρᾶξις and θεωρία not only on their functional interrelation but also on the analogous inseparability within scripture between Old Testament and New, and in human nature between the innate practical and contemplative faculties of the soul:

The two olive trees, as I said before, may be interpreted as the two Testaments. At the left of the lampstand is the Old Testament, which, in the manner of the olive tree, produces the modes of the virtues, pertaining to the practical life (οἱ κατὰ τὴν πρᾶξιν τρόποι τῶν ἀρετῶν), in the gnostic, or contemplative faculty (τὸ θεωρητικόν) of the soul. At the right is the New Testament, which unceasingly produces the spiritual principles, pertaining to contemplation (οἱ κατὰ τὴν θεωρίαν πνευματικοὶ λόγοι), in the passible, or practical faculty (τὸ πρακτικόν) of the soul. In turn we may accurately comprehend the mystery of our salvation (τὸ τῆς σωτηρίας ἡμῶν μυστήριον) through them both. One's way of life (βίος) demonstrates reason (λόγος), while reason constitutes the glory of one's way of life. Practical conduct (πρᾶξις) is contemplation in action (θεωρία ἐνεργουμένη), while contemplation (θεωρία) is mystagogical practice (πρᾶξις μυσταγωγουμένη). In short, virtue (ἀρετή) is the manifestation of knowledge (γνῶσις),[171] while knowledge is the sustaining power behind virtue, and there is one wisdom of both (I mean, of virtue and knowledge).[172]

The Old Testament, since it contains the λόγοι of the commandments, is generally identified with πρᾶξις, both with regard to the purgation of the passions and the attainment of virtue; and the New Testament, with θεωρία, in view of its conjunction with higher mystagogy.[173] Anthropologically, the coinherence of the two phases is founded on the very function of reason (λόγος) itself, which not only supervises the practice of virtue[174] but also, since it is conjoined with the mind (νοῦς), supports the mind's higher contemplative activity.[175]   In another anthropological allusion, Maximus identifies θεωρία with the "glory" of being created in God's image (κατ' εἰκόνα), and πρᾶξις with the "honor" of attaining to the exact imitation (μίμησις) of God by assimilation (κατ' ὁμοίωσιν).[176]

It is in fact possible to see a certain analogy between the interrelation of the "three ways" of the spiritual life (πρακτική, θεωρητική, μυστική) and that of the "three laws" (γραφικός, φυσικός, πνευματικός), though Maximus does not press this analogy too far. Indeed it is impossible to draw exact correspondences between πρακτική and γραφικός, θεωρητική and φυσικός, μυστική and πνευματικός since, as Maximus demonstrates in Question 39, πρᾶξις acquires the τρόποι of the virtues from the natural law, just as θεωρία looks to the spiritual law for the true λόγοι of knowledge.[177] Moreover, as we shall see more clearly below, the written law is just as much the object of θεωρία as the natural. Nonetheless, there is an observable similarity between the "synthesis" established between the three laws[178] and the interplay of the three phases of the spiritual life: first, a necessary reciprocity between πρᾶξις and θεωρία; second, an elevation from the lower, or negative, to the higher, or positive, aspect in each phase (in ascetic practice, from mortification of passions and ἀπάθεια to positive performance of virtue and ἀγάπη, and in contemplation, from natural contemplation to a higher contemplation ἐν πνεύματι); and third, the fulfillment and transcendence of πρᾶξις and θεωρία by the third phase, μυστικὴ θεολογία, implying a mystical union κατὰ χάριν. This "synthesis" conveys, furthermore, that in Maximus' mind each of the three phases—πρᾶξις, θεωρία, θεολογία—is properly irreducible in its salvific function, being drawn together, without violation to any of the three, toward the ultimate grace of mystical union.

Natural (φυσική) and Scriptural (γραφική) Contemplation

Having outlined this important integration of the whole spiritual life in Maximus' understanding of the *diabasis*, I would turn specifically to the instrumental role of θεωρία, both in its natural and scriptural application, in this *transitus*.

The close connection between Maximus' hermeneutics and his spiritual anthropology is especially in evidence here, for he cannot conceive of the contemplation of sensible and intelligible objects without the right ordering of sense (αἴσθησις) and intellect (νοῦς) within human nature itself. Indeed, the mind's power to discern the spiritual λόγοι in the sensible images gleaned from the contemplation of phenomena (i.e., the σχήματα or ἐπιφανείαι of creation, the γράμμα of scripture) will hinge on its ability to reorient the senses away from any hedonistic proclivity (σχέσις) toward sensible objects and to elevate them to the service of intellect.[179] This will entail a radical mortification of sense itself:

> It is impossible for the mind to cross over (διαβῆναι) to intelligible realities, despite their connatural relation, without contemplating intermediary sensible things, but it is also absolutely impossible for contemplation to take place without sense (which is naturally akin to sensible things) being joined with the mind. Thus it is fair to say that if the mind encounters and is entangled in the appearances of visible things, believing that its companion, sense, is its natural activity, the mind by nature falls

away from noetic things and unnaturally lays hold of corporeal objects with both hands, so to speak. It does so irrationally, because it has been taken over by sense. It fathers the grief of a soul tormented by repeated scourges of conscience, and becomes the creator of sensible pleasure, and fattens itself with notions of how to preserve the flesh. On the other hand, if the mind, in its encounters with the appearance of visible things to sense, simultaneously cuts through that appearance and beholds the pure spiritual principles (λόγοι) of created beings free of the external forms (σχήματα) of those beings, it acquires the pleasure of the soul by subjecting itself to none of the things observed by sense. It produces the grief of sense by depriving itself of everything that is by nature sensible. For when reason takes precedence over sense in the contemplation of visible things, the flesh is naturally deprived of all pleasure, since sense is no longer free and loosed from the bonds of reason to pursue sensual pleasures.[180]

The human subject stands existentially, as it were, in the position of Adam in paradise, forced to choose between the "tree of life" (interpreted allegorically as the νοῦς) and the "tree of the knowledge of good and evil" (rendered allegorically as αἴσθησις), between wisdom and irrationality.[181]

Yet while Maximus often stresses this radical mortification of the sensible faculties by reason as part of the process of natural contemplation,[182] he also still envisions a higher collaboration between all the faculties,[183] and, within the same scope, a natural reunion of νοῦς and αἴσθησις.[184] True contemplation will entail not merely the vision of external objects but also a certain self-contemplation in which the mind, by comprehending the lower faculties of the soul in a spiritual way, harmonizes and integrates them.[185]

In Question 49, Maximus shows quite clearly the ideal collaboration of sense and intellect in natural contemplation (φυσικὴ θεωρία), and indicates as well the dynamics of θεωρία itself:

"The river flowing through the middle of the city" (2 Chron. 32:4) signifies knowledge (γνῶσις) gathered from concepts of sensible things in the practice of natural contemplation (φυσικὴ θεωρία), a knowledge that is conveyed by means of the soul, since the soul is a kind of borderland (μεθόριος) between the mind (νοῦς) and sense (αἴσθησις). For the knowledge of sensible things is not completely removed from one's noetic faculty, nor wholly assigned to the activity of sense, but is at the middle, as it were, of the junction (σύνοδος) of the path from the mind to sense, and sense to the mind. In turn, this knowledge forms, in itself, the union (συνάφεια) of mind and sense to one another. It is shaped by the external forms (σχήματα) of sensible things in relation to sense; but in relation to the mind, it translates (μεταβιβάζουσα) the figures (τύποι) of these external forms into principles (λόγοι). Hence the knowledge of visible things has been called a "river flowing through the middle of the city" with good reason, since it is a mean (μεταίχμιος) between extremes, that is, between mind and sense.[186]

The sources and the fuller scope of φυσικὴ θεωρία in Maximus' thought have been thoroughly worked over in earlier studies,[187] so I need not delve into an extensive analysis here. It is enough to note that its principal objective is the apprehension of the Logos-Christ (and thus too the whole Trinity) as Creator and Cause, and as Instigator of the redemptive economy concealed within the λόγοι of the natural creation and of scripture.[188] One could call it, in general terms, a kind of "informed intuition," a kataphatic or affirmative confession of the magnificence (μεγαλουργία) of the God of creation[189] and the Mighty Acts (μεγαλουργήματα) of the God of salvation history.[190] This contemplation is itself a grace, an open-ended kind of knowledge that is constantly needing to be elevated and spiritualized (thus Maximus' notion of ἡ ἐν πνεύματι φυσικὴ θεωρία)[191] by the Logos himself, who is conducting the human subject toward a participation in his redemptive μυστήριον.[192]

Of special interest to us at this point is his conception of "scriptural contemplation" (γραφικὴ θεωρία) as a corollary of natural contemplation (φυσικὴ θεωρία).[193] I have already indicated above the philosophical foundation of this idea in Maximus' application of his λόγοι doctrine to scripture.[194] The notions of λόγος and πνεῦμα are integrally related in Maximus' thought,[195] as is argued exegetically in his long response in *Ad Thalassium* 65. Here it is precisely the one who becomes another "Saul" dispositionally, by clinging to the letter of the law, who is responsible for murdering the "Gabaonites" (Gibeonites; cf. 2 Kings 21:1), or natural principles (οἱ κατὰ φύσιν λόγοι).[196] Throughout this extended exposition, "Saul," who variously prefigures the γράμμα of the law, the Judaizing interpretation of scripture, the fettish for external appearances, materialism, passion, is set in opposition to "David," the redeemer of the "Gabaonites,"[197] who figuratively embraces in himself ὁ κατὰ πνεῦμα νόμος, the salvation of the gentiles, the mystery hidden beneath natural phenomena and scriptural letters, virtue, and spiritual knowledge.[198] Maximus concludes by bringing in the analogy of the three laws:

> Therefore the "three-year famine" (2 Kings 21:1) signifies the lack of knowledge proportionately in each of the three laws (that is, in the natural law, the written law, and the law of grace) that befalls those who are not diligent in the contemplative elevation (ἡ κατὰ θεωρίαν ἀναγωγή) of those three laws. *For whoever rejects the natural principles of created beings apprehended through contemplation, clinging only to material symbols and conceiving no higher spiritual expression for them, cannot fully cultivate the knowledge of the scriptures* (ἡ τῶν Γραφῶν ἐπιστήμη). For, as long as the mere factual narration (ἱστοριωδὴς ἀφήγησις) of the scriptures prevails, the mind's power is not free from transitory and temporal things, and instead, the sons and grandsons of the dead Saul live on. They number seven, signifying, that is, the corporeal and transitory observance of the law, from which a passionate disposition (for the reason that has been explained) is usually produced in the self-indulgent, a disposition that has, as a help for its error, the mere ordinance obvious in the law's symbols. Therefore I do not think that famine occurred in the days of Saul, which is to say that the lack of knowledge in the Spirit was not perceived in the time of the carnal observance of the law, but in the

time of the grace of the gospel, insofar as whenever we fail to interpret all of scripture spiritually, after the passing of the dominance of the letter, we are utterly starving, since we are not enjoying the mystical, spiritual observance of the law which is proper for Christians. But whenever we come to our senses like David and seek the face of the Lord (cf. 2 Kings 21:1), we are taught clearly that the grace of knowledge is deprived us *because we do not apprehend natural principles as an access to mystical contemplation but cleave to the corporeal thoughts in the letter of the law.*[199]

Maximus further reveals this parallelism of "natural" and "scriptural" contemplation when he has occasion to speak of the levels and modes of such contemplation. This order is already articulated in *Mystagogia* 23, where Maximus distinguishes a lower contemplation of natural things, and of the Law and Prophets, on the one hand, and, on the other hand, a higher contemplation of the λόγοι in their more immediate relation to the unifying Logos, and also of the gospel.[200] In outlining φυσικὴ θεωρία, Maximus speaks of five different modes by which the created world and its beings can be contemplated in a way that leads back to the Logos-Christ: (1) essence (οὐσία); (2) motion (κίνησις); (3) difference (διαφορά); (4) mixture (κρᾶσις); and (5) position (θέσις).[201] These contemplative modes reflect Maximus' vision of the orderly relation of creation and history to the Logos in opposition to radical Origenist-Evagrianist notions of creation, providence, and judgment.[202] But, as we see in *Ambiguum* 37,[203] Maximus also draws on Aristotelian and Pseudo-Dionysian "categories" in conceiving of ten modes of γραφικὴ θεωρία which may, in principle, ultimately "contract" all of scripture into its comprehending logos. This decad of scriptural contemplation commences with its own fivefold tropes of (1) time (χρόνος);[204] (2) place (τόπος);[205] (3) genus or race (γένος);[206] (4) person (πρόσωπον);[207] and (5) dignity (ἀξία) or occupation (ἐπιτήδευμα).[208] These are in turn contracted into (6) practical (πρακτική), (7) natural (φυσική), and (8) theological (θεολογική) philosophy, which in turn are contracted into (9) present (ἐνεστώς) and (10) future (μέλλον) (or figure, τύπος, and truth, ἀλήθεια), which are drawn into the one comprehending logos that is contained in the person of the Logos himself. In a classic text, Maximus describes how the five initial modes of scriptural contemplation would be effectively contracted into the three, then into the two, and lastly into the one:

> The logos of scripture displays all these things (as many as there are included in the original five modes) as constituted of essence (οὐσία), potency (δύναμις), and operation (ἐνέργεια), the primary distinctions about these things: whether overall they move or are moved, whether they act or are acted upon, whether they contemplate or are contemplated, whether they speak or are spoken, whether they teach or are taught, whether they receive accession or aversion, and plainly and concisely, whether by either performing or being the object of practical, natural, and theological philosophy, they combine with one another variously so as to initiate us in these three forms of philosophy. In turn, each of the things multifariously specified in scripture is interpreted, with ideas about it gathered through contemplation, either laudably (ἐπαινετῶς) or censoriously (ψεκτῶς), as showing forth principles (λόγοι) of what we should or what we should not do, meanings natural or unnatural, intelligible or nonintelligible. For...there is a double mode (διττὸς τρόπος) for each scriptural meaning (λόγος), according to the capacity of the one who carries out the research of contemplation on them intelligently. As a result, through affirmation (θέσις) of the principles, and by negation (ἀφαίρησις) of what we should not do and of unnatural and nonintelligible illusions, the pious embrace practical, natural, and theological philosophy, which is the same thing, so to speak, as the love of God. And those three forms of philosophy are furthermore divided into both present and future, since they comprehend both shadow and truth, figure and archetype. Insofar as it is possible, albeit in a transcendent and sublime way, for humanity, in this present age, attaining to the ultimate measure of virtue and knowledge and wisdom, to reach the knowledge of divine things, it is possible through a figure and an image of archetypes. For actually a figure

is the whole truth that we judge to be present now, and an image is also a shadow of the superior Logos. For seeing that the Logos creative of the universe both exists and manifests himself in the universe according to the relation of the present to the future, he is understood as figure and truth; and inasmuch as he transcends present and future, he is understood as transcending figure and truth, by containing nothing that could be considered as contrary. But truth has a contrary: falsehood. So then beyond truth the Logos gathers all things unto him[self], being as he is man and God, and indeed also beyond all humanity and divinity.[209]

This passage presents us with a classic translation problem in Maximus: his use of λόγος with so many subtle shades of meaning. In the discussion here, he is speaking of the unitive logos (or "purpose," or "meaning") operative in the whole of scripture, a general logos (paralleling the γενικὸς λόγος that binds together the created cosmos); yet the transcendent Logos in a certain sense *is* this logos, insofar as it is contained *in him*, and he accommodates his self-revelation through it. The important point here is that the whole macrocosm or "universe" (τὰ ὅλα) of scripture, through contemplation according to the tropes proper to its general logos, is seen as integrated in the Logos-Christ, who fully indwells scripture and yet (as Maximus indicates in his concluding syllogism above) far and away transcends its limitations.

The obvious question is this: Does the Confessor carry over this pattern of γραφικὴ θεωρία and apply it in his actual exegesis of scripture? In observing the responses in the *Quaestiones ad Thalassium*, Maximus does not appear, to my knowledge at least, to be concerned systematically with executing the full decad of tropes for any given passage. Again, this is a thoroughly ideal pattern. As we will see in chapter three, Maximus knows there is a good bit of pious speculation involved in researching the spiritual profundities of the Bible. Therefore he more frequently concentrates only on pieces of the puzzle, so to speak, here and there occupying himself with a reflection on one or more of the different tropes: time,[210] place,[211] genus, person,[212] and dignity or occupation,[213] or (as is also suggested as a possibility in the text above from *Ambiguum* 37) a combination of all of these.[214] An especially evocative example is found in Question 51. Here Maximus works from an interpretation of certain natural phenomena by genus (κατὰ γένος) or species to a contemplation of practical and natural philosophy (κατὰ πρακτικὴν καὶ φυσικὴν φιλοσοφίαν). He catalogues a variety of natural exemplars for the intellect (νοῦς) to imitate and thus attain to true philosophy:

> The discerning mind, when it imitates the natural law of the heavens, receives "donations" (cf. 2 Chron. 32:23) by preserving the most even and ever-consistent movement of virtue and knowledge within itself, a movement that steadfastly bears, like stars, the shining and most radiant principles of created beings. When the mind imitates the natural law of the sun, changing alternately to different positions for everything's use, it receives as another "donation" the necessary comprehension for adjusting to all circumstances with wisdom, without diminishing any of its illuminating identity, as based on virtue and knowledge.
>
> When the mind imitates the eagle, it acquires eyes fastened directly on the divine radiance of pure light, enabling the intellectual pupil not to-be smarted in the least by the brilliant rays of light. The mind imitates the deer when, for example, it pursues the highest mountains of divine speculations; and destroys, by the principle of discretion, the passions which lurk like poisonous animals in the nature of created beings; and dispells, through numerous and diverse sources of knowledge, the poison of evil that is confined in its memory during adversity.
>
> The mind imitates the sharp-sightedness of the gazelle and the stability of the bird: like the antelope, it eludes and leaps across the snares of the hostile demons, and, like a bird, it flies over the traps of the spirits that contend against knowledge.
>
> The mind becomes "wise as a serpent and pure as a dove" (Matt. 10:16) when it constantly guards, like its head, the uninjurable faith, and like the dove, having clearly removed from itself the malice of the soul's irascible element, refuses to bear malice toward those who, like persecutors, are anxious to insult it (Matt. 5:44).

From the turtledove too the mind receives, as a "gift" (2 Chron. 32:23), the imitation of temperance, performing works all of which necessarily characterize (created) natures.

In this way, then, the supremely philosophical mind comes with knowledge to the source of created beings by the natural principle (λόγος) and mode (τρόπος) of each thing. Insofar as it is gnostic (γνωστικός), it receives, like "gifts," the spiritual principles of created beings, offered by the creation. Insofar as it is practical (πρακτικός), it receives "donations" when it imitates the natural laws of created beings in its own conduct. It reveals in itself, by its way of life, all the magnificence of the divine wisdom contained invisibly in created beings.[215]

Maximus' exegeses are indeed abundant in examples where his initial interpretation is reduced to a contemplation in terms of practical, natural, and theological philosophy.[216] The mystery of the Logos is in turn seen as comprehending the whole scheme of contemplation, such that there is no exhaustive spiritual interpretation for any one given text (as we will observe in more detail in the next chapter) but a whole host of possible meanings of a scripture, all of which are ultimately tributary to the Logos-Christ.

The overall notion of γραφική θεωρία thus provides a kind of conceptual groundwork and scientific ideal for spiritual or anagogical exegesis; it is a guideline for determining the christocentric σκοπός of all of scripture, but is not to be taken as a strictly defined exegetical methodology in and of itself.

Recapitulation: Communion with the Incarnate Logos-Christ as the Goal of the Spiritual Diabasis

The descent of the Logos-Christ in his self-revelation and the reciprocal spiritual *diabasis* and ascent of the believer is the very heart of Maximus' hermeneutics. This "theandric"[217] mystery expresses itself in various imageries in the *Quaestiones ad Thalassium*. At times, as we observed above in the discussion of the symbolic structure of the spiritual *diabasis*,[218] Maximus draws upon the Pseudo-Dionysian motifs of procession and return, expansion and contraction, or the more Origenian and Evagrian imagery of differentiation and unification, to depict the Logos' self-disclosure in the λόγοι of scripture (and creation) for the purpose of conducting the human subject back to himself. But as a teacher of monks, Maximus introduces abundant biblical images as well. Thus the Logos-Christ is an "intelligible David,"

> the true Shepherd, King, and Destroyer of opposing powers. He is Shepherd of those who pursue practical philosophy and who feed on natural contemplation like grass, as it were. He is the King of those who, through spiritual laws and principles, restore the beauty of the God-given image to its original pattern.[219]

As the "intelligible Zerubbabel," pioneering our *diabasis* to noetic truth,

> He is the one who returns the captives of the true Israel, not from one earthly location to another, as the ancient Zorobabel did when he transported the people from Babylon to Judah, but from earth to heaven, from evil to virtue, from ignorance to knowledge of the true God (cf. 1 Tim. 2:4), from corruption to incorruption, from death to immortality, and in short, from the phenomenal and transitory world to the fixed and intelligible world, and from the dissolving life to the indissoluable and enduring life.[220]

All these revelatory imageries are nonetheless subservient to Maximus' central leitmotif of incarnation-deification, descent-ascent—a reflection, of course, of his determination to integrate Christology, the foundation of his system, into the wider spectrum of his spirituality and hermeneutics. The "three incarnations" of the Logos-Christ, which have already been discussed in detail,[221] work prospectively toward yet another, revelatory and salvific "incarnation" of Christ in the believer, an inhabitation that manifests itself precisely in the human subject's own active communion with the Logos, and appropriation of his presence through moral practice and contemplation. Already present or "incarnate," as it were, in the τρόποι of virtue and λόγοι of things natural and scriptural, says Maximus, God "ever wills to become human in those who are worthy (ἀεὶ θέλων ἐν τοῖς ἀξίοις ἄνθρωπος γίνεται)."[222]

Maximus' exegesis in the *Quaestiones ad Thalassium* abounds in this incarnational and communal language, the indwelling of Christ in the believer's spiritual life.[223] But perhaps nowhere does the Confessor so profoundly convey this theme than in his response to Question 35:

> Question: "The Logos became flesh" (John 1:14), and not only flesh but blood and bones. We are commanded to eat the flesh and to drink the blood (John 6:53) but not to crush the bones (cf. Exod. 12:46; John 19:31-36). I seek to learn what is the tripartite power itself of the Word made man.
>
> Response: As he alone knew how, the superessential Logos and Creator of all beings, having desired to enter a [created] essence, bore in himself, along with the incomprehensible ideas of his proper divinity, the natural principles of all phenomenal and intelligible beings. The principles of intelligible things would be the "blood" of the Logos, the principles of sensible things his "flesh." Since, then, the Logos is himself the Teacher of spiritual principles (πνευματικοὶ λόγοι) in phenomenal and in intelligible things, he appropriately and rationally grants to those who are worthy the knowledge (ἐπιστήμη) of the principles of visible things, which is like the eating of his flesh; and he grants the knowledge (γνῶσις) of the principles of intelligible things, which is like the drinking of his blood. God's wisdom long ago prepared these principles mystically in the book of Proverbs, through the ancient figures of the bowl for mixing wine and of the animals for sacrifice (cf. Prov. 9:1-2). But the Logos does not grant us his bones—that is, the principles of his divinity that transcend our intelligence—since they are equally and infinitely distanced from every created nature, none of whom has any faculty capable of relating to those principles.
>
>   It could also be said that the flesh of the Logos is true virtue (ἀρετή), his blood infallible knowledge (γνῶσις), and his bones

ineffable theology (θεολογία). In the same way that blood is physically changed into flesh, knowledge is transformed through ascetic practice into virtue. And, like the bones that hold together flesh and blood, the principles of his divinity, which transcend all intelligence, inhere in created beings and create, in a way unknown to us, the essences of those beings and sustain those beings in existence. These principles, moreover, are constitutive for all knowledge and virtue.

If someone were to claim that the flesh and blood are the principles of judgment and providence, at some point to be completely consumed and drunk, while the bones are the ineffable principles of divinity that mingled in with them, then that person would not be erring, it seems to me.

It could perhaps be said as well that the flesh of the Logos is the return and restoration of human nature to itself through virtue, while his blood is the future deification (θέωσις) that will sustain human nature by grace unto eternal well-being (τὸ ἀεὶ εὖ εἶναι). His bones are the unknown power itself that sustains human nature, through the process of deification, unto that eternal well-being.

Finally, if someone were to render an even more desirable explanation, and say that the flesh is voluntary mortification through virtue, that the blood is the perfection through death resulting from tribulations for the sake of truth, and that the bones are the primary and inaccessible principles of divinity, he would have a good interpretation and would in no way deviate from the proper meaning of this text.[224]

Maximus expresses much the same idea, albeit focusing more specifically on πρᾶξις and θεωρία, in Question 36. Here it is asked why the Israelites consumed the meat of their sacrifices but poured out the blood (cf. Deut. 12:27). Maximus, indicating again that the Logos incarnates himself in the *spiritual* meaning of the commandments of scripture,[225] explains that the ancients failed to grasp the λόγοι ("blood") of the commandments together with their literal aspects (τὰ φαινόμενα), their "flesh," and in turn fell short of μυστικὴ γνῶσις.[226]

> "But Christ, who appeared as a high priest of future benefits" (Heb. 9:11), offers the ineffable sacrifice, giving himself through flesh and blood to those who, with a view to perfection, are having the senses of their soul "trained to distinguish between good and evil" (Heb. 5:14).[227]

The one who is perfected in the spiritual life therefore not only eats the "flesh" of the virtues in the practical life but drinks the "blood" by contemplating the λόγοι of the scriptural commandments, thereby "elevating the sensible activity of what he does to the level of intellectual knowledge" (πρὸς τὴν κατὰ νοῦν γνῶσιν ἀναβιβάζων τὴν τῶν γινομένων κατ' αἴσθησιν κίνησιν).[228]

In these two pivotal texts from *Ad Thalassium* 35 and 36, Maximus summarizes his christocentric vision of the spiritual *diabasis* from sensible to intelligible truth. The incarnational mystery of the Logos-Christ, in its full spiritual power ("flesh"—"blood"—"bones"), brings about a communion with himself that engages the believer's whole spiritual life: πρακτική, θεωρητική, θεολογική. The implications for Maximus' interpretation of scripture are clear. Whoever would pierce to the true meaning of the scriptures, making the *diabasis* from γράμμα to πνεῦμα, must do so not merely scientifically but at once morally, intellectually, and mystagogically.

Notes

1. This opening statement presents an interesting textual problem. The critical text of Laga and Steel reads: Τῆς σαρκὸς κατὰ τὴν σχέσιν λογικῶς τὴν ψυχὴν ἀποχωρίσας καὶ τῆς αἰσθήσεως ὁλικῶς διὰ τοῦ πνεύματος ἐκσπάσας τὸν νοῦν, ἄνθρωπε τοῦ θεοῦ, τὴν μὲν ἀρετῶν κατέστησας μητέρα πολύγονον, τὸν δὲ θείας πηγὴν ἀέναον ἀπέδειξας γνώσεως (CCSG 17,1-5). The parallel τὴν μέν and τὸν δέ clearly refer respectively to the preceding ψυχή and νοῦς. The 1675 edition of François Combefis has, for the parallel τὴν μέν and τὸν δέ, τὴν μέν and τὴν δέ (PG 244D);

Combefis thereupon notes parenthetically in his Latin translation, "id est, carnem...sensum" respectively (246A). Christoph von Schönborn has argued in a recent study ("Plaisir et douleur," 283-284) that the MS used by Combefis is equally ancient and that the Laga-Steel text registers an interpretative correction that overlooks the fact that Maximus, having already lauded Thalassius' transcendence of the carnal and sensible, is precisely emphasizing the inversion that will allow for a positive integration of the flesh and the senses. Schönborn's opting for Combefis' reading fits his argument that Maximus has an ultimately balanced and positive view of the carnal and sensible aspects of human nature. I would reject the reading of Combefis/Schönborn for the following reasons. First, their rendering appears grammatically impossible, since ψυχή and νοῦς are the dominant elements in the original statement and would thus be the natural referents of the parallel that follows. Second, Maximus is known elsewhere in his works to speak already of the *soul* as a "mother" (cf. A. K. Squire, "The Idea of the Soul as Virgin and Mother in Maximus the Confessor," *StPatr* 8, TU 93 [Berlin: Akademie-Verlag, 1966], 456-461), which would make his application of the same metaphor to the flesh all the more dubious. Last, Maximus' phrase "toward the implementation of an arrangement of better proportions" (εἰς χρῆσιν τῆς οἰκονομίας τῶν κρειττόνων) breaks his thought and provides the transition into what follows (CCSG 17,6-18), which elaborates how σάρξ has come to mirror ψυχή, and αἴσθησις has rendered service to νοῦς. This is the "inversion" of which Schönborn speaks, incorporating the healthy economy of the flesh and sense in the spiritual life. The reciprocity thus established between σάρξ and ψυχή, and between αἴσθησις and νοῦς, is fundamental for Maximus' notion of the continuity in the spiritual διάβασις from sensible to noetic truth.

2. *Q. Thal.* intro. (CCSG 17,1-18).

3. Cf. Philo, *De spec. leg.* 2.147 (see below, n. 8); Origen, *Comm. in Matt.* 15.20.621 (GCSO 10.407,29-32): Ὁ μὲν οὖν διαβεβηκὼς ἐν σοφίᾳ καὶ λόγῳ; *Comm. in Joann.* 10.10.453 on those who must first advance in basic spiritual teaching (ἐπὶ πλεῖον διαβῆναι τῆς στοιχώσεως) and then advance (διαβάς) toward perfection, citing Heb. 6:1 (GCSO 10.11,20ff); *C. Cels.* 6.14 on men who have passed (διαβεβηκότες) from carnal to divine wisdom (GCSO 2.85,2-5); *C. Cels.* 8.22 on the one who truly understands Christ's Passover sacrifice being as one who passes over in thought, word, and deed from worldly affairs to God (διαβαίνων ἀεὶ τῷ λογισμῷ καὶ παντὶ λόγῳ καὶ πάσῃ πράξει ἀπὸ τῶν τοῦ βίου πραγμάτων ἐπὶ τὸν θεόν) (GCSO 2.239,20-24). Marguerite Harl includes διαβαίνειν in Origen's regular vocabulary of spiritual-pedagogical progress. See her *Origène et la*

fonction révélatrice du Verbe incarné, Patristica sorbonensia 2 (Paris: Éditions du Seuil, 1958), 222. Also Gregory of Nyssa, *De vita Moysis* 2.202 (GNO 7, pt. 1, 103,13ff): "He who has progressed (διαβάς) this far through the ascents (διὰ τῶν ἀναβάσεων) which we have contemplated carries in his hand the tables, written by God, which contain the divine Law" (trans. Ferguson-Malherbe, 107). Gregory's cherished terms throughout the *Vita Moysis* and his other works are ἀναβαίνειν-ἀνάβασις.

4. Ἀνάβασις as a favorite term for the larger process of deification in grace, having as its counterpart the κατάβασις of God in the incarnation, has already been highlighted in Josef Loosen's classic study of Maximus' soteriology, *Logos und Pneuma im begnadeten Menschen bei Maximus Confessor*, Münsterische Beiträge zur Theologie 24 (Münster: Aschendorff, 1941). He writes: "A favorite category in the theological thought of St. Maximus is the conceptual form of the 'ascent' and related images. It is sometimes expressly stated, through words like ἀναβαίνω, ἀνάβασις, διαβαίνω, διάβασις, and so on, and at other times is stated through equivalent paraphrases.... The anabasis, the ascent, is the way the graced man has to go, according to St. Maximus. The anabasis is the framework in which he registers his image of man.... The anabasis of man to God is the corresponding reverse side of the descent of God to man" (p. 7).

5. *Cap. theol.* 2.77 (PG 90.1161A-B; trans. Berthold, *Maximus Confessor*, 164).

6. Ibid. 2.18 (PG 90.1133A-B; trans. Berthold, *Maximus Confessor*, 151).

7. See Laga ("Maximus as a Stylist," 142), who notes that in striving for "economy of words," Maximus habitually opts for different prepositions agglutinated to verbs, rather than using them independently.

8. We see precisely such a use of διάβασις originally in Philo's imagery of the spiritual Pasch. In *De spec. leg.* 2.147, he gives the moral-allegorical interpretation of the Passover and says that "...the Crossing-festival (τὰ διαβατήρια) suggests the purification of the soul. They say that the lover of wisdom is occupied solely in crossing over (διάβασις) from the body and the passions, each of which overwhelms him like a torrent, unless the rushing current is dammed and held back by the principles of virtue" (Loeb ed., *Philo* VII, trans. F. H. Colson, 396).

9. Cf. *Q. Thal.* intro. (CCSG 17,12-18).

10. Ibid. 51 (CCSG 407,206-207).

11. Ibid. 64 (PG 708C).

12. Ibid. 55 (CCSG 489,144-145); cf. ibid. 63 (PG 673D), where Maximus speaks of those who receive perfection from the Holy Spirit as attaining

to perfect immutability (ἀτρεψία), "since all [sensible] media–in which there exists a danger of sometimes erring in knowledge–will be wholly transcended (διαβαθέντων) by those who are being deified."

13. Ibid. intro. (CCSG 21,71).

14. Ibid. 49 (CCSG 357,114ff): στάσιν λαμβανούσῃ διὰ τῆς μέσης αἰσθήσεως ἡ περὶ τὰ νοητὰ διάβασις τῆς ἐν ἡμῖν λογικῆς ἐνεργείας.

15. Ibid. 65 (PG 756C).

16. Ibid. (PG 740B). Cf. *Qu. et dub.* 192 (CCSG 10.135,5-7): "Those who cross over (οἱ διαβαίνοντες) from the letter (γράμμα) to the spirit (πνεῦμα) behold the Law and Prophets together with the Logos."

17. *Q. Thal.* 63 (PG 669C).

18. Cf. especially *Myst.* 2 (PG 91.669A-C): The created cosmos (like the Church), "is divided into a spiritual world filled with intelligible and incorporeal essences and into this sensible and bodily world which is ingeniously woven together of many forms and natures.... there is but one world and it is not divided by its parts. On the contrary, it encloses the differences of the parts arising from their natural properties by their relationship to what is one and indivisible by itself. Moreover, it shows that both are the same thing with it and alternately with each other in an unconfused way and that the whole of one enters into the whole of the other, and both fill the same whole as parts fill a unit, and in this way the parts are uniformly and entirely filled as a whole. For the whole spiritual world seems mystically imprinted on the whole sensible world in symbolic forms, for those who are capable of seeing this, and conversely the whole sensible world is spiritually explained in the mind in the principles which it contains. In the spiritual world it is in principles (λόγοι); in the sensible world it is in figures (τύποι)" (trans. Berthold, *Maximus Confessor*, 188-189). Cf. also *Q. Thal.* 63 (PG 685D), where Maximus allegorizes the two olive trees flanking the lampstand (Zech. 4:3) as the sensible and intelligible worlds, between which stands the divine Logos, "who determines in a mystical way that the intelligible world appears in the sensible world through figures (τύποι), and who teaches that the sensible world is comprehended in the intelligible world through principles (λόγοι)." On this mutual circumincession (περιχώρησις) of the sensible and intelligible parts of creation, see the analysis of von Balthasar, *Kosmische Liturgie*, 170-171. On the γενικὸς λόγος of all creation, see, int. al., *Myst.* 7 (PG 91.685A-B); *Q. Thal.* 2 (CCSG 51,18-20); ibid. 54 (CCSG 451,159-453,163); and Thunberg, *Microcosm and Mediator*, 426-427. Cf. also *Amb.* 10 (PG 91.1164D-1165A), where the two figures of Moses and Elijah, flanking the transfigured Lord, are interpreted respectively, in a more salvation-historical framework, as the sensible and

intelligible creations in their mutual relation to the Creator-Logos.

19. On these five polarities, see in particular *Amb.* 41 (PG 91.1304D-1316A). The five polarities, in ascending order, are as follows: (1) between male and female (only as a result of the fall); (2) on earth, between paradise and inhabited earth (also contingent on the fall); (3) in the sensible world, between heaven and earth; (4) in creation, between intelligible and sensible; and (5) between God and creation. In *Q. Thal.* 48 (CCSG 333,65-335,81), Maximus indicates how these polarities have been resolved salvation-historically by the Logos in his incarnation. The concomitant spiritual-vocational mediations of these polarities have been analyzed in detail by Thunberg (*Microcosm and Mediator,* 396-459), and, corresponding to each polarity above, include: (1) practical catharsis within the the soul and the spiritual reorientiation of the faculties of concupiscence and anger; (2) practical mortification and equal love for one's neighbor; (3) contemplation of sensible things, and the achievement of likeness to the angels by "ascending with Christ through the heavens"; (4) contemplation of intelligibles and apprehension of the Logos as the common principle of all created reality; and (5) θεολογία proper and mystical union with the Uncreated.

20. See *Q. Thal.* 48 (CCSG 335,74-76): The incarnate Logos has "united sensible things and intelligible things, and showed that they have one nature, common to all created things, that connects them according to a mystical principle."

21. On the foundations of this notion of διάβασις as the penetration through the sensible, see especially *Amb.* 10 (PG 91.1105C-1205C passim); cf. Sherwood's synopsis, *Earlier Ambigua,* 30-40. It is fair to say that διάβασις has to do primarily with the first through fourth cosmic "mediations" described in n. 19 above, and thus with the first and second of what Thunberg has called the "three levels of theology" in Maximus: (1) the "economic" (kataphatic) level of historical revelation proper; (2) "the level of mystical revelation included in, or behind, historical revelation"; and (3) the apophatic level of "non-revelation" (*Man and the Cosmos,* 44). Spiritual *diabasis* begins with the sensible economy of creation and scripture, and moves over to the intelligible economy, the "second level," which Jérome Gaïth, has appropriately termed "the passage from the level of the cosmos to that of the supercosmos...in other words, the second stage of divine immanence" (*La conception de la liberté chez Grégoire de Nysse,* Études de philosophie médiévale 43 [Paris: Vrin, 1953], 35).

22. Cf. Croce, *Tradizione e ricerca,* 35: "Human knowledge is therefore a passage, a transit, a crossing (διάβασις), which aims not to cancel out the the multiplicity of sensible things as though it were an evil, but to climb the scale of the ascent toward the supreme monad, God."

23. *Q. Thal.* 58 (PG 596D-597A).

24. See again the συζυγία of the soul and the flesh that Maximus envisions in Thalassius in the introduction to the *Q. Thal.*, quoted at the beginning of this chapter; cf. also ibid. 63 (PG 677C-D), where Maximus suggests that "the Old Testament causes (διαβιβάζει) the body, so reckoned through the media of the virtues, to cross over to the level of the soul and prevents the mind from being debased (καταβιβάζεσθαι) to the level of the body. The New Testament causes (ἀναβιβάζει) the mind, on fire with love, to ascend to God." The theme of the body mirroring or serving the soul was already standard in Cappadocian anthropology: see, e.g., Gregory of Nazianzus, *Or.* 2.17 (PG 35.428A): "the soul becomes to the body what God is to the soul, training its servant, bodily matter, and assimilating that fellow servant (ὁμόδουλος) to God"; also Gregory of Nyssa, *De hom. opif.* 12 (PG 46.161C) on the body as a "mirror of the mirror."

25. See *Amb.* 10 (PG 91.1113A).

26. The service of αἴσθησις to νοῦς plays heavily in Maximus' spiritual anthropology. On the consequences of this reciprocity of mind and sense, see also von Balthasar, *Kosmische Liturgie*, 285-286.

27. *Earlier Ambigua*, 35, citing *Amb.* 10 (PG 91.1112D-1113B).

28. Cf. *Q. Thal.* 62 (PG 656C): "For only the inclination of the natural law—that is, of the passible element of human nature—toward the passions of disgrace becomes a barrier dividing the body from the soul, and from the reason (λόγος) of the virtues, and prevents its transit (διάβασις) to the flesh via the soul in ethical practice from taking place." Also ibid. 18 (CCSG 117,8-10), where Maximus says that the doers of the "spiritual law" "do not fall away from grace because of the cathartic transit (διάβασις) of reason into the depth of their soul."

29. See also George Berthold, "History and Exegesis in Evagrius and Maximus," in *Origeniana Quarta: Die Referate des 4. internationalen Origeneskongresses (Innsbruck, 2-6. September 1985)*, ed. Lothar Lies, Innsbrucker theologische Studien 19 (Innsbruck and Vienna: Tyrolia-Verlag, 1987), 393. Berthold recognizes that for Maximus, "Macrocosm and Microcosm are related to the Logos each in its own way and on its own level. Throughout the Questions to Thalassius Maximus refers to the correspondence existing between cosmos, human nature, and soul."

30. *Q. Thal.* 32 (CCSG 225,17-33).

31. See, viz., *Myst.* 6 (PG 91.684A-D) on "How and in what manner sacred scripture is said to be a human being," i.e., with the OT as "body" (σῶμα) and the NT as "soul" (ψυχή), "spirit" (πνεῦμα), and "mind" (νοῦς); or else the historical letter of all scripture, NT and OT, as the "body," and the

inner meaning (νοῦς) and purpose (σκοπός) of all scripture as "soul." The same analogy is made in *Cap. theol.* 1.91 (PG 90.1120D-1121A) and can also be found already in Origen, e.g., *Hom. in Lev.* 5.1 (GCSO 6.333-334). Cf. also *Myst.* 7 (684D-688B) on "How the world is said to be a human being, and in what manner a human being is said to be a world." Here Maximus depicts the cosmos as *makranthropos,* with intelligibles corresponding to the soul, and sensible things corresponding to the body; or intelligibles as the "soul" of sensible things, and sensible things as the body of intelligibles, bound together, like soul and body, by a single natural principle. In turn, the human being, as a microcosm of the creation, reveals the indissoluable relation between intelligible and sensible things.

32. *Myst.* 7 (PG 91.685D-688A; trans. Berthold, *Maximus Confessor,* 197). The fundamentally Origenian structure of this correspondence between creation, scripture, and human nature has been noted, with citations from Origen, by Berthold (ibid., 220, n. 71).

33. Berthold, "History and Exegesis," 393.

34. On the same analogy in Origen, see *Comm. in Joann.* 13.42 (GCSO 4.267-269); also the recent study of Karen Jo Torjesen, *Hermeneutical Procedure and Theological Method in Origen's Exegesis,* PTS 28 (Berlin and New York: Walter de Gruyter, 1986), 109.

35. Von Balthasar, *Kosmische Liturgie,* 289. The interrelation of the "three laws" is further discussed below, The Three Laws and the Three Incarnations.

36. Cf. especially Origen's *Comm. in Matt.* 12.36-43 (GCSO 10.150-170). See also Marguerite Harl's important analysis of the symbolic importance of the transfiguration in Origen's own theology and exegesis in *Origène et la fonction révélatrice du Verbe incarné,* 250-254.

37. Cf. Origen, *Comm. in Matt.* 12.38 (GCSO 10.154,19-21), where the garments symbolize only *αἱ τῶν εὐαγγελίων λέξεις καὶ γράμματα,* "the words and letters of the *gospels*"; so too for Maximus in *Cap. theol.* 2.14 (PG 90.1132A): "When the Word of God becomes bright and shining in us, and his face is dazzling in the sun, then also will his clothes be radiant, that is, the clear and distinct words of the Holy Scripture of the Gospels no longer veiled" (trans. Berthold, *Maximus Confessor,* 150).

38. The "book of creation" metaphor was an ancient one in Greek monasticism. Evagrius attributes it in his *Praktikos* to an apophthegm of St. Antony: "A certain member of what was then considered the circle of the wise once approached the just Anthony and asked him: 'How do you ever manage and carry on, Father, deprived as you are of the consolation of books?' His reply: 'My book, sir philosopher, is the nature of created things, and it is

always at hand when I wish to read the words of God'" (*Praktikos* 92, trans. John E. Bamberger, CS 4 [Kalamazoo: Cistercian Publications, 1981], 39).

39. *Amb.* 10 (PG 91.1125D-1129D). Cf. also *Cap. theol.* 2.14 (PG 90.1132A).

40. Certain of the connections with the Ps.-Dionysian symbolism have been noted already by Völker, *Maximus Confessor als Meister des geistlichen Lebens*, 271ff.

41. See especially the two fundamental studies of Irénée-Henri Dalmais, "La théorie des 'logoi' des créatures chez saint Maxime le Confesseur," *RSPhTh* 36 (1952): 244-249; and "La fonction unificatrice du Verbe Incarné dans les œuvres spirituelles de saint Maxime le Confesseur," *Sciences ecclésiastiques* 14 (1962): 445-459; and more recently his "La manifestation du Logos dans l'homme et dans l'Église: Typologie anthropologique et typologie ecclésiale d'après Qu. Thal. 60 et la Mystagogie," in *Maximus Confessor: Actes du Symposium sur Maxime le Confesseur, Fribourg, 2-5 septembre 1980*, ed. Felix Heinzer and Christoph von Schönborn, Paradosis 27 (Fribourg: Éditions Universitaires, 1980), 13-25. Cf. also the excellent analyses of Riou, *Le monde et l'église*, 54-63, 88-92; Prado, *Voluntad y naturaleza*, 154-157; Thunberg, *Microcosm and Mediator*, 76-84; and Thunberg, *Man and the Cosmos*, 132-140. On the wider historical and theological context of Maximus' theory of λόγοι, see John Meyendorff, *Byzantine Theology*, 2nd ed. (New York: Fordham University Press–Rose Hill Books, 1979), 131-134.

42. See, int. al., the strongly anti-Origenist *Amb.* 7 (PG 91.1077C-1085C). On the predecessors of Maximus' doctrine of λόγοι, see the citations listed by Thunberg, *Microcosm and Mediator*, 77-78, n. 1. I quote, more recently, an excellent summary statement of Thunberg (*Man and the Cosmos*, 138) on the character of the λόγοι in Maximus' thought: "What can one state with certainty about Maximus' conception of the *logoi* in their double relationship to God (the Logos) and to the concrete world in its manifold manifestations? Are the *logoi* transcendent or immanent, are they created or noncreated? The answer must be a double one. On the one hand Maximus affirms that the *logoi* are pre-existent in God. On the other hand, he also says that God brought them to their realization in concrete creation, according to the general law of the continual presence of God and of the Logos. In a certain way they are, thus, both *transcendent and immanent*. Yet, this immanence does not invite us to conclude that they are created. As immanent they represent, and *are*, the presence of the divine intention and principle of every single nature and species. And as such this intention presents itself as their natural fixity as well as their existential purpose. As realized in the

existence of things, they materialize in the created order. Yet they are certainly not themselves created or part of that created order in the sense that they are bound by its material appearance or actual realization."

43. *Q. Thal.* 13 (CCSG 95,6-13): "The principles of created beings (οἱ τῶν ὄντων λόγοι), which were prepared in God from eternity, as he alone saw fit, and which are invisible, and customarily called God's 'good intentions' (ἀγαθὰ θελήματα) by the divines, are clearly perceived from the things he has made. For God's natural creations, which we intellectually contemplate with the necessary science, declare to us secretly (κρυφίως) the principles according to which they were made, and display together with themselves the divine purpose (σκοπός) for each created thing." Cf. Ps.-Dionysius, *De div. nom.* 5.8 (PG 3.824C) on the λόγοι as divine θελήματα. See also Dalmais, "La théorie des 'logoi,'" 244.

44. Thus while the λόγοι have a natural ontological fixity in God, their full "historical" and eschatological disclosure by the Logos has yet to be accomplished. As Thunberg writes (*Microcosm and Mediator*, 81), "...the pre-existent unity of the λόγοι in the Logos is ideal and only in an eschatological perspective will their unity be existential (ὑπαρκτικῶς)." Of this unfolding of the λόγοι in the economy, Riou observes (*Le monde et l'église*, 58): "If the logoi are in God from throughout eternity (that is to say, in his knowledge and in his counsel), then they bear within them this favorable time, this appropriate moment. Therefore they do not constitute the intemporal mode of world's presence in God, but its eternal mode, in the economic and non-temporal sense of the word. Their anteriority lies not in an opposition of eternity to time; it is rather a matter of a benedictive pre-existence, a preelection set in relation to the realization-event of the Economy. And the 'favorable moment' contained in the logos of each creature transforms a chronological vision into a 'kairological' and temporally eschatological advent, the succession through passage, through 'passover.' Through this foreknowledge, God can be called the προνοῶν, the 'Provident,' no longer as the one who holds dominion at the summit of the ontological pyramid of hierarchies, but as the Providence that bears in itself the logos and the kairos of each and every being, down to the very smallest. Over against the Dionysian conception, the Deity in his transcendence is for St. Maximus no longer remote, through the multitude of hierarchical mediations...rather, the Word bears in himself, with no intermediary, the logos of the least of beings. Furthermore, the image itself is modified: while fully recapturing the Neoplatonic and Dionysian terminologies of πρόοδος-ἐπιστροφή, St. Maximus enjoys substituting, for the vertical orientation toward a distant summit, the pattern of a furnace, a center which radiates and vivifies in a grand respiration."

45. Originally in Evagrius, the idea of the "λόγοι of providence and judgment" was tied into the Origenist scheme of a double-creation: "judgment" (κρίσις) having to do with God's decision to create the differentiated sensible world as a remedial realm consequent upon the primordial fall of spiritual beings, and "providence" (πρόνοια) being the plan for the restoration of that preexistent unity: cf. Evagrius, *Cent. Gnost.* 1.27 (PO 28.1, ed. A. Guillaumont, p. 29); ibid. 3.38 (p. 113); ibid. 5.16 (p. 183). Maximus, having rejected the myth of double creation, views providence and judgment rather in conjunction with God's leading his positively differentiated creation ontologically and morally toward its consummation in Christ: see, e.g., *Q. Thal.* 53 (CCSG 431,26-29), where Maximus speaks of Christ as the "intelligible David" (Δαυίδ νοητός), whose "beautiful eyes" (1 Kings 16:12) are "the higher principles of providence and judgment–for judgment and providence are, as it were, the 'eyes' of the Logos, with which he supervises the universe, even when he suffers"; cf. ibid. 54 (CCSG 457,238-243), where providence and judgment are his "wings," "by which the Logos, in an unknowable manner, lights upon created beings, on the one hand healing those who want it with the principles (λόγοι) of wisdom, on the other hand restoring, through educative modes (παιδείας τρόποι), those who are slow to virtue"; also ibid. 64 (PG 728C), where Maximus speaks of the Logos' actions leading us to comprehend the "principles of God's providence and judgment" so as to turn us toward eternal realities. On Maximus' correction of the Origenist-Evagrianist notion of the λόγοι of providence and judgment, see von Balthasar, *Kosmische Liturgie*, 131; and Thunberg, *Microcosm and Mediator*, 69-76. George Berthold ("History and Exegesis," 395-398) shows the significance of this criticism for the Confessor's notions of time and history in relation to the exegesis of scripture.

46. These themes recur repeatedly in the *Q. Thal.* Cf. especially *Q. Thal.* 2 (CCSG 51,7-22), where Maximus describes how God, as preserver of his creation, governs the assimilation of particulars (τὰ μερικά) to universals (τὰ καθόλου), which is also a rallying of differentiated λόγοι toward their common universal principle (λόγος). On this theme of "expansion" and "contraction" in Maximus, see especially Thunberg, *Microcosm and Mediator*, 63ff, 85-88, 420; and von Balthasar, *Kosmische Liturgie*, 154-155.

47. Cf. *Q. Thal.* 13 (CCSG 95,13-97,41), where the λόγοι thus contemplated yield a knowledge of the "eternal power and divinity" (cf. Rom. 1:20) of the Creator; also ibid. 64 (PG 709D), where Maximus describes how the λόγοι of incorporeal and corporeal things are able to conduct the mind such that it too is "contracted" (συσταλείς) toward God the Creator.

48. Maximus also speaks, like Evagrius (e.g., *Cent. Gnost.* 4.55, PO

28.1, p. 161) of the "principles of the commandments" (οἱ τῶν ἐντολῶν λόγοι), the ethical teachings of the Logos in scripture, in which, in effect, the Logos himself is present: cf., e.g., *Q. Thal.* 36 (CCSG 243,13-19), where Maximus distinguishes between consuming merely the carnal or literal aspects (τὰ φαινόμενα) of the virtues and apprehending the "λόγοι of the commandments, in which there exists the knowledge of perfect things"; also ibid. 54 (CCSG 461,317-328), where, commenting on Isa. 11:2, Maximus interprets the "spirit of knowledge" as "comprehension of the principles in the commandments (οἱ ἐν ταῖς ἐντολαῖς λόγοι), on which are based the modes of the virtues (οἱ τρόποι τῶν ἀρετῶν)," and the "spirit of understanding" as "acquiescence in the modes (τρόποι) and principles (λόγοι) of the virtues, or more precisely, a reformation according to which the natural faculties are united to the modes and principles of the commandments."

49. This "contraction" must be distinguished in Maximus from a pure ontological "reduction" or collapsing of the diversity of λόγοι.

50. *Amb.* 37 (PG 91.1293A-C). Maximus indicates (ibid. 1296A) that these τρόποι of scriptural contemplation are in fact proper to the λόγος of scripture, i.e., they are themselves to be thought of, in principle, as objective or *revealed*. On this important text in *Amb.* 37, see also the remarks of Croce, *Tradizione e ricerca*, 60-62. Croce draws attention to Maximus' virtually "geometric" view of scripture and scriptural contemplation, and to the strong Ps.-Dionysian motif in this text, especially the double movement implied in the parallel terms κατὰ πρόοδον and ἐνατατικῶς.

51. *Q. Thal.* 22 (CCSG 143,101-103).

52. Ibid. 55 (CCSG 481,20-21). Ps.-Dionysius had already used συνθήματα as a favorite term for scripture's symbolic language about divine realities: cf. *De cael. hier.* 2.3 (PG 3.141B); *Ep.* 9.1 (PG 3.1105B); also *LPGL*, s.v. σύνθημα, 1331.

53. *Q. Thal.* 55 (CCSG 481,18-26).

54. See, e.g., *Cap. theol.* 1.97 (PG 90.1121C-1124A).

55. *Amb.* 10 (PG 91.1160A-B).

56. Cf. *Q. Thal.* 50 (CCSG 379,9-19): "For if the God who speaks is essentially limitless (ἀπερίγραφος), then clearly the Word that he speaks is also limitless."

57. Cf. Origen, *De princ.* 4.2.7-8 (GCSO 5.318-321) on the Spirit's providential authorship of scripture. Maximus too affirms this divine origin of all of scripture (τὰ τοῦ πνεύματος λόγια) merely as traditional: cf. the principal texts already located by Croce, *Tradizione e ricerca*, 36-38.

58. *Q. Thal.* 31 (CCSG 223,4-9).

59. Ibid. 51 (CCSG 395,18-26).

60. This description of scriptural language about God seems to be

directly inspired by Ps.-Dionysius, *De cael. hier.* 2.5 (PG 3.144C-145A): "We will find that the mysterious theologians [=the human authors of scripture] employ these (similarities and dissimilarities) not only to make known the ranks of heaven but also to reveal something of God himself. They sometimes use the most exalted imagery, calling him for instance *sun* of righteousness (Mal. 4:2), *star* of the morning which rises into the mind (2 Pet. 1:19; Rev. 22:16), clear and conceptual light (1 John 1:5). Sometimes they use more intermediate, down-to-earth images. They call him the blazing *fire* which does not cause destruction (Exod. 3:2), water filling up life and, so to speak, entering the stomach and forming inexhaustible streams (John 7:38, from Prov. 18:4; cf. John 4:14). Sometimes the images are of the lowliest kind, such as sweet-smelling ointment (Song 1:3) and corner stone (Isa. 28:16; Eph. 2:20). Sometimes the imagery is even derived from animals so that God is described as a *lion* or a *panther*, a *leopard* or a charging *bear* (Isa. 31:4; Hos. 5:14; 13:7f). Add to this what seems the lowliest and most incongruous of all, for the experts in things divine gave him the form of a worm (Ps. 21:7)" (trans. Colm Luibheid, *Pseudo-Dionysius: The Complete Works*, CWS [Mahwah, N.J.: Paulist Press, 1987], 152, emphasis added). Maximus also speaks at length of the "corner stone" (*Q. Thal.* 48, CCSG 333,40-41) and "worm" (ibid. 64, PG 713A) analogies.

61. Elsewhere, in *Cap. theol.* 2.10, 63, 66-70 (PG 90.1129A-B, 1152C-D, 1153A-1156D), in terms strongly reminiscent of Origen's commentary on the various ἐπίνοιαι of the Logos in scriptural words (cf. especially his *Comm. in Joann.*), Maximus describes how, spiritually contemplated, the Logos is a "mustard seed," "chaff," "dew," "door," etc. (being his incarnation in the λόγοι of scripture). Von Balthasar (*Kosmische Liturgie*, 534- 538, 547) has made definitive comparisons of Maximus here with Origen's commentaries, his notion of ἐπίνοιαι, and his "logology."

62. In elucidating here how scripture is accommodated for our spiritual *diabasis*, Maximus recalls a familiar *topos* in early Christian exegesis. He had already dealt with it in much the same way in *Qu. et dub.* 39 (III,10) (CCSG 10.32,1-33,34), contrasting Abraham as the consummate visionary of the Trinity, with Lot as the one who had "not yet crossed over (διαβάς) visible things." The interpretation of the three and two angels appearing respectively to Abraham (Gen. 18:2) and Lot (Gen. 19:1) stems originally from Philo's triadic speculations on these passages in *De Abrahamo* 119-132 and *Quaest. in Gen.* 4.2. Philo's theory was that Abraham had perceived, through the three angels, the Existent One (τὸ ὄν), or Father, flanked by his primary creative and ruling Powers (αἱ πρῶται δυνάμεις, ἡ ποιητικὴ καὶ ἡ βασιλικὴ), in the "appearance" (still relative) of a Triad (*De Abrahamo* 122-

123; *Quaest. in Gen.* 4.2, Loeb ed., *Philo* suppl. 1, trans. R. Marcus, 270ff). Lot perceived merely a dyad because he was only progressing and had not yet attained to this higher vision (*Quaest. in Gen.* 4.30, Loeb ed., 305-306). The distinction between Abraham and Lot is thus a "natural distinction between the perfect man and the progressor" (ἡ διαφορὰ τοῦ τελείου καὶ τοῦ προκόπτοντος). Trinitarian speculation on this *topos* abounded among both Greek and Latin patristic exegetes. See Thunberg's study, "Early Christian Interpretations of the Three Angels in Genesis 18," *StPatr* 7, TU 92 (Berlin: Akademie-Verlag, 1966), 560-570, and notably 568-569, on Maximus' interpretation and its immediate Christian background.

63. *Q. Thal.* 28 (CCSG 203,4-25); cf. ibid. 44 (CCSG 299,7ff).

64. Ibid. 28 (CCSG 205,51-64). Such an interpretation of the plurality as the Trinity was a fairly standard one in patristic exegesis.

65. Ibid. (CCSG 203,26-205,41; 205,64-69): πρὸς τοὺς ἀσεβεῖς.

66. Ibid. 44 (CCSG 299,11-27). Maximus writes (ibid. 299,28-301,35): "No one would consider the form of speaking in irony (τὸ εἶδος τῆς κατ' εἰρωνείαν λέξεως) to be foreign to scriptural usage, after hearing the scripture that has the person of God saying to Israel, 'If you walk contrary to me, I will also walk contrary to you' (Lev. 26:27-28), knowing full well that this 'contrariness' differs in no way from irony; or again, after discovering how God planned the deception of Ahab, so that falsehood was prophesied to him as truth, by which he sinned and justly incurred punishment" (cf. 3 Kings 22:15-23).

67. Ibid. (CCSG 301,35-39).

68. See especially Ps.-Dionysius, *De cael. hier.* 2 (PG 3.136D-145C), and *Ep.* 9 (PG 3.1104A-1113C) on how scripture uses symbolic "dissimilarities" for the sake of ἀναγωγή. On the Ps.-Dionysian background of this hermeneutical theme, see Paul Rorem, *Biblical and Liturgical Symbols within the Pseudo-Dionysian Synthesis*, Studies and Texts 71 (Toronto: Pontifical Institute of Medieval Studies, 1984), 84-96.

69. *Q. Thal.* 28 (CCSG 205,42-45).

70. Cf. *De princ.* 4.2.9 (GCSO 5.321,3-15), on this notion of purposeful σκάνδαλα in scripture.

71. Cf. *De cael. hier.* 2.3, 5 (PG 3.141B-C, 145B), where the idea of σκάνδαλα is, in effect, extended even to the dissimilarities and crass signs of scriptural terminology.

72. See *Q. Thal.* 48 (CCSG 339,135-143), where, before entering on his anagogical exposition of 2 Chron. 26:9ff, Maximus writes: "I have a difficulty in wondering how it is possible for Uzziah, who was historically the king of Judah, to have vinedressers on Carmel, which was located not in the

kingdom of Judah but in the kingdom of Israel. Indeed, the capital city of the kingdom of Israel was built on Carmel. It seems, however, that the Word has mixed what is untrue into the historical narrative in order to arouse our dull thinking in quest of the truth." Cf. ibid. 65 (PG 752C-753A), where, in his commentary on 2 Kings 21:1-14, Maximus notes: "Where, in the literal record, do we find that the Gabaonites (Gibeonites) wiped out Saul such that he had no standing in all the borders of Israel, when it says that Maribaal, the son of Jonathan the son of Saul, was spared by King David (2 Kings 21:7), and when in 2 Chronicles it mentions many other of Saul's progeny (cf. 2 Chron. 12:2f)? Moreover, how is it possible that, when the Gabaonites took the seven men from Saul's seed, they said, 'We shall wipe him out, such that he has no standing in all the borders of Israel' (2 Chron. 21:5), when Saul had died long beforehand. But it seems that what is irrational was mingled in with the wording of the historical account, so that we would search for the truth of the meaning of the scriptures" (παρεμίγη τῷ ῥητῷ τῆς ἱστορίας τὸ παράλογον, ἵνα τὸ τῆς διανοίας ἀληθὲς τῶν γεγραμμένων ζητήσωμεν).

73. Cf. *Q. Thal.* 10 (CCSG 83,6ff).
74. Ibid. 50 (CCSG 379,23-29).
75. See ibid. 58 (PG 596D-597A), quoted and analyzed below.
76. See, e.g., ibid. 65 (PG 753B-C), where again, still commenting on 2 Kings 21 and the problems of the historical account there that have been inserted providentially by scripture, Maximus indicates how one cannot allow the literal meaning of scripture to become a basis for carnality and passion. "'For the letter kills, but the spirit gives life' (2 Cor. 3:6). For it is totally impossible for the corporeal and the divine elements of the law, or the letter and the spirit, actively to coexist with each other at the same time, since what can destroy life is not inclined to be in harmony with what by nature supplies it." He adds (756A): "Thus when we interpret this passage in the literal sense, we do not find scripture telling the truth (ἀληθεύουσα)." Evagrius similarly notes how when the literal sense contributes to attachment to sensible and carnal things, it is not true: "One must interpret divine scripture noetically and spiritually, for sensible knowledge according to the literal sense is not true" (*Schol. in Prov.* 251 [SC 340, 346]). Yet it is not the historical facts of scripture as such that are attacked or denied, but preoccupation with what satisfies sense alone.

77. *Q. Thal.* 50 (CCSG 381,39-40): ἡ φθορὰ τῶν παρερχομένων. This is equated with interpretation "in the manner of the Jews" (Ἰουδαϊκῶς).

78. Ibid. (CCSG 381,46-58).

79. *Amb.* 10 (PG 91.1160B); cf. Ps.-Dionysius, *De div. nom.* 4.11 (PG 3.708C-D).

80. Cf. Völker, *Maximus Confessor als Meister des geistlichen Lebens*, 261-262: "Scripture corresponds to man as a whole reality, but so too its unity is preserved amid all the differences that lie in nature, and even the baser levels have a relative right to exist, since truth is revealed to us precisely διὰ τῶν γραμμάτων. Just as man must employ σάρξ and αἴσθησις as necessary aids, so too the gospel must employ the Law and the Prophets."

81. See, e.g., the strongly apologetic tone of Henri de Lubac's treatment of Origen's attitude toward the literal sense in *Histoire et esprit: L'intelligence de l'Écriture d'après Origène* (Paris: Aubier, 1950), 92-138.

82. *Q. Thal.* 17 (CCSG 111,19-21).

83. See ibid. 52 (CCSG 417,51-62), where Maximus is faced with the problem of how, in 2 Chron. 32:25-26, the wrath of God came upon Hezekiah *and* the inhabitants of Judah and Jerusalem, when the text only cites Hezekiah's guilt: "The scripture further says that 'Hezekiah's heart was proud.' It does not also go on to say that the heart of the inhabitants of Jerusalem and Judah was proud. Thus I could not understand why God punished those among them who were blameless together with him who was to blame. For it says, 'And Hezekiah's heart was proud; and wrath came upon him and upon Judah and Jerusalem,' but the text has not said about the latter that they too were proud. Therefore, since a solution to difficulties is impossible for those who have given prominence to the literal sense and preferred the specific word (τὸ ῥητόν) to the true meaning, let us approach the spiritual understanding (πνευματικὴ κατανόησις) of the scriptures and discover the inexhaustible truth hidden within the literal sense, like a light shining before the lovers of truth." In his allegorical interpretation (ibid., 417,63-419,88), in turn, Maximus goes on to interpret "Judah" as the "habit of repentance," and "Jerusalem" as the "habit of impassibility," or "Judah" as "practical philosophy" and "Jerusalem" as "contemplative mystagogy." Whenever the contemplative mind ("Hezekiah") falls into pride and takes credit for its own accomplishments, God also allows practical philosophy to be polluted with passions, and contemplation to be defiled with false ideas.

84. See ibid. 55 (CCSG 459,294-461,298): "According to the literal sense (κατὰ τὴν ἱστορίαν), it appears that Zorobabel by no means had in his hand a plummet of tin that contained seven eyes, nor were those the Lord's eyes, nor did they look upon all the earth (cf. Zech. 4:10). Therefore, since it is completely impossible to take the text literally (κατὰ τὴν λέξιν), let us proceed toward the true meaning of the scriptures." In the spiritual sense, then, Zerubbabel is a type of Christ; the "plummet of tin," faith in him; the "seven eyes," the seven operations of the Holy Spirit.

85. Ibid. 52 (CCSG 423,160-425,171).

86. See above, chapter 1, n. 205-207 and related text.
87. *Q. Thal.* 17 (CCSG 115,76-77).
88. See Croce, *Tradizione e ricerca*, 56-57.
89. *Q. Thal.* 7 (CCSG 73,9-27). Citing what was a traditional interpretation, Maximus observes: "Some therefore say that scripture calls men who died before Christ's sojourn 'dead': for example, those in the flood, those at the time of the building of the tower, those in Sodom, those in Egypt, and others who, in different times and ways, received the multifarious punishment and extraordinary impositions of divine judgments." They are able to receive salvation only by the mediation of the Savior, who descended into Hades to proclaim the knowledge of God.
90. Ibid. (CCSG 73,28-75,41).
91. Ibid. 37. See above, chapter 1, n. 195-196 and related text.
92. Ibid. 9 (CCSG 79,2-81,40). Here Thalassius inquires how 1 John 3:2 ("what we shall be did not yet appear") can agree with 1 Cor. 2:10 ("God has revealed to us through the Spirit"). Maximus concludes, after an analysis of other relevant NT texts, that Paul means that only the general future σκοπός of eschatological salvation has been revealed to him. Paul concurs with John in being ignorant of the actual *mode* of future deification. Maximus cites a number of texts where Paul claims not to have laid hold of the fullness of this future experience (e.g., 2 Cor. 5:7; Phil. 3:13-14).
93. *Q. Thal.* 49 (CCSG 355,90-92).
94. On this important notion in Origen's hermeneutics, see Marguerite Harl's discussion in her introduction to *Origène: Philocalie, 1-20 sur les Écritures*, SC 302 (Paris: Les Éditions du Cerf, 1983), 133-135. She observes: "Origen ranks all sorts of biblical phrases among those that must be transposed: not only metaphors that require one to comprehend an interior reality on the basis of what is said of external objects, not only anthropomorphisms where God is concerned, but still also the totality of what is presented in 'the letter' of texts under the mask of history and legislation, and that must be transposed into signs for the spiritual life or teachings on the future world" (p. 134).
95. See also de Lubac, *Histoire et esprit*, especially 187ff, on the internalization of biblical events in terms of the soul's own spiritual combat.
96. Origen, *Comm. in Joann.* 20.10 (GCSO 4.337,30-32): δεῖ πᾶσαν τὴν κατὰ τὸν Ἀβραὰμ ἀλληγοροῦντα ἱστορίαν ἕκαστον πνευματικῶς ποιῆσαι τῶν πεπραγμένων ὑπ' αὐτοῦ.
97. E.g., on the importance of "exemplary" and "allegorical" interpretation of scripture among the desert monks, see Burton-Christie, *Scripture and the Quest for Holiness*, 262ff.

98. *Ep.* 2.223 (PG 79.316B-317A). Emphasis added.

99. This exposition of the struggles of the heroic kings of the OT with the forces of evil (Pharaoh, Nebuchadnezzar, Sennacherib, etc.) was traditional since Origen: see de Lubac's analysis, with citations from Origen's exegesis, in *Histoire et esprit,* 187-191.

100. *Q. Thal.* 49 (CCSG, especially 355,68-359,169).

101. Ibid. 51 (CCSG 407,216-221).

102. This use of μεταβαίνειν closely parallels Maximus' use of διαβαίνειν in another text (*Q. Thal.* 63 [PG 669C]) speaking of this same *transitus* of the letter of scripture over to the intellect.

103. *Q. Thal.* 52 (CCSG 425,173-181).

104. Ibid. 19 (CCSG 119,7-30). Cf. also ibid. 39 (CCSG 259,14-45), where Maximus, commenting on the "three days" the Lord spent in the desert (Matt. 15:32), shows again the Logos as author of the laws and relates them more specifically to the spiritual life: "By a different manner of spiritual interpretation, the three days signify the three more universal laws: the written law, the natural law, and the spiritual law, or law of grace. Every one of these laws is in itself properly able to illuminate human nature, since the Creator of each law's light is none other than the sun of righteousness (Mal. 4:2). For just as it is totally impossible for there to be daylight without sun, so too a law cannot be just without the essential underlying Wisdom, who makes himself to rise in each law and fills the soul's intellectual eyes with intelligible light. The blessed David knew this very fact when he said, 'Your light is a lamp for my feet and a light for my path' (Ps. 118:105). He calls the written law a 'lamp' since, like a burning light, it skillfully sets fire to the wickedness of the passions with the diverse signs of corporeal symbols (σύμβολα), enigmas (αἰνίγματα), and figures (τύποι), for those who enhance their soul's progress (τὰ διαβήματα) by taking action against contrary powers. David calls the spiritual law, or the law of grace, a 'light' (φῶς) because it displays the eternal "path" without any art, without the use of sensible symbols. Along this path the contemplative mind races toward the highest summit of good things, God, who does not limit the mind's activity. For the light of the law of grace is never-ending, and there is no knowledge whatsoever that can confine its radiant beams. It may be, moreover, that what the prophet David calls 'feet' is the entire course of the godly life, or the stirrings of good thoughts in the soul, which are guided by the light of the written law. And what he calls the 'path' are the virtuous modes (τρόποι) of conduct, which accord with the natural law, and the principles (λόγοι) of knowledge, which accord with the spiritual law. This 'path' is made known by the presence of the divine Logos and brings man back to his true nature and Cause."

105. Cf. ibid. 38 (CCSG 255,13-26), where Maximus gives the "anagogical explanation" (ὁ τῆς ἀναγωγῆς λόγος) of the "seven brothers" for the one wife (Matt. 22:23-28) as "those laws given by God to human nature at the proper times for its training (παιδαγωγία) and for the production of the fruits of righteousness." The seven "laws" thus include: (1) the law given Adam in paradise; (2) the law given him after his expulsion from paradise; (3) the law given to Noah at the time of the ark; (4) the law of circumcision given to Abraham (5) the law given to Abraham concerning the sacrifice of Isaac; (6) the law given to Moses; and (7) the law of prophetic inspiration, predictive of the grace of the gospel. The woman's true husband, then, would be the gospel itself. Cf. also ibid. 41 (CCSG 281,33ff), where Maximus interprets the five ex-husbands of the Samaritan woman (John 4:16-18), who again represents human nature, as (1) the law in paradise; (2) the law after paradise; (3) the law operative during the flood in Noah's time; (4) the law of circumcision in Abraham's time; and (5) the law of the sacrifice of Isaac. All these died because of their inability to conceive with her the fruits of righteousness. The woman's present companion, then, is (6) the Mosaic law, an illegitimate husband either because it too failed to achieve righteousness, or because it was about to give way to a new husband, or law, the gospel of Christ. "For the Mosaic law was not given to human nature forever, but rather as an economy (ἐπ᾽ οἰκονομίᾳ) to train (παιδαγωγούσῃ) it for the greater and more mystical gospel (τὸ εὐαγγέλιον...μειζόν τε καὶ μυστικώτερον)." On a possible Augustinian connection of these texts, see the recent study of George Berthold, "Did Maximus the Confessor Know Augustine?" StPatr 17, ed. Elizabeth Livingstone (Oxford and New York: Pergamon Press, 1982), 16-17.

106. See, int. al., Q. Thal. 60 (PG 621A), where Maximus speaks of the incarnation expressly as "the terminus (πέρας) of providence" and "the recapitulation (ἀνακεφαλαίωσις) of the things God has created"; cf. also Amb. 41 (PG 41.1308D, 1309C-1312A).

107. Kosmische Liturgie, 288ff. Cf. also Dalmais, "La manifestation du Logos," 21; and his "La fonction unificatrice du Verbe Incarné," 459.

108. In a long exposition of the three laws in Q. Thal. 64 (PG 724C-728A), Maximus explains the peculiar mode of life (ἀναστροφὴ βίου) and disposition of the will (ἡ κατὰ τὴν γνώμην διάθεσις) proper to each law. The *natural law* (724C-725A) prevents sense from overpowering reason, and teaches the Golden Rule (Matt. 17:12; Luke 6:31) as a norm for all connatural beings; in this way, it leads all humanity voluntarily to a common will based on their common "natural principle" (ὁ τῆς φύσεως λόγος). The *written law* (725A-B) uses the fear of punishment to train the will, but, by gradually sustaining the good disposition of the will until it acquires a good *habitus*

(ἕξις), teaches the will a new love of others (τὸ φιλάλληλον), the biblical ἀγάπη (cf. Rom. 13:10). Thus human beings do not merely recognize their mutual best interest based on their common natural principle, but acquire a new charitable desire (πόθος). The fulfillment of the written law is thus "the natural principle obtaining a spiritual principle (ὁ λόγος πνευματικός)." This is the difference between "being" (τὸ εἶναι) and "well-being" (τὸ εὖ εἶναι). Through the *law of grace* (725C-728A), however, this love acquires a new and transcendent referent in the imitation of God's own love, the love of others more than ourselves (John 15:13); its fulfillment is the bestowal of a "transcendent principle" (ὁ ὑπὲρ φύσιν λόγος) that transforms human nature, without violating it, unto deification, or "eternal well-being" (τὸ ἀεὶ εὖ εἶναι). See also the discussion of Carl Laga, "Maximi Confessoris," 210-212. Laga notes that in this exposé of the three laws, Maximus "discloses the 'mechanism' that puts the laws in gear" (p. 211). But clearly it is a "mechanism," I would add, only relatively, conceived as such in a way that does not override free human interaction in the laws.

109. See *Q. Thal.* 15 (CCSG 101,7-103,40), where Maximus (commenting on how the Spirit can be "in all things," Wisd. 12:1) speaks of the three activities of the Holy Spirit (συνεκτικόν... νομοθετητικόν... θεοποιόν) commensurate with the operation of the three laws: "The Holy Spirit is not absent from any beings, especially inasmuch as they partake of reason. For he is *conserving* of each being's knowledge, because he who is God and Spirit of God in power providentially and eternally comprehends and arouses the natural principle (ὁ κατὰ φύσιν λόγος) of every being and thereby leads the sensory faculty to an awareness of sins committed against the law of nature, a law that keeps the free will complaisant with the reception of thoughts that are naturally right.... In this way the Holy Spirit is clearly in all things. In another respect, the Holy Spirit is in those who are under the (written) law, in virtue of being *lawgiver* and predictor of future mysteries, instilling in them a sense of the transgression of the commandments and a knowledge of the predicted fulfillment of the law in Christ.... In addition to the aforementioned manners, the Holy Spirit is also in all those who through faith have been allotted the divine and truly *deifying* name of Christ. He is present in them not only as guardian and providential motivator of the natural principle of beings, as demonstrator of the transgression of the commandments and protector thereof, as proclaimer of the prophecy of Christ, but also as creator of the sonship given them by grace through faith. For as worker of wisdom he comes into those who alone have been cleansed in body and soul by the exact observance of the commandments. He converses with them as his own, by simple and immaterial knowledge, and stamps their minds with

the undefiled grasp of ineffable realities, leading to deification." See also Berthold, "History and Exegesis," 395.

110. See *Kosmische Liturgie*, 288-300.

111. See above, A *Locus Classicus: Ambiguum* 10.

112. See von Balthasar, *Kosmische Liturgie*, 300-310.

113. See ibid., 310-312. Cf. Dalmais, "La manifestation du Logos," 22ff.

114. The mystery of *incarnation* is a fundamental principle for Maximus' whole theological enterprise: see *Amb.* 7 (PG 91.1084C-D): "The Logos of God, who is also [fully] God, wills to bring about the mystery of his embodiment always and in all things" (Βούλεται γὰρ ἀεὶ καὶ ἐν πᾶσιν ὁ τοῦ Θεοῦ Λόγος καὶ θεὸς τῆς αὐτοῦ ἐνσωματώσεως ἐνεργεῖσθαι τὸ μυστήριον). See also Thunberg, *Microcosm and Mediator*, 68-69, 342-350, 461.

115. This notion of different "incarnations" (analogically considered) of the Logos was basic to Origen. On the "incarnation" of the Logos in scripture in particular, see, int. al., *Comm. in Matt.* frag. (PG 17.289A-B); also *Comm. in Joann.* 1.19 (GCSO 4.23,28), where Origen declares that "the Logos in scripture is none other than Christ, God, the Logos, who 'was with God.'" Cf. also the Origenian texts assembled by von Balthasar under the theme of "The Scripture as Body," in *Origen: Spirit and Fire: A Thematic Anthology of His Writings*, trans. Robert J. Daly (Washington: The Catholic University of America Press, 1984), 86-88. An excellent study of the incarnation of the Logos in scripture in Origen's hermeneutics is Rolf Gögler, *Zur Theologie des biblischen Wortes bei Origenes* (Düsseldorf: Patmos-Verlag, 1963), especially 260-270. Gögler demonstrates that for Origen too, the Logos incarnate in scripture is indeed the *personal* Logos-Christ (pp. 262-263), who is also the very content of the intelligible mystery in scripture (pp. 268-270). See also De Lubac's important discussion in *Histoire et esprit*, 363-373.

116. Gregory of Nazianzus, *Or.* 38.2 (PG 36.313B).

117. *Amb.* 33 (PG 91.1285C-1288A). See also above, note 39 and related text, where the motif of the Logos "thickening" or incarnating himself in creation and scripture is introduced in *Amb.* 10 as well. See also Thunberg (*Microcosm and Mediator*, 81-82), who notes again the way Maximus, with his notion of three incarnations, ties together his "ontological" and "salvation-historical" perspectives in the person of the Logos: "The cosmological (ontological), the providential and the historical Logos are not separate elements in Maximus' theology, but consciously depicted as one and the same: Christ, the Son of God the Father, and the Lord

of the Church. He is the centre of the universe in the same manner as he is the centre of the economy of salvation. This fact is particularly made evident in a passage in Amb 33, where Maximus indicates a three-fold incarnation of the Logos.... This three-fold incarnation seems to be closely linked with Maximus' idea of three general laws in the world: natural law, written law, and the law of grace. Thus in Maximus' view, the Logos, on account of his general will to incarnate himself, holds together not only the λόγοι of creation but also the three aspects of creation, revelation (illumination) and salvation."

118. Thunberg, *Man and the Cosmos*, 160.
119. *Q. Thal.* 62 (PG 648A-B).
120. Ibid. (PG 649C-652A).
121. See, e.g., Thunberg, *Man and the Cosmos*, 162ff; and René Bornert, *Les commentaires byzantins de la divine liturgie, du VIIe au XVe siècle*, Archives de l'Orient chrétien 9 (Paris: Institut Français d'Études Byzantines, 1966), 112-113.
122. Thunberg, *Man and the Cosmos*, 163.
123. *Q. Thal.* 20 (CCSG 121,6-123,49).
124. *Cap. theol.* 1.66 (PG 90.1108A-B; trans. Berthold, *Maximus Confessor*, 139-140).
125. Ibid. 2.46 (PG 90.1237A-B). Cf. Thunberg, *Man and the Cosmos*, 164: "It is the historical Incarnation and its fulfilment in Christ's glorification (and then also the activities of the Spirit in the Church) that makes the content and reality of the symbols alive."
126. *Q. Thal.* 65 (PG 740B).
127. See *Myst.* 6 (PG 91.684A-D), and above, n. 31-32 and related text.
128. *Q. Thal.* 63 (PG 681A-B). Emphasis added.
129. Frequently in the *Q. Thal.* Maximus opposes the three terms "shadow" (σκιά), "figure" (τύπος) and "riddle" (αἴνιγμα) to their counterpart, the spiritual "truth" (ἀλήθεια): int. al., *Q. Thal.* 20 (CCSG 121, passim); ibid. 62 (PG 648A-B). See also the list of parallel hermeneutical terms gathered by Völker, *Maximus Confessor als Meister des geistlichen Lebens*, 273, n. 5-6.
130. Bornert, *Les commentaires byzantins*, 115.
131. Ibid., 115-116, citing principally *Q. Thal.* 46 (CCSG 309,16ff) and *Amb.* 21 (PG 91.1253C-D) on the parallel between ἐικών and ἀρχέτυπος.
132. Bornert, *Les commentaires byzantins*, 115-116.
133. The issue is complicated by the fact that, while the normal subordination is between τύπος and ἀλήθεια, Maximus can also sometimes

subordinate τύπος to ἀρχέτυπος (e.g., *Q. Thal.* 55, CCSG 481,24-26).

134. Dalmais, "La manifestation du Logos," 21.

135. Thunberg, *Man and the Cosmos*, 165-166, citing *Q. Thal.* 63 (PG 677B) on the superiority of the Prophets to the Law; and *Cap. theol.* 1.90 (PG 90.1120C), where the Law is a "shadow" (σκιά) of the gospel, and the gospel an "image" (εἰκών) of the good things to come (cf. Heb. 10:1); cf. ibid. 2.14 (PG 90.1132A) on the shining clothes of the transfigured Christ as representing the gospels, and Moses and Elijah, on each side of him, as the Law and the Prophets. (See above, n. 37, on the Origenian source of this distinction). However, Maximus also speaks of the shining garments as the literal words of scripture in general in *Amb.* 10, quoted above.

136. Cf. *Comm. in Joann.* 1.9 (GCSO 4.12); also *Comm. in Rom.* 4.8 (PG 14.992B-C), where Origen envisions the order of Mosaic event—Christ event—the future reality of the Church culminating in Christ's second coming in glory.

137. Thunberg, *Man and the Cosmos*, 166.

138. *Q. Thal.* 60 (PG 620D-621B, 624B-D). Cf. the detailed discussion of the larger significance of this text in Maximus' thought in Riou, *Le monde et l'Église* 92-103; also the study of Juan Miguel Garrigues, "Le dessein d'adoption du Créateur dans son rapport au Fils d'après s. Maxime le Confesseur," in *Maximus Confessor: Actes du Symposium sur Maxime le Confesseur, Fribourg, 2-5 septembre 1980*, ed. Felix Heinzer and Christoph von Schönborn, Paradosis 27 (Fribourg: Éditions Universitaires, 1980), 173-192.

139. *Q. Thal.* 60 (PG 637A); cf. ibid. 50 (CCSG 381,56) and ibid. 54 (CCSG 457,231-232): τὸ τῆς σαρκώσεως μυστήριον also ibid. 64 (PG 697D): τὸ μυστήριον τῆς οἰκονομίας.

140. Ibid. 22 (CCSG 137,25-26).

141. Ibid. 42 (CCSG 289,71); ibid. 64 (PG 713B).

142. Ibid. 27 (CCSG 191,12-14).

143. Ibid. 63 (PG 665C).

144. The mystery of the incarnation and its effects are the subject of detailed exegesis throughout the text; beside *Q. Thal.* 60, cf. especially the following: *Q. Thal.* 21 (CCSG 127,5-133,114); ibid. 22 (CCSG 137,4-16 and passim); ibid. 53 (CCSG 431,6ff; 435,101-437,122); ibid. 54 (CCSG 455,203-467,406); ibid. 61 (PG 629Aff and passim); ibid. 62 (PG 648A-652C; ibid. 63 (PG 672C); ibid. 64 (PG 697D-700C).

145. Here, as François Combefis noted (PG 720D-721D) in his edition of the *Q. Thal.*, the "three days" before Nineveh's destruction in the LXX, as opposed to the "forty days" in the Hebrew text, turns out to be of pivotal

importance to Maximus' Christian typology.

146. *Q. Thal.* 64 (720C-721B).

147. See Berthold ("History and Exegesis," especially 391-394), who wants to compare the more "gnosticizing" allegory of Evagrius with Maximus' more salvation-historical interest. Berthold insists that for Maximus, "the mystery (in scripture) is not the noetic contemplation of the One but the deep consideration of the Father's βουλή and the σκοπός of redemption and the spiritual work of deification" (p. 394). Thus although Maximus, like Evagrius, can interpret many events in the gospels and the life of Jesus in terms of a higher referent (Berthold notes *Cap. theol.* 1.60-63, 65-67, 71, 72, 75, 76 (and I could add *Q. Thal.* 3, 4, 20, 38, 39, 40, 41, 47), the historical element is in no way slighted but gives way symbolically to deeper levels of reflection on the wider implications of their reference to Christ (p. 394). Again, Maximus' principal concern in his exegesis is with the second level, or intermediate phase, of theological speculation, the level of the mystery behind the letter, not the trans-intelligible or apophatic level that is the subject of θεολογία proper.

148. The basis of this distinction is the dialectic established between the two references in Paul: (1) the "coming ages" when "God will show his riches" (Eph. 2:7); and (2) the "end of the ages" which already "has come upon us" (1 Cor. 10:11). Thalassius has asked (CCSG 137,2-3) how the end could be said to have already occurred and yet still be future, the classic problem of "realized eschatology" in Paul.

149. *Q. Thal.* 22 (CCSG 137,4-141,82). This very same mystery of incarnation-deification is also dramatically laid out in Maximus' *Commentary on the Lord's Prayer* (see Berthold's translation, *Maximus Confessor*, 101-119).

150. See *Q. Thal.* 32 (CCSG 225,17-33), and above, n. 30 and related text.

151. Ibid. 65 (PG 737B-741B).

152. Ibid. 27 (CCSG 193,48-64).

153. Cf. Dalmais, "La fonction unificatrice du Verbe incarné," 447: "before being a metaphysician, Maximus is a monk and all his thought is arranged according to the perspectives of a spiritual anthropology."

154. The same is true of human sensibility itself, as described by Maximus in the opening of *Q. Thal.* 61 (PG 628A-B), where he contrasts the archetypal sensibility of human nature to its existential reality: "When God created human nature, he did not create pleasure or pain along with it as regards its sensibility. Instead, he furnished it with a certain intellectual capacity (δύναμις) for pleasure, whereby humanity would be able to enjoy God ineffably. But at the instant of his creation (ἅμα τῷ γενέσθαι), the first man

forfeited this intellectual power (I mean the natural desire of the mind for God) to sense. Indeed at his very first movement he unnaturally produced in himself, by the medium of sense (αἴσθησις) a pleasure (for which he had received the capacity) in sensible things (τὰ αἰσθητά)." See also on this text and anthropological theme, Sherwood, "Maximus and Origenism," 9-10; Schönborn, "Plaisir et douleur," 278-279.

155. Cf. *Q. Thal.* intro. (CCSG 31,227-39,381), a long exposition of the fall as a deification of the corporeal and a deviation into the "composite knowledge" (ἡ σύνθετος γνῶσις) of sensible things. See notably ibid. (37,331ff), where Maximus (in dependence on Gregory of Nyssa, *De hom. opif.* 19-20 [PG 44.196Cff]) allegorizes the "tree of the knowledge of good and evil" as the phenomenal creation, which, he explains, gives rise to a composite knowledge "since creation contains the spiritual principles of visible things that nourish the mind, and since it has the natural ability to please sense as well as to sustain the mind."

156. *Q. Thal.* 27 (CCSG 195,65-91). Emphasis added.

157. *DS* 2.2, s.v. "Contemplation"–III. Contemplation chez les grecs et autres orientaux chrétiens (II. La θεωρία φυσική), col. 1820.

158. See Thunberg's observations on Maximus' dependence on Evagrius' threefold scheme in *Microcosm and Mediator*, 354ff.

159. See the various designations of Maximus for the three phases as compiled by Loosen, *Logos und Pneuma*, 8. Cf. also Völker's thorough analysis of the terminology of the three phases in *Maximus Confessor als Meister des geistlichen Lebens*, 236-248.

160. Cf. Dalmais, "La doctrine ascétique," 24; Völker, *Maximus Confessor als Meister des geistlichen Lebens*, 234ff.

161. Thunberg, *Microcosm and Mediator*, 357-363.

162. E.g., *Q. Thal.* 55 (CCSG 501,325ff), where Maximus speaks of the νοῦς which, in its practical life, having determined the length of service for virtue of its "servants," practical reason (λόγος) and reflection (διάνοια), passes over to contemplation (θεωρία). Even in this text, however, there is really no necessary implication that πρᾶξις is transcended by θεωρία.

163. Cf. ibid. 36 (CCSG 243,13-19, 24-29): "Whoever is initiated in piety and instructed about works of righteousness fulfills only ethical practice through an absolute obedience and faith, just as he consumes, like meat, only the literal aspects (τὰ φαινόμενα) of the virtues. In faith he concedes to God the principles of the commandments (οἱ ἐν τῶν ἐντολῶν λόγοι), in which principles lies the knowledge (γνῶσις) of perfect things; but meanwhile he is unable to extend his mind the length of that knowledge.... Everyone who is unable through knowledge discreetly to enjoy the strong drink of inaccessible

kinds of knowledge from the bowl of God's wisdom, in effect 'pours out' the principles (λόγοι) at the 'base' of faith (cf. Deut. 12:27). In other words, he concedes to faith the knowledge of the principles that are beyond his own ability." Elsewhere too (e.g., *Cap. car.* 1.86, PG 90.980C), Maximus makes statements which could, if isolated, be taken as meaning a "chronological" succession from πρᾶξις to θεωρία.

164. *Q. Thal.* 3 (CCSG 55,18-20); cf. ibid. 52 (CCSG 419,72-73). The same principle obtains at ibid. 24 (CCSG 157,5-18), where, in an allegory on Acts 12:10 (Peter's passing by a first guard and then a second guard before coming on the "iron gate"), Maximus indicates how, after passing beyond the passions and acquiescence in those passions through πρακτική φιλοσοφία, the mind comes to the "iron gate" of the proclivity of sense toward sensible things; here φυσική θεωρία lays open the gate and conducts the mind toward intelligible truths.

165. Ibid. 49 (CCSG 357,104-109); cf. ibid. (359,137ff), where Maximus again notes that the mind that has knowledge on a spiritual level need neither pursue natural contemplation, nor flee the demons, nor do anything else when the demons attack save pray alone (Mark 9:29) and subdue the body with remedial toils, destroying pride and safeguarding the soul with virtues like self-control and patience; and again the same principle, ibid. (365,257ff). This text is noted by Lemaître ("Contemplation chez les grecs et autres orientaux chrétiens," II. La θεωρία φυσική, col. 1808-1809) as indicative of the sensitivity of the Eastern Fathers to the danger of illusion through contemplation by itself. In *Ep.* 2 (PG 91.392-408), Maximus speaks as well of a certain deification or union with God attained purely through love and the *vita practica*, without mention of natural contemplation at all (see also Thunberg, *Microcosm and Mediator*, 370).

166. *Q. Thal.* 55 (CCSG 507,426-430, 434ff). Such is the difference between the vainglorious Absalom and David, who perfected his virtue with knowledge.

167. Ibid. 48 (CCSG 339,151-154).

168. The same holds true in general throughout the ascetic works of Maximus. George Berthold (*Maximus Confessor*, 90-91, n. 67) suggests that Gregory of Nazianzus may be a likely inspiration for Maximus' balance of πρᾶξις and θεωρία.

169. *Q. Thal.* 58 (PG 596A).

170. Ibid. 3 (CCSG 55,23-42). Cf. *Amb.* 57 (PG 91.1380D-1381B), where Maximus similarly allegorizes Peter and John respectively as πρᾶξις and θεωρία, running in competition with one another from the empty tomb (cf. John 20:1-10) yet coinciding in their purpose. See similar such allegories

in Q. Thal. 52 (CCSG 417,63ff); ibid. 27 (CCSG 197,113ff; 199,134ff); ibid. 54 (CCSG 447,62ff). See also ibid. 45 (CCSG 305,5ff).

171. Cf. Q. Thal. 35 (CCSG 239,15ff, 27ff).

172. Ibid. 63 (PG 680D-681A).

173. Cf. ibid. 3 (CCSG 55,17-22), where, in a preliminary allegory of Peter and John as forerunners preparing human nature for the "mystical feasting" (i.e., μυστική θεολογία), Maximus says that Peter symbolizes "the law of the old covenant," and John "the law of the new covenant": "While the former scours human nature of all defilement by practical philosophy (πρακτική φιλοσοφία), the latter, through contemplative mystagogy (θεωρητική μυσταγωγία), lifts the mind spiritually from corporeal objects to wonders related to intelligible realities..." In a similar vein, see ibid. 63 (PG 677C-D); also ibid. 52 (CCSG 425,178-181), where Maximus speaks of the tropes (τρόποι) of the divine words (λόγοι) of OT scripture, interpreted spiritually, being able to cleanse the body of passions and make it a "rational factory of virtue"; also ibid. 39 (CCSG 259,26ff), where again Maximus speaks of the corporeal σύμβολα, αἰνίγματα, and τύποι of the written law being able to rid the body of the passions.

174. See ibid. 64 (PG 709B), where Maximus suggests that this λόγος is fundamental to πράξις because it comprehends the λόγοι of the commandments. He also indicates (ibid. 708C-D) that rational knowledge is necessary in order to acknowledge God as the source of virtue and to achieve (in Aristotelian terms) the true mean (μεσότης) in virtue between excess (ὑπερβολή) and defect (ἔλλειψις). Throughout the Q. Thal., Maximus reiterates the pivotal role of reason in πράξις: cf. ibid. 54 (CCSG 445,27 [ἡ μετά λόγου πράξις]); ibid. (CCSG 461,315-320); ibid. (CCSG 493,205ff); ibid. 55 (CCSG 497,285ff) on how λόγος and διάνοια serve a term as "slaves" to πρακτική φιλοσοφία.

175. See Amb. 10 (PG 91.1112D-1116C). Cf. also Myst. 5 (PG 91.672D-673A), where Maximus discusses the close relation between τό πρακτικόν and τό θεωρητικόν in the soul, and so too between λόγος and νοῦς.

176. Q. Thal. 53 (CCSG 435,91-95), referring to 2 Chron. 32:33.

177. Ibid. 39 (CCSG 259,24-261,45; also quoted above, 165, n. 104). This is is not to say that a certain correspondence is not still applicable. Cf. ibid. (CCSG 261,46-58), where Maximus describes how the believer is rewarded for faithfulness to the written law by complete deliverance from the passions (=the mortification aspect of πράξις), for faithfulness to the natural law by the infallible operation and mutual interrelation of the natural faculties (=the precondition for θεωρία), and for their faithfulness to the spiritual law

by separation from natural creatures and union with God (=the substance of μυστικὴ θεολογία).

178. See above, n. 110-113 and related text.

179. Cf. *Q. Thal.* 58 (PG 596D) on the natural tension between the operations of αἴσθησις and νοῦς. Cf. also ibid. 62 (656B-C).

180. Ibid. 58 (PG 597A-B).

181. Cf. ibid. 43 (CCSG 293,33-295,39), for this interpretation of the trees.

182. On the role of reason (λόγος) in contemplation, see ibid. 49 (CCSG 355,89-357,109): "The 'waters from outside the city' (2 Chron. 32:3)–that is, outside the soul–which formed the river flowing through the city are the concepts (νοήματα) that, in the course of natural contemplation, are conveyed from the sensible object through every one of the senses and stream into the mind. By these 'waters,' or notions, reason (λόγος) passes like a river through the city of the soul and achieves the knowledge (ἐπιστήμη) of sensible things. Until reason passes through it, the soul cannot repel the images and illusions of sensible things, through which the wicked and destructive (demonic) power impends, and is prone to wage war on the soul. Therefore Hezekiah says, '...lest the king of Assyria come and find a lot of water, and be strengthened' (2 Chron. 32:4), as if he were the discerning mind (νοῦς) telling its faculties, at the moment when the passions are attacking, 'Let us cease from natural contemplation and engage in prayer alone, and in mortification of the body by practical philosophy.'" See also ibid. 49 (CCSG 357,131ff), where Maximus speaks of reason's task being to destroy the *habitus* conducive to evil and the operation of the senses in relation to the faculties of the soul; cf. ibid. 53 (CCSG 435,75ff) on "death" to sensible objects by elimination of sensible activity in the soul. Cf. ibid. 34 (CCSG 235,20ff), where Maximus envisions one role of πρακτικὴ φιλοσοφία being the "separation of sense from its proclivity toward sensible objects."

183. Cf. *Amb.* 10 (PG 91.1112D-1116C), where Maximus discusses the three distinctive psychic powers of νοῦς, λόγος, and αἴσθησις, each of which is directed toward its own kind of knowledge, and all of which are interrelated and culminate in the function of the νοῦς, which dwells in a non-conceptual contemplation of God supported "from beneath" by reason and sense. On the positive evaluation of sense and the sensible, see *Amb.* 10 (PG 91.1160A-B).

184. Thus in *Q. Thal.* 48 (CCSG 341,187-193) Maximus indicates that the mind not only seeks to establish intellectually the union of particulars to the universal among the beings it contemplates, but also "the union *of the*

mind (νοῦς) to sense (αἴσθησις), of heaven to earth, of sensible things to intelligible things, and of nature to its principle. At all of these unions, the contemplative mind (ὁ θεωρητικὸς νοῦς), using its own science, and establishing true doctrines for each particular thing, wisely builds 'the towers at the angles' (2 Chron. 26:9): in other words, it builds, at all of these particular unions, dogmas that serve to bind them together" (emphasis added).

185. See ibid. 16 (CCSG 109,72-93), where Maximus discusses the actual transformation of the passions themselves through such a self-contemplation. For he writes here that: "All passion is, in an interconnected fashion, composed entirely of a sensible object (τὸ αἰσθητόν), sense (αἴσθησις), and a natural faculty (φυσικὴ δύναμις)–that is (of the natural faculties) wrath (θυμός), concupiscence (ἐπιθυμία), and reason (λόγος) deviated from its natural function. Thus if the mind contemplates the goal (τέλος) of the sensible object, of sense itself, and of the natural faculty dependent on sense, with a view to something different in constitution; and if it is able, discriminating each of these things, to lead them back to their proper natural principle; and if the mind is able to contemplate, in relation to itself, the sensible object independent of the attachment of sense to that object, and sense apart from the kinship of the sensible object to it, and concupiscence, or, let us say, any other natural faculty apart from its impassioned state in conjunction with sense and the sensible object–such that this sort of agitation of passion triggers this contemplation–then the mind 'melts down the calf' (Exod. 32:4). By that I mean that whatever passion arises, the mind 'spreads' the composition of that passion 'over the water' (Exod. 32:20) of knowledge and causes the mere image itself of the passions to disappear by restoring to their true stature the deeds of those who perform them absolutely in accordance with nature. May it be us who 'melt down the calf' in the soul and make it disappear, such that the soul has the genuine divine image alone, absolutely undefiled by external things." For this theme of the transformation of the passions, heavily influenced by Gregory of Nyssa's theological anthropology, see ibid. 1 (CCSG 47,18-49,33) and above, n. 171. See also the discussion of Thunberg, *Microcosm and Mediator*, 219.

186. *Q. Thal.* 49 (CCSG 363,210-224). This positive role of the senses in the intellectual life of the soul is developed in detail in *Amb.* 21 (PG 91.1248A-1259C); on this pivotal text and the importance of αἴσθησις in Maximus' spiritual anthropology, see Panayiotis Nellas, *Deification in Christ: Orthodox Perspectives on the Nature of the Human Person*, trans. Norman Russell (Crestwood, N.Y.: St. Vladimir's Seminary Press, 1987), 54-57, 216-218.

187. Cf. von Balthasar, *Kosmische Liturgie*, 302ff; Völker, *Maximus*

Confessor als Meister des geistlichen Lebens, 296-318; Thunberg, *Microcosm and Mediator*, 368-374; Lemaître, "Contemplation chez les grecs et autres orientaux chrétiens" (II. La θεωρία φυσική), cols. 1806-1827.

188. See, e.g., *Q. Thal.* 13 (CCSG 95,18-97,41): "Or perhaps the 'invisible things' of God (Rom. 1:20) are none other than his 'eternal power and divinity,' the salient indicator of which is the surpassing majesty of created things. For just as we believe on the basis of existent things that there is a God who exists as Lord, so too we are taught, on the basis of the essential diversity (διαφορά) of created beings according to species, the wisdom that God has essentially infused in them, a wisdom that underlies and comprehends beings. Furthermore, we learn, from the essential movement (κίνησις) of beings according to species, of the life which God has essentially infused in them, a life that underlies those beings and is indispensible to them. These beings apprehend, through wise contemplation of creation, the principle (λόγος) of the Holy Trinity (I mean, of the Father, Son, and Holy Spirit). The condemned therefore have not been taught through the contemplation of beings (ἡ τῶν ὄντων θεωρία) the Cause (αἰτία) together with his natural attributes (that is, his 'power and divinity'). So then the creation cries aloud through the things made therein and, as it were, announces, to those who are intellectually capable of hearing it, their proper Cause, triadically recited: I am speaking of the God and Father and his ineffable power and divinity, that is, his only-begotten Logos and Holy Spirit. For these are the 'invisible things' of God that are intellectually perceived from the creation of the world." This text captures the essence of natural contemplation in Maximus; it is based on a knowledge of God in his attributes, through which we perceive him *qua* Cause, and not *in se*. Indeed creation only affords us "adumbrations" of the "economic" Trinity, not a knowledge of its inner being. On this concept of contemplation, see also Thunberg, *Man and the Cosmos*, 32, 45-46.

189. Cf. ibid. 32 (CCSG 225,12-16); ibid. intro. (CCSG 17,7-8); ibid. 13 (CCSG 95,19: ἡ μεγαλοπρέπεια τῶν γεγονότων).

190. See, e.g., *Amb.* 10 (PG 91.1165B). For Maximus, again, natural (and *ipso facto* scriptural) contemplation remains strictly at the "second level" of theology, the transit from the sensible to the intelligible, from historical to mystical revelation, which anticipates but does not accede to the level of apophatic or mystical θεολογία proper, the level of union to God.

191. Cf. *Q. Thal.* 25 (CCSG 161,34-35); ibid. 10 (CCSG 87,86-87); ibid. 65 (γνῶσις ἐν πνεύματι, PG 744C, 745C,748A-B); ibid. (πνευματικὴ γνῶσις, 745D); ibid. 52 (πνευματικὴ θεωρία, CCSG 417,40); cf. ibid. 63 (PG 677A). Maximus can also speak (ibid. 65, PG 745C) of ἡ ἐν πνεύματι μυστικὴ θεωρία and ἡ ἐν χάριτι πνευματικὴ θεωρία.

192. See, e.g., ibid. 25 (CCSG 161,46-53).

193. See also René Bornert, "Explication de la liturgie et interprétation de l'Écriture chez Maxime le Confesseur," *StPatr* 10, TU 107 (Berlin: Akademie-Verlag, 1970), 323-327. Bornert, through his close analysis of the *Mystagogia*, observes how Maximus also applies this θεωρία to the investigation of the liturgical mysteries, in a way parallel to natural and scriptural contemplation..

194. See above, The *Logoi* of Scripture and Maximus' Notion of Accommodation in the *Quaestiones ad Thalassium*, 106ff.

195. Maximus frequently speaks, in fact, of the πνευματικοὶ λόγοι: cf. *Q. Thal.* 51 (CCSG 397,63-64); ibid. (407,206-207); ibid. 53 (433,61). See also Loosen (*Logos und Pneuma*, 91-92), who observes: "The pneumatic character of things is thus an order that, in the view of our religious contemplation, preserves them according to their intentional being; yet it is an order that is at once independent of this human observation and is grounded in the essential God-likeness and God-relatedness of created things." Cf. also Lemaître, "Contemplation chez les grecs et autres orientaux chrétiens" (II. La θεωρία φυσική), col. 1820: "The logos of things would thus be like the pneumatic sense of things."

196. *Q. Thal.* 65 (PG 741C-744A). "For no one who relies solely on the corporeal observance of the law could ever entertain at all a natural principle or thought, since symbols are not the same thing as nature. But if symbols are not the same thing as nature, then obviously he who remained caught up in the law's symbols as prototypes can never naturally see the Source of created beings, and therefore irrationally rejects natural principles" (744A).

197. See ibid. (PG 744A-B), where Maximus adduces a passage from Josh. 9:3ff (Joshua's endeavors to defend the Gabaonites from their enemies and preserve them by making them "wood-bearers" and "water-carriers") as suggesting allegorically the incarnate Logos, who redeems the natural λόγοι from our impassioned thoughts and conduct and makes them into bearers of the mysteries of the divine tabernacle (cf. Josh. 9:27), that is, the Church.

198. See ibid. (PG 737B-745D passim).

199. Ibid. (PG 745D-748A). Emphasis added.

200. *Myst.* 23 (PG 91.697D-700B): "And consider how the soul in fleeing (sensible things) headlong comes as into a church to an inviolable shelter of peace in the natural contemplation in the Spirit (ἡ ἐν πνεύματι φυσικὴ θεωρία), and how free of any fighting or disorder it enters it together with reason and before the Word and our great and true High Priest of God. There it learns, by symbols of the divine readings which take place, the principles (λόγοι) of beings and the marvelous and grand mystery of divine

Providence revealed in the Law and the Prophets, and it receives in each, by the beautiful instruction divinely given in them through the holy angels who spiritually communicate to it the true understanding, the peaceful meanings with the strengthening and preserving enchantment of the divine and ardent desire for God by means of the spiritual appeal of the divine chants singing it mystically. And consider again how the soul passes beyond this and concentrates on the one and only summit, the holy Gospel, which collects these principles together into one and in which pre-exist in one form all the principles both of Providence and of existing things in a single burst of meaning" (trans. Berthold, *Maximus Confessor,* 204-205).

201. *Amb.* 10 (PG 91.1133A-1136B).

202. See Thunberg, *Microcosm and Mediator,* 72-74. Contemplation of the οὐσίαι of creatures indicates God as Cause of existents. Κίνησις deals with the movements of beings in relation to the Creator-Logos and thus focuses on the *providence* of God. Maximus makes clear that this is a movement of diverse species in their irreducible identity and toward a transcendent self-realization (in Aristotelian terms), contra the Origenist-Evagrianist "myth" of the return of fallen beings back to their primordial spiritual unity. Διαφορά elicits God's *judgment* in diversifying his creatures and leading them back to himself in their own moral freedom. Θέσις and κρᾶσις in turn have to do with the peculiar moral and spiritual status of beings in relation to God.

203. See the text from *Amb.* 37 quoted above.

204. Maximus explains (*Amb.* 37 [PG 91.1293C]) that scripture is contemplated in terms of "time" (κατὰ χρόνον) whenever it indicates the category of "when" (τὸ Ποτέ), "was" (τὸ Ἦν), "is" (τὸ Ἔστι), "will be" (τὸ Ἔσται), "before this or that" (τὸ Πρὸ τοῦδε), "now" (τὸ Παρόν), "after this or that" (τὸ Μετὰ τόδε), "in the time of this or that" (τὸ Ἐπὶ τοῦδε), "from the beginning of" (Ἀπ' ἀρχῆς), "the past" (τὸ Παρελθόν), "the future" (τὸ Μέλλον), years, seasons, months, weeks, days, nights, and parts of these, and anything else of this sort.

205. Under the contemplation in terms of place (κατὰ τόπον) Maximus includes (ibid., PG 91.1293C-D) designations in scripture of heaven, earth, air, sea, inhabited earth, far limits of the earth, countries, islands, cities, shrines, villages, fields, mountains, valleys, roads, rivers, deserts, cisterns, threshing floors, vineyards, and anything else of this nature.

206. Maximus includes (ibid., PG 91.1293D) under contemplation according to genus or race (κατὰ γένος) two categories: (1) the "general" (καθολικῶς), that is, indications of angels, or intellectual essences in the heavens, and the sun, moon, stars, fire; indications of things existing in the

air, on land, or in the sea; and whether they be animals, zoophytes, plants, minerals mined from the earth by human engineering, and the like; (2) the "peculiar" (ἰδιοτρόπως), that is, designations of human beings, nations, peoples, languages, tribes, homelands, and anything else of this sort that it names, with or without reference to number.

207. Maximus (ibid., PG 91.1293D) sees the contemplation in terms of person (κατὰ πρόσωπον) as embracing significations *by name* of this or that angel, archangel, or other intellectual essences, or of an Abraham, Isaac, Jacob, or other such figures referred to praiseworthily (ἐπαινετῶς) or censoriously (ψεκτῶς) in the scriptural text.

208. Under contemplation according to dignity or occupation (κατ' ἀξίαν or κατ' ἐπιτήδευμα), Maximus includes (ibid., PG 91.1296A) scriptural designations of king or kingdom, shepherd or flock, priest or priesthood, farmer, general, architect, or anything else differentiating human professions.

209. Ibid. (PG 91.1296A-D).

210. Int. al., see *Q. Thal.* 7 (CCSG 73,5-75,41), where Maximus deals with the "dead" in 1 Pet. 4:6 ("For this reason, the gospel was preached even to the dead, so that, while judged in the flesh like men, they might live in the Spirit like God"). Maximus sees this case, he says, as indicative of how scripture frequently scrambles the different tenses of time (the future as though it were the past, the past as though it were future) and speaks of the present as the time before and after itself. He further explains that this has led some to interpret the "dead" (past tense) here simply as sinners who died "before Christ's earthly sojourn" (πρὸ τῆς ἐπιδημίας Χριστοῦ). But he suggests that the "dead" here may be those who in the present carry the death of Jesus in their bodies (2 Cor. 4:10), that is, those who mortify themselves spiritually here and now. Cf., in turn, ibid. 55 (CCSG 509,459-460), where Maximus speaks of the penitent mind as "entering intellectually into the time before grace" (εἰς τὸν πρὸ τῆς χάριτος χρόνον τῇ διανοίᾳ γενόμενος).

211. Cf. ibid. 27 (CCSG 197,113-199,133) on the spiritual significance of "Joppa" (Acts 10:5) as the scene of Peter's vision of the descending sheet: "'Joppa' is translated 'inspection' (κατασκοπή), signifying the watchful care that befits those who are practical. For, unless the city was situated on the heights, lying on the very hill above the sea, it would have fallen into scores of waves. Therefore it seems to me to indicate that person who builds virtue, like a city, upon the heights of knowledge. Such a person is not far away from involuntary trials, since he has close by, like the sea, the sensual condition that has not yet been completely beaten back and thus requires his close inspection" (197,116-124). Cf. also ibid. 28 (CCSG 203,26ff) on "the East" (Gen. 11:2) as the true knowledge of God, and "Senaar" (rendered

etymologically) as the multiple doctrines of God into which the builders of the tower of Babel sank.

212. Cf. Maximus' extensive exposition (ibid. 49, CCSG 355,75ff) of Hezekiah's "elders" and "captains" as being the faculties of the soul in their service to the νοῦς.

213. Int. al., ibid. 54 (CCSG 445,41-42; 459,260-265) and ibid. 55 (CCSG 483,59-485,70), where Maximus interprets *King* Darius as the "*ruling* law of nature." He explains that because scripture speaks of Darius with good repute (i.e., ἐπαινετῶς) for having cooperated with the grace of the release of God's people, he cannot be allegorized as the Devil (like many of the other foreign kings) but symbolizes rather the natural law prevailing over the moral life.

214. Maximus reaffirms such combinations. See ibid. 26 (CCSG 179,132-137), where, in commenting on the gentile "kings" in 3 Kings 11, he also suggests that "the spiritual man" will come to know their significance by the interpretation of their names (which is part of κατὰ πρόσωπον), or the geographic location of their places (ἡ τῶν τόπων θέσις) (=κατὰ τόπον), or the native tradition (γενικὴ παρδδοσις) that prevails in those lands (i.e., κατὰ γένος), or the particular occupation (ἐπιτήδευσις) pursued among them (i.e., κατ'ἐπιτήδευμα), or the sort of antipathy each shows toward Israel.

215. Ibid. 51 (CCSG 399,97-403,144).

216. Int. al., ibid. 5 (CCSG 65,27-67,44), where the "ground," "grass," and "bread" in the curse of Adam in Gen. 3:17-19 are contemplated as πρακτικὴ φιλοσοφία (purgation of the conscience), φυσικὴ θεωρία (renewed knowledge of material bodies and of God's providence and judgment), and θεολογία (acquisition of mystical teaching based on true γνῶσις). Cf. ibid. 27 (CCSG 195,65-91, also quoted in full above); ibid. 37 (CCSG 249,49-251,78). This tripartite reduction of the scriptural senses is clearly reminiscent of similar forms of reduction in Origen's exegesis (e.g., "body"/"soul"/"spirit;" "ethics"/"physics"/"enoptics," etc.): see the discussion of Harl in her introduction to *Origène: Philocalie, 1-20* (SC 302, 110-118) for an elucidation of the various tripartite divisions developed by Origen.

217. A term of Ps.-Dionysius that Maximus on occasion uses. Thunberg (*Man and the Cosmos*, 72) suggests that "the term 'theandric' becomes (Maximus') *preferred expression of the divine-human reciprocity in action.* The goal of the Incarnation is precisely to make possible a communion of (divine and human) energies, which alone can bring into being the divinization that is the final goal of human life."

218. On the model of the Logos' "procession" and "return" (and related

philosophical imagery of "expansion" and "contraction;" "differentiation" and "unification") with regard to scripture, see above, n. 46-47 and related text.

219. *Q. Thal.* 53 (CCSG 433,57-62).
220. Ibid. 54 (CCSG 457,244-252).
221. See above, n. 114-117 and related text.
222. *Q. Thal.* 22 (CCSG 141,101-104). Cf. ibid. 47 (CCSG 325,211-227), where Maximus describes this incarnation in the believer as realized through virtue and knowledge: "it is perhaps possible for those who search after loftier sorts of visions to see differently, as in a desert, with their soul void of passions, the voice (cf. Luke 3:4) of divine wisdom and knowledge resounding through the virtues, a voice crying out invisibly. It is possible because the one and the same Logos 'becomes all things to all men' (1 Cor. 9:22) proportionately in each man. The Logos is extended ($\chi\omega\rho\tilde{\omega}\nu$) through each man and presents him beforehand with the grace that, like a precursory voice, prepares each man beforehand for his presence. In some men, this grace is like a forerunner of future righteousness and becomes repentance. In others it is like a preliminary realization of knowledge expected in the future and becomes virtue. In still others, this grace is like a stamp of a future divine habitus and becomes knowledge. Time simply fails the mind that is making the divine ascents of the Logos, and adapting to his supernatural and philanthropic intentions for each individual, of which is it said that 'he becomes all things to all men, that he may save all' (1 Cor. 9:22) on account of 'the richness of his goodness' (Rom. 2:4)."
223. Cf. ibid. intro. (CCSG 23,99-107), on the Logos as "watering" human beings and manifesting himself in them as fruit, both intellectually and practically, through their virtuous life; ibid. 16 (CCSG 105,26ff) on the $\pi\alpha\rho\text{o}\upsilon\sigma\acute{\iota}\alpha$ of the Logos in one's contemplative life; ibid. 47 (CCSG 317,77ff) on the good and glorious "way" (Luke 3:4) as the virtuous life, "in which the Logos paves the course of salvation, indwelling ($\dot{\epsilon}\nu\text{o}\iota\kappa\tilde{\omega}\nu$) it through faith and walking around on it through the diverse laws of virtue and knowledge"; ibid. 52 (CCSG 427,209-217) on the sun of righteousness "rising" in the mind that engages in $\pi\rho\tilde{\alpha}\xi\iota\varsigma$ and $\theta\epsilon\omega\rho\acute{\iota}\alpha$. The motif of the incarnation of the Logos in the believer's spiritual life is indeed predominant in Maximus' larger corpus of writings. See Thunberg, *Microcosm and Mediator*, 342-350.
224. *Q. Thal.* 35 (CCSG 239,2-50).
225. On this "incarnation" in the $\lambda\acute{o}\gamma\text{o}\iota$ of the commandments, see ibid. 62, quoted above.
226. Ibid. 36 (CCSG 243,6-245,34).
227. Ibid. (CCSG 245,34-38).

228. Ibid. (CCSG 245,38-44). Cf. also Thunberg (*Man and the Cosmos*, 160-161), who remarks on *Q. Thal.* 35 and 36 in the context of his larger study of communion terminology in Maximus' scriptural interpretation and Eucharistic doctrine.

Chapter Three

Anagogical Exegesis as a Theological and Pedagogical Use of Scripture in the *Quaestiones ad Thalassium*

In the preceding chapter we have investigated Maximus' multifaceted vision of spiritual *diabasis* in its broader theological and hermeneutical dimensions. At this theoretical level, Maximus' understanding of scripture and its interpretation cannot in principle be isolated from his larger christocentric *Weltanschauung*.[1] The mystery of the incarnation, in all its aspects, is the axis of Maximus' whole system of thought, to which the λόγος of things created and the πνεῦμα (or λόγος) of things scriptural is ultimately tributary. Spiritual *diabasis* will entail the sort of transition in which the mind is to be contracted toward ever more subtle insights into the underlying, unifying mystery of all being: Jesus Christ in the flesh.

For Maximus, the same christocentric principle obtains *ipso facto* for the science and practice of exegesis itself. This has already been touched upon preliminarily in the analysis of Maximus' notion of γραφικὴ θεωρία, with the proposed contraction of all the particulars, the πράγματα of scripture, into practical, natural, and theological philosophy, and thereupon into its one comprehending logos in Christ.[2] But how does this ideal translate itself in the actual manner in which Maximus, the monastic pedagogue, works with and from the text of scripture so as to arrive at new spiritual (i.e., christological and soteriological) insights into its meaning? In this chapter I shall explore what might best be called "working principles" of anagogical exegesis in the *Quaestiones ad Thalassium*. Further on I shall examine some of the classic methods of Maximus' anagogy and analyze some exemplary texts in an effort to demonstrate that for him, exegesis functions primarily and precisely as a theological and pedagogical use of scripture. Exegesis is not an isolated science but, in the tradition of Cappadocian and Pseudo-Dionysian θεολογία, a basis of inquiry, of probing and continuing initiation in the multifaceted μυστήριον of the Logos.

Anagoge and Multiple Meanings of Scripture in Maximus' Exegesis

Maximus the Confessor, needless to say, stands in a long patristic tradition of "anagogical" exposition of scripture. A few general remarks are in order on the Alexandrian background of ἀναγωγή and its significance for Maximus.[3] In Origen ἀναγωγή had already grown into a *terminus technicus* for the spiritual meaning of scripture in general, this in opposition to its literal or historical sense (ἡ ἱστορία).[4] But as Samuel Laüchli has cogently argued, Origen more often than not sees in ἀναγωγή the full "tracing of the historical situation," the full horizon of a scriptural text for the Church and for the soul.[5] Historical events are, to be sure, subordinated hierarchically to their noetic significance, but that significance will actualize itself in that "history," properly understood, which is a redemptive movement of creation toward eschatological consummation.[6] The inspired text of scripture is seen to conceal an "objective" order of relations of pneumatic meaning that need to be disclosed through anagogical interpretation.[7] Laüchli points out that Origen, sensing "the conflict between the objectivity of the text and the constraint of the interpreter," conceives of various possible interpretations, various exegetical starting points (ἀφορμαί) for speculating about that objectivity.[8] Anagogical exegesis in turn represents "no longer objectivity itself, but only the basis for objectivity."[9]

In Didymus the Blind too, deeply indebted to Origen and influential on later Greek monastic exegesis, ἀναγωγή is similarly the "leading up," the "pedagogical act" that embraces at once the mediation of knowledge by God through inspired scripture and the human subject's ascent to its higher meaning; it implies not a direct communication of objective knowledge so much as an ongoing progress (eschatologically) toward the truth.[10]

Maximus for the most part presupposes this Alexandrian tradition of ἀναγωγή, or anagogical exegesis,[11] and, within his Greek monastic milieu, finds no need to define his exegetical terms or defend his appeal to anagogy.

His understanding of anagogy is best demonstated from what he *does* exegetically. For Maximus, as for most of his predecessors, ἀναγωγή embraces the spiritual meanings of scripture in general, elevated from the literal sense.[12] The anagogical meaning is what "can accommodate everyone," yet is distinguishable from the most mystical or esoteric sense, the one Maximus proposes on a few occasions to "honor with silence."[13] The anagogical interpretation of scripture would *in principle* (and I shall indicate below that Maximus does not always adhere in practice to that principle) lead up, according to the diverse needs of believers, from the literal sense to this highest mystical meaning, the one presumably revealed by the Logos himself in the fullness of his incarnational mystery. Maximus states this principle in the *Chapters on Knowledge*:

> Just as before his visible and fleshly appearance the Word of God dwelt spiritually with the patriarchs and prophets prefiguring the mysteries of his coming, so after this presence he comes not only to those who are still infants, spiritually supporting them and bringing them to the age of perfection in God, but he comes also to the perfect and in a hidden way he delineates in advance in them as in a picture the features of his future coming.
>
> Just as the understanding of the Law and the Prophets as precursors of the coming of the Word in the flesh instructed souls about Christ, so has the same glorified Word of God incarnate become a precursor of his spiritual coming and he instructs souls by his words about the acceptance of his visible divine coming. This coming he always effects by changing those who are worthy from the flesh to the spirit through the virtues. And he will do this also at the end of time, clearly revealing to all what is still secret.[14]

Divine pedagogy aside, anagogical exegesis, from the subjective standpoint of the exegete, can claim no direct or immediate apprehension of the mystical depth of scripture. Since the higher meanings of a text will be discovered only through sensible words, letters, and syllables, the Confessor admits that there will be considerable "stumbling and staggering over the determination of the truth" (τὸ πταίειν περὶ τὴν κρίσιν τῆς ἀληθείας καὶ σφάλλεσθαι).[15]

The anagogical postulations of the exegete can in the meantime be put forward only as "good and pious speculations" (καλὰ καὶ εὐσεβῆ θεωρήματα)[16] based on an ongoing and disciplined research (ἐξέτασις) into scripture.[17] In Question 55, Maximus suggests that pious conjecture is not at all out of order:

> It is not improper, in view of that faculty within us that naturally longs for the knowledge of divine things, to undertake a conjecture (στοχασμός) about higher truths, as long as two good things from the conjecture exhibit themselves to those who possess genuine reverence for divine realities. For the one who approaches divine realities conjecturally either attains to intelligible truth and, rejoicing, offers the "sacrifice of praise" (Ps. 49:14, 23; Heb. 13:15), thanksgiving, to the Giver of the knowledge of what was sought, or he finds that the meaning of the scriptures eludes him, and reveres the divine truths all the more by learning that the acquisition of them exceeds his own ability.[18]

Maximus here draws upon an important exegetical principle of Gregory of Nyssa. For Gregory, the words and names in scripture, while not allowing access to God in his inner essence, are nonetheless energies (ἐνέργειαι) or effects of his being that allow us a limited access to him.[19] Through scripture we can form conjectures or analogies about God that suit our limited intellect. In his *Commentary on the Song of Songs,* for example, Gregory proposes such a conjecture with regard to the signification of God as "perfume" in the scriptural text: we can form an analogy of his good fragrance but are left without an insight into his essence.[20] For Gregory, this notion of στοχασμός carries with it a profound apophaticism and an intense philosophical concern for symbolic language about God. While certainly sympathetic with this concern for the limitations of scriptural discourse about divine truths, Maximus in Question 55 assumes "conjecture" more or less as a general expression for cautiously speculative exegesis.

As in Origen, the anagogical interpretation will entail for Maximus more than one possible meaning, indeed many possible senses discovered through multiple intuitions (κατὰ πολλὰς ἐπινοίας)[21] or interpretative readings (ἐπιβολαί)[22] of a given scriptural text. The inherent diversity in the πράγματα of scripture makes for a diversity of contemplations that find their unity only through spiritual interpretation. In Question 64, Maximus writes:

> None of the persons, places, times, or other things recorded in Scripture–animate and inanimate, sensible and intelligible–when always interpreted according to the same trope, shows up the whole spiritual meaning (ἡ θεωρία) together with the literal (ἡ ἱστορία). Whoever, therefore, is infallibly trained in the divine knowledge of holy scripture, through the diversities (διαφοραί) of the things that occur and are said therein, must interpret each of the things recounted in a different way (διαφορῶς) and assign to each thing having to do with time and place its fitting spiritual meaning (ἡ ἁρμόζουσα θεωρία). For the name (ὄνομα) of each thing signified in scripture lends itself to many meanings (πολυσήμον ἐστι), according to the force (δύναμις) of the Hebrew language.[23]

Maximus takes seriously the principle that "because of the abundance of grace, every syllable of divine scripture is capable of being interpreted in multifarious ways (πολυτρόπως) for the benefit (ὠφέλεια) of those who long for virtue (ἀρετή) and knowledge (γνῶσις)."[24] Indeed, in certain cases it is legitimate to offer contrasting, even apparently divergent interpretations of a given thing in scripture. I have mentioned above the idea of divergent interpretations on the basis of whether some scriptural thing or person is cast laudably (ἐπαινετῶς) or censoriously (ψεκτῶς),[25] a principle we find in Evagrius[26] as well as in Origen. Maximus applies this, for example, with certain of the foreign kings in the Old Testament narratives, who, he says, "are not always interpreted in the same way or according to one meaning but are interpreted with a view to their underlying utility and prophetic power" (πρὸς τὴν ὑποκειμένην χρείαν καὶ τῆς προφετεία τὴν δύναμιν).[27] Nebuchadnezzar might normally be allegorized as the devil who assaults the soul, but in Jeremiah 34:2-11 (likewise Baruch 1:11), where he is alleged to be

God's servant, he can be interpreted still as the devil insofar as God allows him to inflict sufferings on human beings for corrective chastening;[28] or rather, quite by contrast, he may be understood as the natural law lording over the soul.[29] The same holds true of the other kings:

> Scripture knew that the Pharaoh was to be rendered as the devil when he sought to destroy Israel, but then again as the law of nature when he served Israel during the dispensation of Joseph.... Likewise the king of Tyre was intended to represent the devil when he waged war on Israel through Sisera, but elsewhere he signifies the law of nature when he made peace with David and contributed so much to Solomon for the building of the divine temple. Each of the kings recounted in scripture is interpreted in many different meanings (πολλά σημαινόμενα) according to their underlying prophetic power.[30]

As I noted briefly above, the anagogical interpretation would in principle consist in different levels of elevation from the literal sense proportionate to the needs of those to whom it is ministered. Yet Maximus rarely indicates any peculiar taxis in his various speculations on a text, other than occasionally proposing one interpretation as "more gnostic" (γνωστικώτερον)[31] or "more sublime" (ὑψηλοτέρως)[32] than another. On some very rare occasions, he chooses to "honor with silence" a passage or an object in scripture that he sees as carrying a mystical interpretation too sublime for open speculation and discussion. This is the case in Maximus' treatment of the distinction between the "tree of life" and the mysterious "tree of the knowledge of good and evil" in Genesis 2:16-17, a classic patristic and monastic *topos* that he takes up at length in his introduction to the *Ad Thalassium* and in Question 43,[33] as well as earlier in *Quaestiones et dubia* 44. The real problem is the significance of the tree of knowledge: Is it wholly an aberration?

> So then it is necessary here to interpret the tree according to the anagogical method that is able to accommodate everyone. The

more mystical and better meaning of the tree is reserved for the mystics and is honored by us with silence.[34]

Similarly in Question 43, Maximus respects the earlier doctors of the Church who, he says, have also chosen to honor this passage of scripture in silence for the sake of those intellectually incapable of grasping its deeper sense; he thus proposes to give the meaning that can accommodate small and great minds alike.[35]

Already in his introduction, Maximus had suggested that the tree of knowledge symbolized the sensible or phenomenal creation that, if contemplated in a spiritual way, could yield a knowledge of the good.[36] In Question 43, he notes the interpretation of Gregory of Nyssa, who distinguishes the trees as "tree of life" and "tree of death";[37] but wishing, as Thunberg suggests,[38] to avoid Gregory's purely pejorative evaluation of the tree of knowledge, Maximus advances a further possibility, in which the tree of life is νοῦς and the tree of knowledge is αἴσθησις. The mind distinguishes intelligible and sensible things, while sense merely discriminates pleasure and pain. To choose only the tree of knowledge, which differentiates between pleasure as "good" and pain as "evil" doubtless leads to bodily hedonism and transgression of God's commandment. Yet Maximus adds the important caveat that

> you who are wise through grace know that what is plainly called "evil" is not entirely evil, but in relation to one thing evil and in relation to another thing not evil. Likewise that which is plainly called "good" is not entirely good, but in relation to one thing good and in relation to another thing not good.[39]

Rather than simply equating the tree of knowledge with disobedience, Maximus hints that there may be a relative value to the knowledge gained from pleasure and pain: namely, the experience of a healthy pain or suffering that plays a positive or rehabilitative role in the economy of salvation, curbing hedonistic desires.[40] This has led scholars like von Balthasar and Thunberg to conclude, for different reasons, that the more mystical interpretation Maximus "honors in silence" here is an ultimate identification of the "tree of the knowledge of good and evil" with the "tree of life."[41]

Again, such "honorable silence" and engagement in more esoteric speculations on scripture are very rare in Maximus' exegesis.[42] His principal interest in the *Quaestiones ad Thalassium* is not merely to address the perfect, despite his basic conviction, rooted in the legacy of Origen and Evagrius, that the spiritual interpretation of scripture should ultimately lead to the formation of a truly Christian "gnostic." For all intents and purposes, Maximus supposes everyone to be at varying levels of initiation in the deeper meaning of scripture. His occasional references to his addressees as γνωστικοί should not, it seems, be taken as much more than a rhetorical courtesy.[43] And the Confessor continually insists on his own inability to exhaust the limitless depths of scripture.[44] Most often he negotiates between a variety of orthodox possibilities of interpretation and normally introduces them with ἢ πάλιν,[45] ἢ μᾶλλον,[46] ἢ τάχα,[47] τυχόν,[48] κατ' ἄλλον τρόπον,[49] εἴ τις φήσειε...οὐκ ἔξω βέβηκεν τοῦ εἰκότος,[50] and other similar expressions.[51] A prime example of this is found in the response to Question 63, where Maximus, in an extensive typological interpretation of the vision of the lampstand in Zechariah 4, designates no less than eight possible anagogical meanings of the two olive trees flanking the "lampstand" (the Logos): the Old Testament and the New, the natural law and the spiritual law, providence and judgment (=τὸ γνωστικώτερον), practice (πρᾶξις) and contemplation (θεωρία), faith and a good conscience, gentiles and Jews, soul and body, and intelligible world and sensible world.[52] In this specific text, and in numerous other instances as well,[53] Maximus has a limited interest in setting out an order of progressively more refined and more gnostic interpretations suited to beginners, intermediates, and the perfect, though he speaks often of spiritual progress. Maximus, moreover, does not, strictly speaking, segregate, in the manner of Cassian and other monastic exegetes especially in the Latin Christian tradition, the "allegorical," "tropological," and "anagogical" senses of the nonliteral meaning of a scriptural text,[54] all of which he simply subsumes under ἀναγωγή.[55] He is concerned principally with offering a full horizon of meanings that engage cosmology, salvation history, ecclesiology, anthropology, ethics, all under the rubric of the saving μυστήριον of Christ.[56]

Again, Maximus' macrocosmic perspective of diverse particulars bound together and unified by an all-encompassing γενικὸς λόγος of the world and of scripture, itself contained in the person of the Logos-Christ, holds the clue to the Confessor's exegetical practice as well. The true unity between these diverse senses of scripture will be realized ultimately only through reflection on them as aspects of the work of Christ, who, in the fullness of his incarnation, is leading spiritual subjects toward deification. But in the intellectual *diabasis* that this entails, the particulars of scriptural meaning, even at the baser "sensible" level, are not in principle nullified by the higher and more mystagogical insights; rather, they continue to undergird the mind in its research into the more sublime truths. Maximus carefully depicts the contemplation of scripture not as a pure "reduction" of the πράγματα of scripture to its comprehending mystical logos, but as a gradual and orderly "contraction" of integral particular meanings toward that subtle, central mystery.

Anagogical Exegesis as a Use of Scripture in the *Quaestiones ad Thalassium*

I must now seek to validate the earlier, preliminary suggestion that Maximus' anagogy in the *Ad Thalassium* is best understood as a theological and pedagogical *use* of scripture, an attempt to articulate new insights into the christocentric μυστήριον of the world and scripture on the basis of the inter-connections of scriptural words, symbols, and language.

It has become common in modern biblical-hermeneutical analysis to speak of a theologian's "use" of scripture in theological or doctrinal discourse. Theologians do not purely and simply interpret scripture, critically or otherwise; consciously or unconsciously they are *doing* something with it, in a manner that is informed by their particular understanding of the nature of scripture and its authority and exigency. Appropriating such an analytical idea here need not be seen as forcing a modern critical category on an ancient author since, in fact, the idea of the theological utility of scripture was one acknowledged and embraced—even in a quasi-technical sense—by patristic exegetes as well. They too were fully conscious that in interpreting scripture they were doing something with it, be it modulating the text to a diversified audience, propounding a way of salvation, or both.⁵⁷ The prospect, however, of manipulating the text or engaging in an abusive "eisegesis" was to a great degree alleviated by the conviction that the spiritual usefulness, the "utility" (χρεία) or "profitability" (ὠφέλεια) of scripture,⁵⁸ was something fully intrinsic to the text itself. Maximus himself thoroughly embraced this established principle, rooted in Origenian hermeneutics, of the ὠφέλεια of the scriptures, a notion closely related to the perceived salvific goal (σκοπός) of scripture as a whole.⁵⁹

In an excellent study, the methodology of which could prove valuable for analyzing biblical exposition in various historical epochs, David Kelsey has isolated a number of divergent models by which modern theologians "use" scripture to support, shape, and warrant theological arguments.⁶⁰ Kelsey notes that in each model, the theologian ascribes a certain authority to an aspect or aspects of scripture that enables him or her in turn to use that scripture to authorize doctrinal statements or other sorts of theological proposals.⁶¹ Kelsey evaluates the model of the Anglican theologian Lionel Thornton under the title "Image and Mystery."⁶² This model provides a particularly helpful analogy for the present study of Maximus' use of scripture because, as Kelsey observes, Thornton's work draws deeply upon the early Christian form of typological exposition of scripture in order to substantiate what is, in effect, a "subtle essay in Christology."⁶³

According to Thornton, it is precisely the symbolic imagery (i.e., symbolic pictures, or events symbolically described) in scripture that holds authority for theology. The Bible—Old and New Testaments—is itself a complex network of symbols, all organically related, that have their unifying nucleus in the revelation of Jesus Christ, the Restorer of creation.⁶⁴ In his analysis, Kelsey shows, for example, how Thornton interrelates the "six-day" symbolic pattern shared by the creation story, the events leading up to the transfiguration (cf. Mark 9:2), and the passion week (cf. Mark 11:1-16:8) within a common expression of the divine victory of Christ over chaos, and the recreation of humanity in him.⁶⁵ Such a construct is interestingly reminiscent of the way Maximus himself associates the "three-day" patterns in Jonah and in the resurrection story within the framework of the unfolding incarnational μυστήριον of Christ.⁶⁶

Kelsey continues his analysis of Thornton's typological model:

> Moreover, because each (scriptural) image has its symbolic value only as it stands in a network of relationships with other images, the symbolic value of the whole is implicit in any image in the network taken alone. This backs a hermeneutical rule that Thornton uses to warrant reading symbolic value into passages where that value is not explicitly evident.[67]

These various scriptural symbols hold authority only to the extent that they are able to serve as vehicles or "mysteries" linking us to the revelation of divine creativity; in turn,

> the incarnation of divine creativity in Jesus Christ is the central mystery because Jesus is the one link between the "human foreground" of history and its "cosmic background" in the creative process. What is manifested in Jesus Christ is a process that has been going on all along anyhow. "What happened at Calvary," for example, "is in principle that which has been happening in the historical foreground from the fall of man onwards, namely a turning away from light to darkness, a refusal of response to the Word." So too, when "creativity in the person of the God-man" overcomes chaos by entering it, he overcomes it by following an eternal law of the cosmos, viz., that nature "dies to live...." Thus the central Christian mystery, the historical life of Jesus, is revelatory precisely because it is a "foreground" instance, albeit the uniquely archetypal instance, of an eternal law of the "background" cosmic process. And biblical images are authoritative for theology because by symbolizing that mystery they put us in touch with the creative process it reveals.[68]

Kelsey attempts to show how scripture (specifically its images or symbols), construed in this way by Thornton, can in turn be brought to bear or "used" theologically. One principal use of scripture is the description of the recreative work and victory of Jesus Christ "by mapping the relations among these images and noting their subtly diverse symbolic significance":

This is thoroughly Christocentric theology; it consists in an elucidation of christological symbolism in biblical writings. Done this way theology seems a species of literary criticism in which the critic, far from translating the image-rich text into a paraphrase, confines himself to identifying and sorting out the symbols and suggesting how they "work" in the text.[69]

Kelsey's analysis of Thornton's theological use of scripture is helpful to our study of Maximus' exegesis first because of the striking similarity already existing between the hermeneutical enterprises of the two theologians, one modern and one ancient. This is not to say that there are not important differences commensurate with their divergent contexts and peculiar notions of divine inspiration of scripture.[70] Yet Thornton's integration of cosmology and history in the event of Christ, his notion of the cosmic "background" and historical "foreground" convergent in the mystery of the incarnation, clearly recalls Maximus' own constant concern, in his scriptural typology, to integrate cosmological and salvation-historical ("economic") perspectives in the μυστήριον of Christ.[71] Indeed, Thornton's notion of divine recreation in Christ functions as a scriptural σκοπός and hermeneutical axis in much the same way (although, it seems, in much more systematic terms) as Maximus' incarnation theme. Likewise Thornton's understanding of the organic connection of scriptural symbols in their relation to and fulfillment in Christ is closely akin to Maximus' vision of diverse scriptural λόγοι and τύποι focused on the incarnate Logos. Because of this organic relation of symbols, Thornton, like his ancient predecessor, sees each individual symbol as bearing the weight of the whole symbolic system; and this justifies, as Kelsey has indicated, his ascription of symbolic value to passages of scripture where that value may not be overt. This is a common feature of Maximus' exegesis, frequently using a single scriptural symbol or set of symbols in order to substantiate a thoroughgoing spiritual or theological resumé, even where those symbols may not explicitly invite such an exposition.

Perhaps the most interesting aspect of the analogy between Thornton and Maximus the Confessor lies in the theological function of their exegesis, their use of scripture as a "mapping out" of the organic relation of diverse scriptural symbols to the central mystery of Christ. I shall examine in more detail below some favored exegetical techniques by which Maximus maps the configurations of scriptural symbols and their meanings as representations of this saving μυστήριον. To be sure, Maximus is hardly to be seen in the mold, say, of a Gregory of Nyssa, who, with the consummate artistry of a literary critic, moves through the text of scripture with a view to uncovering methodically its inner ἀκολουθία, the underlying "organic liaison"[72] of symbols that conducts us to its ultimate saving σκοπός. Maximus, by his own admission neither a seasoned exegete nor indeed a prolific composer of commentaries, is far more utilitarian, some would argue almost cavalier,[73] in his treatment of scriptural symbols than his predecessors like Gregory or other refined exegetes in the Greek patristic tradition. While holding intently to the ideal that the panorama of scriptural words and symbols all interplay and ultimately converge in the mystery of Christ, the Confessor's main concern is not always the pure exegetical consistency or elegance, as it were, of his typologies or allegories, but the end product itself, namely, interpretations of scripture κατὰ Χριστόν.

Forms of Anagogy in the *Quaestiones ad Thalassium*

Holding to the notion of the "use" of scripture in the *Quaestiones ad Thalassium* as a "mapping out" of scriptural symbols and a demonstration of their bearing on the saving mystery of Christ, we turn now to some of this use's more characteristic manifestations in the text. All of the devices described below are classic exegetical methods in earlier patristic exegesis for extracting spiritual meanings from the Bible. There will be occasion to remark on some of the more important connections of Maximus' anagogy with the Origenian methods. But in the *Ad Thalassium*, Maximus exploits these methods, not only as exegetical techniques in working with the scriptural text, but also as means for working *from* the text, deciphering the symbolic structures in scripture to shape his expositions of spiritual doctrine. The intention here is to view Maximus' anagogical exegesis more precisely in the light of its theological and pedagogical functions within the setting of monastic spiritual direction.

Typology, Allegory, and Tropology

To begin, a few observations are in order on typology and allegory as exegetical techniques in the *Quaestiones ad Thalassium*. Maximus, like Origen, does not draw any sharp distinction in purpose between "typology" and "allegory." He would seemingly have had little use for the convenient division, sometimes made by modern scholars, between "typology" as an expression of the "objective" correspondence among salvation-historical events in scripture, and "allegorism" as a purely subjective imposition of correspondences having to do with the soul or the Church that are not self-evident.[74]

To be sure, Maximus is not altogether ignorant of more subjective forms of symbolic exegesis like allegory and tropology as distinct from typology proper. In the *Quaestiones et dubia*, he tenders a curious definition of "allegory" as the interpretation of inanimate things (mountains, hills, trees, etc.) and "tropology" as interpretation of our body parts (head, eyes, etc.).[75] This brief note, however, has the look of a handbook definition that Maximus has perhaps reproduced, and in the *Quaestiones ad Thalassium* there is no evidence that he ever binds himself to this distinction. On the few occasions where he actually uses ἀλληγορικῶς[76] or τροπικῶς,[77] he simply has in mind a scriptural symbolism bearing on the interior moral-spiritual life of the soul and its faculties.[78]

In his actual exegesis, however, Maximus does not distinguish sharply between a more objective typology that is based on the progressive order of type and fulfillment in salvation history, and a more subjective allegorism that applies scriptural symbols to the individual soul (or to the Church). Are not all the λόγοι of creation, of scripture,[79] and indeed of the present moral-spiritual life of the individual as well,[80] intrinsically and organically related as prefigurations of one and the same eschatological μυστήριον in Christ?

It is all to one purpose. Such an ethos allows Maximus, in effect, to render a single τύπος both "typologically" and "allegorically" at the same time. In Question 55, in his exegesis of Zorababel (Zerubbabel) leading the Israelites from captivity back to their promised land (1 Esd. 5:41-43), Maximus moves immediately from an exposition of "Zorobabel" as a τύπος of Christ's incarnational descent for the purpose of leading fallen humanity back to the heavenly Jerusalem, to a spiritual-anthropological exposition in which "Zorobabel" is the contemplative mind (ὁ νοῦς θεωρητικός) leading its thoughts, virtues, and faculties toward perfection.[81] King Uzziah, with his ambitious building projects (cf. 2 Chron. 26:9ff), is a τύπος of Christ, who, through his incarnation, constructs unions and the principles of his doctrines in the Church, in the cosmos, and in human nature;[82] but Uzziah is also a τύπος of the individual νοῦς, which apprehends those unions and principles in its contemplative, moral, and ecclesiastical life.[83]

A most evocative example of this underlying correlation of typology and allegory appears in Question 54. Maximus indicates that the "plummet of tin" in the prophet Zechariah's vision (Zech. 4:10) can be allegorized as the individual's faith in Christ, the "tin" in this case being an alloy of the "lead" of training, retribution, punishment, and condemnation, and the "silver" of brightness, glory, and splendor.[84] Next he adduces another interpretation, culled from some unnamed authority, wherein the "plummet of tin" is rendered typologically as the incarnate Christ, the "tin" alloy being his hypostatic composition from two natures (ἐκ δύο φύσεων), divine and human.[85] At last, however, positing what should probably be taken as his own unique contribution, Maximus adds:

> Yet if someone wishes to interpret faith in Christ, or Christ himself [i.e., the "plummet of tin"] in a more gnostic fashion (γνωστικώτερον), the "lead" is *faith and also Christ himself,* since it is he who trains the soul, punishes the flesh, avenges the passions, and condemns the demons; yet he is also "silver," since he illuminates the mind through the virtues, glorifies it with knowledge, and, through deification, makes the mind a light, an image of the primal Light.[86]

Most striking here is the fact that the "more gnostic" interpretation is precisely the one that conflates the moral-spiritual "allegory" for the soul (the "plummet of tin" *qua* faith) with the christological "typology" (the "plummet of tin" *qua* Christ incarnate). What joins them together is none other than the μυστήριον of Christ, the axis of Maximus' hermeneutics, comprehending simultaneously the objective, salvation-historical reality of the incarnation and the prospective and existential reality of deification.[87]

Having examined typology (and so too allegory) as an exegetical method *per se*, it is helpful to analyze it more precisely as a pedagogical exercise and a use of scripture for spiritual instruction. For Maximus, the purpose of typology, working from the diverse τύποι and images of scripture as starting points, is to portray the christocentric drama of salvation history which is, in principle, continuing to unfold in the present with the individual soul and the Church as its *dramatis personae*.[88] Mapping scriptural symbols and types in their organic configurations and relations, typological and allegorical exegesis itself becomes a deliberative catechetical exercise in the *Ad Thalassium*, postulating multiple possibilities from the text of scripture that are both illuminating and uplifting but also grounded "objectively" in the μυστήριον of Christ.

Here, as in the other sections below, I shall limit myself to a few of Maximus' more salient examples. Question 63 exhibits one of his most elaborate demonstrations, an exegesis of the lampstand vision in Zechariah 4:2-4. Maximus provides two long resumés of the text. The first is a grand *ecclesiological* typology, in which he sets out the various figures in the vision in a seven-part structure, each figure the subject of an excursus of varying length: (1) the "lampstand" is the Church in its unity and purity; (2) the "bowl" is the incarnate Christ, the central mystery of the Church; (3) the "lamp" is the incarnate Christ, who continues to be the illuminator and dispeller of darkness; (4) the "bushel" is the Synagogue of the Jews, or the literalism that threatens the Word of God; (5) the "seven lamps" are the seven charisms of the Holy Spirit, offered to the Church through Christ, or else the seven grades (βαθμοί) of believers in the Church commensurate with those charisms; (6) the "seven funnels" are the habits (ἕξεις) of the soul proper to those seven charisms; and (7) the "two olive trees" flanking the lampstand are the Old Testament and the New, without which there is no true knowledge of God.[89]

In a second, *anthropological* exposé, Maximus rehearses the same order of figures with some shifting of nuances: (1) the "lampstand" is the individual soul (ἡ ἑκάστου ψυχή); (2) the "bowl" is the incarnate Christ who is the source of faith; (3) the "lamp" is the word of knowledge (γνῶσις); (4) the "bushel" is earthly mindedness of the flesh, or the impassioned law of the body; (5) the "seven lamps" are the charisms of the Holy Spirit necessary for deification; (6) the "seven funnels" are the habits of πρᾶξις and θεωρία; and at last (7) the "two olive trees" are rendered, as already noted above,[90] in terms of eight different possibilities.[91] The plasticity of the scriptural τύποι and the religious vision of the exegete in this *responsio* combine to produce a précis of the grace of Christ and his Spirit at work in the Church and in the soul. The integration of ecclesiological and anthropological symbolism is, of course, a standard procedure in Origenian exegesis, so it is little surprise to find it developed here.

This kind of typological exposition is common, indeed dominant, in the exegeses in the *Quaestiones ad Thalassium*. The general pattern is the same. Maximus sets forth the different possible meanings of the τύποι of the text in question and organizes them into his own spiritual-doctrinal summaries, the themes of which, doctrinal and ascetic, vary for each response. Sometimes the Confessor is led to extraordinary lengths of detail to produce these doctrinal expositions. A *locus classicus* is Question 25, where Thalassius has petitioned him to explain Paul's curious regulations on prayer in 1 Corinthians 11:3-5:

> What is the significance of this passage from Paul: "I want you to know that the head of every husband is Christ, the head of a wife is her husband, and the head of Christ is God. Every husband who prays and prophesies with his head covered dishonors his head; but every wife who prays or prophesies with her head uncovered dishonors her head—for it is the same as if her head were shaven?"[92]

Responding, Maximus uses every detail and figure in the text to structure his own exposition, reworking them into three resumés where they are fully transposed in terms of the three integral phases of the spiritual life (πρακτική, φυσική, θεολογική), each of which focuses on the μυστήριον of Christ:

(1) Not limiting ourselves to one interpretation as we proceed toward the anagogical meaning, we say that the *husband* here is the

practical mind (ὁ πρακτικὸς νοῦς), whose *head* is the word of faith (ὁ λόγος τῆς πίστεως). The mind orders its own life, a life edified, through practical deeds, by the gifts of the commandments, according to this word of faith, which it sees as *Christ*. It does not dishonor its *head* (that is, its faith) with any external material covering, nor put anything transitory and fleeting above faith. On the other hand, we say that the *wife* of such a mind signifies the very habit of ascetic practice, bedecked and veiled with man different practical thoughts and customs; moreover, she has covered the mind itself, as it is her own *head*, with the thickness and beauty of such ethical thoughts and conduct. We say that *Christ* is faith made actual (ἡ ἐνυπόστατος πίστις),[93] whose *head* is God, toward whom the Word of faith leads, exhibiting the God who exists in him by nature to the the mind who follows.

(2) Still again, the *husband* here is the mind that diligently engages in natural contemplation in the Spirit (ἡ φυσικὴ θεωρία ἐν πνεύματι) and that has as its *head*, by faith, the Creator and Logos of the entire world, who is revealed through the order (διακόσμησις) of visible things. The mind does not cover him, nor place him below anything visible, nor put anything else at all above him. The *wife* of such a mind is its companion sense (αἴσθησις), through which the mind enters upon the nature of sensible things and gathers up the principles of the more divine truths within them. The mind does not allow sense, shed of its rational coverings, to be used in the service of irrationality and sin, wherein it might, as its *head*, substitute irrational passion for the mind by throwing off the veils of the more divine principles. The *head* of *Christ*—that is, of the Creator-Logos who manifests himself proportionately to created beings by faith through the natural contemplation of created things—is the ineffable Mind who begets him of his own essence. Through himself, the Logos conducts the mind led by devout contemplation of created beings to this divine Mind and supplies it with intellectual reflections of the divine realities proportionate to its knowledge of visible things.

(3) From still another perspective, the *husband* is the mind that enters into mystical theology (μυστικὴ θεολογία). It has an uncovered *head*, which is *Christ*: that is, him who is conceived of without normal knowledge, through indemonstrable mystical doctrines (μυσταγωγίαι), or, more precisely, the Word of faith who is known without knowledge (ἀγνώστως γινοσεκομένος). No existent thing is placed above him: neither sense, reason, mind, thought, knowledge; nor anything known, conceived, spoken, sensed; nor anyone who uses the senses. The mind cherishes this laudable and utter void that transcends itself and created beings, and that is, in a different respect, a deifying void. The *wife* of such a mind is the discursive faculty (ἡ διάνοια), purged of every sensible illusion, having the mind as its *head,* which is itself covered with interpretations of unknowable and ineffable dogmas, eternal interpretations that transcend intelligence. But the *head* of *Christ*—that is, of the Logos who is, through his preeminence, manifested mystically—is that Mind which is unconditionally, absolutely, and infinitely removed from all things. In turn, Christ, who is conceived of as being by nature the Logos of that Mind, makes the divine Mind known to those who are worthy. For, as he says, "he who has seen me has seen the Father" (John 14:9). And truly the clear intelligence (νόησις) of the Logos consists in the knowledge of the Mind who has begotten him, since the Logos exhibits in himself the essentially subsisting Mind. The Logos leads the mind, as it yearns for identity with God by grace (κατὰ χάριν), up to the divine Mind. Therein the mind is released from the difference in, and quantity of, intelligence that is found in the multitude of created beings and is admitted into a godlike unity through both the fixity and simplicity of intensive eternal movement in relation to God.[94]

What is interesting, in this text and elsewhere, is that Maximus sees absolutely no contradiction in the three different possible typological expositions he sets forth. Nor is any one of the three designated here as necessarily superior; even the third, regarding μυστικὴ θεολογία, is not set apart in this instance as γνωστικώτερον. All are equally valid in terms of their unifying focus, the mystery of Christ.

Etymology

The science of names was an important resource in early biblical exposition, as the recensions of early Christian onomastica indicate. Origen, heavily influenced by Philo, exploited the study of names in his commentaries and homilies, and later monastic exegetes diligently followed suit.[95] Maximus also willingly integrated the "spiritual research through the interpretation of names" (ἡ πνευματικὴ ἔρευνα ἐκ τῆς τῶν ὀνομάτων ἑρμηνείας) into his exegesis.[96]

> Whoever interprets holy scripture in terms of Christ (κατὰ Χριστόν), in an intellectual way (γνωστικῶς) for the soul, must also diligently study the interpretation of names, which can elucidate the whole meaning of the scriptures, if indeed he cares about the precise intellectual comprehension of the scriptures.[97]

Great emphasis was laid on the possibility of a Hebrew name in scripture giving way, through its venerable derivation, to some new spiritual insight. "For the name of each thing in scripture lends itself to multiple meanings (πολυσημόν ἐστι) according to the force (δύναμις) of the Hebrew language."[98]

Etymological speculation in fact engendered its own science. In Origen we find, though probably attributable for the most part to earlier sources, two classes of etymologies: in one, the syllables of words from the Greek Bible were transliterated into Hebrew, then an interpretation derived from the Hebrew; in the other, speculation started with words from the Hebrew Bible itself, in some cases dividing those words into syllables as well.[99] Maximus, in fact, mentions what appears to be a standard etymological procedure in Question 54, where he gives an interpretation of "Zorobabel" that undoubtedly draws on an earlier source or sources:

According to the precision of the Hebrew language, "Zorobabel" is capable of a rough (δασεῖα) and a smooth (ψιλή) reading and can be rendered by synthesis (σύνθεσις), division (διαίρεσις), and orderly arrangement (στιχισμός) of its parts. With a smooth pronunciation, the name signifies "seed of confusion" (σπορὰ συγχύσεως);[100] with a rough pronunciation, it means "rising of confusion" (ἀνατολὴ συγχύσεως).[101] As a synthesis, it means "rising in confusion" (ἀνατολὴ ἐν συγχύσει).[102] Broken down, it means "rising from dispersion" (ἀνατολὴ διασπορᾶς).[103] By an orderly arrangement of its parts, it signifies "he who is rest" (αὐτὸς ἀνάπαυσις[104]).[105]

Similar renderings of "Zorobabel," through variously reworking its syllables in the Hebrew so as to arrive at different cryptic meanings, can be found in earlier recensions of onomastica.[106] Clearly Maximus had access to these venerable traditions and used them like other Christian exegetes. There are more than forty different etymologies in the *Ad Thalassium*, some of which match up with derivations from the recensions studied by Wutz. Some are familiar from Origen and Philo.[107] Others, Wutz claims the majority, are new with Maximus,[108] at least by comparison with extant onomastic lists.

For Maximus, the names in scripture (personal, geographical, and otherwise) are themselves τύποι of spiritual realities, and are basic especially to the contemplation of individual personages in scripture.[109] As Ilona Opelt notes, in this early hermeneutical tradition "the name is a telling exponent of the salvation history of the deeper, allegorical meaning. This notion is the methodical presupposition of Christian exegesis and preaching."[110] In practice, Maximus' understanding of etymology as an exegetical technique for extracting spiritual interpretations differs in no observable way from that of Origen or other earlier patristic exegetes. In the *Ad Thalassium*, he exploits it to the fullest, like typology, as a means of deriving from the text multiple possibilities to be organized pedagogically.

The "Zorobabel" etymology, noted above, yields no fewer than five different possibilities upon which Maximus, in Question 54, sets forth an initial anthropological interpretation:

Zorobabel represents a philosophical mind (νοῦς φιλόσοφος). He is so first in the sense of sowing himself with righteousness, by repentance, in the confusion of captivity to the passions [="seed of confusion"]. Second, in the sense of a "rising of confusion," by making manifest the disgrace of the confusing passions. Third, in the sense of a "rising in confusion," by giving illumination, through knowledge, amid the chaos of the activity of the senses in relation to sensible objects, and by not allowing the senses to attach themselves to sensible objects. Fourth, in the sense of a "rising from dispersion," by causing righteous deeds to rise up through the faculties of the soul that have been dispersed in relation to sensible things. It is of this emergence of righteous deeds that ascetic practice (πρᾶξις), supported by reason, is composed, having the benefit of gnostic contemplation (γνωστικὴ θεωρία), which leads the soul's dispersed faculties up to intelligible objects. Fifth, in the sense of "he who is rest," since the philosophical mind creates total peace and unites its practical life naturally to the good, its contemplative life naturally to truth. For all practice is by nature disposed to the good, while all contemplation seeks after knowledge with a view to truth. Once these things have been perfected, nothing at all will batter the practical life of the soul, nor annoy its contemplative life with strange visions, since the soul will have transcended all being and thought and entered (εἰσδυσάσης) into God himself, who is alone good and true and exists beyond all being and intelligence.[111]

Interestingly, the five possible etymological derivations of "Zorobabel" provide the framework here, not for a gradually "more gnostic" insight *per se*, but for a complete initiation in the spiritual life of the monk, a paradigmatic "scheme of ascent" (*Aufstiegsschema*),[112] stressing the balance of πρᾶξις and θεωρία and their culmination in deification (the "entry" into God).[113]

Nowhere in the *Ad Thalassium* do we see such an extensive use of etymology (and typology) as in Question 64, which has all the makings of a general Christian catechism—an *Allerweltkatechismus*[114]— that could easily have accommodated a larger forum of readers than the monks. Thalassius' question initially asks merely for an anagogical explanation (ὁ τῆς ἀναγωγῆς λόγος) of Jonah 4:11, specifically the curious statement about Nineveh containing "more than twelve myriads of men who do not know their right hand or their left." What Maximus embarks upon is, in effect, a miniature commentary on the book of Jonah. At the outset of his response, he proposes "the elements with the help of which the edifice will be constructed."[115]

> The name "Jonah" is translated according to various pronunciations so as to mean: "repose of God" (ἀνάπαυσις Θεοῦ), "donation of God" (δόμα Θεοῦ), "healing of God" (ἴαμα Θεοῦ), "God's grace to them" (Θεοῦ χάρις αὐτοῖς), "labor of God" (πόνος Θεοῦ), "dove" (περιστερά), "flight from beauty" (φυγὴ κάλλους), and "their toil" (διαπόνησις αὐτῶν). Moreover, Jonah went into Joppa, and into the sea, and into the whale, and into Nineveh, and under the gourd. "Joppa" is translated "contemplation of joy" (κατασκοπὴ χαρᾶς), "wondrous beauty" (καλλονὴ θαυμαστή), and "powerful joy" (χαρὰ δυνατή). Therefore Jonah the prophet is a figure of Adam and our human nature, of Christ, of prophetic grace, and of the ungrateful Jewish people who weary in the face of everything good and who constantly envy the graces of God.[116]

The ostensible contradiction of Jonah prefiguring both prophetic grace and the Jewish people does not hinder Maximus, who holds true to the principle that things can be interpreted both laudably (ἐπαινετῶς) and censoriously (ψεκτῶς) according to the manner in which they appear in a narrative.[117] More remarkable is the fact that, in the passage just quoted, Maximus sets up an enormous range of possible significances through the prospective combination of: 8 translations of "Jonah" x 5 situations from Jonah's career x 4 τύποι of Jonah.[118] In his initial exposition of Jonah as Adam (or human nature), however, we discover that he is aiming at a more modest—though still impressive—combination of these elements:

> For example, Jonah is a figure of Adam and of our common human nature when he flees from Joppa to the sea, for which reason he is

called "flight from beauty," insofar as his name can be so rendered. It is clear that Joppa constitutes a figure of paradise, which truly is, as well as being named, a "contemplation of joy," since there is an abundance of incorruption in paradise....

...We should observe that human nature is always fleeing Joppa (that is, the habit [ἕξις] of virtue and knowledge), just as Adam fled paradise by his disobedience, because human thinking is diligently engrossed in evil things and is willingly dragged down into the sea (I mean, into the brine of sin). It is like our forefather Adam, who, when he fell, was tossed from paradise into this world, the unstable sea of material things, an alien sea that engenders and fosters error and confusion. The more those who cling to this error and confusion profit from it, the deeper they are merely plunged [into the brine], and swallowed by the whale, and drenched in water up to the soul (cf. Jon. 1:17, 2:6); the more too they are engulfed by the deepest abyss, and their head sinks into the clefts of the mountains, and they descend into the earth, whose bars are its eternal constraints (cf. ibid. 2:6-7). For it is obvious that the earth—the truly remote and dark earth, the earth of eternal darkness—is like the depths of the deepest abyss. "There is no light in it," nor can one see any life of mortal men therein, as is affirmed somewhere by the great Job (cf. Job 10:21), who struggled with great ordeals for the sake of truth.[119]

In fact, Maximus never carries through an exhaustive combination of the initial elements (i.e., the 8 etymological possibilies x 5 situations x 4 potential typologies) but structures the main body of his exposition in four general parts based on the four τύποι of Jonah. I have noted the first typology, on Adam and our human nature.[120] In the second, on Jonah as a Christ-figure, he deploys a further combination of these "situations" and "translations":[121]

When Jonah prefigured the God who came for our sake, among our kind, and became like us through flesh endowed with an intellectual soul, save only without sin, he delineated in advance (προδιαγράφει) the mystery of the economy [incarnation] (τὸ μυστήριον τῆς οἰκονομίας) and of the sufferings accompanying the incarnation. He signifies the descent from heaven to this world through his migration from Joppa to the sea. His being swallowed by the whale and his impassible submission for three days and three nights indicates the mystery of the death, burial, and resurrection. For this reason his name is appropriately able to be translated "repose of God," "healing of God," and "God's grace to them." Perhaps he is also rightly called "labor of God" because of his voluntary suffering. For the prophet prefigured in advance, in a mystical way (μυστικῶς) by his own actions (δράματα), the true *repose* of those who have labored in physical pains, the *healing* of those who have been broken, the *grace* of the forgiveness of sins, and the true God Jesus Christ. For our Lord and God himself became a man and entered the sea of life like ours, insofar as he descended from the heaven of "Joppa" (translated "contemplation of joy") into the sea of this world. As the scripture says, he is the one "who for the joy that was set before him endured the cross, despising the shame" (Heb. 12:2). He descended voluntarily into the heart of the earth, where the Evil One had swallowed us through death, and he drew us up by his resurrection, leading our whole captive nature to heaven. Truly he is our repose, healing, and grace. The Lord is our repose insofar as he freed the law, by virtue of his timely life, from its circumstantial carnal bondage. He is our healing insofar as he thoroughly cured us of the destruction of death and corruption. Finally, he is our grace insofar as he was the distributor of adoption in the Spirit by faith and of the grace of deification for each who is worthy. For it was necessary, necessary in truth, for him to become the light in that world (cf. John 1:9), the power of our God and Father (cf. 1 Cor. 1:18) in the earth where there exists darkness and "eternal bars" (Jon. 2:7), in order that, having dispelled the darkness of ignorance, and being, as it were, a spiritual light, and having crushed the bars of evil by virtue of being the very power of God in person (ἡ ἐνυπόστατος δύναμις), he might liberate human nature, which was imprisoned in these things by the Evil One, and endow it with the unquenchable light of true knowledge and with the indefatigable power of the virtues.[122]

In his third, ecclesiological, typology, with Jonah prefiguring prophetic grace, Maximus enters on a very long exposition,[123] underpinned once again by a novel combination of "translations" and "situations":

When Jonah the prophet mystically leaves Joppa, he is a figure in himself of prophetic grace, which transfers, as from Joppa, from the observance of the law, considered beforehand to be glorious, over to the gentiles, by way of the gospel (εὐαγγελικῶς), leaving the Jewish people barren of joy because of their unbelief. He represents as well the Church of the gentiles, in the manner of Nineveh, turning to God through the course of numerous tribulations, dangers, adversities, toils, persecutions, and deaths. By withdrawing distinctly from the religion of law, he signifies the prophetic grace that entered the sea of unsought adversities, and of the struggles, toils, and dangers therein, and which was swallowed by the whale of death, but in no way completely destroyed....

...Those who innocently endure death amid voluntary sufferings for the sake of truth and who have become heralds of the word of grace keep effecting life in the Spirit for the gentiles through knowledge of the truth. They are just like Jonah who, prefiguring this same grace in himself mystically, suffered and endured these sorts of perils in order to turn the Ninevites from their sin to God. This is why Jonah, by the inherent power of his name, is rightly rendered "donation of God" and also "labor of God," for he was a donation (δόμα)—and, in truth, a beloved and philanthropic gift (δῶρον)—of God.[124] He is also commended as the divine "labor," which is the prophetic grace destined for the gentiles. This grace is God's donation, since it gives out the light of true knowledge and presents an incorruptible life to those who await it. On the other hand, this grace is God's "labor" because it persuades its servants to take pride in their labors for the sake of truth.[125]

In his fourth and final typology, with Jonah signifying the Jewish people, Maximus is left with one last etymological derivation of "Jonah" ("their toil"), and one last "situation" ("under the gourd"), on which to build his instruction.[126] Herein he also weaves an exegesis of Jonah 4.

> I said earlier that the great Jonah prefigured in himself the madness of the Jews: by no means did he become subject to any of the Jews' own attributes; rather, he refuted in himself in advance the impiety on account of which the Jews fell from their former glory, as from a "Joppa." This is why the Holy Spirit mystically conferred on him such a name as Jonah, a name that was able, through different translations, to demonstrate the condition of all the things prefigured in it. Since, therefore, he refutes in himself, figuratively ($\tau v \pi \iota \kappa \hat{\omega}_S$), the Jews' derangement ($\pi \alpha \rho \alpha \phi \rho o \sigma \acute{v} \nu \eta$)—a derangement that grieves over the salvation of the gentiles, and is confused over the paradox of the gentiles' calling; a derangement that even renounces, contrary to God's will, the life [that was offered], and instead prefers death because the gourd was withered (Jon. 4:1-8)—Jonah is translated "their toil."[127]

Maximus goes on, at great length, to explain the various figures in the text of Jonah 4 in terms of the indictment of the Jews. Nineveh represents the Church of the gentiles; the booth built by Jonah is the earthly Jerusalem and its artificial temple; the gourd is the literalist observance of the Law; and the worm who destroys it is the incarnate Christ, usurping the old order; the wind that smites Jonah is the Jews' own pride.[128]

The four basic typologies are followed by a further digression in which Maximus engages in an extensive interpretation of the anthropological and ecclesiological significance of the "three days" in Jonah 3:4.[129] A recapitulation ensues where he tries to summarize the eight etymological renderings of "Jonah" in relation to the original four typologies that he has set forth:

It has been clearly demonstrated that the prophet Jonah had multifarious spiritual significance (πολύτροπος θεωρία) attached to him in accordance with the power of his name (κατά τήν δύναμιν τοῦ ὀνόματος). This power, when translated, appropriately fits the topics (τόποι) of his scriptural prophecy. Translated "flight from beauty," Jonah signifies Adam and our common human nature. Being called "healing of God" and "labor of God," he represents our Lord and God, as we explained this meaning. He reveals the kerygmatic grace (="God's grace to them") through the riches of the Spirit within him. He is called "dove," "donation of God," and "labor of God" in view of the many struggles of those who have become ministers of the same true vocation. His name is translated "their toil" since he hinted at the derangement of the Jews against the truth.[130]

This is not the end. There comes still a θεωρία of the "three days" as the "three laws"[131] and finally a concluding digression aimed at summing things up.[132] Maximus has been led far afield of his original structure, but its basic skeleton remains the various creative combinations established between the "translations," "situations," and "types" of Jonah. The upshot is a *tour de force* of spiritual doctrine that integrates anthropology, Christology, ecclesiology, and ascetic teaching.

Arithmology

In a pericope in the *Apophthegmata patrum*, a monk inquires of Epiphanius why there are ten commandments in the Law, and only nine Beatitudes of Jesus. Epiphanius promptly replies: "The Decalogue corresponds with the number of plagues of Egypt, while the figure of the Beatitudes is three times the image of the Trinity."[133] The tacit symbolic value of numbers fascinated early Christian exegetes, the monks included, just as speculative arithmology had intrigued pagan and Christian philosophers in late antiquity. Once again it was principally the Alexandrians, Clement and Origen, inspired by Philo and by the distilled Pythagorean tradition, who appropriated arithmology as a workable tool in early Christian allegorical exegesis.¹³⁴ In a characteristic example from his *Commentary on the Song of Songs*, Origen conveys the particular soteriological and christological mystery behind two scriptural numbers:

> And the number five hundred, or two hundred and fifty (Exod. 30:22-25), either contains the mystery of the five senses perfected a hundredfold in Him; or else, as being the pardonable number fifty multiplied five times, it signifies the remission of sins that is bestowed through Him.¹³⁵

Maximus is constantly inserting similar speculations in the course of his exegeses in the *Quaestiones ad Thalassium*. Number in fact may enter in as a consideration in the contemplation of scriptural things "according to genus or race" (κατὰ γένος).¹³⁶ Commenting, for instance, on 4 Kings 19:35, the "185,000 Assyrians" slain by the angel of the Lord—which symbolically signifies the wicked *habitus* of the soul subdued by the νοῦς—Maximus focuses on the spiritual-anthropological meaning of the "185":

> The number that contains six, when compounded by ten, makes sixty. Sixty, when tripled by the three universal faculties of the soul, added with five, for the innate senses, makes the number 185, and indicates the habit of the natural faculties that is productive of evil in relation to the senses, since this number appears in a culpable light (ψεκτῶς) in this passage of holy scripture. The mind that relies by prayer more on its own power, and which leads an entirely upright life, and which considers God the Cause of every victory over the demons, kills this number.¹³⁷

Besides Maximus' fascination with this spiritual valuation of numbers born of earlier patristic exegesis, there are occasional glimpses, in the *Quaestiones ad Thalassium*, of a deeper philosophical and theological interest in the numbers designated in the scriptural text, an interest clearly informed by his Christian Neoplatonic background—namely, of course, his assiduous reading of Pseudo-Dionysius.[138] There is also in Maximus' arithmology, as von Balthasar has observed, an underlying urge to overcome the negative evaluation of number and plurality in the Origenist system (wherein they are indicative of the fall of creation from its primordial unity) by affirming number and multiplicity as expressive of created nature itself—in consonance with the perspective of the Cappadocians and Pseudo-Dionysius.[139] Maximus often occupies himself in his larger corpus with the mystery of numbers, the problem of unity and multiplicity, and the relation of numbers to the primal μονάς.[140] Though such discussions often appear as digressions from the scriptural commentary, they betray Maximus' profound sense of the inner logocentric and "cosmic" symmetry of scripture, the proportionality and unity of its many particular elements of meaning. An important example of this interest, worked into the context of his exegesis, comes in Question 55, of which more is to be said below. In other instances in the *Ad Thalassium*, there is certainly no sharp distinction between technical arithmological speculation and the simple allegorical demonstration of the spiritual value of numbers.

A good case in point is *Ad Thalassium* 54, where Maximus comments on the significance of the three young men who delivered speeches before King Darius (1 Esd. 3:4-4:32). Accordingly, the first "two" symbolize evil spirits associated with the more material body, since "two" characteristically implies what is passionate and mortal. But the third "one," Zorobabel, who in his speech defends "women" as the strongest thing (cf. 1 Esd. 4:13ff), symbolizes the νοῦς, which is "one" (εἷς) and which defends the soul, which is simple in its essence. For the mind, Maximus explains, "bears the reflection of the indivisible Monad."[141] He appears in this text to be echoing discussions from earlier Middle-Platonic and Neoplatonic speculations about first principles, where δυάς was occasionally regarded as having a sort of moral inferiority to μονάς by its association with matter, evil, compositeness.[142] But Maximus pursues the philosophical explanation, in this instance, only so far as it can shed further light on the inner moral and spiritual health of the soul.

Most importantly for our purposes here, arithmology is, in close association with typology and etymology, another fundamental method by which Maximus grounds his spiritual-doctrinal expositions in scripture. A *locus classicus* in the *Quaestiones ad Thalassium* is his response to Question 55. Thalassius is perplexed here by the minutiae included in 1 Esdras' account of the return of the captives from Babylon to Judah.

> "All those of Israel, twelve or more years old, not including children and women, numbered four myriads, three thousand, three hundred and sixty [43,360]. Their menservants and maidservants numbered 7,307, and there were 855 musicians and singers. There were 435 camels, 7,736 horses, 845 mules, and 5,525 asses" (1 Esd. 5:41-43). Instill in us a love for these great and sublime things which were uttered by the Holy Spirit through the prophets concerning the return from captivity. Is it not rather base, and an unseemly narrative, unworthy of the Spirit, to have recalled these things with the exactness of giving the number of camels, horses, mules, and asses?[143]

The bulk of Maximus' long *responsio* consists in a rehearsal of the return from captivity to Jerusalem as a figure of the spiritual *diabasis* of the soul, initiated and guided by "Zorobabel" (the incarnate Christ). At the outset Maximus makes clear that the Spirit has a definite purpose for this curious precision of numbers, even though his own interpretation of them is to be considered a pious conjecture ($\sigma\tau o\chi\alpha\sigma\mu\acute{o}s$).[144] Since the incarnate Christ is the one who is conducting souls back to the spiritual Jerusalem, it rightly follows that

> the Logos, by symbolically variegating ($\sigma\upsilon\mu\beta o\lambda\iota\kappa\hat{\omega}s\ \delta\iota\alpha\pi o\iota\kappa\acute{\iota}\lambda\alpha s$) the excellence of their virtue and knowledge, matches it with the species and numbers about which you questioned. For every devout and righteous man returns in an intelligible manner ($\nu o\eta\tau\hat{\omega}s$) to the Jerusalem above and himself fills in the cited numbers of the different species, gathering the principles ($\lambda\acute{o}\gamma o\iota$) of every species and number into one fulfillment ($\dot{\epsilon}\kappa\pi\lambda\acute{\eta}\rho\omega\sigma\iota s$) of virtue and knowledge.[145]

With that Maximus launches into a systematic treatment of the different numbers recorded in the text in question. For the sake of convenience, let us concentrate here on the first number of migrants noted, the "43,360 women and children." Even in this one number, however, one discovers a self-contained resumé of spiritual doctrine, and a remarkable example of the Confessor's extensive arithmological speculation.

Having initially dealt with the allegorical significance of the "women and children,"[146] Maximus proceeds to break down the parts of their number, dealing with each part in order. With the "four myriads" (40,000), Maximus presents no fewer than four different possibilities of interpretation, all of which revolve around the theme of virtue. In the first he suggests:

> The "four myriads" signify the four cardinal virtues with which the mind passes over (διαβάς) nature and time and is restored to the blessed state of impassibility (ἀπάθεια). Now the myriad is known only through the basic unit of the monad (μονάς) and cannot be designated by any other character at all—(since it is fundamentally the same thing as the monad, even if, like the relation between end and beginning, the myriad is capable of difference by conception alone—for the myriad is the end of the monad and the monad is the beginning of the myriad; or, more precisely, the myriad is the monad moved, and the monad is the immobile myriad). In the same way, then, every cardinal virtue has, as its beginning and end, the divine and ineffable Monad, God. For every cardinal virtue begins with him and ends in him; each one is the same before God and differs only according to the conceptual principle from which, in which, and for which every source of virtue manifestly exists.[147]

In this θεωρία Maximus exhibits the extraordinary interplay of scriptural symbol, philosophical arithmology, and application to ascetic teaching.[148] The number in the scriptural text at once points the reader back to its "monadic" origin in God, and forward to the quadruplicate manifestation of virtue, which, like all realities in the "myriad" is ultimately comprehended (without being annihilated) in the reality of the monad.

His second speculation on the meaning of the "four myriads" opens a no less sophisticated, yet pragmatically oriented, contemplation of number. Here Maximus suggests that they signify "the four progressions (προκοπαί) in the decad of divine commandments that span the length of contemplation and knowledge."[149] In this way, he asserts, the one who completes these progressions in the commandments "gathers together (συνήγαγεν) the 'four myriads'...(and) is esteemed according to each progression in the mystery of the Monad, toward whom the principle (λόγος) of the myriad is drawn (συνάγεται)."[150] It is clear at this point that Maximus is striving toward a precise, symmetrical, quasi-geometric configuration of the scriptural number-symbols in elucidating his doctrine of the spiritual life. The spiritual mind is called to be "contracted," to move in orderly fashion from the multiplicity of number to the unity and subtlety of the comprehending logos in the Monad.

In his third and final interpretation of the "four myriads," again associating them with virtue but also drawing them even more directly into the sphere of πράξις, Maximus proposes that they are the "four cardinal impassibilities (ἀπάθειαι)."[151] Again the one who fulfills these is said to comprehend the "four myriads" and, departing from material objects, to press on toward intelligible realities.[152]

Continuing his exegesis of the "43,360 women and children" Maximus moves from the four myriads to the 3000. His interpretation here consists in a short, nonspeculative doxology on the impenetrable principle of the Trinity:

> The "three thousand" signifies the perfect, correct, and godly theological principle (λόγος) of the holy and consubstantial Trinity, by which we praise and believe in the Holy Monad in three Persons (ἡ ἁγία μονὰς τρισυπόστατος).[153]

The 300 opens up a new line of considerations, a mixture of typology and arithmology, with the central theme being the christocentric mystery of divine providence:

> The "three hundred" here indicates the principle of providence, not only because the power that extends from things above to things

Forms of Anagogy in the *Ad Thalassium* 217

below it, and which embraces the extremities on each side of it, is signified in the shape of the character [300=T]—(this fact alone ineffably indicates the providence that binds the universe tightly)— but also because this power is honored by the figure (τύπος) of the cross, in which the great and primary and hidden mystery of providence was fulfilled. For the great mystery of the incarnation of God constitutes the ineffable mode of his providence. The great patriarch Abraham probably had confidence in this figure, along with the name of him who was nailed to it for our sake, when, together with 318 men—that is, with the figure and name of Jesus [318=T + ιη]¹⁵⁴—he overthrew the opposing powers signified by the kings (Gen. 14:14ff). For scripture frequently knows how to manifest its peculiar purpose to those who are being purified on the basis of that purpose, through the outward forms (σχήματα) of its characters (γράμματα).

If someone wishes to view the intention (βούλημα) of holy scripture through a number, so also he will discover the providence indicated by that number. For the effect of providence is to sustain human nature undiminished not only in its own principle of being (κατά τὸν ἑαυτῆς τοῦ εἶναι λόγον) but to display human nature infallibly holding fast in the acquired principle of well-being through grace (κατά τὸν ἐπίκτητον τοῦ εὖ εἶναι χάριτι λόγον). Therefore when someone combines one hundred with two hundred, he gets three hundred, which signifies nature and virtue. For they say the number two hundred often signifies nature, since nature is composed of matter and form: matter is identified with four because of the four elements, while form is identified with five because of sense, which molds the material mass into a form. When you multiply forty by five or fifty by four, you have two hundred. The number one hundred, on the other hand, signifies perfect virtue, since it contains the divine decad of commandments multiplied by ten. Having attained in age to this decad-times-ten, Abraham became the father of the great Isaac, and though naturally dead, he became spiritually a begetter of life and joy (cf. Gen. 21:1-5). Thus if you add the one hundred with the two hundred, you would have the number three hundred, which indicates the providence that maintains human nature according to its principle of well-being.[155]

Maximus finally adduces that the 60 in the 360 is a symbol of one's "natural ability to perform the commandments" (ἡ κατὰ φύσιν ποιητικὴ τῶν ἐντολῶν δύναμις), an ability perfected through the λόγοι of the virtues.[156]

> For if the number six, since it is perfect and composed of its own parts (for which reason too it is written that God created the world in six days), signifies the natural ability to act, while the number ten indicates the perfection of virtue in the commandments, then the number sixty clearly represents the natural ability to apprehend the divine principles (λόγοι) which are inherent in the commandments.[157]

This last elucidation completes his anagogical exposition of the "43,360 women and children," which Maximus ends in a summation and exhortation:

> Therefore the "four myriads," joined with the "three thousand, three hundred and sixty," indicates the perfect principle of virtue (ὁ τέλειος περὶ ἀρετῆς λόγος), the holy mystery of theology (τὸ σεπτὸν τῆς θεολογίας μυστήριον), the true purpose of providence (ὁ ἀληθὴς τῆς προνοίας σκόπος), and the ability of human nature to act, which is informed by the virtues (ἡ ἀρεταῖς ποιωθεῖσα πρακτικὴ τῆς φύσεως δύναμις). He who, with these things, has separated out his mind in the Spirit and departed completely from the flesh and world of sense, abandoning, among other things, their chaos and confusion, like the ancients leaving Babylon, presses on toward the city above, his mind free of attachment to anything whatsoever.[158]

When one considers that this is only the first in a series of numbers from Thalassius' original inquiry, one gets an idea of the complexity of this response, though in fact Maximus' later arithmological expositions are more modest by comparison. The "7307 menservants and maidservants" occasions a tropology in which Maximus describes the "slaves" as the faculties of the soul in their service to νοῦς,[159] but his very brief treatment of the "7307" engenders a long note from a scholiast who is either Maximus himself or someone quite knowledgeable of his exegetical arithmologies.[160] The later interpretations of the "855 musicians and singers," "435 camels," "7736 horses," "845 mules," and "5525 asses" also consist for the most part of expansions of ascetic teaching framed in number symbolisms.[161]

Throughout his response Maximus generally maintains (a few digressions notwithstanding) his original scheme of transposing the pilgrimage from captivity to Jerusalem (1 Esd. 5:41-43) in terms of the *diabasis* to God inaugurated by the incarnational mystery of "Zorobabel"-Christ. Since scripture has providentially accommodated the text for our salvation, it is the task of the monk—aided of course by the exegete's doctrinal and ascetic illuminations of the symbolic value of the numbers cited—to grasp the λόγοι of the numbers and so, as Maximus says, "fill them in" existentially in his own life, and thereby participate in the return to God.[162] One observes in this *responsio* to Question 55 a consummate example of the spiritual-pedagogical nature of Maximus' exegesis of scripture. Scripture is, to recall the Confessor's own analogy, a "cosmos," a world of multiplicity and diversity to be explored through every aspect, every activity of the monk's vocation.

Extrapolations from Biblical Terms or Language

While typology, etymology, and arithmology all function in much the same way exegetically for Maximus, opening up symbolic patterns in scripture, another prevalent anagogical method in the *Quaestiones ad Thalassium* focuses more on semantic peculiarities of individual scriptural words, or finepoints of biblical grammar and their capacity to convey higher spiritual or theological truths. This is not, at bottom, allegory, though it can lead to allegory; it is, rather, an assiduous attentiveness to the literal words (τὰ ῥήματα) of the Bible and an attempt to extrapolate, directly from their grammatical and syntactical placement in the text, indications of their special force. The conviction, of course, is that the literal text, the very εὐταξία[163] of the words as they appear, is God-inspired, purposeful, and indeed saving.

Once again it is Origen who instigated this kind of attention to biblical words and terms with the precision of a grammatical and philological science. His commentaries are full of observations on homonymy, metaphor, tropes, and other linguistic phenomena, as well as comments on the peculiar force of certain words and phrases in the Greek Bible, all of which are thought to point us to a more precise understanding of a scriptural text.[164] Maximus is hardly the exegetical scientist that Origen is, but he does in his responses to Thalassius occasionally remark on special grammatical features or semantic finepoints in the scriptures in question, in a way which he hopes will bolster his interpretation. This may include a philological note,[165] an observation on homonymy,[166] or a speculation on the syntax of a given text.[167] In Question 51, Maximus derives no fewer than three possible spiritual interpretations of the text in question—(2 Chron. 32:23: "And many brought gifts [δῶρα] for the Lord to Jerusalem, and donations [δόματα] for King Hezekiah...")—on the basis of the important semantic distinction he finds between the terms δῶρα and δόματα.[168]

Sometimes Maximus concentrates his exegesis on particularly poignant terms in the text of scripture that already invite a moral or spiritual exposition. This too can be found in abundance in Origen and Evagrius.[169] In certain instances, like Question 10, in which Maximus discourses at length on the meanings of "fear" (φόβος, 1 John 4:18; Ps. 33:10) and its larger ramifications for the ascetic life, the moral-spiritual definition of a scriptural term is derived from its various "literal" possibilities.[170] Similarly, in Question 58, the appearance of a cognate of λύπη in 1 Peter 1:6 ("In this you rejoice, though now for a little while you must be grieved [λυπηθέντας] by various trials") affords Maximus a platform for entering into the deeper ascetic significance of λύπη as a privation of sensible pleasure (ἡδονή).[171] In Question 50, where he speculates on the meaning of Hezekiah and Isaiah "praying and crying aloud to heaven" (2 Chron. 32:20), the terms "praying,"[172] "crying aloud,"[173] and "heaven"[174] each give way to varying degrees of moral-spiritual transposition.

These are all examples of how Maximus employs grammatical and semantic analysis as a means of deriving a spiritual interpretation from scripture. But let us once more observe an example of how this kind of analysis can function pedagogically, or as a theological use of scripture, in the *Quaestiones ad Thalassium*. The premier case in point is Maximus' answer to Question 59. Thalassius' query reads:

> "The prophets who prophesied concerning the grace intended for you sought out (ἐξεζήτησαν) and investigated (ἐξηρεύνησαν) this salvation; they inquired (ἐρευνῶντες) as to what person or time the Spirit of Christ within them was revealing when he testified to sufferings for Christ and the glory that would follow" (1 Pet. 1:10-11). If the blessed prophets themselves were taught these very things directly by the Holy Spirit and left them in writing for us to research and investigate, then how did the ones who were taught directly by the Holy Spirit and who wrote down these things revealed to them carry out their own sort of *research* (ποίαν ἐκζήτησιν ἐξεζήτουν) or conduct their own sort of *investigation* (ἐξερεύνησιν ἐξηρεύνων)?[175]

Maximus' response is a full exposition of the συνέργεια of grace and nature, the cooperation of the Spirit and the mind, in the human "research" and "investigation" into salvation. But it is framed by an analysis of the semantic possibilities of the couplet ἐκζητεῖν-ἐξερευνᾶν found here in the text from 1 Peter 1:10-11 (and also the couplet ζητεῖν-ἐρευνᾶν, doubtless suggested by the appearance of ἐρευνᾶν too, minus the intensive ἐξ- prefix, in vs. 11). This very kind of a grammatical analysis of intensive prefixes of scriptural verbs, for purposes of extrapolating a spiritual or theological intepretation, can be found already in Origen.[176]

Roughly the first half or more of Maximus' exposition elaborates the inner mechanics of the synergy of grace (Spirit) and nature (mind). He sets up his argument by suggesting that the Creator originally endowed human nature with faculties for "researching" and "investigating" divine realities (ἡ ἐκζητική τε καὶ ἐξερευνητικὴ δύναμις), but that these were deluded by the Evil One and had to be restored by the Holy Spirit:

Having recovered this faculty as purified by grace, human beings first *sought* (ἐζήτησαν) and *inquired* (ἠρεύνησαν), and then *researched* (ἐξεζήτησαν) and *investigated* (ἐξηρεύνησαν) — through the grace of the Spirit, of course.[177]

Maximus insists that it is absolutely a cooperative effort of our own intellectual ability and of the grace of the Holy Spirit that brings about the knowledge of the divine mysteries, the "salvation" of which Peter speaks: this has always been the case,[178] and it was the case for the prophets who authored scripture.[179] "It is clear too," adds Maximus, "that grace in no way negates the ability of human nature; rather, since humanity's natural ability has been voided by unnatural conduct, grace makes it effective again through natural conduct."[180] Grace restores, not overrides, nature.

A key to Maximus' exposition is his subtle distinction between, on the one hand, "seeking" (ζητεῖν) and "inquiring" (ἐρευνᾶν), both of which he seems to identify with the Spirit informing our own initial efforts, and, on the other hand, the "researching" (ἐκζητεῖν) and "investigating" (ἐξερευνᾶν), wherein our natural abilities and efforts are perfected by the operation of the Spirit.[181] This insight, based (however artificially) on the distinction of terms in 1 Peter 1:10-11, will be clarified in more detail further into his exegesis. Most important, this distinction gives Maximus a scriptural frame with which, through progressive glossing, he will outline his doctrine of divine-human synergy in the attainment of salvation.

Only later in his exposition, after an involved treatment of the soteriological and christological scope of the synergy, and of the deification which is its goal,[182] does Maximus propose to support his theological interpretation of 1 Peter 1:10-11 more explicitly by expanding his original grammatical insight into this text. At this point, in his usual style, a number of different possible glosses (three in all) are proposed for the soteriological significance of the distinction between ζητεῖν-ἐρευνᾶν (unprefixed) and ἐκζητεῖν-ἐξερευνᾶν (with intensive ἐξ- prefix).

(1) Perhaps when they first searched (ζητήσαντες) and inquired (ἐρευνήσαντες) into these things, the saints attained through the Holy Spirit to practical philosophy (πρακτικὴ φιλοσοφία). Then

Forms of Anagogy in the *Ad Thalassium* 223

they were made pure, as it were, of all defilement, and, through the agency of the Spirit, moved their soul's intellectual eyes toward the goal of created beings. They researched (ἐκζητοῦντες) the resurrection of free choice and of the incorruption of human nature, and they investigated (ἐξερευνῶντες) the means and principles of the divine immortality that accompanies that incorruption. For they were not still seeking (ἐζήτουν) the resurrection of free choice, which they already had received from the Holy Spirit through practical philosophy; nor were they inquiring (ἠρεύνων) into the means of attaining it. Rather, they were researching (ἐξεζήτουν) the incorruption of human nature, which they did not have; and they were investigating (ἐξηρεύνων) the principles of the deification that accompanies that incorruption. Desiring the glory that comes in Christ, they pressed on toward that deification, in order that, just as they suffered with him in this present age...so too they might be glorified with him in the future age, becoming supernatural heirs by grace and, in the economy of salvation (κατ'οἰκονομίαν), joint heirs of Christ, who by the power of his incarnation assumed the whole of human nature.[183]

In this case the couplets ζητεῖν-ἐρευνᾶν and ἐκζητεῖν-ἐξερευνᾶν represent a two-stage development in the spiritual life, to which Maximus sometimes refers by distinguishing between πρακτικὴ φιλοσοφία and θεωρητικὴ μυσταγωγία.[184] As already noted briefly above, this kind of glossing of scriptural verbs with intensive prefixes in terms of a progress or development in the spiritual life is not without precedent in Origen or Didymus the Blind, among others.[185] We find it, for example, in their exegesis of Psalm 118, a psalm that is full of such verbs, including our own ἐκζητεῖν and ἐξερευνᾶν no less. In his gloss on Psalm 118:2 ("Blessed are those who investigate [οἱ ἐξερευνῶντες] his testimonies, and research [ἐκζητήσουσιν] him with their whole heart"), Didymus takes the two verbs here as respectively signifying "being removed from every human concern" and "approaching God through virtuous actions and right thought."[186] Likewise in the catena on Psalm 118:29 ("Wondrous are your testimonies, and so my soul investigates [ἐξηρεύνησεν] them"), Didymus (or Origen) comments:

> 'Wondrous are your testimonies' means they are great and have much meaning. I do not approach them randomly; on the contrary, 'my soul investigates (ἐξερευνᾷ) them' intensely (ἐπιτεταμένως). When I contemplate them, I find how very far removed I am from them, and I examine them a second time. Then, finding that I am hardly even a beginner, I press further the inquiry (ἔρευνα) that I am able to conduct, until I lay hold of the purer truth of their science. But those who decide to resist steadfastly and hold to the letter and the text (of the testimonies) shall not consider them 'wondrous,' nor 'investigate (ἐξερευνήσουσιν) them with their whole soul.'[187]

Returning to Maximus' exposition of the verbs in 1 Peter 1:10-11, we find him obviating the potential objection of those who would say that this scripture speaks not of ζήτησις and ἐρεύνησις, but specifically of ἐκζήτησις and ἐξερεύνησις.[188] The Confessor replies with a second explanation that he claims to have learned from a certain sage (τις σόφος),[189] and that allegedly holds the clue to the intensive ἐξ- prefix.

(2) For, in considering the more mystical principle (μυστικώτερος λόγος) of the beginning (ἀρχή) and the end (τέλος), and of the search (ζήτησις) and research (ἐκζήτησις), the sage said that the search (ζήτησις) was naturally oriented toward the beginning, while the research (ἐκζήτησις) was oriented toward the end. For one naturally does not research (ἐκζητεῖ) the beginning, nor search (ζητεῖ) for the end, but rather searches (ζητεῖ) for the beginning and researches (ἐκζητεῖ) the end. The sage further said that man, having put his own beginning, together with his existence, behind him through disobedience, was unable to seek (ζητεῖν) what lay behind him; and since the beginning delimits the motion of the beings that owe their existence to it, it is rightly called the end as well, at which, *qua* beginning, the course of movement of moved beings has its terminus (πέρας).

Therefore when man researches (ἐκζητῶν) his own end (τέλος), he arrives at his beginning (ἀρχή), which is naturally found within his end. Having abandoned the search (ζήτησις) for his beginning, he naturally pursues the research (ἐκζήτησις) of that beginning *qua* end. For man could not defy the limits of his beginning, which encompassed him on all sides and delineated his movement. He could not seek (ζητῆσαι) his beginning, which, as I said, lay behind him. He tried rather to research (ἐκζητῆσαι) his end, which lay in front of him, so that he might know the beginning that he deserted through the end, since he did not know the end through the beginning.[190]

The explanation of the distinction between ζητεῖν and ἐκζητεῖν given here appears somewhat curious *prima facie*. In effect, it introduces and seeks to obviate the errant soteriology of the Origenists in a way that clarifies and bolsters Maximus' own spiritual-doctrinal position. According to the Origenist myth of a primordial unity of pure spirits fallen through disobedience, the salvific end (τέλος) would be nothing but an absolute reduplication of the preexistent beginning (ἀρχή). Maximus does not reject the *moral* principle of humanity's eschatological "end" paralleling its original purpose from the "beginning" (thus the idea, in the passage above, of the "beginning" being found immanent in the "end"); but, as Sherwood and others have emphasized,[191] Maximus disclaims a sheer ontological identification of ἀρχή and τέλος and the quasi-cyclic view of salvation history that it presupposes. Human life and the process of salvation take place on a continuous and linear field of movement from an *irretrievable* beginning to an eschatological end. Translated in terms applicable to the ascetic life, the purpose of our own knowledge is not to "seek (ζητεῖν) the beginning" but to "research (ἐκζητεῖν) the end," and thereupon discover the secret to our created beginning as well.

This particular distinction between ζητεῖν and ἐκζητεῖν thus invites a reflection on a most important cosmological and soteriological theme in the Confessor's monastic catechesis—one which to the modern critical eye appears artificial or forced unless it is kept in mind that the scriptural "world," understood through its particular words as well as its symbols, is always for Maximus a primary indicator of the origins and movements of created beings. He thereupon appeals in his commentary to other biblical testimonia to corroborate his view:

> The wise Solomon was probably also revealing this fact when he said, "What is that which has been? It is that which will be." And "What is that which has been done? It is that which will be done" (Eccl. 1:9). It is as if Solomon was wisely indicating the beginning through the end. For after humanity's transgression, the end can no longer be exhibited through the beginning, but only the beginning through the end. Nor does one seek ($\zeta\eta\tau\epsilon\hat{\iota}$) the principles of the beginning but rather researches ($\dot{\epsilon}\kappa\zeta\eta\tau\epsilon\hat{\iota}$) those beings which, being moved, are leading toward the end.
>
> If, however, someone notes that the term "seeking" ($\zeta\acute{\eta}\tau\eta\sigma\iota\varsigma$) is frequently used in scripture, as when it says, "Seek ($\zeta\acute{\eta}\tau\eta\sigma o\nu$) peace, and pursue it" (Ps. 33:15), or "Seek ($\zeta\eta\tau\epsilon\hat{\iota}\tau\epsilon$) first the Kingdom of God, and its righteousness" (Matt. 6:3), he does not consider its meaning certain, and with a prudent trust spontaneously maintains the credibility of what was said. For the Word, when it says "Seek ($\zeta\acute{\eta}\tau\eta\sigma o\nu$) peace, and pursue it," has enjoined us to pursue the beginning in the end ($\dot{\epsilon}\nu\ \tau\hat{\omega}\ \tau\acute{\epsilon}\lambda\epsilon\iota\ \tau\grave{\eta}\nu\ \dot{\alpha}\rho\chi\grave{\eta}\nu\ \delta\iota\hat{\omega}\xi\alpha\iota$). And it has commanded us to research ($\dot{\epsilon}\kappa\zeta\eta\tau\hat{\eta}\sigma\alpha\iota$) the "kingdom," which is the beginning, through the "righteousness" that is the end of the kingdom. For the Kingdom of God is prior to all righteousness; or, more precisely, the Kingdom is righteousness in itself ($\alpha\dot{\upsilon}\tau o\delta\iota\kappa\alpha\iota o\sigma\acute{\upsilon}\nu\eta$), toward which, *qua* end, all earnest movement presses.[192]

Concluding his soteriological exposition, Maximus offers a third and final possible interpretation of the distinction between $\zeta\eta\tau\epsilon\hat{\iota}\nu$-$\dot{\epsilon}\rho\epsilon\upsilon\nu\hat{\alpha}\nu$ and $\dot{\epsilon}\kappa\zeta\eta\tau\epsilon\hat{\iota}\nu$-$\dot{\epsilon}\xi\epsilon\rho\epsilon\upsilon\nu\hat{\alpha}\nu$. This time, however, he introduces a division between the cognates $\zeta\acute{\eta}\tau\eta\sigma\iota\varsigma$-$\dot{\epsilon}\kappa\zeta\acute{\eta}\tau\eta\sigma\iota\varsigma$ and the cognates $\dot{\epsilon}\rho\epsilon\acute{\upsilon}\nu\eta\sigma\iota\varsigma$-$\dot{\epsilon}\xi\epsilon\rho\epsilon\acute{\upsilon}\nu\eta\sigma\iota\varsigma$ and sorts out the importance of each for the ascetic life and gnostic life:

(3) If, in a different way, someone were to desire to know the method of seeking (ζήτησις) and inquiry (ἐρεύνησις), and of research (ἐκζήτησις) and investigation (ἐξερεύνησις), he would find that seeking (ζήτησις) and research (ἐκζήτησις) are movements of the mind (νοῦς), and inquiry (ἐρεύνησις) and investigation (ἐξερεύνησις) are movements of reason (λόγος). For seeking (ζήτησις), if we might put it in a definition, is simple, affective (μετ' ἐφέσεως) movement of the mind toward something known. Inquiry (ἐρεύνησις) is a simple discretion (διάκρισις) of reason about something known, with an intention (μετά τινος ἐν νοίας). Research (ἐκζήτησις) is the scientific, gnostic movement of the mind, with just such a gnostic affection, toward something known. Investigation (ἐξερεύνησις) is the effective (κατ' ἐνέργειαν) discretion of reason about something known, with just such an effective intention. Translated into the context of divine things, we say that seeking (ζήτησις) is the primary, simple, and affective movement of the mind toward its proper Cause. Inquiry (ἐρεύνησις) is the primary and simple discretion of reason, with an intention, about its proper Cause. Furthermore, research (ἐκζήτησις) is the scientific, gnostic movement of the mind, with a burning affection, toward its proper Cause. Finally, investigation (ἐξερεύνησις) is the discretion of reason, effective through the virtues, about its proper Cause, and with a prudent and wise intention.

Therefore the holy prophets, who researched (ἐκζητήσαντες) and investigated (ἐξερευνήσαντες) the salvation of souls (1 Pet. 1:10), had an affective movement of their minds toward God, a movement fiery hot and fervent with science and knowledge; and they had the prudent, wise, and effective discretion about divine things. Those who imitate them research (ἐκζητοῦσι) the salvation of souls with knowledge (γνῶσις) and science (ἐπιστήμη), and investigating (ἐξερευνῶντες) it with prudence (φρόνησις) and wisdom (σοφία), pursue discretion through divine deeds.[193]

By his conclusion here, Maximus recalls for the reader that, though he has been drawn into a highly developed excursus on synergism and on the cognitive nature of our human "search" for salvation, his whole exposition has been framed and shaped by this original analysis of the distinction in the scriptural text between the terms ἐκζήτησις and ἐξερεύνησις (and so too between ζήτησις and ἐρεύνησις), to which he has consistently returned throughout the discourse. What we discover is a use of scripture distinct from typology or allegory but fully "anagogical" in Maximus' sense. The biblical words and diction provide the springboard for a full range of possible theological and ascetic significances, all of which are nonetheless within semantic range of the "literal" sense of the text in question (1 Pet. 1:10-11), namely, the nature of the prophets' own ancient "research" and "investigation" into salvation.

Notes

1. As Völker notes (*Maximus Confessor als Meister des geistlichen Lebens*, 274), "Like the Areopagite, Maximus builds his doctrine of scripture into the whole of his fundamental theological position." Thunberg too (*Man and the Cosmos*, 159), commenting on Maximus' treatment of scripture in conjunction with his larger enterprise, puts it quite simply: "Things belong together in Maximus' theological universe. The key to it is the doctrine of the incarnation." Cf. also Florovsky (*The Fathers of the Sixth through Eighth Century*, 216-217), who suggests that rather than making Christology an aspect of the doctrine of revelation, as in Origenism, Maximus' "conception of revelation is developed within Christological perspectives...the mystery of Revelation is discernible in Christology. It is not that Christ's person demands explanation, but that everything is explained in Christ's person–the person of the God-Man."

2. See above, chapter 2, n. 204-216 and related text.

3. For a fuller treatment of the exegetical usage of ἀναγωγή, see Wolfgang Bienert, *'Allegoria' and 'Anagoge' bei Didymos dem Blinden von Alexandria*, PTS 13 (Berlin and New York: Walter de Gruyter, 1972), especially 58-68, 69ff, 160ff; cf. also Samuel Laüchli, "Die Frage nach der Objectivität der Exegese des Origenes," *Theologische Zeitschrift* 10 (1954): 183-197. See also *LPGL*, s.v. ἀναγωγή, 100-101.

4. See, e.g., *Hom. in Jer.* 19.14 (GCSO 3.171.1-3; also above, chapter 1, n. 231); *Comm. in Matt.* 10.23 (GCSO 10.32.1-2); ibid. 15.7 (GCSO 10.369.24-26). Laüchli notes that, despite the use of ἀναγωγή in Platonic tradition and in earlier Christian sources, Origen is the first to apply the term systematically to scriptural exegesis ("Die Frage nach der Objectivität," 183).

5. Laüchli, "Die Frage nach Objektivität," 184-185.

6. Ibid., 187-192.

7. Ibid., 192-195.

8. Ibid., 196.

9. Ibid.

10. Bienert, *'Allegoria' und 'Anagoge,'* 160-161.

11. Maximus variously calls it "anagogical contemplation" (ἡ ἀναγωγικὴ θεωρία, *Q. Thal.* intro. [CCSG 19,28]; cf. *Myst.* 6 [PG 91.684A]), "contemplative anagogy" (ἡ κατὰ τὴν θεωρίαν ἀναγωγή, *Q. Thal.* 65 [PG 745D]; cf. *Amb.* 46 [PG 91.1356C]) or "anagogical explanation" (ὁ τῆς ἀναγωγῆς λόγος, *Q. Thal.* 25 [CCSG 161,17-18]; ibid. 38 [CCSG 255,11]; ibid. 64 [PG 704C]), or simply "anagogy" (ἀναγωγή, ibid. intro. [CCSG 37,351]). Maximus doubtless knows the Ps.-Dionysian conception of ἀναγωγή (cf. Rorem, *Biblical and Liturgical Symbols,* 99-116), but the classic Alexandrian understanding, in my estimation, predominates in his exegesis.

12. See Henri de Lubac, *Exégèse médiévale: Les quatre sens de l'Écriture,* pt. 1, vol. 2, Théol 41 (Paris: Aubier, 1959), 622. De Lubac notes that ἀναγωγή was the general term for the spiritual meaning of scripture in Origen, Gregory of Nyssa, Didymus, and Jerome. Only later medieval Christian exegetes began to give it various nuances.

13. See below, n. 34-35 and related text. See also the important allusion to the anagogical sense of scripture given in Schol. 2 to *Q. Thal.* 55 (CCSG 515,12-19): "The gnostics of truth, who teach the words of the mysteries in the scriptures, have used figures (τύποι) from within the literal account as paradigms. For the purpose of the elevation of the ones being taught (πρὸς τὴν τῶν διδασκομένων ἀναγωγήν), they accommodate the spirit of the spiritual meaning (τὸ πνεῦμα τῆς θεωρίας) to the letter of the literal meaning (τὸ γράμμα τῆς ἱστορίας), in order that the figure (τύπος), for the sake of sense, and the word (λόγος), for the sake of the mind, might be preserved for man (περὶ τὸν ἄνθρωπον) who, as a single whole human being, consists of soul and body, in relation to which naturally exist mind and sense." This definition comports with Maximus' general principle, continuously reiterated throughout the *Q. Thal.,* of the wholeness of scripture as analogous to the wholeness in human nature.

14. *Cap. theol.* 2.28-29 (PG 90.1137B-D; trans. Berthold, *Maximus*

Confessor, 153-154).
   15. *Amb.* 10 (PG 91.1160B).
   16. *Q. Thal.* 63 (PG 677D).
   17. Ibid. 40 (CCSG 269,51-53): "For all of these things (in scripture) are left for investigation (πρὸς ἐξέτασιν) by the initiate and the mystagogue of the divine realities and meanings (λόγοι) and concepts (νοήματα), since we are pleased intellectually wholly by the mode of anagogical interpretation." On this same principle of ἐξέτασις, see also *Amb.* 37 (PG 91.1296B).
   18. *Q. Thal.* 55 (CCSG 481,26-483,36).
   19. For a deeper discussion of Gregory's notion of conjecture (στοχασμός) in his exegesis of scripture, see the important study of Mariette Canévet, *Grégoire de Nysse et l'herméneutique biblique: Étude des rapports entre le langage et la connaissance de Dieu* (Paris: Études Augustiniennes, 1983), 52-55.
   20. Gregory of Nyssa, *Comm. in Cant.* Or. 1 (GNO 6, 37,1-3): "Our discourse conjectures (καταστοχάζεται) about the invisible by means of what is perceptible, by portraying the incomprehensible on the basis of an analogy." Gregory further explains (ibid. 6, 37,6ff) that "we make a certain conjecture" (στοχασμόν τινα ποιούμεθα) about the perfume itself (viz., God's essence) from the good "odor" that is made available to us (an ἐνέργεια).
   21. *Amb.* 10 (PG 91.1160D).
   22. Int. al., *Q. Thal.* 3 (CCSG 55,12-13); ibid. 63 (PG 676A). See also Bornert, "Explication de la liturgie et interprétation de l'Écriture," 326-327.
   23. *Q. Thal.* 64 (PG 693B-C).
   24. Ibid. 47 (CCSG 315,63-317,65).
   25. Cf. *Amb.* 37 (PG 91.1296B); and above, chapter 2, n. 209 and related text.
   26. See Géhin, intro. to the *Scholies aux Proverbes*, SC 340, 18-19.
   27. *Q. Thal.* 26 (CCSG 179,37-181,138).
   28. Ibid. (CCSG 173,14-179,120).
   29. Ibid. (CCSG 181,167-185,229).
   30. Ibid. (CCSG 181,140-143, 145-152). The similar polyvalence of the figure of Jonah is the object of a long exposition in *Q. Thal.* 64.
   31. Ibid. 54 (CCSG 465,386-387); ibid. 63 (PG 681B).
   32. Ibid. 50 (CCSG 391,203).
   33. (CCSG 293,1-5).
   34. *Q. Thal.* intro. (CCSG 37,350-353):   Οὕτω μὲν οὖν ἐνταῦθα ληπτέον περὶ τοῦ ξύλου κατὰ τὴν πᾶσιν ἁρμόσαι δυναμένην ἀναγωγήν, τοῦ μυστικωτέρου λόγου καὶ κρείττονος φυλαττομένου τοῖς

μυστικοῖς τὴν διάνοιαν καὶ παρ' ἡμῶν διὰ τῆς σιωπῆς τιμωμένου.

35. Ibid. 43 (CCSG 293,6-18).

36. Ibid. intro. (CCSG 37,331ff). Cf. *Qu. et dub.* 44 (II,22) (CCSG 10.37,6-15): "The 'tree of life' is interpreted as the principle of intelligible things. The 'tree of the knowledge of good and evil' is interpreted as the principle of sensible things, for it is this principle that contains the knowledge of good and evil. For those who ponder the Creator through the beauty of created things, and ascend through these things to their Cause, it is a knowledge of good; but for those who are content with sense alone, who deceive themselves with the outward appearance of sensible things, and who orient their soul's whole desire toward matter, it is a knowledge of evil."

37. *Q. Thal.* 43 (CCSG 293,19-27). Cf. especially Gregory of Nyssa, *De hom. opif.* 19-20 (PG 44.196Cff).

38. Thunberg, *Microcosm and Mediator,* 176.

39. *Q. Thal.* 43 (CCSG 295,67-297,72).

40. This doctrine of the quasi-necessary experience of pain is spelled out by Maximus in detail, ibid. 58 (PG 592D-600B).

41. Von Balthasar (*Kosmische Liturgie,* 179ff, 356-358) was the first to make this argument based on comparisons of Maximus with Origen and Gregory of Nyssa. He compared the two texts on the "trees" from *Q. Thal.* intro. and 43, as well as another text "honored in silence" (*Q. Thal.* 21 [CCSG 133,108ff]) on how Christ's death despoiled the Powers and Principalities (Col. 2:15), with Origen's exegesis in *Hom. in Jesu Nave* 8.3-6 (GCSO 7.338-342). Origen had suggested an identification of the tree of the knowledge of good and evil with the cross, implying that its redemption would subsume all good and evil (including the devil) in the ἀποκατάστασις τῶν πάντων. It is a short step for Origen, then, to an equation, in the cross itself, of the tree of life and the tree of knowledge. For von Balthasar, Maximus' "honorable silence" implies the fact that he entertains this equation, together with the Origenian doctrine of apokatastasis but, realizing the limited powers of speculation, stops short of affirming it openly. Numerous Maximian scholars have expressed skepticism about von Balthasar's thesis. Sherwood (*Earlier Ambigua,* 210-214) finds von Balthasar's argument plausible, but, pointing out Maximus' caveat at the end of *Q. Thal.* 43 (quoted above), contends that Maximus is disputing Origen's overly facile identification of Christ with the "good" and the devil with the "evil" in regard to the tree of knowledge; such a view is what has allowed Origen's controversial and mistaken notion of a restoration of the devil. Maximus honors in silence the Origenian position on apokatastasis in view of this tragic flaw of the temporariness of hell. Another approach, which appears

especially satisfying, is proffered by Thunberg (*Microcosm and Mediator*, 177), who, also noting the caveat at the end of *Q. Thal.* 43, asserts that for Maximus, the "tree of the knowledge of good and evil" represents the dialectic of pleasure and pain introduced into the economy of salvation in view of the fall: "Fallen man gains eternal life through abstaining from a vicious pleasure and accepting a healthy pain, and though this is not the way God had indicated from the beginning, it is not entirely outside God's plan and intention." In this way, the tree of knowledge can be equated ("in silence") with the tree of life without either a positive evaluation of the fall or an implication of the Origenian apokatastasis.

42. See Brian Daley, "Apokatastasis and 'Honorable Silence' in the Eschatology of Maximus the Confessor," in *Maximus Confessor: Actes du Symposium sur Maxime le Confesseur, Fribourg, 2-5 septembre 1980*, ed. Felix Heinzer and Christoph von Schönborn, Paradosis 27 (Fribourg: Éditions Universitaires, 1982), 309-339. Included here is a thorough criticism of von Balthasar's thesis on the connection of Maximus' views "honored in silence" with the Origenian apokatastasis. Daley notes (ibid., 318-319) that Maximus should not, by this reticence, be seen as always concealing a reserve of esoteric speculations; sometimes he is simply expressing his own sincere modesty.

43. Cf. *Q. Thal.* intro. (CCSG 21,70-71); ibid. 40 (CCSG 269,40).

44. See, e.g., ibid. 55 (CCSG 391,202-211).

45. Cf. ibid. 7 (CCSG 73,28); ibid. 11 (CCSG 89,16, 25); ibid. 20 (CCSG 123,50); ibid. 22 (CCSG 139,66); ibid. 45 (CCSG 305,14); ibid. 52 (CCSG 415,32); ibid. 55 (CCSG 493,200); ibid. 61 (PG 640C); ibid. 63 (PG 665ff passim); ibid. 64 (PG 716A and passim); ibid. 65 (PG 740B, C).

46. Cf. ibid. 5 (CCSG 65,27); ibid. 10 (CCSG 85,52); ibid. 12 (CCSG 93,10); ibid. 22 (CCSG 139,60); ibid. 64 (PG 721C: μᾶλλον δέ); ibid. 65 (PG 756D).

47. Ibid. 13 (CCSG 95,18).

48. Cf. ibid. 11 (CCSG 89,14); ibid. 35 (CCSG 241,39); ibid. 49 (CCSG 361,170; 367,277); ibid. 52 (CCSG 427,209); ibid. 53 (CCSG 435,91); ibid. 54 (CCSG 467,402); ibid. 55 (CCSG 487,123; 489,159); ibid. 59 (PG 612B); ibid. 61 (PG 640A); ibid. 62 (PG 653C, 656A); ibid. 63 (PG 672A, 685C); ibid. 64 (PG 721B and passim).

49. Cf. ibid. 55 (CCSG 507,434); ibid. 48 (CCSG 337,132: καθ' ἕτερον τρόπον); likewise ibid. 39 (CCSG 259,14).

50. Ibid. 35 (CCSG 241,34-38). Variants of the same can be seen, int. al.: ibid. 4 (CCSG 63,39ff); ibid. 28 (CCSG 205,51ff); ibid. 35 (CCSG 241,45ff); ibid. 38 (CCSG 257,46ff); ibid. 50 (CCSG 391,203ff); ibid. 51

(CCSG 397,58ff; 403,145ff); ibid. 55 (CCSG 495,240ff; 511,498ff); ibid. 59 (PG 616C); ibid. 62 (PG 657A-B); ibid. 63 (PG 681B); ibid. 64 (PG 709D).

51. Such expressions are fairly typical in Evagrius' speculative exegesis as well. See Géhin (introduction to the *Scholies aux Proverbes* [SC 340, 19]), who lists the following: ἤ, ἤ τάχα, ἄλλως, καὶ ἄλλως, Ἄλλος δέ τις ἐρεῖ, Δύναται δέ...λέγειν.

52. *Q. Thal.* 63 (PG 680D-685D). Cf. similarly *Amb.* 10 (PG 91.1161A-1165A), where Maximus proposes no less than ten possible θεωρίαι of the figures of Moses and Elijah flanking the transfigured Christ. They are, respectively: the word of the law and the prophetic word; the wisdom and goodness of the Logos; gnosis and paideia; practice and contemplation; the mysteries of marriage and celibacy; life and death; the fact that everyone is living before God and no one at all dead before him save by one's own willful sin; the figures (τύποι) of the mysteries both of the achievement of the the Law and of the Prophets; nature (i.e., the cosmic order of salvation) and time (i.e., the order of salvation history); the intelligible and sensible creation.

53. See, e.g., *Q. Thal.* 11 (CCSG 89,12-91,28), where Maximus comments on "the domain which the angels did not keep," the "dwelling" they abandoned, and the "eternal chains" in which they are kept (Jude 6). The "domain" could be (1) the principle according to which they were created; or (2) the natural sovereignty accorded to them by which they may attain to deification by grace; or (3) the stational order in which they are deserving of grace. The "dwelling" they left could mean: (1) heaven; or (2) habitual wisdom; or (3) the watchful care of the undefiled Godhead. The "eternal gifts" are (1) complete and continual inability to choose the good, whereby they never in any way enjoy God's loosening of those bonds; or (2) the providential power of God that holds their rage against us in check for the sake of our salvation.

54. See Cassian, *Coll.* 14.8 (CSEL 13.404ff). See also de Lubac, *Exégèse médiévale*, pt. 1, vol. 1, 191ff; on the roots of this division of senses in Origen, see 198ff. De Lubac's larger study details the way in which these sorts of divisions proliferated in later monastic exegesis in the West.

55. See also Croce, *Tradizione e ricerca*, 54 and n. 84.

56. Sherwood recognized this preliminarily in his early essay on Maximus' exegesis ("Exegesis and Use of Scripture," 204): "What is the principle which permits several, perhaps contrasting interpretations of the same Scriptural text? I have not found Maximus giving a direct answer to such a question: but I believe I am not far off the mark in affirming that these various interpretations are but diverse representations of the one central mystery of Christ and of our unity in Him."

57. Indeed, Sherwood ("Exegesis and Use of Scripture," 207) suggested that what Maximus was doing in the *Q. Thal.* could better be described as a "use" of scripture than an "exegesis" in an "Antiochene" or modern sense. Perhaps, however, this evaluation begs the question, since for Maximus exegesis *is* a use of scripture.

58. See, in particular, *Q. Thal.* 47 (CCSG 315,63-317,65).

59. On this principle of exegetical usefulness ($\omega\phi\epsilon\lambda\epsilon\iota\alpha$) in Origen's hermeneutics, see, e.g., *Hom. in Jesu Nave* 20 (frag.), *Philocalia* 12.1-2 (SC 340.388-392); also Harl, intro. to *Origène: Philocalie, 1-20* (SC 302, 147-151); Torjesen, *Hermeneutical Procedure and Theological Method*, 124ff.

60. *The Uses of Scripture in Recent Theology* (Philadelphia: Fortress Press, 1975).

61. Kelsey (ibid., 2-3, 15) asks four questions of each model by which the theologian in question uses scripture: (1) What aspect(s) of scripture are taken to be authoritative (e.g., concepts, doctrines, historical reports, liturgical utterances, "symbols," or a combination of these)? (2) What is it about this aspect of scripture that makes it authoritative? (3) What sort of logical force seems to be ascribed to the scripture to which appeal is made (e.g., the impact of descriptive report or recital, injunction, emotive ejaculation, etc.)? And (4) How is the scripture that is cited brought to bear on theological proposals so as to authorize them?

62. Kelsey focuses particular attention on Thornton's *The Dominion of Christ* (London: Dacre Press, 1952), part of the trilogy, *The Form of a Servant*.

63. *Uses of Scripture*, 57.

64. Ibid., 61-62.

65. Ibid., 57-61. Kelsey notes numerous other parallel symbols besides the "six days" through which Thornton develops this typological integration of the creation story, the events leading up to the transfiguration, and the passion week.

66. Cf. *Q. Thal.* 64 (720C-721B), a text discussed above in chapter 2.

67. *Uses of Scripture*, 62.

68. Ibid., 62-63. (Kelsey quotes from Thornton, *The Dominion of Christ*, 113).

69. Kelsey, *Uses of Scripture*, 63.

70. Maximus' "high" view, characteristically patristic, of the divine inspiration both of the sensible or literal text of scripture and its underlying intelligible substance evokes the utterly and mysteriously *intrinsic* authority of scripture. Scripture, even in its letter, carries its own authority as *divine oracle*. Needless to say, the pattern described by Kelsey of a theologian

consciously ascribing authority to scripture in order, in turn, to use it as an authority, would have been thoroughly foreign to patristic exegetes. In principle, scripture is a unified and yet mysterious whole, and its inherent logical and symbolic structures—if Maximus can, as he hopes, decipher them—serve to substantiate his spiritual and doctrinal pedagogy, much more than, as Kelsey would say, they "warrant" or "authorize" theological proposals in a modern analytical idiom. After all, there is really no distinction between "theological" and "exegetical" tasks among the Greek Fathers.

71. This concern is perhaps most outstanding in Maximus' attempt to integrate the "three laws" (natural, scriptural, and spiritual).

72. See Jean Daniélou, *L'être et le temps chez Grégoire de Nysse* (Leiden: E. J. Brill, 1970), 49 (from ch. 2 on the theme of "Enchaînement," ἀκολουθία). Cf. also Canévet, *Grégoire de Nysse et l'herméneutique biblique*, 268-273; and Bertrand de Margerie, *Introduction à l'histoire de l'exégèse*, vol. 1: *Les Pères grecs et orientaux* (Paris: Les Éditions du Cerf, 1980), 240-247. On Gregory's profound understanding of symbolic patterns in scripture, see Canévet, *Grégoire de Nysse et l'herméneutique biblique*, 289-361, on "Symbolisme et exégèse."

73. See Völker, *Maximus Confessor als Meister des geistlichen Lebens*, 285: "in contrast with Gregory of Nyssa, in whose allegory one can observe a smooth self-restraint, Maximus' allegory threatens to overflow all dams."

74. See, e.g., Bornert, *Les commentaires byzantins*, 44-45. Bornert suggests that typology "refers to the oneness of the salvific plan and to its progressive realization in several stages.... Typology can be prophetic and announce the eschatological or commemorative future and show the fulfillment of the past. Allegorism, by contrast, interprets Scripture and the liturgy without taking into account the real relation between the successive stages in the divine economy. Typology revels in an objective historical foundation. Allegorism, which sets aside the analogy between the different phases of the same divine plan, constitutes an arbitrary innovation." Elsewhere Bornert ("L'explication de la liturgie et l'interprétation de l'Écriture," 327; cf. idem, *Les commentaires byzantins*, 114-115) claims to find in Maximus a general distinction between authentic typology (designated by the term τυπικῶς) and allegorism (designated by μυστικῶς). I have discovered only one brief allusion, in *Q. Thal.* 50 (CCSG 379,20ff), where Maximus says, "as we interpret the things that happened and ended in Hezekiah's time figuratively (τυπικῶς), and interpret spiritually (πνευματικῶς) the upshot of the things recorded at that time, we will marvel at the wisdom of the Holy Spirit who put them to scripture: how the Spirit determines the meaning of the scriptures that is proper and fitting for every human being." Maximus is

perhaps distinguishing loosely between τυπικῶς (=typology) and πνευματικῶς (=allegory), but they are clearly to one purpose. In my view, as I hope to show below, it is hard to hold Maximus to any rigid distinctions of this kind, since the purpose of typology and allegory is indeed ultimately one and the same.

75. *Qu. et dub.* I,8 (CCSG 10.141): Question: "Do allegories entail a certain number of modes? And what is tropology (τροπολογία)?" Response: "Allegory is used for the interpretation of inanimate things such as mountains, hills, trees, and so forth. Tropology is used for the interpretation of our body parts, such as the head, eyes, and so forth. For it is called tropology instead of alteration (τὸ τρέπεσθαι)."

76. E.g., *Q. Thal.* 52 (CCSG 419,71), here with reference to the interpretation of "Jerusalem" as the "peaceful habit of impassibility" (ἡ εἰρηνικὴ τῆς ἀπαθείας ἕξις).

77. Cf. ibid. 25 (CCSG 167,148), referring to the interpretation of the "angels" (1 Cor. 11:10) τροπικῶς as "reflections of conscience" (οἱ κατὰ συνείδησιν λογισμοί); ibid. 50 (CCSG 383,77), on the etymology of "Ahaz," meaning "strength," which is rendered τροπικῶς as performance (πρᾶξις) of the commandments; ibid. 51 (CCSG 403,162) on "Hezekiah" (the νοῦς) as exalted by the gentiles (2 Chron. 32:23), the gentiles being rendered τροπικῶς as "the passions of the flesh and all the so-called natural bodies, and, in short, all the species perceptible to sense"; ibid. 62 (PG 653D) on the "wood" (Zech 5:4) interpreted τροπικῶς as the soul's desire (ἐπιθυμία), which is a fuel for the fire of the passions, and the "stones" as its irascible faculty (τὸ θυμικόν), which is prone to resist the rule of reason.

78. "Tropological" expositions are frequent in the *Q. Thal.*, most often dealing with the moral consequences of the relationship between the three faculties of the soul (τὸ ἐπιθυμητικόν, τὸ θυμικόν, and τὸ λογικόν). Cf. ibid. 16 (CCSG 107,57-109,93); ibid. 27 (CCSG 197,102-112); ibid. 49 (CCSG 353,58-359,136); ibid. 55 (CCSG 499,302-322). See also Thunberg, *Microcosm and Mediator*, 206-210.

79. For Maximus, just as the λόγοι of created nature are "types" (τύποι) and "foreshadowings" (προχαράγματα) of God's *future* benefits (*Q. Thal.* 22 [CCSG 143,101-103]), so too the true (eschatological) meanings of scripture are veiled by "figurative signs" (τυπικὰ συνθήματα) (ibid. 55 [CCSG 481,20-21]).

80. See ibid. 47 (CCSG 315,50-56), where Maximus affirms that every saint is, existentially, by his proper way of life (ἀναστροφή), a "voice" and a "forerunner" (πρόδρομος) of the Logos of God proportionate to his faith and righteousness.

81. See the whole of Maximus' response in *Q. Thal.* 55, and especially

(CCSG 485,91-487,99) where he states: "If Zorobabel–whether he signifies the contemplative mind like ours, or the Logos, the Creator who transcends us, who became like us in our midst and thus because a human being, in order to restore us to himself, by his incarnation, those who drove themselves from impassibility and life to passion and death–presses toward Jerusalem and leaves behind the principles of time and nature, then it is fitting that he brings with him those who have become like him insofar as that is humanly possible, and that he is leading them back to the heavenly Jerusalem."

82. Ibid. 48 (CCSG 333,35-337,129).

83. Ibid. (CCSG 337,130-345,243). See also ibid. 54, where "Zorobabel" is the subject of an extensive anthropological exposé (CCSG 443,17-455,202: *qua νοῦς φιλόσοφος*), then of a wholly new christological typology (455,203-467,406).

84. Ibid. 54 (CCSG 463,358-465,382). Maximus, having already allegorized the "plummet" as faith, continues: "Some say that tin is an alloy of silver and lead. On the one hand, then, lead is a symbol (σύμβολον) of training (παιδεία), retribution (τιμωρία), punishment (κόλασις), and the heavy burden of condemnation (κατάκρισις), while, on the other hand, silver is in the same way a figure of brightness (λαμπρότης), glory (δόξα), and splendor (περιφάνεια). If this is the case, then faith is also signified by the tin. It trains, avenges, punishes, and condemns those who have become reprobate in faith by laxity in performing the commandments, since, like lead, it seems, faith contains the weakness of the flesh, which is strengthened in the Logos by union with him. Yet faith also brightens, glorifies, illuminates, and leads to deification those who have become acceptable in faith by fulfilling the commandments, since, like silver, it seems to contain the divinity of the Logos, which radiates universally in those who are worthy, insofar as this is possible for them."

85. Ibid. (CCSG 465,383-385): Ἔλαβον δέ τινες τὸν κασσιτήριον λίθον εἰς τὸν κύριον ἡμῶν Ἰησοῦν Χριστόν, ὡς ἐκ δύο συγκείμενον φύσεων, θεότητός τε καὶ ἀνθρωπότητος. This ἐκ δύο φύσεων was of course a classic Neo-Chalcedonian christological formula. Maximus himself recognizes it but prefers the formula ἐν δύο φύσεων, with its greater sense of inner hypostatic unity (e.g., *Ep.* 13 [PG 91.524D-525A]; ibid. 15 [573A]). On this christological background, see Piret, *Le Christ et la Trinité*, 205-214, 236-239.

86. *Q. Thal.* 54 (CCSG 465,385- 391). Emphasis added.

87. On incarnation and deification as the two sides of the μυστήριον of Christ, see again *Q. Thal.* 22 (CCSG 137,4-141,82), which is quoted above, chapter 2, n. 149 and related text.

88. Maximus' exegesis aims, like Gregory of Nyssa's, precisely "...to introduce the reader or the hearer at every moment into the movement of the history of salvation, of which, as a member of humanity, he is simultaneously subject and actor" (Mariette Canévet, *Grégoire de Nysse et l'herméneutique biblique*, 234).

89. *Q. Thal.* 63 (PG 666B-677D).

90. See above, n. 52 and related text.

91. *Q. Thal.* 63 (PG 677D-685D).

92. Ibid. 25 (CCSG 159,2-7).

93. Cf. ibid., Schol. 3 (CCSG 167,8-11), which explains that Ἐνυπόστατος πίστις ἐστὶν ἡ ἐνεργὴς καὶ ἔμπρακτος, καθ' ἣν ὁ τοῦ θεοῦ λόγος ἐν τοῖς πρακτικοῖς δείκνυται ταῖς ἐντολαῖς σωματούμενος, δι' ὧν ὡς λόγος πρὸς τὸν ἐν ᾧ κατὰ φύσιν ἐστὶν ἀνάγει πατέρα τοὺς πράττοντας. The scholiast here (perhaps Maximus himself–see Laga and Steel, introduction to the CCSG edition, xiii) views this passage as suggestive of the Maximian motif of Christ's incarnation in the commandments to conduct the spiritual subject to God through the performance of those commandments.

94. *Q. Thal.* 25 (CCSG 159,17-163,80). The original figures drawn from the Pauline text are given in italics in my translation.

95. See the foundational study of Franz Wutz, *Onomastica sacra: Untersuchungen zum Liber Interpretationis Nominum Hebraicorum des Hl. Hieronymus*, 2 parts, TU 41.1-2 (Leipzig: J. C. Hinrich, 1914-1915); also Ilona Opelt, *RAC* 6, s.v. "Etymologie." See also the studies of Ursula Treu, "Etymologie und Allegorie bei Klemens von Alexandria," *StPatr* 4, TU 79 (Berlin: Akademie-Verlag, 1961), 191-211; and R. P. C. Hanson, "Interpretations of Hebrew Names in Origen," *VigChr* 10 (1956): 103-123.

96. *Q. Thal.* 50 (CCSG 383,70-71).

97. Ibid. (CCSG 379,32-381,37).

98. Ibid. 64 (PG 693C).

99. See Hanson's study ("Interpretations of Hebrew Names in Origen," 105ff), which gives abundant examples from each etymological class.

100. Heb. *zera^c be-bal*.

101. Heb. *zerech be-bal* (with *be-* as construct marker).

102. Heb. *zerech be-bal* (with *be-* as preposition "in").

103. Perhaps Heb. *zerech [be]zera^c* as a basis for ἀνατολὴ [δια]σπορᾶς, or instead, through a play on "Babel" as the proper symbolic name for the place of the dispersion, *zerech bebal* once again. Since the etymology is forced, these can only be conjectures.

104. Presumably Heb. *zeh ru^{a}ch [bebal]*. Maximus has only αὐτὸς

ἀνάπαυσις as the Greek translation here, without συγχύσεως, but in certain earlier onomastic traditions listed by Wutz (*Onomastica sacra*, pt. 1, 153, 367, 617) we find the similar οὗτος ἀνάπαυσις ἀπὸ συγχύσεως.

105. *Q. Thal.* 54 (CCSG 443,10-16).

106. One especially common derivation is αὐτὸς διδάσκαλος ἀπὸ συγχύσεως =Heb. *zeh rab be-bal*. See Wutz, *Onomastica sacra*, pt. 1, 153, 367, 617; and pt. 2, 711, 761.

107. E.g., "Jerusalem" as "vision of peace" (ὅρασις τῆς εἰρήνης): *Q. Thal.* 27 (CCSG 199,137); ibid. 49 (CCSG 351,14-15); cf. Origen, *Hom. in Jer.* 9.11; Philo, *De somn.* 2.38.692. Also "Cain" as "possession" (κτῆσις): *Q. Thal.* 49 (CCSG 367,292-293); cf. Philo, *cherub.* 15.148; 20.151. "Gilead" (Γαλαάδ) as "migration of testimony" (μετοικία τῆς μαρτυρίας): *Q. Thal.* 55 (CCSG 509,449-450); cf. Philo, *leg. alleg.* 3.6.91. "Judah" as "confession" (ἐξομολόγησις): *Q. Thal.* 52 (CCSG 419,68-69); cf. Philo, *plant.* 33.349; Origen, *Hom. in Jer.* frag. 11; *Hom. in Gen.* 17 (*confessio*). "Isaachar" as "hire" (μισθός): *Q. Thal.* 27 (CCSG 199,128); cf. Philo, *plant.* 33.349. "Hilkiah" (Χελκίας) as "part of God" (μερὶς θεοῦ): *Q. Thal.* 49 (CCSG 353,42); cf. Origen, *Hom. in Jer.* frag. 55. (References here from Philo and Origen have been culled from the etymological lists compiled by Wutz, *Onomastica sacra*, pt. 2, 733-748).

108. See Wutz, *Onomastica sacra*, xxii: "By far the majority of etymologies is totally new and thereby properly peculiar to Maximus: e.g., Ἀρμενία παράθεσις ἀναπαύσεως [*Q. Thal.* 49, CCSG 361,199-200]...Αἱμάθ ὅρασις φαινομένων [*Q. Thal.* 56, PG 580A]...Σενναάρ βλασφήμοι[-εις] ὀδόντες [*Q. Thal.* 28, CCSG 203,29]...Νινευή μελάνωσις αὐχμηρά ἢ ὡραιότης λειοτάτη [*Q. Thal.* 64, PG 721C]. On the basis of some individual errors like...Σαούλ αἰτητὸς ᾅδης [=*Q. Thal.* 65, 737B, 748C, etc.] (Paraphr.), Δαυίδ ἱκανὸς [ἰσχυρὸς] ὁράσει [=*Q. Thal.* 65, PG 745B, etc.], Maximus is not to be regarded as the author of these etymologies." (Square brackets show my own additions).

109. As mentioned above (chapter 2, n. 207), Maximus indicates in *Amb.* 37 that name is a key element in contemplations of scripture "according to person" (κατὰ πρόσωπον).

110. "Etymologie," col. 837.

111. *Q. Thal.* 54 (CCSG 443,17-445,39).

112. So Völker (*Maximus Confessor als Meister des geistlichen Lebens*, 281, n. 6), noting briefly this same text.

113. Maximus further uses two of these five etymological derivations in his later christological typology of "Zorobabel." Cf. *Q. Thal.* 54 (CCSG 455,203-225), where Christ ("Zorobabel") is the "scion in confusion" by his

incarnation amid the "confusion" of human passibility; and ibid. (455,226-467,406), where he is a "rising of a dispersion" by pioneering the liberation of the "true Israel" from captivity and its return to build the "true temple."

114. So Beck (*Kirche und theologische Literatur*, 91) describes some of the early kinds of Byzantine monastic *Erotapokriseis*.

115. Laga, "Maximi Confessoris," 205.

116. *Q. Thal.* 64 (PG 693C-D).

117. Laga, "Maximi Confessoris," 205-206. On this principle see also *Amb*. 37 (PG 91.1296A-D); and *Q. Thal.* 64 (PG 712A).

118. See also Laga, "Maximi Confessoris," 206.

119. *Q. Thal.* 64 (PG 693D-696D). This is followed by a larger and more detailed expansion on the same combination of elements, ibid. (696D-697C).

120. Ibid. (PG 693D-697D).

121. The christological typology runs from PG 697D to 700C.

122. Ibid. (PG 697D-700C). There is, of course, much traditional material here: see the significant study of Y.-M. Duval, *Le livre de Jonas dans la littérature chrétienne grecque et latine*, vol. 1 (Paris: Études Augustiniennes, 1973), 381-395.

123. *Q. Thal.* 64 (PG 700C-705C?). As Laga notes ("Maximi Confessoris," 206), there is some confusion as to where this section ends, since Maximus becomes involved (at 705C-709D) in detailed discussions on human nature and the individual soul, at which point it becomes clear that he is really concentrating on answering Thalassius' immediate question about the men who "do not know their right hand or their left." Laga is probably right in suggesting that Maximus becomes distracted here from his original structure of four typologies.

124. Cf. *Q. Thal.* 51 (CCSG 397,50- 407,237), where the same play on δόμα/δῶρον, based on 2 Chron. 32:23 (δῶρα for the Lord, δόματα for King Hezekiah), gives occasion for an extensive spiritual interpretation by Maximus.

125. Ibid. 64 (PG 700C-D, 701C-D). This is just a brief excerpt from this long exposé, but it shows how Maximus uses his initial "translations" and "situations" of Jonah as a frame for his exegesis.

126. Ibid. (PG 712A-720B).

127. Ibid. (PG 712A-712C).

128. Ibid. (PG 712D-720B). Maximus works here (see especially 717A) from an etymological play on τύφος, "pride," and the burning wind in Jonah 4:8, which he identifies with the "Typhonic wind" (cf. Acts 27:14).

129. Ibid. (PG 720B-724A). On the "three days," see above, chapter 2,

n. 145-146 and related text.

130. Ibid. (PG 724A-B).

131. Ibid. (724B-728A).

132. Ibid. (728A-D).

133. Epiphanius 13 (PG 65.165C-D; trans. Ward, 50).

134. On Clement's arithmological speculations in particular, see Jean Daniélou, *Gospel Message and Hellenistic Culture*, vol. 2 of *A History of Early Christian Doctrine before the Council of Nicaea*, trans. J. A. Baker (Philadelphia: Westminster Press, 1973), 246-247.

135. Origen, *Comm. in Cant.* 1.3 (GCSO 8.99,19-23); the translation here is that of R. P. Lawson in ACW 26 (Westminster, Md.: Newman Press, 1957), 72. For similar mystical speculation on the number 50, see Philo, *De mut. num.* 228; Origen, *Comm. in Matt.* 11.3 (GCSO 10.38). On the number 5 as symbolizing the senses, see Philo, *De migr. Abr.* 204; Origen, *Hom. in Gen.* 16.6 (GCSO 6.143). See also Lawson, ACW 26, 325-326, n. 45.

136. *Amb.* 37 (PG 91.1293D).

137. *Q. Thal.* 49 (CCSG 365,256-267). Similar allusions to 5 as symbolizing the human senses are found ibid. 53 (CCSG 431,31-433,32); ibid. 55 (CCSG 487,117); ibid. 64 (PG 708B). For further examples, see Völker, *Maximus Confessor als Meister des geistlichen Lebens*, 281-282, n. 7.

138. On the pagan and Christian Neoplatonic background for Maximus' arithmology, see Stephen Gersh, *From Iamblichus to Eriugena: An Investigation of the Pre-History and Evolution of the Pseudo-Dionysian Tradition*, Studien zur Problemgeschichte der Antike und mittelalterischen Philosophie 8 (Leiden: E. J. Brill, 1978), 137ff; also von Balthasar, *Kosmische Liturgie*, 104-109.

139. Von Balthasar, *Kosmische Liturgie*, 101: "Maximus has basically opted for the second solution, even though he occasionally uses the terminology of the Alexandrians."

140. See, e.g., the arithmologies in *Amb.* 65-67 (PG 91.1389D-1404C). Thunberg (*Microcosm and Mediator*, 65) points out that number for Maximus is precisely a positive expression of the multiplicity of things. Numbers are indivisible, irreducible significations of "quantity," which *ipso facto* manifest the "qualitative" differentiation between created things, a differentiation comprehended by the God who transcends number. See also the remarks of von Balthasar, *Kosmische Liturgie*, 104-107.

141. *Q. Thal.* 54 (CCSG 449,99-112; 451,139ff).

142. See *Q. Thal.* 28, CCSG 203,4-25, on the pejorative implications of Lot's vision of only two angels (Gen. 19:1).

143. Ibid. 55 (CCSG 481,2-14).

144. Ibid. (CCSG 483,48ff); cf. Maximus' statement ibid. (481,26-483,36) on the possibility of "conjecture" ($\sigma\tau o\chi\alpha\sigma\mu\acute{o}\varsigma$).

145. Ibid. (CCSG 487,99-106).

146. Ibid. (CCSG 486, 107-489,142).

147. Ibid. (CCSG 489,143-158).

148. Certainly one of the inspirations for Maximus' reflection here on the fundamental sameness of monad and myriad in their relation to God appears to be Ps.-Dionysius, *De div. nom.* 13.1-3 (PG 3.977B-981B). Unity and multiplicity (or monad and myriad) are the same through participation in the One, who, as Ps.-Dionysius emphasizes, transcends even the monad (cf. ibid. [especially 977C-980A]). Maximus, recalling older Pythagorean terminology (cf. von Balthasar, *Kosmische Liturgie*, 101) speaks here more in terms of the movement and dynamism of the myriad in its relation to the monad (the myriad=monad moved; monad=myriad immobile); nevertheless, his fundamental emphasis is again the comprehending God (Monad). Von Balthasar (ibid., 107-109) has compared Maximus' arithmology with Ps.-Dionysius' in detail.

149. *Q. Thal.* 55 (CCSG 489,159-491,192). Maximus establishes a pattern of 10 x 10 x 10 x 10 = myriad and applies it to the progress in the spiritual life: (1) the practice of the 10 commandments among beginners who have fled sin; (2) the inclusion of all 10 commandments in the practice of each individual one, thus making the original 10 commandments 100; (3) the multiplication of this century of commandments by another 10, the law of (human) nature (=5 senses + 3 faculties of the soul + vocal faculty + natural fecundity), a combination into 1000 which is the integration of the whole person in the spiritual life; and finally (4) the final progression to the 10000 being "the ascent ($\dot{\alpha}\nu\acute{\alpha}\beta\alpha\sigma\iota\varsigma$) through contemplation and knowledge of the natural law...to the more primary principle ($\lambda\acute{o}\gamma o\varsigma$) of every commandment." By this ascent, says Maximus, the myriad is seen as contracted and known only through the primary unit of the monad.

150. Ibid. (CCSG 491,197-199).

151. Ibid. (CCSG 493,200-211). The four $\dot{\alpha}\pi\dot{\alpha}\theta\epsilon\iota\alpha\iota$ are designated as (1) complete abstention from active evils, observable in beginners; (2) total mental rejection of consent to evil thoughts ($\lambda o\gamma\iota\sigma\mu oi$), realized by those who pursue virtue with reason; (3) complete immobility of one's concupiscible faculty in relation to the passions, realized by those who intellectually contemplate the $\lambda\acute{o}\gamma o\iota$ of visible things; and (4) total purgation of even the mere fantasy of the passions, which is accomplished in those who have made their intellectual faculty ($\tau\grave{o}$ $\dot{\eta}\gamma\epsilon\mu o\nu\iota\kappa\acute{o}\nu$) a mirror of God through knowledge and contemplation.

152. Ibid. (CCSG 493,212-218).
153. Ibid. (CCSG 493,219-223).
154. Maximus recalls here a classic exegetical *topos* from the Alexandrian heritage, the cross-symbolism of the sacred number 318: cf. *Epistle of Barnabas* 9.8; also Clement of Alexandria, *Strom.* 6.11.84.
155. *Q. Thal.* 55 (CCSG 493,224-495,260).
156. Ibid. (CCSG 495,261ff).
157. Ibid. (CCSG 493,262-268).
158. Ibid. (CCSG 497,269-278).
159. Ibid. (CCSG 497,279-501,334).
160. Ibid., Schol. 26 (CCSG 529,246-259). Cf. also Schol. 30 (CCSG 529,267-531,294) on the "855" musicians and singers; and Schol. 32 (CCSG 533,318-326) on the "435" camels. On the possibility of Maximus being his own scholiast in the *Q. Thal.*, see Laga-Steel, introduction to the CCSG edition, xiii.
161. E.g., ibid. (CCSG 509,470-479) on the "845" mules: "The present number indicates the perfect impassibility ($ἀπάθεια$) of the mind toward sensible things and sense itself, based on a habit barren of evil–that is, a habit that does not produce evil. For the number eight hundred signifies the impassibility characteristic of the future age, when understood in a laudable way ($ἐπαινετῶς$), while the number forty indicates sensible things, and five signifies sense." The "eight hundred," or "eight," as referring to the eschaton is frequent in Maximus (and other earlier patristic exegetes), contrasted with "seven" as symbolic of the terminus of time. Cf. *Cap. theol.* 1.51-60 (PG 90.1101C-1105A) on the sixth, seventh, and eighth "days" as signifying the transition from the realm of time and nature to deification (the eschatological "eighth day").
162. *Q. Thal.* 55 (CCSG 487,99-106).
163. Ibid. 10 (CCSG 83,6).
164. On Origen's philological and grammatical precision in his exegesis, see the important analysis of Marguerite Harl in her introduction to *Origène: Philocalie, 1-20*, SC 302, 127-132. See also her study "Y a-t-il une influence du 'grec biblique' sur la langue spirituelle des chrétiens? Examples tirés du psaume 118 et des commentateurs, d'Origène à Théodoret," in *La Bible et les pères (Colloque de Strasbourg, 1er-3 octobre 1969)* (Paris: Presses Universitaires de France, 1971), 245-262. Harl notes (pp. 245-246) that often in his exegesis, Origen (and other patristic exegetes like him) goes through a three-stage process: (1) the paraphrasing of the text under examination, in a way that introduces the particular idea that he wants to convey in his own exegesis; (2) grammatical observations about peculiarities of words or

constructions; and finally (3) the transcription or transposition of words judged to be symbolic. Origen, convinced of the verbal inspiration of the LXX, often occupies himself with the peculiarities of its Greek terms. Thus, "One can, in this sense, speak of the literalism of Origen who, without reference to context, interprets the words of the text in themselves, seemingly ignorant of the Hebrew twists that gave birth to these bizarre Greek expressions. The strangeness of biblical Greek, considered in an initial literal explication, gives rise to allegory" (p. 247).

165. See, e.g., *Q. Thal.* 63 (PG 668C), where, commenting on the "lamp" (Zech. 4:2) as a figure of Christ, Maximus notes how the philologists (οἱ περὶ λόγους σπουδάζοντες) say that the term λύχνος is a compound originally derived from τὸ λύειν ("release") + τὸ νύχος (=νύξ, "night"), thus meaning delivery from darkness, which is precisely the work of Christ the Lamp.

166. Without doubt the classic example here is the two "trees" in Genesis 2, which take Maximus (ibid. 43 [CCSG 293-297]) into an extended discussion of the difference between them, at the end of which he advises that we beware of the damage that can be done by equivocal words in scripture: τὴν ἐκ τῆς ὁμωνυμίας βλάβην φυλάξασθε (297,72-73). Cf. also ibid. 42 (CCSG 287,35ff), where Maximus comments on the crucial double meaning (ὁμωνυμία) of the term "sin." Thalassius' question concerns how it is that Christ became sin but did not know sin (2 Cor. 5:21). Maximus suggests that Christ *became* "consequential sin" (ἡ ἁμαρτία δι' ἐμέ), i.e., the corruption precipitated by our deliberate sin, but did not *know* the "deliberate sin" (ἡ ἐμὴ ἁμαρτία) that we commit. Later he affirms this as the proper distinction in view of the *equivocality* of the word "sin" (ἡ κατὰ τὴν ἁμαρτίαν ὁμωνυμία) (289,85-86). Elsewhere he makes a similar distinction with the term "curse" regarding Adam's curse (cf. ibid. 62 [PG 652B-D]). For examples of this concern in earlier exegetes, cf. Origen, *De princ.* 2.3.6 (GCSO 5.121-124) and *Comm. in Gen.* 3 (*Philocalia* 14.1-2, SC 302, 410), on the homonymy of the term "cosmos" in scripture, which might be this world or another world beyond us, etc. Cf. also Gregory of Nyssa, *De vita Moysis* 2.210 (GNO 7, pt. 1, 106,11-19) on how Aaron could still be called Moses' "brother" even after he helped the apostate Israelites fashion the idol: the secret lies in the homonymy of "brotherhood."

167. See, e.g., *Q. Thal.* 3 (CCSG 55,9ff), where, commenting on Luke 22:7-13, the story of the man carrying the jar of water in the city and leading the disciples to the householder, Maximus makes a deduction from the fact that the text leaves out the name of the man carrying the water, and the name of the city: "For this reason, on a first reading, I would conjecture (ὑπονοῶ)

that the sensible world is indicated by the 'city,' and human nature in general by the 'man.'" A classic example of such extrapolation is found in *Qu. et dub.* III,1 (CCSG 10.170,2-20), where Maximus initially asks how it is that in Gen. 1:26 we find "Let us make man in the image *and likeness* of God," while in Gen. 1:27 it says "God made man in his image" and leaves out "in his likeness." Maximus suggests that "likeness" is left out in Gen. 1:27 because God gave man his "image" as an original natural endowment, but humanity must attain to God's "likeness" eschatologically. This argument is not new; it appears already in Origen, *De princ.* 3.6.1 (GCSO 5.280,6-17).

168. See *Q. Thal.* 51 (CCSG 397,34- 403,153). (1) Initially Maximus comments (397,34-50) that the δῶρα signify allegorically the λόγοι of created things, and the δόματα represent the τρόποι of virtue, both of which we creatures offer to God through our contemplation and practice. He then adds (397,50ff) that the text deliberately distinguishes semantically (σεσημει- ωμένως) between δῶρα, gifts given to one who is self-sufficient, and δόματα, donations given to one who stands in need. But that does not fit his initial interpretation if God is the recipient of both, for God is in need of nothing. Thus (397,64-399,71) he circumvents this by saying that, in effect, we give the δῶρα (λόγοι) to God as being in his debt, but, with the δόματα (τρόποι of virtue), it is really we who are the beneficiaries of these δόματα when we practice philosophy. Yet (2) Maximus suggests (399,72-96) that δῶρον can also be taken ἄλλως to mean a gift given to those who have nothing to offer beforehand (τοῖς προεισενεγκοῦσι). In this case we can say that the δῶρα are the "principles of faith" (λόγοι τῆς πίστεως) which are given to the mind in its contemplation of created things apart from rational proofs, and which it in turn offers to the Lord. Likewise, then the δόματα are the τρόποι of virtue which we receive as donations when we undergo sufferings and hardships. There is (3) one more orthodox possibility (403,145-153), that God receives both δῶρα and δόματα as if he were in need of them, simply as an act of his infinite grace, though in fact the real benefit is ours.

169. On Origen's (and other patristic exegetes') spiritual valuation and appropriation of Greek terms from the LXX into his own spiritual-doctrinal vocabulary, see Harl, "Y a-t-il une influence du 'grec biblique' sur la langue spirituelle des chrétiens?" 253ff. In Evagrius, see Géhin (intro. to *Évagre le Pontique: Scholies aux Proverbes* [SC 340], 15-16), who notes how Evagrius often "reinterprets in his own way moral and religious notions from the biblical text and furnishes equivalents to the words that he considers symbolic. The great number of these definitions tends to give his commentary the look of a glossary in which scriptural terms find themselves accompanied in some way by their 'translation.'"

170. See *Q. Thal.* 10 (CCSG 83ff), on "fear" as both the lower fear of punishment and the higher "fear" of reverence (see also above, chapter 1, n. 178-186 and related text). Cf. ibid. 14 (CCSG 99,4-12), a straightforward excursus on the literal meaning of "worship" (σέβας) and "service" (λατρεία) in Rom. 1:25.

171. Ibid. 58 (PG 592Dff). The antithesis λυπή-ἡδονή is one found in abundance in Philo and earlier Christian ascetic writers: see Thunberg, *Microcosm and Mediator*, 168.

172. *Q. Thal.* 50 (383,87-93). Maximus' definition of prayer is straightforward: "'Prayer' is a petition for those things that God is naturally disposed to give to human beings for their salvation. And indeed, it is very reasonably so. For if a 'vow' (εὐχή) is an undertaking of the good things men offer to God according to a promise, 'prayer' (προσευχή) clearly would be, by a reasonable explanation, the petition for the good things that God furnishes to human beings for their salvation, inferring a retribution for the good disposition of those who are praying."

173. Ibid. (383,94-385,99). The "crying" is merely transposed to the soul: "A 'cry' (βοή) is the advancing and increasing of virtuous conduct, by practice (πρᾶξις), and of gnostic speculations, by contemplation (θεωρία) at the moment when the wicked demons attack. God naturally hears this cry above all: instead of a loud voice, he hears the disposition of those who are cultivating virtue and knowledge."

174. Ibid. (CCSG 385,100-115). Here Maximus notes first that "heaven" may be a metaphor already in scripture, then moves to a thorough allegorical transposition of his own: "'Heaven' frequently refers in holy scripture to God himself, as where John the forerunner, the great herald of truth, says, 'Man can receive nothing' on his own 'unless it is given him from heaven' (John 3:27). He says 'from heaven' instead of 'from God' because 'every good endowment and every perfect gift is from above, descending from the Father of lights...' (James 1:17). One must understand a passage of scripture according to what is meant in an earlier passage of scripture.... However, if someone were to say that 'heaven' is the human mind when it is purified of every material illusion and adorned in the divine principles of intelligible things, that person would not, in my view, have stepped outside the truth. Too, if someone were to say that 'heaven' is the summit of intellectual knowledge in human beings, that person also would not miss what is proper."

175. Ibid. 59 (PG 604A-B). Emphasis added.

176. A most striking example of this is Origen's commentary on Ps. 118:114 ("You are my helper and my supporter; I have hoped in your words [εἰς τοὺς λόγους σου ἐπήλπισα]"): "I ask, why does it not say 'I hoped for

(ἤλπισα) your word,' but rather 'I hoped in (ἐπήλπισα) it?' Those who hope (ἐλπίζοντες) do not remain as beginners in hoping, but, if they progress toward God, they increase (ἐπαυξάνουσι) their hope, such that the more their love increases, the more their hope increases. And, in particular, when we are aided by God, we increase our hope relative to our desire for God. Moreover, I have found another way of putting this text: When I had faith in your Law and Prophets, I hoped for you (ἐπὶ σὲ ἤλπιζον). But once your Christ became present, I added to my hope for you (ἡ ἐπὶ σὲ ἐλπίς) the hope for your word, and I hoped in your word (εἰς τὸν λόγον σου ἐπήλπισα)." Translation here of the Greek text of *La chaîne palestinienne sur le Psaume 118*, ed. Marguerite Harl, SC 189 (Paris: Les Éditions du Cerf, 1972), 374-376 (section 114a).

177. *Q. Thal.* 59 (PG 604B-C). Emphasis added.

178. Ibid. (PG 604D-605B). Maximus supplies scriptural *testimonia* to support his idea of the synergy of grace and human nature (Prov. 16:23; James 1:17; 1 Cor. 12:7-11). He summarizes: "Therefore, the grace of the Holy Spirit does not bring about wisdom in the saints without the mind that receives it; nor knowledge without the faculty of reason capable of apprehending it; nor faith without the full assurance (πληροφορία) of the mind and reason of the future things that are meanwhile invisible to everyone; nor gifts of healing without natural philanthropy; nor any other of the remaining gifts without the capacity and faculty for receiving each gift. Nor indeed does a human being acquire a single one of the things enumerated above by natural ability without the power of God that supplies them."

179. See ibid. (PG 605C-608A), where Maximus provides *exempla* of the great OT saints who, when receiving a revelation from God, always inquired about the reasons for the revelation. Thus "when Abraham received the promise of the inheritance of the land which was shown to him...(Gen. 15:7), he was not, upon receiving what he researched (ἐκζητῶν), content and did not just leave the land of the Chaldeans; rather, desiring also to know the manner of the inheritance, he inquired (ἠρεύνησε) and said to God, 'Sovereign Lord, how shall I know that I will inherit it?' (Gen. 15:8). And when Moses received the power to perform signs and wonders, he also sought (ἐζήτει) to be taught the modes (τρόποι) and reasons (λόγοι) necessary for assuring their credibility..." (605C). Other examples are David, Daniel, and Zachariah (605D-608A).

180. Ibid. (PG 608A).

181. Interestingly, Maximus avoids a mere identification of ζητεῖν-ἐρευνᾶν with "nature" and of ἐκζητεῖν-ἐξερευνᾶν with "grace"–for in fact he wants to show, not a sequential development from nature to grace, but that

nature and grace are always cooperating.

182. See *Q. Thal.* 59 (PG 608A-609D). Maximus concludes (608C-D) that this synergy, deification, the participation in supernatural realities κατά χάριν, is precisely the "salvation" which, according 1 Pet. 1:9-11, the prophets "researched and investigated."

183. Ibid. (PG 612B-D).

184. See above, chapter 2, n. 164 and related text. This distinction stands in contrast with, though not necessarily in opposition to, his usual threefold development of πρακτική-θεωρητική-θεολογική.

185. See above, n. 176. Cf. also Didymus (or Origen) on Ps. 118:129 ("Wondrous are your testimonies, and so my soul investigates them").

186. *Le chaîne palestinienne*, SC 189.194 [3b]).

187. Ibid. 398 [129a]).

188. *Q. Thal.* 59 (PG 613B).

189. Maximus gives no further indication of this figure. I have noted already (introduction, n. 43 and related text) how Maximus occasionally defers to a certain anonymous γέρων. Some argue that this is probably Sophronius, Maximus' monastic mentor. Sophronius could, it seems, be a candidate for the σόφος mentioned here, but there is simply no way of identifying him with certainty, and there remains the possibility that he is a literary fiction.

190. *Q. Thal.* 59 (PG 613B-D).

191. Cf. Sherwood, *Earlier Ambigua*, 90-91, 164-180 (on *Amb.* 7); and "Maximus and Origenism," 6- 25; also Thunberg, *Man and the Cosmos*, 68-69.

192. *Q. Thal.* 59 (PG 613D-616B).

193. Ibid. (PG 616C-617A).

Conclusion

This study was originally motivated as a preliminary attempt to satisfy the need, suggested over thirty years ago by Polycarp Sherwood, for a concentrated investigation of the *Quaestiones ad Thalassium* of Maximus the Confessor. Rather than treating the work solely as another register of Maximus' developing theological and spiritual synthesis, or delivering the "thorough doctrinal analysis" for which Sherwood called, I looked for an access into the *Ad Thalassium* from the standpoint of its own intentionality and purview as a commentary for monks on scriptural ἀπορίαι. Not only is this work a "treatise of spiritual anthropology,"[1] and a crucial resource for Maximus' spiritual doctrine in general, but the work is also his exegetical *tour de force,* however modest it might appear in a technical comparison with the commentaries and homilies of earlier, more prolific patristic exegetes. The *Ad Thalassium* is, in a word, Maximus' most significant attempt to bring his theology and spirituality to bear on the interpretation of scripture.

To be sure, the *Quaestiones ad Thalassium* is not an extended, running commentary on selected books of the Bible. It is a set of scholia or "notes," of varying length and depth of analysis, on some problematic spots in scripture as introduced by his friend, the Libyan hegumen Thalassius. This format conforms very well to Maximus' larger scheme of writing and teaching. As Georges Florovsky has rightly remarked, the Confessor preferred to leave "sketches" of his thought—opuscula, chapters, scholia—rather than a thoroughly condensed system.[2]

Even as scholia on scripture, however, the literary genre of the *Quaestiones ad Thalassium* defies easy categorization. Genre often poses a knotty problem in dealing with early Christian writings, and especially so in the exegetical tradition, where there are few analytical studies on the genres of commentaries, homilies, and the like. Gustave Bardy's foundational study of the *quaestiones* literature as a breed of exegetical scholia is still too broad in scope to illuminate the *Ad Thalassium* in its native context. Even the identification of the work in the reasonably uniform category of Greek exegetical ἀπορίαι proves too general to carry great weight. The secret to its genre lies in its monastic milieu, and even there, rigid strictures of literary form seem to be lacking, since the monastic literature of *quaestiones et responsiones* was tied to variant emerging patterns of monastic pedagogy and treatment of scripture.

Good teachers improvise, and the plasticity of the *quaestio-responsio* format, as applied to the interpretation of scripture, proved effective to Maximus as it had for many of his predecessors in the monastic tradition. In the early conferences of the desert fathers and in the letters of later rigorists like the Palestinians Barsanuphius and John, speculative queries on scripture had been discouraged outright in the ongoing γέρων-disciple relationship. More "philosophically" inclined monastic teachers had used scriptural ἀπορίαι as an effective means of bringing scripture to bear on the increasingly complex problems of ascetic doctrine and ethics, or else as an artificial platform for their own extrapolations. Maximus was the beneficiary of a gathering momentum initially impelled by Evagrius, Cassian, and others to fuse the devotional "interrogation" of scripture among the monks with the interests of a more speculative, openly theological, and Alexandrian-inspired exegesis. Still, Maximus inherited no simple prefabricated forms. For the *Ad Thalassium*, perhaps the best antecedent is to be found in certain of Evagrius' *Scholia on Proverbs* styled in the pattern of question-and-response. Yet in the *Ad Thalassium*, Maximus goes far beyond the limitations that Evagrius imposed on his exegetical scholia and adapts the scriptural ἀπορία as a spiritual-pedagogical medium *par excellence*.

The *Quaestiones ad Thalassium* grew out of a fertile and increasingly sophisticated monastic literary culture. There is, nonetheless, an important continuity with the primitive eremitic tradition that must always be kept in view. The involvement of many of Maximus' answers to Thalassius' scriptural difficulties in "speculative" theology and anthropology should never, in principle at least, be considered in strict opposition to their "pragmatic" value for spiritual direction. Heuristically, Maximus aims in the *Ad Thalassium* to integrate θεωρία and πρᾶξις even in the most sublime reaches of his thought. His intellectual reflections on scripture are directed toward a discipline of the monastic mind and a devotion to evangelical asceticism that indicate their ancestry, however distant, in the conferences of the desert fathers. Did not Maximus enjoy a living link to the desert tradition in the person of his own venerable spiritual father, Sophronius?

I have attempted to provide an insight not only into the tradition-historical, literary, and heuristic background of the *Quaestiones ad Thalassium*, but also into its theological conceptuality, its hermeneutical "scheme," and its central spiritual theme. This is no simple task. Florovsky argues that Maximus is aiming throughout his writings to construct primarily a "system of asceticism" rather than a purely dogmatic system:

> It is the rhythm of spiritual life rather than a logical connection of ideas which defines the architechtonics of his vision of the world, and one could say that his system has more of a musical structure than an architectural one. This is more like a symphony—a symphony of spiritual experience—than a system. It is not easy to read St. Maximus.... [His] language is really unwieldy and astringent, burdened by allegories and tangled in rhetorical figures. At the same time, however, one constantly perceives the intensity and condensation of his thought.... The reader has to divine St. Maximus' system in his sketches. When he does, the inner access to the integral world of St. Maximus' inspired experience is revealed.[3]

Indeed, the diffuse subject matter of the *Ad Thalassium* is held together, not by any defined structural taxis, nor even by a strictly systematic hermeneutics, but by Maximus' vision of a spiritual $\delta\iota\acute{a}\beta\alpha\sigma\iota\varsigma$, a dynamic transition at work already in the very fabric of creation and scripture. It is an essentially integrating vision. Cosmology, scriptural revelation, anthropology, asceticism hang together as aspects of the unfolding christocentric mystery of salvation and deification. Within that framework, Maximus' biblical hermeneutics, properly speaking, and his understanding of the task of exegesis are corollaries of his larger spiritual theology. And yet, in response to Florovsky's assessment, I would not want to sell short the underlying logical and philosophical subtlety that informs the Confessor's exegesis of scripture. There is a foundational "architectural" framework in Maximus' conception of the very nature of scripture itself. He presupposes at all times that there is a harmonious, albeit mysterious, "logic" to scripture as a whole, traces of which he hopes to uncover in his own mapping of the organic relations between biblical words and symbols, and his application of them to the ascetic life.

The fundamentally Origenian inspiration of his hermeneutics and doctrine of revelation goes without saying. The Logos' gradual self-communication—through the λόγοι of creation, the πνεῦμα of scripture, and the person of Jesus Christ—is depicted as commensurate with the human *transitus* toward him in the spiritual life. Maximus, however, brings all aspects of revelation and the whole "magnetic field"[4] of scriptural figures to focus on the central μυστήριον of the historical incarnation. This we saw in the analysis of the "three laws" and "three incarnations."[5] It is the Logos-*Christ,* not simply the transcendent mediatorial Logos (as enhanced in the Origenist system that Maximus was seeking to correct), who authors the natural law and the written law, and who initiates his "incarnation" in creation and scripture, leading them all to a culmination in the person of Jesus Christ, the very embodiment of the eternal law of grace. After the historical incarnation, then, the λόγοι and τύποι of creation and scripture do not suddenly lose their force but continue to be the effective instruments of Christ's self-communication in the Church and in individual souls. Indeed, his continuing "incarnation" in the λόγοι of creation and scripture provides the channel of human communion with him in all aspects of the spiritual life: practical, contemplative, mystagogical.

This christocentric perspective regulates Maximus' whole treatment of scripture, his understanding both of the deeper scheme of scriptural symbolism and of the contemplation of scripture (γραφικὴ θεωρία). He adapts the mature symbolic system and λόγοι theory of Pseudo-Dionysius and engages a hierarchical scheme of revelation—seen in the configurations of τύπος-ἀλήθεια, ἀλήθεια-ἀρχέτυπος, etc.—to the extent that it provides a structural framework for understanding the "contraction" of all the λόγοι of scripture toward the one comprehending Logos-Christ. In using this symbolic pattern, however, Maximus makes clear that the transition from the particular and most apparent objects of contemplation—the letter of scripture, the

Conclusion   253

phenomenon in creation—to their inner principles (λόγοι) as contained in the Logos-Christ is not a pure *reduction* of the external reality, the πρᾶγμα, to its spirit. Such was the penchant Maximus had observed in the radical forms of Origenist—or better yet, Evagrianist—spirituality which had continued to hold sway in certain monastic circles even, it seems, into his own lifetime. Symbols, scriptural and otherwise, serve not just to point the mind to spiritual archetypes, but also indicate the *irreducible* relation between material realities and their archetypes. Through contemplation of symbols, the mind is drawn in or "contracted" toward the unifying plan, the comprehensive λόγος of all things, and so too toward the ineffable Logos-Christ himself; but so long as human beings are striving toward ultimate deification, the final revelation, images and concepts derived from sensible realities will always in principle be necessary to undergird the mind in its spiritual *diabasis*.

As was seen in the earlier analysis of the heavily "Dionysian" *Ambiguum* 37 and its bearing on the hermeneutics of the *Ad Thalassium*, Maximus treats this subordinationist or hierarchical symbolism as an ideal pattern of contemplation that he does not always carry out systematically in his actual exegesis of particular passages of scripture. Scriptural symbols are organically related to the one μυστήριον of Christ, but for Maximus the exegetical goal is not to determine exhaustively all the possible configurations and interrelations of those symbols, but simply to recover something of the deeper "rational" (λογικός) structure of scripture that points his readers toward the mystery of salvation in Christ. More than once in the *Ad Thalassium*, Maximus indicates that his own exegeses are a modest beginning in the direction of a deeper penetration of the christological content of scripture.

The exegete, like every other Christian, sees through a glass darkly. Scripture is a "cosmos" and an elusive one at that.[6] Maximus would certainly have concurred with the sentiments of a modern Russian theologian who has written:

> The Bible is an entire universe, it is a mystical organism, and it is only partially that we attain to living in it. The Bible is inexhaustible for us because of its divine content and its composition, its many aspects; by reason, also, of our limited and changing mentality. The Bible is a heavenly constellation, shining

above us eternally, while we move on the sea of human existence. We gaze at the constellation, and it remains fixed, but it is also continually changing its place in relation to us.[7]

Andrew Louth, in a trenchant analysis of the nature of patristic allegory, notes that its primary purpose for the Fathers was not to deal with "contingent difficulties" so much as to be "a means of ensuring that we do not evade the fundamental 'ontological difficulty' which opens us to the ultimate mystery of Christ contained in the Scriptures." The real "difficulty" of scripture "arises from the depth of its signification, and forces us to find a point of stability, or is rather a warning that we have yet to find it."[8]

For Maximus the essence of ἀναγωγή, the spiritual interpretation of scripture generally speaking, consists precisely in arriving at a host of possible insights or speculations into the stabilizing mystery of Christ. A given scriptural symbol or set of symbols may evoke a whole number of different, sometimes even divergent, interpretations. Maximus thrives on the diversity of possible meanings, which do not always warrant a reduction to the most "gnostic" interpretations. Where such a "more gnostic" (γνωστικώ-τερον) explanation is proposed, it might very well entail none other than an insight into the mystery of the incarnation as it relates to the *practice* of the spiritual life.[9] Frequently, as in his long response to Question 64 on the figure of Jonah, Maximus arrives at a wide variety of insights that span the whole range of spiritual doctrine: the fall and anthropology, salvation and Christology, the spiritual life of the soul, the Church and eschatology, and so on. Yet these insights, even if they entail some measure of pious speculation or "conjecture" (στοχασμός), are not mere stabs in the dark, so long as they are engaged by the historical and ontological reality of the incarnation.

The instinct of Maximus' hermeneutics, as of his entire theological enterprise, is toward unity in diversity. His exegesis only manifests further his underlying vision of the healthy and thoroughly profitable diversity of material symbols in scripture and creation. The value of those symbols lies not in their sheer reducibility to one unifying spiritual logos in a timeless moment of contemplation. Maximus envisions the Logos-Christ, himself the final revealer of the comprehensive logos of all things, working precisely through the diversity of symbolic meanings in scripture and creation that are ever illuminating the practical, contemplative, and mystagogical aspects of the monk's spiritual *diabasis*. Set in the context of Maximus' ongoing criticism of radical intellectualism in the Byzantine monastic tradition, authentic revelation is a process not of extreme spiritualization but of a *transfiguration* in which material realities disclose their created fullness κατὰ Χριστόν.[10]

This hermeneutical principle informs all of the Confessor's exegetical techniques, and the whole of what I have called his theological and pedagogical use of scripture: typology and allegory, etymology, arithmology, and extrapolation from the grammar and syntax of the biblical texts. All of these provide Maximus an entry and a means of research into the logical and symbolic structures in scripture, upon which basis he telescopes his interpretations in individual expositions of spiritual doctrine: be it an exposé of the three modes of the spiritual life (Question 25), a summary of ecclesiology and anthropology (Question 63), a miniature commentary on the prophecy of Jonah (Question 64), a rehearsal of the spiritual *diabasis* inaugurated by Christ (Question 55), an excursus on the "researching" of our salvation (Question 59), or something more modest.

The analysis of Maximus' exegesis of scripture in the *Quaestiones ad Thalassium* brings us full circle: not to a towering figure in the history of patristic exegesis or a grand innovator in hermeneutical method, but to the spiritual father and teacher of monks called upon in this instance to discover spiritual benefits even in the most obscure corners of scripture. Maximus pleads in his introduction to Thalassius that he is not a scientist of scripture, and we can take him at his word. Like numerous monastic exegetes of his time, he was all too willing to build upon the genius of Origen and the Alexandrian masters. But seeing Maximus out of his element in the *Ad Thalassium* perhaps gives us a most important insight into the depth of his Christocentrism. As an exegete he is an eclectic in method, and something of a "researcher" still in the science of scripture, but a theologian and indeed a philosopher of the incarnation in his deepest intuitions.

For Maximus, all of scripture converges in the double-sided μυστήριον of the incarnation, which embraces the incarnational descent of the Logos-Christ on the one hand, and the ascent and deification of humanity on the other. In *Ad Thalassium* 22, a *locus classicus* dealt with earlier, Maximus describes this mystery precisely in its "historical" dimensions, the consecutive "ages" of incarnation (or "activity") and deification (or "passivity").[11] His exegetical legacy lies in the fact that it is this *salvation-historical* reality that is the summit, the axis, of the symbolic structure of scripture. Types, foreshadowings, prefigurations, images, all find their "future" or teleological significance in the *archetype* of this *mysterium Christi*. The "intelligible" sense of scripture is none other than the truth that Christ is bringing to completion in the historical and eschatological reality of salvation. Here I am reminded again of I.-H. Dalmais' remark that Maximus gives ultimate precedence, not to the hierarchical antithesis of figure and reality, but to the salvation-historical dialectic of preparation and fulfillment.[12] Yet the "historical" culmination of the mystery of Christ in the contingent realms of creation and scripture—and at last in the lives of the faithful who contemplate the world and the scriptures—vindicates precisely the archetypal and "ontological" truth of that mystery.

Christ has himself completed the incarnational "preparation," but the "fulfillment" of the mystery, in the Church and in individual believers, is an ongoing, open-ended reality that is still unfolding. At present, the monk must find himself drawn up into it, captivated by it, making the mystery real for himself in the whole of his spiritual life, and especially now in his meditation on scripture. He must research the spiritual sense of scripture as the *eschatological* sense in which he is summoned now to live.[13] This mystery is, after all, the very substance of his salvation. And it is Maximus the Confessor's ultimate "answer" to the petitions of Thalassius, albeit one that comes less as a final resolution of $ἀπορίαι$ than as a basis for further probing and searching.

Notes

1. See above, introduction, n. 83 and related text.
2. *The Byzantine Fathers of the Sixth to Eighth Century*, 213.
3. Ibid.
4. This analogy is picked up by Andrew Louth from the work of Paul Claudel to describe how patristic exegetes consistently aim to show the inner

organic relation of scriptural figures to the *mysterium Christi*; Louth adds: "The idea of a *magnetic field* is an attractive one: one could develop the analogy by thinking of the mystery of Christ as a magnetic pole and the field of force as the *regula fidei*, the rule of faith, in the context of which the Scriptures are to be interpreted and which is itself derived from the Scriptures" (*Discerning the Mystery: An Essay in the Nature of Theology* [Oxford: Oxford University Press, 1983], 121).

5. See the section on The Three Laws and the Three Incarnations in chapter 2 above.

6. See the celebrated passage from *Ambiguum* 10 as quoted above, chapter 2, n. 39 and related text.

7. Sergius Bulgakov, *The Orthodox Church*, revised ET by Lydia Kesich from the original 1935 Russian ed. (Crestwood, N.Y.: St. Vladimir's Seminary Press, 1988), 20-21.

8. Louth, *Discerning the Mystery*, 112. Louth further observes that patristic allegory "is a way of holding us before the mystery which is the ultimate 'difficulty' of the Scriptures—a difficulty, a mystery, which challenges us to revise our understanding of what might be meant by meaning; a difficulty, a mystery, which calls on us for a response of metanoia, change of mental perspective, repentance" (p. 111).

9. See above, chapter 3, n. 86 and related text.

10. On the importance of this principle in Maximus' larger philosophical theology, see Paul Plass, "'Moving Rest' in Maximus the Confessor," *Classica et mediaevalia* 35 (1984): 183-185.

11. See above, chapter 2, n. 149 and related text.

12. See above, chapter 2, n. 134 and related text.

13. Here Maximus touches on a concern of some modern theologians who would instead seek to retrieve the *eschatological* sense of scripture in the name of the *literal* sense. In an insightful recent study, Rowan Williams appeals for a recapturing of the diachronic, and indeed "dramatic" reading of the literal narrative of scripture: "...we might try reconceiving the literal sense of Scripture as an *eschatological* sense. To read diachronically the history that we call a history of *salvation* is to 'read' our own time in the believing community (and so too the time of our world) as capable of being integrated into such a history, in a future we cannot but call God's because we have no secure human way of planning it or thematising it" ("The Literal Sense of Scripture," *Modern Theology* 7 [1991]: 132).

Bibliography

Primary Literature

Editions of the Quaestiones ad Thalassium

Maximi Confessoris Quaestiones ad Thalassium 1-64. Greek text edited by François Combefis. Patrologia graeca, vol. 90, cols. 244-785. Edited by J.-P. Migne. Paris, 1850.

Maximi Confessoris Quaestiones ad Thalassium. I. Quaestiones I-LV una cum latine interpretatione Ioannis Scotti Eriugenae. Edited by Carl Laga and Carlos Steel. Corpus christianorum, series graeca, no. 7. Turnhout: Brepols—Leuven University Press, 1980.

Editions of Other Works of Maximus the Confessor

Maximi Confessoris Quaestiones et dubia. Greek text edited by José Declerck. Corpus christianorum, series graeca, no. 10. Turnhout: Brepols—Leuven University Press, 1982.

S. P. N. Maximi Confessoris opera omnia. Greek texts edited by François Combefis and Franz Oehler. Patrologia graeca, vols. 90 and 91. Edited by J.-P. Migne. Paris, 1850, 1863.

Translations of Works of Maximus the Confessor

Maximos der Bekenner, All-Eins in Christus. Selected and translated by Endre von Ivánka. Einsiedeln: Johannes-Verlag, 1961.

Maximus Confessor: Selected Writings. Translated with notes by George C. Berthold. Preface by Irénée-Henri Dalmais. Introduction by Jaroslav Pelikan. Classics of Western Spirituality. Mahwah, N.J.: Paulist Press, 1985.

Maximus the Confessor: The Ascetic Life and Four Centuries on Charity. Translated with an introduction by Polycarp Sherwood. Ancient Christian Writers, no. 21. Westminster, Md.: Newman Press, 1957.

Saint Maxime le Confesseur: Le mystère du salut. Texts presented with a French translation by Astérios Argyriou. Introduction by I.-H. Dalmais. Namur: Les Éditions du Soleil Levant, 1964.

Editions of Other Patristic Sources

Anastasius Sinaïta. *Quaestiones et responsiones centum quinquaginta quatuor.* Greek text edited by Jacob Gretser (1617). Patrologia graeca, vol. 89, columns 312-824. Edited by J.-P. Migne. Paris, 1865.

Apophthegmata patrum. Collectio alphabetica. Greek text edited by J.-B. Cotelier (1647). Patrologia graeca, vol. 65, cols. 71-440. Edited by J.-P. Migne. Paris, 1864.

Barsanuphius and John: Questions and Answers. Greek text edited with an English translation by Derwas Chitty. Patrologia orientalis, vol. 31, fasc. 3. Paris: Firmin-Didot, 1966.

S. P. N. Basilii Cesareae Cappadociae archiepiscopi opera omnia quae extant. Patrologia graeca, vol. 31. Edited by J.-P. Migne. Paris, 1985.

La chaîne palestinienne sur le Psaume 118. 2 vols. Greek text with a French translation and notes by Marguerite Harl. Sources chrétiennes, nos. 189-190. Paris: Les Éditions du Cerf, 1972.

Diadoque de Photiké: Œuvres spirituelles. Greek text edited with a French translation by Édouard des Places. Revised ed. Sources chrétiennes, no. 5. Paris: Les Éditions du Cerf, 1966.

S. Dionysius Areopagitae opera omnia quae extant. Greek texts edited by Balthasar Cordier (1634). Patrologia graeca, vol. 3. Edited by J.-P. Migne. Paris, 1889.

Dorothée de Gaza: Œuvres spirituelles. Greek text with a French translation, introduction, and notes by L. Regnault and J. de Préville. Sources chrétiennes, no. 92. Paris: Les Éditions du Cerf, 1963.

Évagre le Pontique: Scholies aux Proverbes. Greek text edited with a French translation by Paul Géhin. Sources chrétiennes, no. 340. Paris: Les Éditions du Cerf, 1987.

Evagriana Syriaca: Textes inédits du British Museum et de la Vatiacane. Bibliothèque du *Muséon,* vol. 31. Syriac texts edited with a French translation by J. Muyldermans. Louvain: Publications Universitaires, 1952.

Die 50 geistlichen Homilien des Makarios. Greek texts edited by Hermann Dörries, Erich Klostermann, and Matthias Kroeger. Patristische Texte und Studien, vol. 4. Berlin: Walter de Gruyter, 1964.

Gregorii Nysseni Opera. 9 vols. with a supplement. Edited by Werner Jaeger, Hermann Langerbeck, and Heinrich Dörrie. Leiden: E. J. Brill, 1960-67.

S. P. N. Gregorii episcopi Nysseni operae quae reperiri potuerunt omnia. Patrologia graeca, vols. 44-46. Edited by J.-P. Migne. Paris, 1863.

Johannis Cassianus: Conlationes XXIIII. Latin text edited by Michael Petschenig. Corpus scriptorum ecclesiasticorum latinorum, vol. 13. Vienna: C. Geroldi, 1886.

Makarios/Symeon: Reden und Briefe: Die Sammlung I des Vaticanus Graecus 694 (B). Greek texts edited by Heinz Berthold. Die griechischen christlichen Schriftsteller der ersten Jahrhunderte. Berlin: Akademie-Verlag, 1973.

Mark the Hermit. *Opuscula.* Greek texts edited by Andrea Gallandi (1772). Patrologia graeca, vol. 65, cols. 905-1140. Edited by J.-P. Migne. Paris, 1864.

Nilus of Ancyra. *Epistulae.* Greek text edited by L. Allatius (1668). Patrologia graeca, vol. 79, columns 81-581. Edited by J.-P. Migne. Paris, 1865.

Origène: Philocalie, 1-20 sur les Écritures. Greek text edited with a French translation by Marguerite Harl. Sources chrétiennes, no. 302. Paris: Les Éditions du Cerf, 1983.

Origenes Werke. 12 vols. Greek and Latin texts edited by P. Koetschau et al. Die griechischen christlichen Schriftsteller der ersten drei Jahrhunderte. Leipzig: J. C. Hinrichs; and Berlin: Akademie-Verlag, 1899-1955.

Les six centuries des 'Kephalaia Gnostica' d'Évagre le Pontique. Syriac text edited with a French translation by Antoine Guillaumont. Patrologia orientalis, vol. 28, fasc. 1. Paris: Firmin-Didot, 1958.

Vita ac certamen. Greek text of the Life of Maximus. Edited by François Combefis. Patrologia graeca, vol. 90, cols. 68-109. Edited by J.-P. Migne. Paris, 1850.

Translations of Other Patristic Sources

The Ascetical Homilies of Saint Isaac the Syrian. Translated by the Holy Transfiguration Monastery. Boston: Holy Transfiguration Monastery, 1984.

The Ascetic Works of Saint Basil. Translated with an introduction and notes by W. K. L. Clarke. Translations of Christian Literature, series I: Greek Texts. London: S. P. C. K., 1925.

Evagrius Ponticus: The Praktikos; Chapters on Prayer. Translated with an introduction and notes by John E. Bamberger. Cistercian Studies, no. 4. Kalamazoo: Cistercian Publications, 1981.

Gregory of Nyssa: The Life of Moses. Translated with an introduction and notes by Everett Ferguson and Abraham Malherbe. Classics of Western Spirituality. Ramsay, N.J.: Paulist Press, 1978.

John Cassian: Conferences. Translated by Colm Luibheid. Introduction by Owen Chadwick. Classics of Western Spirituality. Mahwah, N.J.: Paulist Press, 1985.

Markus Eremita: Asketische und dogmatische Schriften. German translation with an introduction and notes by Otmar Hesse. Bibliothek der griechischen Literatur, vol. 19. Stuttgart: Anton Hiersemann, 1985.

Origen: On First Principles. Translated with an introduction by G. W. Butterworth. New York: Harper and Row—Harper Torchbooks, 1966; reprint ed., Gloucester, Mass.: Peter Smith, 1973.

Origen: The Song of Songs: Commentary and Homilies. Translated and annotated by R. P. Lawson. Ancient Christian Writers, no. 26. Westminster, Md.: Newman Press, 1957.

The Philokalia: The Complete Text. Compiled by St. Nikodimos of the Holy Mountain and St. Makarios of Corinth. Edited and translated by G. E. H. Palmer, Philip Sherrard, and Kallistos Ware. 2 vols. London and Boston: Faber, 1979 and 1981.

Pseudo-Dionysius: The Complete Works. Translated by Colm Luibheid. Foreward, notes, and translation collaboration by Paul Rorem. Preface by René Roques. Introductions by Jaroslav Pelikan, Jean Leclercq, and Karlfried Froehlich. Classics of Western Spirituality. Mahwah, N.J.: Paulist Press, 1987.

The Sayings of the Desert Fathers. Translated by Benedicta Ward. Foreword by Metropolitan Anthony. Cistercian Studies, no. 59. Kalamazoo: Cistercian Publications, 1975.

Three Byzantine Saints: Contemporary Biographies of St. Daniel the Stylite, St. Theodore of Sykeon, and St. John the Almsgiver. Translated by Elizabeth Dawes and Norman Baynes. Oxford: Basil Blackwell, 1948. Reprint ed. Crestwood, N.Y.: St. Vladimir's Seminary Press, 1977.

Secondary Literature

Aubineau, Michel. "Dossier patristique sur Jean XIX, 23-24: La tunique sans couture du Christ." In *La Bible et les pères (Colloque de Strasbourg, 1er-3 octobre 1969)*, 9-50. Paris: Presses Universitaires de France, 1971.

Balthasar, Hans Urs von. *Kosmische Liturgie: Das Weltbild Maximus' des Bekenners*. 2nd ed. Einsiedeln: Johannes-Verlag, 1961.

―――. *Origen: Spirit and Fire: A Thematic Anthology of His Writings*. Translated by Robert J. Daly. Washington: The Catholic University of America Press, 1984.

Bardy, Gustave. "La littérature patristique des 'Quaestiones et Responsiones' sur l'Écriture sainte." *Revue biblique* 41 (1932): 210-236, 341-369, 516-537; and 42 (1933): 14-30, 211-229, 328-352.

Baynes, Norman. "The *Pratum Spirituelle*." *Orientalia christiana periodica* 13 (1947). Reprinted in *Byzantine Studies and Other Essays*, 261-270. London: University of London—Athlone Press, 1955.

Beck, Hans-Georg. *Kirche und theologische Literatur im byzantinischen Reich*. Handbuch der Altertumswissenschaft, section. 12. Byzantinisches Handbuch, part 2, vol. 1. Munich: C. H. Beck, 1959.

Berthold, George. "The Cappadocian Roots of Maximus the Confessor." In *Maximus Confessor: Actes du Symposium sur Maxime le Confesseur, Fribourg, 2-5 septembre 1980*, 51-59. Edited by Felix Heinzer and Christoph von Schönborn. Paradosis, no. 27. Fribourg: Éditions Universitaires, 1982.

―――. "Did Maximus the Confessor Know Augustine?" *Studia patristica*, vol. 17, 14-17. Edited by Elizabeth Livingstone. Oxford and New York: Pergamon Press, 1982.

―――. "History and Exegesis in Evagrius and Maximus." In *Origeniana Quarta: Die Referate des 4. internationalen Origeneskongresses (Innsbruck, 2-6. September 1985)*, 390-404. Edited by Lothar Lies. Innsbrucker theologische Studien, vol. 19. Innsbruck and Vienna: Tyrolia-Verlag, 1987.

Bienert, Wolfgang. *'Allegoria' und 'Anagoge' bei Didymos dem Blinden von Alexandria*. Patristische Texte und Studien, vol. 13. Berlin and New York: Walter de Gruyter, 1972.

Bornert, René. *Les commentaires byzantins de la divine liturgie, du VIIe au XVe siècle*. Archives de l'Orient chrétien, no. 9. Paris: Institut Français d'Études Byzantines, 1966.

———. "Explication de la liturgie et interprétation de l'Écriture chez Maxime le Confesseur." *Studia patristica*, vol. 10, 323-327. Texte und Untersuchungen, vol. 107. Berlin: Akademie-Verlag, 1970.
Bousset, Wilhelm. *Apophthegmata: Studien zur Geschichte des ältesten Mönchtums*. Tübingen: J. C. B. Mohr, 1923. Reprint ed. Aalen: Scientia-Verlag, 1969.
Brock, Sebastian. "An Early Syriac Life of Maximus the Confessor." *Analecta bollandiana* 91 (1973): 299-346.
Brown, Peter. *Society and the Holy in Late Antiquity*. Berkeley: University of California Press, 1982.
Bulgakov, Sergius. *The Orthodox Church*. Revised translation by Lydia Kesich from the original 1935 Russian ed. Crestwood, N.Y.: St. Vladimir's Seminary Press, 1988.
Burton-Christie, Douglas. "Scripture and the Quest for Holiness in the *Apophthegmata patrum*." Ph.D. dissertation, Graduate Theological Union, 1988.
Campenhausen, Hans von. "The Ascetic Idea of Exile in Ancient and Medieval Monasticism." In *Tradition and Life in the Church*, 231-251. Translated by A. V. Littledale. Philadelphia: Fortress Press, 1968.
Canévet, Mariette. *Grégoire de Nysse et l'herméneutique biblique: Étude des rapports entre le langage et la connaissance de Dieu*. Paris: Études Augustiniennes, 1983.
Ceresa-Gestaldo, A. "Tradition et innovation linguistique chez Maxime le Confesseur." In *Maximus Confessor: Actes du Symposium sur Maxime le Confesseur, Fribourg, 2-5 septembre 1980*, 123-137. Edited by Felix Heinzer and Christoph von Schönborn. Paradosis, no. 27. Fribourg: Éditions Universitaires, 1982.
Chadwick, Henry. "The Identity and Date of Mark the Monk." *Eastern Churches Review* 4 (1972): 125-130.
———. "John Moschus and His Friend Sophronius the Sophist." *Journal of Theological Studies* N.S. 25 (1974): 49-74.
Chitty, Derwas. *The Desert a City: An Introduction to the Study of Egyptian and Palestinian Monasticism under the Christian Empire*. Oxford: Basil Blackwell, 1966.
Colombás, García. "La biblia en la espiritualidad del monacato primitivo." *Yermo* 2 (1964): 113-129.
Croce, Vittorio. *Tradizione e ricerca: Il metodo teologico di san Massimo il Confessore*. Studia patristica mediolanensia, no. 2. Milan: Vita e Pensiero, 1974.

Daley, Brian. "Apokatastasis and 'Honorable Silence' in the Eschatology of Maximus the Confessor." In *Maximus Confessor: Actes du Symposium sur Maxime le Confesseur, Fribourg, 2-5 septembre 1980*, 309-339. Edited by Felix Heinzer and Christoph von Schönborn. Paradosis, no. 27. Fribourg: Éditions Universitaires, 1982.

Dalmais, Irénée-Henri. "L'anthropologie spirituelle de saint Maxime le Confesseur." *Recherches et débats* 36 (1961): 202-211.

———. "La doctrine ascétique de saint Maxime le Confesseur d'après le *Liber Asceticus*." *Irénikon* 26 (1953): 17-39.

———. "La fonction unificatrice du Verbe Incarné dans les œuvres spirituelles de saint Maxime le Confesseur." *Sciences ecclésiastiques* 14 (1962): 445-459.

———. "La manifestation du Logos dans l'homme et dans l'Église: Typologie anthropologique et typologie ecclésiale d'après Qu. Thal. 60 et la Mystagogie." In *Maximus Confessor: Actes du Symposium sur Maxime le Confesseur, Fribourg, 2-5 septembre 1980*, 13-25. Edited by Felix Heinzer and Christoph von Schönborn.Paradosis, no. 27. Fribourg: Éditions Universitaires, 1980.

———. "Maxime le Confesseur." *Dictionnaire de spiritualité*. Vol. 10.

———. "Saint Maxime le Confesseur et la crise de l'origénisme monastique." In *Théologie de la vie monastique: Études sur la tradition patristique*, 411-421. Théologie, no. 49. Paris: Aubier, 1961.

———. "La théorie des 'logoi' des créatures chez saint Maxime le Confesseur." *Revue des sciences philosophiques et théologiques* 36 (1952): 244-249.

———. "Un traité de théologie contemplative: Le commentaire du Pater Noster de saint Maxime le Confesseur." *Revue d'ascétique et de mystique* 29 (1953): 123-159.

Daniélou, Jean. *L'être et le temps chez Grégoire de Nysse*. Leiden: E. J. Brill, 1970.

———. *Gospel Message and Hellenistic Culture. A History of Early Christian Doctrine before the Council of Nicaea*, vol. 2. Translated by J. A. Baker. Philadelphia: Westminster Press, 1973.

Desprez, Vincent, and Mariette Canévet. "Macaire" (8. Pseudo-Macaire; Macaire-Symeon). *Dictionnaire de spiritualité*. Vol. 10.

Devreesse, Robert. "La fin inédite d'une lettre de saint Maxime: Un baptême forcé de juifs et de samaritains à Carthage en 632." *Revue des sciences religieuses* 17 (1937): 25-35.

———. "La vie de s. Maxime le Confesseur et ses recensions." *Analecta bollandiana* 46 (1928): 5-49.

Diehl, Charles. *L'Afrique byzantine: Histoire de la domination byzantine en Afrique (533-709)*. 2 vols. Paris: E. Leroux, 1896.
Disdier, M.-Th. "Les fondements dogmatiques de la spiritualité de saint Maxime le Confesseur." *Echos d'Orient* 29 (1930): 296-313.
———. "Le témoignage spirituel de Thalassius le Lybien." *Études byzantines* 2 (1944): 79-118.
Dorival, Gilles. "Des commentaires de l'Écriture aux chaînes." In *Le monde grec ancien et la Bible*, 361-383. Directed by Claude Mondésert. Bible de tous les temps, vol. 1. Paris: Beauchesne, 1984.
Dörrie, Heinrich. "Erotapokriseis" (A. nichtchristlich). *Reallexikon für Antike und Christentum*. Vol. 6.
Dörries, Hermann. "Die Bibel im ältesten Mönchtum." *Theologische Literaturzeitung* 72 (1947): 215-222.
———. "Erotapokriseis" (B. christlich). *Reallexikon für Antike und Christentum*. Vol. 6.
———. *Symeon von Mesopotamien: Die Überlieferung der messalianischen Makarios-Shriften*. Texte und Untersuchungen, vol. 95.1. Leipzig: J. C. Hinrich, 1941.
———. *Die Theologie des Makarios/Symeon*. Abhandlungen der Akademie der Wissenschaften in Göttingen (philosophisch-historische Klasse), series 3, no. 103. Göttingen: Vandenhoeck und Ruprecht, 1978.
Duval, Y.-M. *Le livre de Jonas dans la littérature chrétienne grecque et latine*. 2 vols. Paris: Études Augustiniennes, 1973.
Evans, G. R. *The Language and Logic of the Bible: The Earlier Middle Ages*. Cambridge: Cambridge University Press, 1984.
Florovsky, Georges. "The Anthropomorphites in the Egyptian Desert." In *Creation and Redemption*, 89-96. The Collected Works of Georges Florovsky, vol. 4. Belmont, Mass.: Nordland, 1975.
———. *The Byzantine Ascetic and Spiritual Fathers*. The Collected Works of Georges Florovsky, vol. 10. Translated by Raymond Miller, Anne-Marie Döllinger-Labriolle, and Helmut Schmiedel. Vaduz: Büchervertriebsanstalt, 1987.
———. *The Byzantine Fathers of the Sixth to Eighth Century*. The Collected Works of Georges Florovsky, vol. 9. Translated by Raymond Miller, Anne-Marie Döllinger-Labriolle, and Helmut Schmiedel. Vaduz: Büchervertriebsanstalt, 1987.
Gaïth, Jérome. *La conception de la liberté chez Grégoire de Nysse*. Études de philosophie médiévale, no. 43. Paris: Vrin, 1953.

Garrigues, Juan Miguel. "Le dessein d'adoption du Créateur dans son rapport au Fils d'après s. Maxime le Confesseur." In *Maximus Confessor: Actes du Symposium sur Maxime le Confesseur, Fribourg, 2-5 septembre 1980*, 173-192. Edited by Felix Heinzer and Christoph von Schönborn. Paradosis, no. 27. Fribourg: Éditions Universitaires, 1980.

———. *Maxime le Confesseur: La charité, avenir divin de l'homme*. Théologie historique, no. 38. Paris: Beauchesne, 1976.

———. "La Personne composée du Christ d'après Maxime le Confesseur." *Revue thomiste* 74 (1974): 181-204.

Geerard, Maurice, ed. *Clavis patrum graecorum*, vol. 3. Corpus christianorum. Turnhout: Brepols, 1979.

Gersh, Stephen. *From Iamblichus to Eriugena: An Investigation of the Pre-History and Evolution of the Pseudo-Dionysian Tradition*. Studien zur Problemgeschichte der Antike und mittelalterischen Philosophie, no. 8. Leiden: E. J. Brill, 1978.

Gögler, Rolf. *Zur Theologie des biblischen Wortes bei Origenes*. Düsseldorf: Patmos-Verlag, 1963.

Gorce, Denys. *La lectio divina des origenes du cénobitisme à saint Benoît et Cassiodore*, vol. 1. Wépion-sur-Meuse, Belgium: Monastère du Mont-Vièrge; Paris: Librairie A. Picard, 1925.

Gribomont, Jean. "Marc le Moine." *Dictionnaire de spiritualité*. Vol. 10.

Guillaumont, Antoine. *Les 'Kephalaia gnostica' d'Évagre le Pontique et l'histoire de l'origénisme chez les grecs et chez les syriens*. Patristica sorbonensia, no. 5. Paris: Éditions du Seuil, 1962.

Guy, Jean-Claude. "Les *Apophthegmata patrum*." In *Théologie de la vie monastique: Études sur la tradition patristique*, 73-83. Théologie, no. 49. Paris: Aubier, 1961.

Guy, Jean-Claude, and Jean Kirchmeyer. "Écriture sainte et vie spirituelle" (II. Écriture et vie spirituelle dans la tradition [A. Époque patristique; 4. Le monachisme]). *Dictionnaire de spiritualité*. Vol. 4, part 1.

Hanson, R. P. C. "Interpretations of Hebrew Names in Origen." *Vigiliae christianae* 10 (1956): 103-123.

Harl, Marguerite. *Origène et la fonction révélatrice du Verbe incarné*. Patristica sorbonensia, no. 2. Paris: Éditions du Seuil, 1958.

———. "Y a-t-il une influence du 'grec biblique' sur la langue spirituelle des chrétiens? Examples tirés du psaume 118 et des commentateurs, d'Origène à Théodoret." In *La Bible et les pères (Colloque de Strasbourg, 1er-3 octobre 1969)*, 243-262. Paris: Presses Universitaires de France, 1971.

Hausherr, Irénée. "Centuries." *Dictionnaire de spiritualité*. Vol. 2, part 1.
Heinzer, Felix. "L'explication trinitaire de l'économie chez Maxime le Confesseur." In *Maximus Confessor: Actes du Symposium sur Maxime le Confesseur, Fribourg, 2-5 septembre 1980*, 159-172. Paradosis, no. 27. Edited by Felix Heinzer and Christoph von Schönborn. Fribourg: Éditions Universitaires, 1982.
Heinzer, Felix, and Christoph von Schönborn, eds. *Maximus Confessor: Actes du Symposium sur Maxime le Confesseur, Fribourg, 2-5 septembre, 1980*. Paradosis, no. 27. Fribourg: Éditions Universitaires, 1982.
Ivánka, Endre von. "Κεφάλαια: Eine byzantinische Literaturform und ihre antiken Wurzeln." *Byzantinische Zeitschrift* 47 (1954): 285-291.
―――. "Der philosophische Ertrag der Auseinandersetzung Maximos des Bekenners mit dem Origenismus." *Jahrbuch der Österreichischen Byzantinischen Gesellschaft* 7 (1958): 23-49.
Jaeger, Werner. *Two Rediscovered Works of Ancient Christian Literature: Gregory of Nyssa and Macarius*. Leiden: E. J. Brill, 1954.
Jordan, Hermann. *Die Geschichte der altchristlichen Literatur*. Leipzig: Quelle und Meyer, 1911.
Kelsey, David. *The Uses of Scripture in Recent Theology*. Philadelphia: Fortress Press, 1975.
Kirchmeyer, Jean. "Écriture sainte et vie spirituelle" (II. Écriture et vie spirituelle dans la tradition [F. Dans l'église orientale]). *Dictionnaire de spiritualité*. Vol. 4, part 1.
Laga, Carl. "Maximi Confessoris ad Thalassium Quaestio 64." In *After Chalcedon: Studies in Theology and Church History Offered to Professor Albert Van Roey for His Seventieth Birthday*, 203-215. Edited by Carl Laga, J. A. Munitz, and L. van Rompay. Orientalia lovaniensia analecta, no. 18. Leuven: Departement Oriëntalistiek, 1985.
―――. "Maximus as a Stylist in *Quaestiones ad Thalassium*." In *Maximus Confessor: Actes du Symposium sur Maxime le Confesseur, Fribourg, 2-5 septembre 1980*, 139-146. Edited by Felix Heinzer and Christoph von Schönborn. Paradosis, no. 27. Fribourg: Éditions Universitaires, 1982.
Laga, Carl, J. A. Munitz, and L. van Rompay, eds. *After Chalcedon: Studies in Theology and Church History Offered to Professor Albert Van Roey for His Seventieth Birthday*. Orientalia lovaniensia analecta, no. 18. Leuven: Departement Oriëntalistiek, 1985.

Lampe, G. W. H., ed. *A Patristic Greek Lexikon*. Oxford: Oxford University Press, 1961.
Laüchli, Samuel. "Die Frage nach der Objektivität der Exegese des Origenes." *Theologische Zeitschrift* 10 (1954): 175-197.
Leclercq, Jean. *The Love of Learning and the Desire for God: A Study of Monastic Culture*. 3rd ed. Translated by Catharine Misrahi. New York: Fordham University Press, 1982.
Lemaître, J. "Contemplation" (Contemplation chez les grecs et autres orientaux chrétiens [II. La Θεωρία φυσική). *Dictionnaire de spiritualité*. Vol. 2, part 2.
Léthel, François-Marie. *Théologie de l'agonie du Christ: La liberté humaine du Fils de Dieu et son importance sotériologique mises en lumière par saint Maxime le Confesseur*. Théologie historique, no. 52. Paris: Beauchesne, 1979.
Loosen, Josef. *Logos und Pneuma im begnadeten Menschen bei Maximus Confessor*. Münsterische Beiträge zur Theologie, vol. 24. Münster: Aschendorff, 1941.
Louth, Andrew. *Discerning the Mystery: An Essay on the Nature of Theology*. Oxford: Oxford University Press, 1983.
Lubac, Henri de. *Exégèse médiévale: Les quatre sens de l'Écriture*. 2 parts, 4 vols. Théologie, nos. 41, 42, 59. Paris: Aubier, 1959, 1961, and 1964.
―――. *Histoire et esprit: L'intelligence de l'Écriture d'après Origène*. Paris: Aubier, 1950.
McGinn, Bernard, John Meyendorff, with Jean Leclercq, eds. *Christian Spirituality (I): Origins to the Twelfth Century*. World Spirituality: An Encyclopedic History of the Religious Quest, vol. 16. New York: Crossroad, 1985.
Madden, Nicholas. "The *Commentary on the Pater Noster*: An Example of the Structural Methodology of Maximus the Confessor." In *Maximus Confessor: Actes du Symposium sur Maxime le Confesseur, Fribourg, 2-5 septembre 1980*, 147-155. Edited by Felix Heinzer and Christoph von Schönborn. Paradosis, no. 27. Fribourg: Éditions Universitaires, 1982.
Margerie, Bertrand de. *Introduction à l'histoire de l'exégèse*. Vol. 1: *Les Pères grecs et orientaux*. Paris: Les Éditions du Cerf, 1980.
Meyendorff, John. *Byzantine Theology*. 2nd ed. New York: Fordham University Press—Rose Hill Books, 1979.
―――. *Christ in Eastern Christian Thought*. Crestwood, N.Y: St. Vladimir's Seminary Press, 1975.

―――. "Messalianism or Anti-Messalianism: A Fresh Look at the 'Macarian' Problem." In *Kyriakon: Festschrift Johannes Quasten*, 585-590. Edited by Patrick Granfield and Josef Jungmann. Münster: Aschendorff, 1970.

Neiman, David, and Margaret Schatkin, eds. *The Heritage of the Early Church: Essays in Honor of Georges Florovsky*. Orientalia christiana analecta, no. 195. Rome: Pontifical Institute of Oriental Studies, 1973.

Nellas, Panayiotis. *Deification in Christ: Orthodox Perspectives on the Nature of the Human Person*. Translated by Norman Russell. Crestwood, N.Y.: St. Vladimir's Seminary Press, 1987.

O'Laughlin, Michael. "Origenism in the Desert: Anthropology and Integration in Evagrius Ponticus." Th.D. dissertation, Harvard Divinity School, 1987.

Olphe-Galliard, Michel. "Conférences spirituelles." *Dictionnaire de spiritualité*. Vol. 2, part 2.

Opelt, Ilona. "Etymologie." *Reallexikon für Antike und Christentum*. Vol. 6.

Ostrogorsky, George. *History of the Byzantine State*. Rev. ed. Translated by Joan Hussey. New Brunswick, N.J.: Rutgers University Press, 1969.

Parys, Michel van. "Un maître spirituel oublié: Thalassios de Lybie." *Irénikon* 52 (1979): 214-240.

Pelikan, Jaroslav. "Council or Father or Scripture: The Concept of Authority in the Theology of Maximus the Confessor." In *The Heritage of the Early Church: Essays in Honor of Georges Florovsky*, 277-288. Edited by David Neiman and Margaret Schatkin. Orientalia christiana analecta, no.195. Rome: Pontifical Institute of Oriental Studies, 1973.

Piret, Pierre. *Le Christ et la Trinité selon Maxime le Confesseur*. Théologie historique, no. 69. Paris: Beauchesne, 1983.

Plass, Paul. "'Moving Rest' in Maximus the Confessor." *Classica et mediaevalia* 35 (1984): 177-190.

Podskalsky, Gerhard. *Theologie und Philosophie in Byzanz: Der Streit um die theologische Methodik in der spätbyzantinischen Geistesgeschichte (14./15. Jh.), seine systematischen Grundlage und seine historische Entwicklung*. Byzantinisches Archiv, no. 15. Munich: C. H. Beck, 1977.

Prado, José J. *Voluntad y naturaleza: La antropología filosófica de Maximo el Confesor*. Rio Cuata, Argentina: Ediciónes de la Universidad Nacional de Rio Cuarto, 1974.

Regnault, Lucien. "Théologie de la vie monastique selon Barsanuphe et Dorothée (VIe siècle)." In *Théologie de la vie monastique: Études sur la tradition patristique*, 315-322. Théologie, no. 49. Paris: Aubier, 1961.

Richard, Marcel. "Florilèges spirituels grecs." In *Dictionnaire de spiritualité*, vol. 5, cols. 475-512. Reprint ed. *Opera Minora*, vol. 1. Edited by E. Dekkers, M. Geerard, A. van Roey, and G. Verbeke. Turnhout: Brepols, 1976.

———. "Les véritables 'Questions et réponses' d'Anastase le Sinaïte." *Bulletin de l'Institut de Recherche et d'Histoire des Textes*, no. 15 (1967-1978): 39-56. Reprint ed. *Opera Minora*, vol. 3. Edited by E. Dekkers, M. Geerard, A. van Roey, and G. Verbeke. Turnhout: Brepols, 1977.

Riou, Alain. *Le monde et l'église selon Maxime le Confesseur*. Théologie historique, no. 22. Paris: Beauchesne, 1973.

Rorem, Paul. *Biblical and Liturgical Symbols within the Pseudo-Dionysian Synthesis*. Studies and Texts, vol. 71. Toronto: Pontifical Institute of Medieval Studies, 1984.

Rousse, Jacques. "Lectio divina et lecture spirituelle" (I. La lectio divina). *Dictionnaire de spiritualité*. Vol. 9.

Rousseau, Philip. *Ascetics, Authority, and the Church in the Age of Jerome and Cassian*. Oxford: Oxford University Press, 1978.

Schönborn, Christoph von. "Plaisir et douleur dans l'analyse de saint Maximus d'après les *Quaestiones ad Thalassium*." In *Maximus Confessor: Actes du Symposium sur Maxime le Confesseur, Fribourg, 2-5 septembre 1980*, 273-284. Edited by Felix Heinzer and Christoph von Schönborn. Paradosis, no. 27. Fribourg: Éditions Universitaires, 1982.

———. *Sophrone de Jérusalem: Vie monastique et confession dogmatique*. Théologie historique, no. 20. Paris: Beauchesne, 1972.

Sherwood, Polycarp. *An Annotated Date-List of the Works of Maximus the Confessor*. Studia anselmiana, fasc. 30. Rome: Herder, 1952.

———. *The Earlier Ambigua of St. Maximus the Confessor and His Refutation of Origenism*. Studia anselmiana, fasc. 36. Rome: Herder, 1955.

———. "Exposition and Use of Scripture in St. Maximus, as Manifest in the *Quaestiones ad Thalassium*." *Orientalia christiana periodica* 24 (1958): 202-207.

———. "Maximus and Origenism: Ἀρχή καὶ Τέλος." *Berichte zum XI. internationalen Byzantinisten-Kongreß*. Munich, 1958.

―――. "Survey of Recent Work on St. Maximus the Confessor." *Traditio* 20 (1964): 428-437.
Squire, A. K. "The Idea of the Soul as Virgin and Mother in Maximus the Confessor." *Studia patristica,* vol. 8, 456-461. Texte und Untersuchungen, vol. 93. Berlin: Akademie-Verlag, 1966.
Starr, Joshua. "St. Maximos and the Forced Baptism at Carthage in 632." *Byzantinisch-neugriechische Jahrbücher* 16 (1940): 192-196.
Tatakis, Basile. *La philosophie byzantine.* Histoire de la philosophie, fasc. supplémentaire, no. 2. Edited by Émile Bréhier. Paris: Presses Universitaires de France, 1949.
Thornton, Lionel. *The Dominion of Christ.* London: Dacre Press, 1952.
Thunberg, Lars. "Early Christian Interpretations of the Three Angels in Genesis 18." *Studia patristica,* vol. 7, 560-570. Texte und Untersuchungen, vol. 92. Berlin: Akademie-Verlag, 1966.
―――. *Man and the Cosmos: The Vision of St. Maximus the Confessor.* Crestwood, N.Y.: St. Vladimir's Seminary Press, 1985.
―――. *Microcosm and Mediator: The Theological Anthropology of Maximus the Confessor.* Lund: C. W. K. Gleerup, 1965.
Torjeson, Karen Jo. *Hermeneutical Procedure and Theological Method in Origen's Exegesis.* Patristische Texte und Studien, vol. 28. Berlin and New York: Walter de Gruyter, 1986.
Treu, Ursula. "Etymologie und Allegorie bei Klemens von Alexandria." *Studia patristica,* vol. 4, 191-211. Texte und Untersuchungen, vol. 79. Berlin: Akademie-Verlag, 1961.
Tsirpanlis, Constantine. "Praxis and Theoria: The Heart, Love, and Light Mysticism in Saint Isaac the Syrian." *Patristic and Byzantine Review* 6 (1987): 93-120.
Viller, Marcel. "Aux sources de la spiritualité de saint Maxime: Les œuvres d'Évagre le Pontique." *Revue d'ascétique et de mystique* 11 (1930): 156-184, 239-268, 331-336.
Völker, Walther. *Maximus Confessor als Meister des geistlichen Lebens.* Wiesbaden: Franz Steiner, 1965.
Ware, Timothy. "The Sacrament of Baptism and the Ascetic Life in the Teaching of Mark the Monk." *Studia patristica,* vol. 10, 441-452. Texte und Untersuchungen, vol. 107. Berlin: Akademie-Verlag, 1970.
Williams, Rowan. "The Literal Sense of Scripture." *Modern Theology* 7 (1991): 121-134.
Wutz, Franz. *Onomastica sacra: Untersuchungen zum Liber Interpretationis Nominum Hebraicorum des Hl. Hieronymus.* 2 parts. Texte und Untersuchungen, vol. 41.1-2. Leipzig: J. C. Hinrich, 1914-1915.

General Index

Abraham, 29, 30, 50, 110-111, 115, 160-161n, 166n, 217, 247n

Adam, 30, 34, 35, 82n, 111, 138, 166n, 206, 244n

allegorical interpretation (see Holy Scripture, allegorical interpretation of)

anagogical interpretation, 11, 14, 35, 54, 56, 61, 72, 100, 113, 114, 128, 140, 145, 161n, 166n; and arithmology, 211-219; and etymology, 203-211; and grammatical-syntactical exegesis, 219-228; meaning of ἀναγωγή, 185-192; "more gnostic" interpretations, 189, 191, 198, 203, 254; as a theological use of scripture, 192-228

Anastasius Sinaïta, 49-52, 70

anthropomorphism, 34, 60, 164n

Antony, 94n, 155n

Augustine of Hippo, 75n, 118, 166n

baptism, 31, 44, 45, 58, 115

Barsanuphius and John, 4, 47-49, 71, 250

Basil of Caesarea, 10, 39-40, 71, 78n, 79n, 87n, 88n, 89n

body, the, 99, 116-117, 125, 134, 154n, 155n, 173n, 174n, 175n, 200, 213

Clement of Alexandria, 211, 241n, 243n

conferences, monastic, 37-38, 39, 40-41, 52, 53, 84n

"conjecture" (στοχασμός), 187, 214, 230n, 242n, 254

contemplation (θεωρία), 55, 61, 96, 97, 99, 131, 133, 134, 135, 136, 146, 149, 172n, 173n, 174n, 175n, 176n, 178n, 181n, 182n, 205, 252-253; natural (φυσική), 54-55, 63, 104, 107, 132, 134, 137-139, 140, 141, 146, 157n, 158n, 173n, 175n, 176n, 177n, 178-179n, 181n, 201; paired with ascetic practice (see practice, ascetic); scriptural (γραφική), 71, 72, 108, 109, 139-145, 149, 159n, 160n, 179-180n, 212, 252, 253

creation, 15, 16, 30, 34, 62, 63, 66, 75n, 82n, 99, 100-106, 107, 108, 109, 111, 112, 117-119, 120, 122, 124, 128, 131, 132, 133, 137, 139, 141, 145, 152n, 153n, 155n, 156n, 157n, 158n, 168n, 169n, 171n, 172n, 177n, 185, 190, 193, 197, 213, 251, 252, 253, 254, 255, 256

David, 23n, 50, 68, 75n, 140, 141, 146, 158n, 162n, 165n, 173n, 189, 247n

deification, 90n, 101, 119, 127, 128-130, 146, 148, 151n, 164n, 167n, 168n, 171n, 173n, 192, 198, 199, 200, 205, 208, 222, 223, 233n, 237n, 243n, 248n, 251, 253, 255-256
demons, 41, 44, 47, 48, 49, 51, 53, 55, 57, 62-63, 71-72, 78n, 116, 144, 173n, 198, 212, 246n
desert fathers, 37-39, 47, 71, 77n, 78n, 250, 251
desire, 59, 67, 85n, 89n, 167n, 172n, 179n, 190, 231n, 236n, 247n
diabasis (spiritual "transit"): as grounded in creation and scripture, 100-117, 251; as human vocation, 95-96, 137-138; pioneered by Christ, 146, 214; terminology of, 96-99; as transition from letter to spirit in scripture, 98, 101, 112-117, 119, 149
Diadochus of Photice, 5, 58, 59, 89n
Didymus the Blind, 4, 7, 185, 223-224, 229n, 248n
Dionysius the Areopagite (Pseudo-Dionysius), 5, 15, 96, 102, 106, 107, 111-112, 125, 141, 145-146, 157n, 159n, 160n, 181n, 184-185, 213, 242n, 252, 253
Dorotheus of Gaza, 58, 59, 89n
Eusebius of Caesarea, 29-30
Evagrius Ponticus, 4, 5, 6, 7, 8, 9, 10, 16, 21n, 24n, 25n, 67-69, 70, 71, 72, 93n, 94n, 107, 113, 128, 133, 134, 155n, 158n, 162n, 171n, 188, 191, 220, 233n, 245n, 250
exegesis (See anagogical interpretation; Holy Scripture)
faith, 47, 60, 64, 90n, 92n, 105, 127, 130, 132, 144, 163n, 167n, 172-173n, 182n, 191, 198, 199, 201, 202, 208, 237n, 245n, 247n
fear of God, 32, 41, 44, 58-59, 68, 72, 89n, 90n, 134, 220, 246n
grace, 43, 44, 45, 58, 62, 72, 82n, 83n, 97, 117, 124, 125, 127, 129, 130, 135, 139, 141, 148, 151n, 166n, 169n, 180n, 181n, 182n, 188, 200, 202, 206, 208, 209-210, 211, 217, 221, 222, 223, 233n, 245n; law of, 117, 118, 119, 120, 122, 140, 165n, 167n, 252; and nature, 61, 114, 221-222, 247-248n
Gregory of Nazianzus, 5, 75n, 87n, 119, 154n, 173n
Gregory of Nyssa, 4, 5, 21n, 42, 58, 60, 76n, 81n, 83n, 89n, 93n, 96, 151n, 154n, 172n, 176n, 187, 190, 196, 229n, 230n, 231n, 235n, 238n, 244n
Hebrew language, 188, 203-204
Hesychius of Jerusalem, 30
Hezekiah, 112, 113, 115, 116, 134, 163n, 175n, 181n, 220, 235n, 236n
Holy Scripture: accommodation of, 106-112, allegorical interpretation of, 4, 30, 34, 38, 48, 60, 61, 63, 65, 70, 94n, 113, 114-115, 121, 131, 134, 138, 151n, 152n, 163n, 164n, 171n, 172n, 173-174n, 188, 191, 197-199, 219, 228, 235-236n, 237n, 254,

255, 257n; anagogical interpretation of (see anagogical interpretation); difficulties (ἀπορίαι) in, 14, 15, 29-36, 40, 46, 54-56, 57, 58-70, 72, 87n, 93n, 112, 249, 250, 256; incarnation of the Logos in, 103-104, 119-124, 146, 148-149, 160n, 168n; literal sense of, 30, 35, 38, 58, 60, 62, 63, 64, 65, 99, 100, 111, 112-115, 117, 131, 132, 149, 159n, 162n, 163n, 172n, 185, 186, 188, 189, 219, 220, 228, 229n, 244n, 246n, 257n; monastic use of, 35-36, 37-38, 39-40, 41-42, 43-45, 46-47, 48-49, 52, 54-56, 61-73, 78n; as object of contemplation, 41-42, 71, 72, 108, 137, 139-145; obstacles (σκάνδαλα) in, 111-112, 113, 161n; practical application of, 37-38, 39-40, 41, 48, 71-72, 78n; profitability (ὠφέλεια) of, 188, 193, 234n; spiritual sense of, 41, 61, 62, 64, 98, 100, 101, 106, 108, 109, 112-117, 124, 125-126, 128, 133, 148, 152n, 162n, 163n, 185, 186, 188, 211, 220-221, 229n, 235n, 254; symbolic structure in, 100, 101, 102-106, 107, 108-112, 119, 124, 125, 131, 196, 219, 235n, 252, 255, 256; tropological interpretation of, 56, 114, 191, 197, 219, 236n; typological interpretation of, 109, 115-117, 122-124, 125, 191, 193, 195, 197-203, 207-211, 216, 235-236n, 255, 256

Holy Spirit, 31, 32, 33, 43, 58, 61, 62, 63, 66-67, 73, 95, 98, 103, 104, 105, 109, 112, 113, 115, 120, 123, 124, 125, 126, 127, 130, 132, 135, 140, 151n, 163n, 167n, 177n, 178n, 199, 200, 201, 208, 209, 210, 211, 214, 218, 221, 222, 223, 235n, 247n

"honorable silence," 186, 189-191, 231-232n

impassibility (ἀπάθεια), 84n, 90n, 98, 163n, 215, 216, 236n, 237n, 242n, 243n

incarnation (see Jesus Christ)

Isaac the Syrian, 36, 46-47, 56, 71, 84n, 85n

Jesus Christ: garments interpreted spiritually, 62-63, 92n; incarnational mystery (μυστήριον) of, 53, 65, 103-104, 105-106, 118, 119-130, 131, 139, 145-149, 168-169n, 170n, 181n, 182n, 184, 185, 186, 191, 192, 193, 194, 195, 196, 197, 198-199, 200, 203, 207-209, 214, 223, 228n, 233n, 237n, 252, 253, 254, 255-256, 257n; transfiguration of, 102-105, 152n, 155n, 170n, 193, 233n

John Cassian, 36, 40-42, 47, 53, 58, 59, 71, 72, 79n, 80n, 91n, 94n, 191, 233n, 250

John Moschus, 3, 5, 19n, 20n, 21n

Jonah, 151, 128, 193, 206-211, 240n

law: Mosaic, 122, 123, 124, 141, 166n, 170n, 179n, 186, 211, 233n, 247n; natural, 102, 104-105, 106, 117-119, 120, 136, 140, 144, 154n, 165n, 166n,

167n, 169n, 174n, 181n, 189, 191, 242n, 252; spiritual (law of grace), 102, 117-119, 120, 136, 140, 146, 154n, 165n, 167n, 169n, 174n, 191, 252; written, 102, 104-105, 106, 117-119, 120, 136, 140, 165n, 166-167n, 169n, 174n, 252

logoi (principles): of the divinity of Christ, 147-148; of the commandments, 136, 148, 149, 159n, 172n, 174n, 218; in creation, 55, 62, 66, 95, 98, 99, 105, 106-107, 108, 109, 119, 120, 131, 132, 137, 138, 139, 140, 141, 146, 147, 152n, 156-157n, 158n, 169n, 178n, 197n, 214, 219, 236n, 242n, 245n, 247n, 252, 253; of providence and judgment, 107, 158n; in scripture, 107, 108-109, 111-112, 116-117, 119, 139, 146, 160n, 174n, 195, 197, 230n, 236n, 252, 253; of virtue, 64, 158n, 159n, 218

Logos (see Jesus Christ)

love, 32, 41, 48, 58, 59, 66, 67, 89n, 90n, 142, 153n, 167n, 173n, 214, 247n

Macarius (Pseudo-Macarius), 6, 21n, 36, 42-44, 45, 46, 47, 56, 58, 60, 71, 81n, 82n, 83n, 84n, 91n, 94n

Mark the Hermit, 36, 44-46, 53, 58, 71, 83n, 84n, 94n

Maximus the Confessor: in contemporary scholarship, 1-2; early years and monastic training, 3-6; as exegete, 112-117, 139-145, 184-228, 253-255; on Jews and Judaism, 6-7, 22-23n, 105, 123, 162n, 191, 199, 206, 209, 210, 211; and Origenism, 4, 7-9, 19-20n, 24n, 98-99, 107, 118, 128, 141, 158n, 179n, 213, 225, 228n, 252, 253; relationship with Thalassius, 9-12, 25n, 26n, 95-96; spiritual pedagogy of, 12, 13-14, 15, 52-56, 58, 59-67, 69, 116-117, 131-149, 196-228 passim, 250-252, 254, 255, 256

Messalianism, 42, 44-45, 58, 81n, 83n

mind ($νοῦς$), the, 15, 54, 56, 61, 62, 63-64, 65, 66, 68, 89n, 90n, 95, 97, 98, 101, 107, 110, 111, 112, 113, 114, 116, 131, 132-133, 134, 135, 136, 137-138, 139, 140, 144-145, 152n, 154n, 158n, 163n, 165n, 172n, 173n, 174n, 175-176n, 180n, 182n, 184, 190, 192, 198, 201-202, 205, 212, 213, 215, 216, 218, 221, 227, 229n, 237n, 243n, 245n, 246n, 247n, 253

monad, 108, 111, 133, 153n, 213, 215, 216, 242n

Moses, 30, 32, 63-65, 93n, 102, 114, 152n, 166n, 170, 233n, 244n, 247n

mystical theology ($θεολογία$), 15, 103, 106, 133, 137, 148, 153n, 171n, 174n, 175n, 177n, 181n, 185, 202, 218

Nilus of Ancyra, 115-116

Origen, 4, 5, 7, 9, 13, 15, 19n, 65, 71, 75n, 92n, 94n, 96, 102, 107, 112, 113, 115, 118, 125, 128, 150n, 155n, 159n, 160n, 163n, 164n, 165n, 168n, 170n,

181n, 185, 188, 191, 197, 203, 204, 211, 212, 220, 221, 223, 224, 229n, 231n, 232n, 233n, 234n, 239n, 241n, 243n, 244n, 245n, 246n, 248n, 252, 255

Origenism, 4, 5, 7-9, 19-20n, 24n, 40, 41, 47, 60, 98, 128, 141, 158n, 179n, 213, 225, 228n, 252, 253

passions, 11, 13, 23n, 26n, 38, 46, 53, 54, 55, 57, 58, 62, 63, 64, 65, 68, 72, 77n, 78n, 85n, 88n, 89n, 90n, 95, 98, 103, 114, 117, 131, 132, 134, 136, 137, 140, 144, 151n, 154n, 162n, 163n, 165n, 173n, 174n, 175n, 176n, 182n, 198, 201, 205, 213, 236n, 237n, 242n

Paul the Apostle, 32, 33, 35, 45, 58, 60-61, 66-67, 91n, 92n, 114, 164n, 171n, 200

Peter the Apostle, 33, 65-66, 92n, 102, 131, 132, 134-135, 173n, 174n, 180n, 222

Philo of Alexandria, 96, 150n, 151n, 160-161n, 203, 204, 211, 239n, 241n, 246n

practice ($\pi\rho\tilde{a}\xi\iota\varsigma$), ascetic, 14, 37, 38, 39, 40, 41, 42, 47, 48, 56, 61, 71, 72, 95, 97, 99, 108, 132, 133, 141, 142, 144, 145, 148, 149, 153n, 154n, 173n, 174n, 175n, 201, 216, 222, 236n, 242n, 254; paired with contemplation ($\theta\epsilon\omega\rho\acute{\iota}a$), 47, 72, 99, 113, 131, 133-137, 146, 148, 149, 163n, 172-173n, 174n, 181n, 182n, 191, 200, 205, 223, 233n, 245n, 246n, 250, 252, 255

prayer, 43, 46-47, 53, 60, 90n, 97, 116, 173n, 175n, 200, 212, 220, 246n

Quaestiones ad Thalassium: critical problems related to, 13-15; earlier research on, 2, 13-14; historical setting of, 6-12; and monastic pedagogical *quaestiones*, 28, 29, 35-36, 56-69, 70, 250; monastic topoi in, 57-61; and patristic exegetical $\dot{a}\pi o\rho\acute{\iota}a\iota$, 28-35, 249-250

Quaestio-responsio genre: in Anastasius Sinaïta, 49-52; in the *Apophthegmata patrum*, 37-39, 77n; in Barsanuphius and John, 47-49; in Basil of Caesarea, 38-40; in Eusebius of Caesarea, 38-40; in Evagrius Ponticus, 67-69, 93n; in Hesychius of Jerusalem, 30; in Isaac the Syrian, 46-47, 84n, 85n; in John Cassian, 40-42; in Mark the Hermit, 44-46, 84n; Maximus' adaptation of, 52-57, 61-70, 71-73, 87n, 88n; and monastic pedagogy, 35-36, 37, 38-52, 69-73; in pagan antiquity, 28; in the Pseudo-Macarian corpus, 42-44, 82n, 83n; in Theodoret of Cyrrhus, 30-31

reason, 99, 134, 136, 138, 154n, 166n, 172n, 174n, 175n, 176n, 178n, 202, 205, 227, 236n, 242n, 247n

Saul, 131, 140, 162n

Scripture (see Holy Scripture)

sense ($a\mathcal{\check{\iota}}\sigma\theta\eta\sigma\iota\varsigma$), 95, 98, 99, 101, 103, 106, 109, 110, 112, 131, 132, 137-138, 139, 150n, 154n,

166n, 171-172n, 173n, 175n, 176n, 190, 201, 202, 205, 212, 217, 218, 229n, 231n, 236n, 241n, 242n, 243n
sin, 31, 32, 34, 40, 43, 44-45, 50, 58, 82n, 119, 129, 201, 208, 209, 212, 244n
Sophronius, 3-4, 5-6, 19n, 20n, 21n, 22n, 248n, 251
soul (ψυχή), the, 43, 48, 55, 58, 64, 65, 68, 72, 73, 77n, 85n, 90n, 95, 96, 99, 100, 101, 114, 116, 123, 124, 125, 128, 138, 139, 150n, 151n, 153n, 154n, 155n, 165n, 167n, 173n, 175n, 176n, 178n, 179n, 182n, 185, 188, 189, 191, 197, 198, 199, 200, 203, 205, 207-208, 212, 213, 214, 224, 229n, 231n, 236n, 246n; faculties of, 58, 85n, 116, 135-136, 138, 144, 149, 174n, 175n, 181n, 197, 205, 212, 219, 223, 236n
spiritual anthropology, 13, 14, 41, 46, 49-50, 52, 54-56, 63-65, 99, 100-102, 116-117, 132-133, 134, 135-136, 154n, 155n, 166-167n, 171-172n, 198, 199-202, 204-205, 212, 249, 250, 251, 254, 255 (see also body; impassibility; mind; passions; reason; sense; soul)
spiritual knowledge (γνῶσις), 11, 12, 55, 56, 63, 72, 89n, 95, 96, 97, 98, 103, 110, 112, 116, 124, 134, 135, 136, 138, 139, 140, 141, 142, 145, 146, 147, 148, 149, 159n, 165n, 167n, 172-173n, 176n, 180n, 182n, 187, 188, 198, 199, 202, 205, 207, 209, 214, 216, 2222, 227, 242n, 246n, 247n
spiritual progress, 43, 49, 59, 63-65, 82n, 96-99, 103, 111, 160-161n, 165n, 182n, 185, 191, 205, 216, 223, 242n, 247n
suffering, 53, 60, 158n, 189, 190, 208, 221, 223, 245n
Thalassius the Libyan: questions posed to Maximus the Confessor; 10-11, 13, 31-35, 46, 57-61, 62, 63, 70, 85n, 171n, 200, 206, 214, 221; relationship with Maximus, 9-12, 25n; as spiritual writer, 10, 25-26n
Theodoret of Cyrrhus, 30-31, 74n, 87n
Thornton, Lionel, 193-195
tree of knowledge, 34, 60, 82n, 90-91n, 138, 172n, 189-191, 231-232n, 244n
tree of life, 34, 60, 90-91n, 138, 189, 190, 191, 231-232n, 244n
Trinity, 111, 127, 139, 160-161n, 177n, 211, 216
typology (see Holy Scripture, typological interpretation of)
virtue/virtues, 46, 47, 59, 62, 63, 64-65, 72, 85n, 89n, 90n, 95, 96, 97, 98, 99, 101, 117, 132, 133, 134, 135, 136, 137, 140, 142, 144, 146, 147, 148, 149, 151n, 154n, 158n, 159n, 172n, 173n, 174n, 180n, 182n, 186, 188, 198, 207, 209, 214, 215, 216, 217, 218, 227, 242n, 245n, 246n
Zorobabel (Zerubbabel), 113, 146, 163n, 197-198, 203-205, 213, 214, 219, 237n, 238-239n

Index of the Works of Maximus the Confessor

Ambiguorum Liber (Ambigua):
1, 2, 4, 5, 6, 8, 19n, 20n, 87n
1-5: 87n
5: 22n
Preface to *Ambigua ad Joannem*: 20n
7: 24n, 156n, 168n
10: 102-105, 119, 152n, 153n, 154n, 159n, 162n, 174n, 175n, 177n, 230n, 233n, 257n
15: 24n
21: 169n
33: 119-120, 169n
37: 108, 141-143, 159n, 179n, 230n, 239n, 240n, 241n, 253
41: 153n, 166n
42: 24n
46: 229n
57: 173n
65-67: 241n

Capita de caritate (Chapters on Charity): 1, 10, 21n, 87n

1.86: 173n

Capita theologica et oeconomica (Chapters on Knowledge):
1, 4, 6, 8, 19n, 87n

1.51-60: 243n

1.60-63, 65-67: 171n
1.66: 169n
1.71-72, 75-76: 171n
1.90: 170n
1.91: 155n
1.97: 159n
2.10: 160n
2.14: 155n, 156n, 160n
2.18: 97
2.28-29: 186
2.46: 169n
2.63, 66-70: 160n
2.77: 96

Epistulae
1: 22n
2: 173n
8: 18-19n, 22n
9: 24n, 25n
12: 19n, 20n, 21n
13: 237n
14: 22n
15: 237n
26: 24n, 26n
40: 11, 24n
41: 11, 24n
42: 22n, 24n

Liber asceticus: 22n, 36, 53, 71-72, 87n, 94n
1: 88n
2: 88n

6: 88n
18: 71-72

Mystagogia: 1, 6, 88n, 178n
Prooemium: 22n, 88n
2: 152n
5: 174n
6: 154n, 169n, 229n
7: 101, 152n, 155n
23: 141, 178-179n

Opuscula theologica et polemica
1: 25n
12: 19n, 20n

Orationis dominicae expositio (Commentary on the Lord's Prayer): 6, 87n

Quaestiones ad Thalassium
Introduction: 11-12, 24n, 25n, 26n, 75n, 85n, 88-89n, 90n, 92n, 95-96, 132, 151n, 152n, 172n, 177n, 182n, 189-190, 229n, 230n, 231n, 232n
1: 57-58, 76n, 89n, 176n
2: 31, 34, 152n, 158n
3: 134-135, 171n, 173n, 174n, 230n, 244-245n
4: 31, 34, 62-63, 171n
5: 75n, 181n, 232n
6: 31, 89n
7: 76n, 114, 164n, 180n, 232n
8: 31
9: 32, 164n
10: 26n, 32, 58, 59, 90n, 162n, 177n, 220, 232n, 243n, 246n
11: 232n, 233n
12: 232n
13: 157n, 158n, 177n, 232
14: 246n
15: 32, 119, 167-168n
16: 176n, 182n, 236n
17: 32, 63-65, 114, 163n
18: 32, 58, 154n
19: 32-33, 117-118
20: 23n, 33, 122-124, 169n, 171n, 232n
21: 170n, 231n
22: 33, 128-130, 159n, 170n, 182n, 232n, 236n, 237n, 255-256
23: 23n, 75n
24: 173n
25: 35, 177n, 200-203, 229n, 236n
26: 75n, 94n, 181n, 189, 230n
27: 33, 65-66, 132-133, 170n, 171n, 174n, 180n, 181n, 236n, 239n
28: 33, 34, 60, 111, 160n, 161n, 180-181n, 241n
29: 33, 66-67
30: 76n
31: 75n, 109-110
32: 76n, 100-101, 171n, 177n
33: 60, 76n, 187n
34: 60, 90n, 175n
35: 75n, 147-148, 149, 174n, 183n, 232n
36: 75-76n, 148-149, 159n, 172-173n, 183n
37: 33-34, 60-61, 92n, 164n, 181n
38: 75n, 76n, 166n, 171n, 229n

39: 76n, 136, 165n, 171n, 174-175n, 183n
40: 26n, 75n, 76n, 171n, 230n, 232n
41: 76n, 166n, 171n
42: 34, 170n, 244n
43: 34, 60, 76n, 90n, 175n, 189, 190, 231n, 232n, 244n
44: 34, 60, 111, 160n, 161n
45: 76n, 174n, 232n
46: 76n, 169n
47: 76n, 94n, 171n, 182n, 230n, 234n, 236n
48: 75n, 153n, 160n, 161-162n, 173n, 175-176n, 232n, 237n
49: 75n, 116, 134, 138-139, 152n, 164n, 165n, 173n, 175n, 181n, 212, 232n, 236n, 239n
50: 26n, 75n, 159n, 162n, 170n, 203, 220, 230n, 232n, 235n, 236n, 238n, 246n
51: 75n, 110, 116-117, 144-145, 151n, 178n, 220n, 232n, 236n, 240n, 245n
52: 75n, 113, 163n, 165n, 173n, 174n, 177n, 232n, 236n, 239n
53: 22-23n, 75n, 109, 146, 158n, 170n, 175n, 178n, 232n, 241n
54: 26n, 75n, 76n, 146, 152n, 153n, 159n, 170n, 174n, 181n, 198-199, 203-205, 213, 230n, 232n, 237n, 239-240n
55: 75n, 98, 159n, 163n, 170n, 172n, 173n, 174n, 180n, 181n, 187, 197-198, 214-219, 229n, 232n, 233n, 236-237n, 239n, 241n, 242n, 243n
56: 57, 75n, 239n
57: 76n, 90n, 94n
58: 25n, 60, 90n, 134, 137-138, 154n, 162n, 175n, 220, 246n
59: 8, 76n, 221-228, 232n, 233n, 246n, 247n, 248n
60: 8-9, 76n, 126-127, 166n, 170n
61: 76n, 132n, 170n, 171n, 232n
62: 75n, 120-122, 154n, 169n, 170n, 175n, 182n, 232n, 233n, 236n, 244n
63: 23n, 75n, 124-125, 135-136, 151n, 152n, 154n, 165n, 170n, 174n, 177n, 191, 199-200, 230n, 232n, 233n, 238n, 244n
64: 23n, 35, 86n, 119, 128, 151n, 158n, 160n, 166-167n, 170n, 174n, 188, 205-211, 229n, 230n, 232n, 233n, 234n, 238n, 239n, 240n, 241n
65: 23n, 24n, 26n, 140-141, 152n, 162n, 169n, 171n, 177n, 178n, 229n, 232n, 239n

Quaestiones ad Theopemptum: 53

Quaestiones et dubia: 4, 13, 53-56, 57, 61, 69, 72
I,8 (CCSG): 197, 236n

III,1 (CCSG): 87n, 245n
19 (I,3 CCSG): 30n
30: 55-56
39 (III,10 CCSG): 160n
44 (II,22 CCSG): 91n, 189, 231n
77: 54
192: 152n

Index of Biblical References

(Note: All Old Testament references follow the Septuagint text).

Genesis	
1:26-27	52, 91n, 245n
1:31-2:2	31
2:2	34, 74-75n
2:8	91n
2:9	34
2:16-17	82n, 189
3:14	11
3:17-19	35, 181n
3:22	34, 111
4:1-16	54
4:8	23n, 54
6:1-4	41
11:2	180n
11:7	33, 111
14:14ff	217
15:7-8	247n
18:1ff	111, 160n
19:1	111, 160n, 241n
21:1-5	217
21:9ff	23n
27:41	23n
30:37-38	55
30:39	55
31:19	55
31:33ff	55
35:1-4	55, 56
38:7-10	23n

Exodus	
3:1	63
3:2	160n
4:21	52
4:24-26	32, 63-65, 114
12:46	76n, 147
30:22-25	212
32:4	176n
32:20	176n

Leviticus	
26:27-28	161n

Deuteronomy	
12:27	148, 173n

Joshua	
9:3ff	178n
9:27	178n

1 Kings	
5	78n
16:12	158n
17:28	23n
24:4f	22n

2 Kings	
13:11-21	23n
21:1	140
21:1-14	162n
21:8-9	131

3 Kings	
6:1	116

11	181n	49:14	187
22:15-23	125n	88:8	90n
		118:2	223
4 Kings		118:14	246n
19:35	212	118:105	165n
21:1-18	23n	118:112	41
		118:129	223-224, 248n
2 Chronicles		119:6	96
12:2	162n		
21:5	162n	Proverbs	
26:4-10	75n	1:26	67
26:9ff	161n, 176n, 198	2:17	68
32:2-4	75n, 116, 138, 175n	3:18	34
		9:1-2	147
32:20ff	75n, 116, 220	9:13	68
32:23	75n, 144, 145, 220, 240n	15:27	68
		16:23	247n
32:25-26	75n, 163n	17:5	67
32:33	75n, 174n, 236n	18:4	160n
Job		Ecclesiastes	
10:21	207	1:9	226
15:15	38		
40:20	86n	Song of Songs	
		1:3	160n
Psalms			
8:4	68	Isaiah	
9:7	23n	1:16	44
17:46	23n	11:2	159n
21:7	86n, 160n	14:13-14	68
30:24	89n	19:12	51
33:10	32, 41, 58, 59, 89n, 90n, 220	28:16	160n
		31:4	160n
33:12	68	47:13-14	51
33:15	226	53:2	103
41:5	96	65:11	51
44:3	103		
46:8	39	Jeremiah	
48:10	154	27:6	94n

Index of Biblical References

34:2-11	75n, 188	**Wisdom of Solomon**	
		1:4	32
Ezekiel		12:1	32, 167n
31:9	68		
		Baruch	
Hosea		1:11	188
5:14	160n		
13:7f	160n	**Matthew**	
		5:22	79n
Jonah		5:44	144
1:17	207	6:3	79n, 226
2:1	128	6:23	84n
2:6-7	207, 208	7:6	79n
3:4	128, 210	9:9	67
4:1-8	210	10:10	31, 62, 92n
4:8	23n, 240n	10:16	144
4:6-9	23n	10:28	46
4:11	35, 206	10:39	46
		12:40	128
Zechariah		13:31	86n
4:2-4	75n, 199-200, 244n	15:32	165n
		17:1-8	102
4:3	152n	17:12	166n
4:10	163n, 198-199	21:18-22	23n, 33, 122, 123
5:1-4	75n, 120-122	22:23-28	166n
5:2	121	25:18	79n
5:4	236n	26:41	46
		28:19	33, 65
Malachi			
4:2	160n, 165n	**Mark**	
		6:9	31
1 Esdras		9:2	193
3:4-4:32	213	9:29	173n
4:48-60	75n	11:1-16:8	193
5:41-43	75n, 197, 214, 219	11:11ff	123
		11:12-14	33, 122, 123
5:66-71	75n		
5:68-69	57n	**Luke**	
		1:32-33	75n

3:4	182n	11:2	33, 65
6:7	84n	12:10	173n
6:29	53	17:27	100
6:31	166n	19:12	33, 60, 114
9:3	31	21:4	33, 66
10:19	48	22:16	44
12:47	40	27:14	240n
13:24	46	28:5	33, 60
18:1-7	84n		
18:6	53	Romans	
22:7-13	134, 244n	1:20	158n, 177n
		1:25	105, 246n
John		2:4	182n
1:1	103	2:12	33, 117, 118
1:9	208	2:13	32, 58
1:14	76n, 103, 147	2:16	33, 117
3:5	31, 58	7:14	46
3:27	246n	7:23	45
4:14	160n	8:6	54
4:16-18	166n	9:31	124
5:17	31, 34, 74-75n	10:4	117
6:27	84n	12:19	84n
6:53	147	13:10	167n
7:38	160n	14:4	84n
8:44	55		
14:9	202	1 Corinthians	
15:13	167n	1:18	208
19:23-24	31, 34, 62, 92n	2:9	44
19:31-36	76n, 147	2:10	32, 164n
20:1-10	173n	3:22	116
20:17	53	4:5	84n
		6:11	44
Acts		7:29-31	51
9:1	23n	9:22	182n
10:5	180n	10:11	33, 116, 129, 171n
10:11	132		
10:11-48	33, 65-66, 131	11:3-5	35, 200-202
10:12	132	11:10	35, 236n
10:13	66, 132	12:7-11	247n
10:16	132	12:8ff	66

Index of Biblical References

13:4	48, 79n	**1 Timothy**	
		2:4	146
2 Corinthians		6:17-19	50
3:6	106, 112, 162n		
3:18	96, 97	**2 Timothy**	
4:10	180n	3:2	79n
5:7	164n		
5:21	34, 244n	**Hebrews**	
6:16	116	4:14	97
7:1	45	5:14	149
7:15	44	6:1	150n
10:5	55	9:11	149
		10:1	170n
Galatians		11:24-26	41
4:6	96	12:2	208
5:4	32, 58	12:22	45, 83n
		13:15	187
Ephesians			
1:10-11	127	**James**	
2:7	33, 129, 171n	1:17	12, 246n, 247n
2:20	160n	5:16	90n
4:26	40		
4:31	40	**1 Peter**	
6:17	132	1:6	90n, 220
6:18	84n	1:10-11	8, 76n, 221-228, 248n
Philippians		1:20	76n, 127
2:5-8	84n	4:6	114, 180n
3:14	64, 164n		
3:19	23n, 105	**2 Peter**	
		1:9	101
Colossians		1:19	123n
2:15	231n		
		1 John	
1 Thessalonians		1:5	31, 160n
5:17	84n	1:7	31
		1:8	34
2 Thessalonians		3:2	32, 164n
2:3	7	3:9	31, 58

4:18   32, 58, 59, 89n,
       90n, 220

Jude
  6   233n

Revelation
  22:18   160n

www.ingramcontent.com/pod-product-compliance
Lightning Source LLC
Chambersburg PA
CBHW030525230426
43665CB00010B/777